OXFORD

TH

THE ODYSSEY has its roots in an ancient tradition of oral , which flourished in the 8th and 7th centuries BC. Nothing certain is known about Homer, who was depicted by the Greeks as a blind beggar and divine singer; they considered him to be the greatest poet that ever lived. To him are credited two astonishing works of genius, the *Iliad* and the *Odyssey*.

ANTHONY VERITY was Master of Dulwich College before his retirement. His previous translations include *Theocritus, The Idylls* (2002), *Pindar, The Complete Odes* (2007), and *Homer, The Iliad* (2011).

WILLIAM ALLAN is McConnell Laing Fellow and Tutor in Classical Languages and Literature at University College, Oxford. His previous publications include *The Andromache and Euripidean Tragedy* (2000), *Euripides: The Children of Heracles* (2001), *Euripides: Medea* (2002), *Euripides: Helen* (2008), *Homer: The Iliad* (2012), and *Classical Literature: A Very Short Introduction* (2014).

OXFORD WORLD'S CLASSICS

*For over 100 years Oxford World's Classics have brought
readers closer to the world's great literature. Now with over 700
titles—from the 4,000-year-old myths of Mesopotamia to the
twentieth century's greatest novels—the series makes available
lesser-known as well as celebrated writing.*

*The pocket-sized hardbacks of the early years contained
introductions by Virginia Woolf, T. S. Eliot, Graham Greene,
and other literary figures which enriched the experience of reading.
Today the series is recognized for its fine scholarship and
reliability in texts that span world literature, drama and poetry,
religion, philosophy and politics. Each edition includes perceptive
commentary and essential background information to meet the
changing needs of readers.*

OXFORD WORLD'S CLASSICS

HOMER

The Odyssey

Translated by
ANTHONY VERITY

With an Introduction and Notes by
WILLIAM ALLAN

OXFORD
UNIVERSITY PRESS

OXFORD
UNIVERSITY PRESS

Great Clarendon Street, Oxford, OX2 6DP,
United Kingdom

Oxford University Press is a department of the University of Oxford.
It furthers the University's objective of excellence in research, scholarship,
and education by publishing worldwide. Oxford is a registered trade mark of
Oxford University Press in the UK and in certain other countries

Translation © Anthony Verity 2016
Introduction, select bibliography, explanatory notes, index © William Allan 2016

The moral rights of the authors have been asserted

First published in 2016
First published as an Oxford World's Classics paperback 2018

Impression: 7

Published in the United States of America by Oxford University Press
198 Madison Avenue, New York, NY 10016, United States of America

British Library Cataloguing in Publication Data
Data available

Library of Congress Cataloging in Publication Data
Data available

ISBN 978-0-19-873647-9

Printed and bound in Great Britain by Clays Ltd, Elcograf S.p.A.

CONTENTS

THE ODYSSEY

INTRODUCTION

THE *Odyssey* rivals the *Iliad* as the greatest poem of Western culture and is perhaps the most influential text of classical literature. Its characters and plot continue to inspire artists in the various media of modern culture, ranging from popular fiction and comic books to classical music and opera. The aim of this brief introduction is to situate the poem in its original cultural context, especially the world of the itinerant epic bard and his audiences, and to consider some of the major themes of the narrative, including hospitality and recognition, the nature of heroism, the relationship between humans and their gods, and the pleasures and tensions of family life.

The Odyssey *and early Greek epic*

The *Odyssey*, like the *Iliad*, seems to embody a double paradox, since Homer's poems are not only the earliest works of Greek literature, but also the best; and Homer is arguably the greatest poet who ever lived, and yet nothing certain is known about him. As we shall see, however, the *Iliad* and *Odyssey* may be the earliest Greek literature to survive, but they are in fact the culmination of a centuries-old tradition of oral epic poetry. Homer's silence about himself, meanwhile, is entirely deliberate and productive, for rather than being a specific person tied to a particular place, the enigmatic narrator becomes a conduit of divine knowledge, inspired by the Muses, whose authority is universal.

Although we do not know who Homer was, there is clearly a single creative intelligence behind each epic. In contrast to nearly all ancient readers, most modern scholars believe that the *Iliad* poet and the *Odyssey* poet are different people (for a variety of linguistic, theological, and geographical reasons). However, as with the identity of Homer (whose poems we can enjoy and interpret without knowing any 'facts' about him), the question of whether he is one person or two is much less important than it seems. For all that really matters is the *Iliad* and *Odyssey* themselves and their shaping by a master poet or poets, who (for the sake of convenience) we will call Homer.

Composed in the late eighth or early seventh century BC, the Homeric epics are the work of a master of the epic tradition. This tradition was the storehouse of epic phrases and characters (such as 'much-enduring Odysseus' or 'Menelaus, master of the war-cry') and story-patterns (for example, 'the hero's return home from war') inherited, and added to, by each generation of epic bards. This 'oral' poetry was not only performed live, but also reshaped every time to suit the occasion and the audience's tastes. In other words, the bard may have sung a version of his story many times before, but his success lay in creating it anew for each performance. The word used by Homer to describe these epic stories is *oimē*, meaning 'path', referring to the 'path of song' which the poet (and his audience) would travel along. Homer gives examples of bards at work in his own poetry. Thus, in the *Odyssey* the bard Demodocus at one point selects the *oimē* of the quarrel of Odysseus and Achilles, moving Odysseus himself to tears at the recollection of his own past (8.73–6). The poet plots his own 'path' through the forests of Greek heroic myth, and his audience admires his skill in doing so.

An itinerant artist, keen to drum up future patronage, Homer takes care to advertise his own skill: the bard Phemius in the *Odyssey* asserts that such skill comes through hard practice as well as divine inspiration: 'My only teacher is myself; some god has planted varied song-paths (*oimas*) in my mind' (22.347–8). And it is no coincidence that Odysseus himself is compared to a bard stringing his lyre as he strings his bow for vengeance against the suitors (21.406–11). The ideal effect of an epic performance is the 'enchantment' (*kēlēthmos*) of the listeners, who are transported back to the world of the heroes and their mighty deeds. To achieve this enchantment the poet must make his account as vivid and authentic as possible, as if he himself had witnessed the events. Thus Odysseus praises the bard Demodocus because he sings of the Greeks' deeds and sufferings at Troy 'as if you had somehow been there yourself, or heard it from one who was' (8.491)—a real compliment, coming from one of those suffering Greek heroes. So, despite his reticence about himself, Homer's presentation of Phemius and Demodocus in the *Odyssey* conveys his conception of both poetry's value and the bard's authority and authenticity in singing of the heroic past.

Unlike Phemius and Demodocus, however, who in his poem are court poets, attached to particular royal families, Homer himself is likely to have been itinerant, performing in a variety of contexts: the halls of wealthy chieftains (especially after feasts, as in the *Odyssey*), but also at weddings, funerals, and public festivals of various kinds. As with his own identity, Homer is deliberately silent about the perform- ance context of his poetry, and for similar reasons: for he wants his work to be as universal as possible, so that it appeals not to one specific family, clan, or city but to all Greek-speaking communities. In that way Homer can perform all over the Greek world, making his poems more portable, flexible, and profitable. Similarly, the *Odyssey*'s varied cast of characters, ranging from kings and aristocrats to pig-farmers and servants, points to the mixed audience of the poem and to its bal- anced ideology, which praises both rich and poor so long as they are good and condemns both groups too if they behave badly, as with the decadent aristocratic suitors and the servants in Odysseus' home who connive with them. The poem ends with 'normal' social and political hierarchy restored, with loyal servants and kind masters triumphant, so it is far from being a revolutionary tale, but its condemnation of arrogance and cruelty is no less powerful and compelling.

The *Odyssey* is a variation on the tale of the wandering and return- ing hero which is known from many cultures around the world. In this story-pattern the hero is typically stranded far from home, and his family suffer in his absence, yet the hero battles against the odds and reclaims his wife and household. Thus the *Odyssey* begins ten years after the end of the Trojan War, but Odysseus has still not returned and his household is in disarray: a gang of over a hundred disorderly and arrogant suitors is vying with one another to claim Odysseus' wife Penelope, and his young son Telemachus is unable to stop them.

In taking up the tale of Odysseus, the *Odyssey* can be seen in some ways as a sequel to the *Iliad*, not least in its frequent references to the fall of Troy and the fate of the other Greek heroes. But whereas the *Iliad* portrays the tragic destruction of an entire society (the kingdom of Troy), the *Odyssey* is a more romantic and optimistic tale of a hero whose return to his community restabilizes it. Nonetheless, despite its more domestic setting, the *Odyssey* is still concerned with the same concepts of honour and revenge that dominate the *Iliad*, for the shameful behaviour of the suitors cannot go unpunished. Ignoring repeated warnings, the suitors persist in their outrageous abuse of the hospitality of Odysseus' household, and even scheme to murder Telemachus. Their complete destruction has struck some modern critics as excessive, but is fully in line with moralizing stories of this kind and with the ethics of ancient Greek society, where punishment is harsh but predictable (the suitors know well the liberties they are taking) and therefore justified.

The many interconnections between the two poems mean that even if not composed by the same bard, they evolved as part of a shared tradition of epic performance. Moreover, the *Odyssey* engages not only with the *Iliad* but also with the wider tradition of early Greek epic, transforming other heroic tales beyond the Trojan War. So as well as referring, for example, to the post-war returns of other Greek heroes, especially the murder of Agamemnon by his wife Clytemnestra (which serves as a foil to the successful homecoming of Odysseus and his reunion with Penelope: cf. 1.29–43, 298–300; 3.248–312; 4.512–37, etc.), the *Odyssey* interacts with the epic tale of the Argonauts, alluding to 'the storied ship Argo' (12.70), and adapting the Argonauts' adventures to expand Odysseus' own wanderings.

In terms of its basic structure, the *Odyssey* falls into two almost equal halves (1.1–13.92, 13.93–24.548). After introducing us to the situation in Ithaca and the crisis facing Telemachus and Penelope, the first half presents Odysseus' adventures since the fall of Troy, and we see his return to Ithaca repeatedly threatened: in the land of the Lotus-Eaters, for example, whose delicious lotus fruit makes the eater lose all memory of home, or in the cave of the monstrous Cyclops, Polyphemus, who kills and eats many of Odysseus' crew, or on the island of the witch Circe, who turns his men into pigs and keeps the hero as her lover for a year. The second half presents Odysseus' struggle on Ithaca, disguised as a beggar, to regain his kingdom, as he and Telemachus slaughter the suitors, and Odysseus and Penelope are finally reunited after twenty years apart. The fundamental structural division thus enhances our sense of the challenge facing Odysseus if he is to reclaim his original status and heroic identity.

The two halves contain three main storylines—centring upon Telemachus, Ithaca (that is, Penelope and the suitors), and Odysseus himself—and the three gradually merge, as Odysseus and Telemachus are reunited on Ithaca in Book 16 and plot their revenge upon the suitors. The narrative is handled with great skill throughout, as when the poet delays the introduction of his central hero until Book 5 (where we find him detained by the goddess Calypso and furthest from home), or has Odysseus recall his post-war sufferings in an extended flashback (Books 9–12). Thus, although the poem's main plot covers only forty-one days in the twentieth year after the Greeks set out for Troy, its use of embedded stories allows the bard to present his hero's tale on a grand scale, from Odysseus' youth to his gentle death at a great age.

Hospitality and recognition

I mentioned above the poet's adaptation of traditional story-patterns to create his own distinctive version of the heroic past. So, for example, we see Odysseus encountering a succession of rebellious young men (Phaeacian youths, his own crew, the suitors), whose threat to his heroic status and homecoming must be overcome. But two story-patterns in particular are central to the shaping of the poem: hospitality and recognition. The code of hospitality (*xenia*) governs the proper conduct of host and guest, and the poem's basic morality is articulated through good hosts (such as Nestor, Menelaus, Eumaeus) and bad ones (like Polyphemus or Circe), as well as by good and bad guests (most notably the suitors). As Eumaeus remarks, guests are sacred to Zeus, the patron god of strangers (14.388–9), but this protection also entails responsibility (to respect the host and his family), and thus the suitors' violation of such a basic ethical and religious principle is inevitably punished, and rightly so.

The early books of the poem chart Telemachus' travels to find out what happened to his father, and here the poet introduces us to the importance of hospitality, as the young man visits the courts of his father's friends and is received by them. Indeed, the importance of hospitality is made explicit by Menelaus, who tells Telemachus (15.69–74):

> I would indeed
> disapprove of any host who is either over-hospitable or
> too lacking in civility; moderation in all things is best. It is,
> I think, an equal failing to speed a guest's departure when he
>   is reluctant
> to leave and to detain him when eager to go. One must
> care for the guest in one's house, but send him on when he wishes.

This respectful relationship between guest and host stands in contrast to the chaos on Ithaca, where the suitors abuse their position as guests by consuming Odysseus' wealth in his absence and disrespect-ing his wife and son. In Odysseus' account of his adventures (Books 9–12) we find these ideas of hospitality explored in a more allegorical fashion, since many of the challenges Odysseus faces can be seen as perversions of the guest–host relationship. Thus, for example, the Cyclops Polyphemus is a host who is not merely unwelcoming but murderous, and rather than offering his guests a meal, he makes a meal of them. Conversely, Circe and Calypso are over-welcoming hosts, who trap their guests rather than facilitating their desire to leave. But guests as well as hosts are responsible for the smooth run-ning of the system, and it is no coincidence that the greatest crime committed by Odysseus' men is the consumption of the cattle of the Sun (12.294–373), which leads to the complete destruction of the fleet. In doing this, the men act like guests who abuse hospitality by consum-ing the host's resources. That this is punished so fearsomely by the gods helps the audience understand how serious the suitors' trans-gressions in Odysseus' household in Ithaca are, and so prepares us for Odysseus' vengeance against them.

Similarly pervasive is the story-pattern of recognition, as a succes-sion of characters (Telemachus, Odysseus' dog Argus, Eurycleia, Eumaeus, the suitors, Penelope, and finally Odysseus' father Laertes) come to realize who the mysterious beggar actually is. Odysseus uses his disguise to test others, a test failed by the suitors and his disloyal servants. The climactic reunion of Odysseus and Penelope is fittingly the most elaborate recognition scene of all, and varies the standard pattern, as Penelope takes control of the process, outwits Odysseus, and tricks him into confirming his identity by pretending that she has destroyed the marital bed he made for them (23.173–230). In beating Odysseus at his own game of disguise and trickery, Penelope proves that she is a worthy match for him, and confirms the validity of their relationship.

Odysseus as hero

While the *Iliad* portrays the pressures of the battlefield, the *Odyssey* explores a different form of heroism through the figure of Odysseus, who has to use intelligence and guile to overcome the many obstacles that keep him from returning to his home and family. We refer to the main figures of Homeric epic as heroes, but it is important that we make clear what being a 'hero' means in this context. For us the term 'hero' conjures up someone who has done something unambiguously positive: a fireman who rushes into a burning building to save people, for example. In ancient Greek culture, however, the 'heroes', often the offspring of unions between gods and humans, are not simply positive figures, but are characterized by their excessiveness, both for good and for ill. The heroes are capable of acts of superhuman and admirable prowess. But their heroic power is double-edged, because it can also lead to less desirable qualities: excessive anger, violence, cruelty, pride, recklessness, and egotism. So there is a tension within heroism itself, in that the very energy which makes the heroes outstanding is also the source of their instability and danger (both to themselves and to others). The *Iliad* and *Odyssey* are sophisticated epics, which not only celebrate the heroic world but also explore the complex nature of heroism itself.

Moreover, as the Homeric epics make clear, heroes come in a variety of forms: Odysseus is not the same as Achilles, nor is Menelaus the same as Nestor. In other words, the basic heroic drive 'always to be the best and to stand out above other men' (*Iliad* 6.208) does not lead to a series of identical characters. Even if we sum up the heroic ideal in terms of being outstanding as 'a speaker of words and a doer of deeds' (*Iliad* 9.443), each hero will possess these abilities in his own individual way. Thus Odysseus and Nestor excel as speakers, Achilles and Ajax as fighters. To us such a close connection between fighting well and speaking well seems odd, but from a Homeric perspective they complement one another perfectly, since the battlefield and the assembly are the foremost arenas in which the hero can excel and thereby benefit both himself and his community.

The ideal Homeric hero, then, has both brains and brawn: Achilles is intelligent and eloquent as well as the supreme fighter, while the wily Odysseus proves himself a formidable warrior too. But insofar as Achilles and Odysseus typify two contrasting forms of heroism (one favouring force, the other intelligence), we can see both Homeric epics exploring this opposition. In the *Odyssey*, Odysseus himself recalls the impetuous Achilles—but dead in Hades, emphasizing his own superiority as a canny and flexible survivor (11.467–540). Odysseus makes clear that, unlike Achilles, he will be reunited with his family, and that whereas Achilles had to choose between a short life with glory and a long life in obscurity, he will achieve both glory and a happy old age.

Thus the poem highlights the benefits of being an Odyssean hero, and suggests that intelligence can be superior to might.

So the protagonist of the *Odyssey* is not a new kind of hero. Nor is he even a new kind of Odysseus, since the Odysseus of the *Iliad* also combines warrior strength and guile. However, the post-war context of the *Odyssey* calls for more of the latter. Thus, for example, he uses his cunning and intelligence to escape the Cyclops' cave when his men are being gobbled up around him, and he deceives everyone he meets when he gets back home to Ithaca. But when cunning has served its purpose, Odysseus drops his disguise and deploys heroic force, ruthlessly killing the suitors and restoring his honour.

Odysseus' typical Homeric epithets—'much-wandering', 'much-enduring', 'of many wiles'—pick out the characteristics that ensure his survival and success: he is driven beyond the limits of the known world, endures the humiliation of life as a beggar in his own kingdom, and conceals his true identity with elaborate lying tales. This latter characteristic, Odysseus' outstanding skill as a liar, could be portrayed negatively in Greek literature (as it was in some tragedies), but the circumstances of the *Odyssey* make such deception necessary for survival, and we (like his patron goddess Athena) enjoy Odysseus' ingenious fictions and relish the irony of the nonchalant and arrogant suitors unaware of the avenger in their midst.

Odysseus' skill as a storyteller is one of the most striking features of the *Odyssey*, which displays an awareness of itself as poetic fiction that would not be out of place in a (post-)modern novel. Odysseus tells his tales to various audiences over many thousands of verses, some of them truly (his past adventures as told to the Phaeacians in Books 9–12), others falsely (most notably his tales of being a wandering beggar, as told on Ithaca in Books 13–24). In each case Odysseus is acting like a bard, celebrating a hero's endurance and glorious past (in this case his own, to impress the Phaeacians), and spinning persuasive falsehoods in order to regain his honour and status on Ithaca. Indeed, the wandering beggar tales (told to Athena, Eumaeus, the suitor Antinous, and Penelope) show Odysseus using a narrative technique that is typical of the epic bard himself, for he presents variations on a basic story (of a wealthy man from Crete who endures various sufferings), whose details are changed to suit the identity of his addressee and the needs of the situation: so, for example, in seeking to gain Eumaeus' sympathy, Odysseus emphasizes the idea of being sold into slavery, since he knows that Eumaeus himself has endured this (14.287–98, 334–59). Like a bard who composes his song anew in each performance, Odysseus recombines the basic elements of his false identity to create a story best suited to his audience at the time. Fittingly, this bardic imagery culminates in the moment of Odysseus' revenge (21.404–13):

> Odysseus, man of many wiles,
> lifted up the great bow, examining it from every side,
> and then, just as a man skilled in lyre-playing and song
> without difficulty stretches a string around a new peg,
> tying the well-twisted gut of a sheep at both its ends,
> so, without any effort, did Odysseus string the great bow.
> Taking it up in his right hand he tested the string,
> and it sang out sweetly, like the song of a swallow.
> At this great distress fell upon the suitors, and the colour
> left their faces.

To lose one ship on the voyage home may be forgiven, but to lose all of them, as Odysseus does, seems less than heroic. Indeed, it is essential to the concept of the hero in Homeric epic that these powerful men are not rampant individualists, but fundamentally social heroes; that is, they exist as part of a wider community whom they have a duty to protect. Hence the opening of the *Odyssey* insists that Odysseus' men 'perished by reason of their own recklessness, | the fools, because they ate the cattle of the Sun, Hyperion' (1.7–9). But we see other members of Odysseus' crew perish because of *his* mistakes, as when his comrades urge him to leave the Cyclops' cave and he refuses, an error he later admits (9.228–30): 'I was not persuaded—though it would have been much better— | as I wanted to see him, hoping he might give me presents; but | when he did appear my crew found him anything but pleasant.' So while most of Odysseus' men do bring about their own destruction, some die due to Odysseus' lack of judgement and personal ambition. Concern for others is an essential part of heroism, and even great figures like Odysseus sometimes fail to balance the pursuit of personal glory with the duty of care they owe to those who honour and depend upon them.

It is sometimes claimed that, in comparison to the *Iliad*, the *Odyssey* displays a more critical attitude to war and heroic glory, but this underestimates the extent to which the *Iliad* too shows the cost of war, and risks obscuring how much pride Odysseus takes in the Greek victory at Troy. Odysseus may grieve for the suffering of the past, as (for example) when he weeps at Demodocus' song of the Trojan horse and the sack of Troy (8.499–531), but he is just as focused on his honour and glory in the *Odyssey* as he is in the *Iliad*, and he secures his victory over the suitors in typically heroic style (22.1–329). Like every other major Greek hero, however, Odysseus is far from perfect. The loss of his men makes it clear that he will have to learn greater self-control if he is to achieve success on Ithaca. Odysseus rises to the challenge, and proves himself truly 'much-enduring' in the midst of the suitors' insults, and this newly learned restraint enables him to defeat his enemies and regain both his family and his kingdom.

Mortals and immortals

The gods' concern for mortals and their constant intervention in human affairs is one of the most striking aspects of the Homeric epics. Yet Homer's gods are not merely figures of literature: they are an expression of a coherent theology. According to the historian Herodotus (2.53), writing in the fifth century BC: 'It was Homer and Hesiod who created for the Greeks a genealogy of the gods, gave the gods their names, assigned their honours and areas of expertise, and described their appearance.' Since there was no established church or priestly caste or sacred book to prescribe religious beliefs in ancient Greece, poets played a fundamental role in shaping religious ideas, and none more so than Homer, who was the foundation of all education, including what the Greeks thought about their gods. It is a measure of the spell of Homer that when the philosopher Xenophanes (who was active in the sixth century BC) wishes to criticize conventional religious belief, he attacks the theology of the great poets (fr. 11): 'Homer and Hesiod have attributed to the gods everything that men find shameful and blameworthy: stealing, adultery, and deceiving one another.' Despite such moral and intellectual criticisms (especially by philosophers such as Plato), the Homeric picture of the gods as powerful anthropomorphic figures, for good and for ill, remained the basis for popular religion throughout antiquity.

To understand ancient Greek religion, then, it is essential that we jettison inappropriate (especially Christian) conceptions of the divine as intrinsically kind and caring. For although the Greek gods do care for humans, they are anything but selfless, and their honour is every bit as important to them as it is to the heroes. If a god is offended, as when Odysseus' men kill the cattle of the sun-god, Helios, or Odysseus himself blinds Polyphemus, son of the sea-god Poseidon, the gods are no less relentless than the angriest of heroes in their pursuit of revenge, and their greater power means that their retribution is all the more terrifying. Indeed, the *Odyssey*'s plot is crucially shaped by the anger of these two gods, as Poseidon's enmity accounts for the extent of Odysseus' wanderings, while Helios' rage leads to the destruction of Odysseus' men.

Poseidon's persecution of Odysseus is motivated by kinship and personal vengeance, not by any abstract sense of morality. The narrator underlines from the very start of the poem the importance of the god's anger to his version of Odysseus' return (1.19–21): 'All the gods had pity for him | except Poseidon, who raged unrelentingly against | godlike Odysseus until the time he reached his homeland.' As Zeus' speeches in Book 1 also make clear, it is Odysseus' fate to return home and punish the suitors, so Poseidon knows that he cannot kill him; nonetheless, the god does his best to make his homecoming as painful as possible. It must be stressed, however, that this is not simply a case of divine cruelty or caprice, for Odysseus' own errors have brought about this suffering: he foolishly rejected his men's advice to leave the Cyclops' cave (9.224–30), then taunted the blinded Polyphemus and boastfully gave away his name, enabling the Cyclops to call on his father Poseidon for vengeance (9.491–536).

Poseidon's anger also harms the kindly Phaeacians, whom he targets for helping Odysseus return to Ithaca. Their punishment seems—from a human perspective—disturbing. For as their king Alcinous makes clear, the Phaeacians offer to help Odysseus because of their concern for strangers and suppliants (8.544–7); yet Zeus, the patron of strangers and suppliants, allows them to be punished. Indeed, Zeus not only approves of Poseidon's plan to smite the Phaeacians' ship as it returns from Ithaca, and to envelop their city behind a mountain, but also suggests turning the ship to stone, making it a permanent memorial of the Phaeacians' punishment (13.154–8). By human standards of justice Zeus' collaboration may appear vindictive, but it embodies a basic feature of his maintenance of divine order, since even Zeus cannot interfere constantly in other gods' spheres of influence. It is also made clear that the Phaeacians, who

have a privileged relationship with the gods, are particularly close to
Poseidon: they are outstanding seafarers and their devotion to sailing
and the sea is repeatedly underlined. Moreover, King Alcinous and
his wife Arete are both descended from Poseidon (grandson and
great-granddaughter respectively: 7.56–66). So whereas Polyphemus,
the son of Poseidon, exploits his kinship to punish his enemy Odysseus, the Phaeacians suffer from their proximity to the god.

Moreover, as we saw with Odysseus' own share of responsibility for
Poseidon's anger, it is important that the Phaeacians have been
warned about their behaviour well before Odysseus' arrival, as Alcinous recalls with an insouciance that alerts the audience to their
future punishment (8.564–71):

> 'I heard from my father Nausithous the tale I shall now tell you.
> He always said that Poseidon would hold a grudge against us,
> because we, remaining unharmed, give safe-conduct to all men.
> He said that one day he will smash a fine ship of the Phaeacians
> as it returns from an escort mission on the mist-shrouded sea,
> and will then hide our city behind a huge encircling mountain.
> This was what the old man said; and the god will either
> make it happen or leave it undone, as his spirit pleases him.'

In failing to heed a warning, the Phaeacians are like Odysseus' men, who
eat the cattle of Helios after swearing an oath that they will leave them
untouched (12.297–303). It makes no difference to Helios or his vengeful response that the men's fatal error is the product of exhaustion and
starvation. For as with Poseidon's anger (whether at Odysseus' blinding
of his son or at the Phaeacians' assistance to Odysseus), Zeus respects
Helios' right to punish those who offend the god or transgress in his
domain. Moreover, Helios' threat to descend to Hades and shine among
the dead (if Odysseus' men are not punished) threatens the whole cos-
mic order (12.382–3). Zeus' response is immediate (12.385–8):

> 'Sun-god, of course you must continue to shine on the immortals,
> and on mortal men who live on the grain-giving ploughland.
> As for these men, I shall at once hurl a shining thunderbolt at
> their swift ship, and smash it in pieces out on the wine-dark sea.'

So these various episodes of divine punishment—of Odysseus, his
men, and the Phaeacians—not only embody the basic principle of a
god's right to control his or her domain, but also show a fundamental

system of divine justice, where punishment may be harsh, but is predictable (that is, based on human actions) and therefore (in ancient
Greek terms) fair.

A further essential aspect of the gods' behaviour—their support
for justice among humans—is best illustrated by the poem's major
and climactic example of punishment, namely the destruction of the
suitors. However, although the punishment of the suitors is unques-
tionably demanded by the honour-based ethics of Homeric society,
the *Odyssey* poet complicates the initial picture of the suitors as a
gang of insolent reprobates. As the narrative develops, we get a more
particularized view of the suitors, revealing that not all of them are
wicked. Their varied natures emerge with greater clarity, significantly,
as the vengeance draws closer.

We first hear of Amphinomus, one of two decent suitors, in
Book 16, where we are told that 'he more than the others found favour
with | Penelope through his words, for he was endowed with good
sense' (16.397–8). He persuades the suitors to reject Antinous' proposal
that they try once more to ambush and kill Telemachus (16.400–6).
And his kind words to 'the beggar' prompt Odysseus to warn him
against remaining any longer with the suitors and even to pray that
some god may save him from Odysseus' vengeance (18.122–50). Yet
the narrator immediately contrasts Odysseus' attitude to Amphinomus with that of Athena (18.153–6):

> Amphinomus...went back through the house, troubled in spirit
> and shaking his head, because in his heart he could foresee evil.
> Even so he did not escape death; he too was bound fast by Athena,
> to be overcome by Telemachus' hands and the force of his spear.

Indeed, Athena's determination to kill all the suitors, regardless of
their individual conduct, is made clear (17.360–4):

> Athena came and stood next to Odysseus, Laertes' son,
> and urged him to go round the suitors and collect crusts, to
> find out which were right-minded and which lawless;
> even so, she did not intend that any should escape ruin.

Athena's intervention simultaneously separates the suitors into
the good and the bad and underlines her indifference to their decency.
Thus the audience know Amphinomus' fate even as he offers the
disguised Odysseus protection and urges the suitors to stop abus-
ing both 'the beggar' and the servants of Odysseus' household

(18.394–5, 414–21). The disjunction between character and fate is even clearer in the case of the suitor Leodes, whom the narrator introduces as the first to attempt to string Odysseus' bow (21.144–7):

> The first to rise to his feet was Leodes, son of Oenops,
> who interpreted their sacrifices, and always sat furthest away,
> next to the fine mixing-bowl; he was the only one who hated
> the suitors' reckless deeds, and was indignant with them all.

The narrator's comment on Leodes' decency is expanded by Leodes himself in his appeal to Odysseus (22.312–19), yet Odysseus rejects the supplication and cuts off Leodes' head while he is still speaking (22.326–9). Thus both Athena and her human protégé kill the two more virtuous suitors with equal ruthlessness. The parameters of vengeance among both gods and mortals are seen to be similarly harsh—but as we saw above with Odysseus' men and the Phaeacians, such punishment (based on collective responsibility in the case of Amphinomus and Leodes) is entirely predictable and avoidable, and the destruction of all the suitors (without exception) embodies the stern but fair system of Homeric justice.

Fortunately, as mention of Athena reminds us, the divine system is not just about punishment of the wicked, but has a positive side too, not least in the gods' protection of their favourites. Athena's care for Odysseus is also a feature of the *Iliad*, where (for example) the goddess protects him in battle (especially in Book 11) and helps him win the running-race at the Funeral Games for Patroclus (in Book 23). In the *Odyssey*, with its focus on her favourite hero and a much smaller cast of divine characters (compared to the *Iliad*), Athena is even more central to the unfolding of the plot and to Odysseus' success. From raising the issue of his return in the divine council of Book 1 through to settling the peace on Ithaca in Book 24, Athena's assistance is crucial.

But why does she do all this for a mere mortal? Their relationship is unusually close, and the reason for this emerges at their first meeting in the poem, as Odysseus finally reaches the shore of Ithaca in Book 13. When Odysseus tries to dupe Athena (who is disguised as a young man) with a lying tale, the goddess strokes him with her hand (13.287–8)—a gesture that elsewhere evokes the closeness of mother and son or the intimacy of man and wife—and remarks fondly on how similar they are to one another (13.296–302):

'Come now, let us not talk like this any longer, since we are both
well versed in deception: among mortals you surpass all men in
plotting and tale-spinning, while among all the gods I am well
known for cleverness and cunning. But you did not recognize
Pallas Athena, daughter of Zeus, I who have always stood
by you in all your trials and have watched over you; it was
I who made sure you were welcomed by all the Phaeacians.'

The goddess clearly recognizes herself in Odysseus, so much so that,
when Odysseus persists in his caution and distrust, asking whether
this really is Ithaca or is she out to deceive him, Athena reacts not with
anger (as one might expect, based on other divine–human inter-
actions), but with renewed affection (13.330–2): 'This is always the
way that the mind within you works! | And that is why I cannot aban-
don you in your unhappy state, | because you are so shrewd, sagacious,
and firm of purpose.' Though not based on ties of blood (as with
Poseidon and Polyphemus), Athena's desire to protect Odysseus is no
less personal, based on her strong sense of similarity and sympathy.

In conclusion, the Homeric poems provide their audience with a
compelling picture of the world, and of the ways in which gods and
humans act and interact within it. For all their personal biases, the
gods act as guarantors of justice, showing a collective concern for
morality, which is seen most clearly in the punishment of the suitors.

Marriage and family life

The importance of domestic life and personal relationships is often
stressed in the *Iliad*, but the post-war context of the *Odyssey* and its
focus on the hero's return to both family and homeland make these
themes even more prominent. Odysseus returns in the nick of time to
prevent the loss of everything—his wife, wealth, kingdom, and identity. Moreover, the restoration of the family unit is the climax of the
narrative, coming after Odysseus' vengeance upon the suitors (and
not before, as in other versions of the 'returning husband' story).

Books 1–4 (known since antiquity as the 'Telemachy') present
Telemachus' search for news of the absent Odysseus. We see the son,
who grew up fatherless, gradually come of age among the wider community of adult men, as he hears exemplary stories of his father from
former comrades, Nestor in Pylos (Book 3) and Menelaus in Sparta
(Book 4). The two storylines ('return of the father' and 'maturation

of the son') eventually converge in Book 16, as father and son are
reunited, and Telemachus takes on the self-control and concealment
of his father, enabling them to exact vengeance together. As Odysseus
prepares to throw off his disguise and kill the suitors, Telemachus
takes his stand beside him, demonstrating that heroic excellence
has been successfully transmitted from father to son (21.431–4):
'Telemachus, | the dear son of godlike Odysseus, slung his sharp
sword | about him and grasped his spear firmly, and took his stand | by
his father, next to his seat, armed in flashing bronze.'

At the beginning of the poem, however, we see disorder in Odysseus' household and kingdom. His prolonged absence has created a
dangerous power-vacuum, since Penelope, as a woman, cannot take
on a full role in governing Ithaca, while Telemachus is as yet too
immature to assert his independence and authority. These tensions
erupt in a dispute between mother and son, as Telemachus rebukes
Penelope when she objects to the bard Phemius singing about the
Greeks' return from Troy (1.353–9):

> 'So let your heart and spirit be strong to listen; Odysseus
> is not the only man at Troy to lose the day of his return
> home, since many other men perished there as well.
> Go back to your rooms and take charge of your own tasks,
> the loom and the distaff, and order your women servants
> to go about their work. Talk must be men's concern, all of
> them, and mine especially, for the power in the house is mine.'

Since Athena (in disguise) had just instructed Telemachus to behave
like an adult male, expelling the suitors from the house and arranging
for his mother's remarriage (1.272–8, 296–7), his sudden assertive-
ness, which astonishes both Penelope and the suitors (1.360–1, 381–
2), marks the beginning of his growth to manhood. But at this stage
(before his meetings with Nestor and Menelaus, and before he can
learn from Odysseus) he is not yet ready, and his claim, 'the power in
the house is mine', is shown to be premature: the suitors ignore his
demand that they leave the house, and Telemachus himself breaks
down in tears as he addresses the Ithacan assembly (2.80–1).

Telemachus' development as a man is one part of the restoration of
family life, but by far the most important element is the reunion of
husband and wife. The marriage of Odysseus and Penelope is con-
trasted with a variety of flawed relationships, particularly those of

Agamemnon and Clytemnestra, and Menelaus and Helen, which act as foils to the hero's ideal union. Thus, for example, the shade of Agamemnon advises Odysseus in the underworld (11.441–5):

'For this reason [i.e. because Clytemnestra killed me] you too should
    never be indulgent to your wife,
nor give her a full account of everything that is in your mind;
you should tell her some of it and keep the rest concealed.
Still, Odysseus, your wife is certainly not likely to murder you;
she is utterly loyal, circumspect Penelope, Icarius' daughter,
and the thoughts in her heart are always right and proper.'

And when Telemachus visits Menelaus and Helen in Sparta, they tell him very different stories from the Trojan War. Helen recalls how she helped the disguised Odysseus escape from a secret mission to Troy because (or so she claims) she desired to return home to her dear husband Menelaus (4.235–64). Menelaus, on the other hand, recalls an episode from the end of the war, as the Greeks crouched inside the Trojan horse; Helen imitated the voice of every Greek hero's wife, trying to make them cry out and reveal their stratagem (4.266–89). The contrasting tales—was Helen an unwilling prisoner or a scheming traitor who tried to get all the Greeks killed?—illustrate the instability of their marriage.

Odysseus' commitment to Penelope is tested by a variety of women, both mortal and divine. The goddesses Calypso and Circe delay him in different ways. Calypso saves him from shipwreck at the end of his wanderings, but then keeps him as her (increasingly unwilling) lover for seven years, before finally succumbing to pressure from Zeus to send him on his way. Circe is more overtly hostile, turning some of his men into pigs, but Odysseus subdues her and departs (albeit after a year of lovemaking). Calypso, whose name ('concealer', from *kaluptō*, 'I hide') suits her function, offers Odysseus immortality, but even this is not enough to deflect him from his desire to return home (5.203–24). The mortal Nausicaa, princess of the Phaeacians, is the last temptation. Their encounter is structured around the familiar 'handsome stranger meets eligible princess' story-pattern, and the fairy-tale possibility that Odysseus might marry her (hinted at by her own father Alcinous, 7.309–16) creates great tension and interest in Books 6–8.

Penelope, the goal of Odysseus' quest, represents the ideal wife (within the poem's patriarchal culture): she oversees the domestic sphere and preserves Odysseus' kingdom without usurping his authority, which is reaffirmed when he returns. Throughout the poem it is made clear that Penelope is not only stunningly beautiful (the suitors go wild whenever she appears to them in the banqueting hall), but also highly intelligent. Indeed, she proves herself more than a match for the clever Odysseus himself, whom she ultimately outwits. For as he stands before her, bespattered with the blood of the suitors, she refuses to believe that this man is her husband. Knowing, however, that their marriage bed is immovable, since Odysseus had built it from the trunk of an olive tree when the house was first constructed, Penelope orders that it be moved, which prompts the angry Odysseus to tell the story of the bed's making (a secret shared by him and Penelope), thus confirming his identity for his wife (23.173–230). Penelope's trick shows her to be her husband's equal in cleverness and the skilled use of language, and proves their worthiness to be reunited as husband and wife.

Penelope's relationship with Odysseus thus embodies the Homeric ideal of marriage, which presents women's excellence as complementary to men's and no less essential to a flourishing human society. Indeed, a harmonious marriage is seen as central to a good life. This cultural ideal of harmony between the sexes is summed up in the notion of *homophrosynē*, or 'like-mindedness', which Odysseus hopes Nausicaa will enjoy (6.180–5):

> '...may the gods grant you all that you desire in your heart,
> and may they bestow on you a husband, a house, and good
> harmony of minds (*homophrosynē*); there is nothing better
>   or more powerful
> than this, when a man and his wife keep house in sympathy
> of mind (*homophroneonte noēmasin*)—a great grief to
>   their enemies, but a joy to those who
> wish them well; and they themselves are highly esteemed.'

It is this principle of harmony that underpins the marriage of Odysseus and Penelope, and its illustration by Penelope's final trick (the marriage bed) makes a fitting climax to their story. Their positive relationship, in contrast to the negative models of Agamemnon and Clytemnestra or Menelaus and Helen, shows the benefits that come from a balanced partnership between the sexes, and celebrates the important roles performed by both women and men in Homeric society.

NOTE ON THE TEXT AND
EXPLANATORY MATERIALS

THE text of the *Odyssey* translated here is the Oxford Classical Text
edited by T. W. Allen (2nd edn. Oxford, 1917–19). The Explanatory
Notes begin with a succinct summary of each book and aim to clarify
mythical references, place-names, and the like, while also discussing
selected passages in the light of the key themes covered in the Introduction. References given in both the Explanatory Notes and the
Index of Personal Names are to the book and line number in the
translation. The Select Bibliography offers a brief guide to further
reading in English.

NOTE ON THE TRANSLATION

THIS translation respects as far as possible the line numeration in standard editions of Homer, which means that references to the original text can easily be matched to the line numbers in the margin of this version. It does not claim to be 'poetic'; my aim has been to use a straightforward English register and to keep closely to the Greek, allowing Homeric directness and power to speak for itself. The *Odyssey* employs a greater variation of voices than the *Iliad*, from the elevated to the everyday, and I am aware that some readers may find the occasional shift from current to archaic idiom awkward; all I can say is that this is the way in which Homer has led me.

I have benefited greatly from the criticism and encouragement of friends in preparing this version, notably Peter Jones, Alistair Elliott, and James Morwood. Bill Allan has been the ideal collaborator. I owe an enormous debt to Paddy Johnston, who read and commented on every word with care; his ear for the telling phrase, and deep knowledge of seafaring and rural life, both improved my early efforts and shed a new light on Homer's world. All surviving infelicities are entirely my own. As always, Judith Luna at OUP was wise, constant, and supportive, everything an editor should be; and Jeff New went beyond copy-editing to suggest useful and clarifying suggestions of his own.

Anthony Verity

SELECT BIBLIOGRAPHY

THIS is a highly selective list, limited to books in English; more detailed bibliographies can be found in the suggested works.

Commentaries

Bowie, A. M., *Homer: Odyssey XIII and XIV* (Cambridge, 2013).

De Jong, I. J. F., *A Narratological Commentary on the Odyssey* (Cambridge, 2001).

Garvie, A. F., *Homer: Odyssey VI–VIII* (Cambridge, 1994).

Heubeck, A., West, S. R., and Hainsworth, J. B., *A Commentary on Homer's Odyssey Books 1–8* (Oxford, 1988).

Heubeck, A., and Hoekstra, A., *A Commentary on Homer's Odyssey Books 9–16* (Oxford, 1989).

Russo, J., Fernandez-Galiano, M., and Heubeck, A., *A Commentary on Homer's Odyssey Books 17–24* (Oxford, 1992).

Rutherford, R. B., *Homer: Odyssey XIX and XX* (Cambridge, 1992).

Stanford, W. B., *Homer: Odyssey*, 2 vols. (London, 1958–9).

Steiner, D., *Homer: Odyssey XVII and XVIII* (Cambridge, 2010).

Companions to Homer

De Jong, I. J. F. (ed.), *Homer: Critical Assessments*, 4 vols. (London, 1999).

Doherty, L. E. (ed.), *Oxford Readings in Homer's Odyssey* (Oxford, 2009).

Finkelberg, M. (ed.), *The Homer Encyclopedia*, 3 vols. (Oxford, 2011).

Fowler, R. L. (ed.), *The Cambridge Companion to Homer* (Cambridge, 2005).

Morris, I., and Powell, B. (eds.), *A New Companion to Homer* (Leiden, 1998).

Wace, A. J. B., and Stubbings, F. H. (eds.), *A Companion to Homer* (London, 1962).

Critical Studies

Austin, N., *Archery at the Dark of the Moon: Poetic Problems in Homer's Odyssey* (Berkeley, 1975).

Burgess, J. S., *The Tradition of the Trojan War in Homer and the Epic Cycle* (Baltimore, 2001).

Camps, W. A., *An Introduction to Homer* (Oxford, 1980).

Clarke, H. W. (ed.), *Twentieth-Century Interpretations of the Odyssey* (Englewood Cliffs, NJ, 1985).

Clarke, M., *Flesh and Spirit in the Songs of Homer* (Oxford, 1999).

Clay, J. S., *The Wrath of Athena: Gods and Men in the Odyssey* (Princeton, 1983).

Cohen, B. (ed.), *The Distaff Side: Representing the Female in Homer's Odyssey* (Oxford, 1995).

Edwards, A., *Achilles in the Odyssey: Ideologies of Heroism in the Homeric Epic* (Königstein, 1985).

Fenik, B., *Studies in the Odyssey* (Wiesbaden, 1974).

Ford, A., *Homer and the Poetry of the Past* (Ithaca, NY, 1992).

Frame, D., *The Myth of Return in Early Greek Epic* (New Haven, 1978).

Griffin, J., *Homer: The Odyssey* (2nd edn. Cambridge, 2004).

Hainsworth, J. B., *The Idea of Epic* (Berkeley, 1991).

Janko, R., *Homer, Hesiod and the Hymns: Diachronic Development in Epic Diction* (Cambridge, 1982).

Lord, A. B., *The Singer of Tales* (Cambridge, Mass., 1960).

Moulton, C., *Similes in the Homeric Poems* (Göttingen, 1977).

Murnaghan, S., *Disguise and Recognition in the Odyssey* (Princeton, 1987).

Nagler, M. N., *Spontaneity and Tradition: A Study in the Oral Art of Homer* (Berkeley, 1974).

Page, D., *Folktales in Homer's Odyssey* (Cambridge, Mass., 1973).

Parry, M., *The Making of Homeric Verse: The Collected Papers of Milman Parry*, ed. A. Parry (Oxford, 1971).

Reece, S., *The Stranger's Welcome: The Aesthetics of the Homeric Hospitality Scene* (Ann Arbor, Mich., 1993).

Ricks, D., *The Shade of Homer: A Study in Modern Greek Poetry* (Cambridge, 1989).

Rubens, B., and Taplin, O., *An Odyssey Round Odysseus: The Man and His Story Traced through Time and Place* (London, 1989).

Rutherford, R. B., *Homer* (2nd edn. Cambridge, 2013).

Schein, S. L. (ed.), *Reading the Odyssey* (Princeton, 1996).

Scodel, R., *Listening to Homer: Tradition, Narrative, and Audience* (Ann Arbor, Mich., 2002).

Segal, C., *Singers, Heroes, and Gods in the Odyssey* (Ithaca, NY, 1994).

Snodgrass, A., *Homer and the Artists: Text and Picture in Early Greek Art* (Cambridge, 1998).

Stanford, W. B., *The Ulysses Theme: A Study in the Adaptability of a Traditional Hero* (2nd edn. Oxford, 1963).

Thalmann, W. G., *The Swineherd and the Bow: Representations of Class in the Odyssey* (Ithaca, NY, 1998).

Thornton, A., *People and Themes in Homer's Odyssey* (London, 1970).

Tracy, S. V., *The Story of the Odyssey* (Princeton, 1990).

West, M. L., *The East Face of Helicon: West Asiatic Elements in Greek Poetry and Myth* (Oxford, 1997).

SELECT BIBLIOGRAPHY xxix

West, M. L., *The Epic Cycle: A Commentary on the Lost Troy Epics* (Oxford, 2013).

West, M. L., *The Making of the Odyssey* (Oxford, 2014).

Wright, G. M., and Jones, P. V. (eds.), *Homer: German Scholarship in Translation* (Oxford, 1997).

Further Reading in Oxford World's Classics

Greek Lyric Poetry, trans. M. L. West.

Hesiod, *Theogony* and *Works and Days*, trans. M. L. West.

Homer, *The Iliad*, trans. A. Verity.

The Homeric Hymns, trans. M. Crudden.

Greece and Asia Minor

THE ODYSSEY

THE ODYSSEY

BOOK ONE

Tell me, Muse, of the man of many turns, who was driven
far and wide after he had sacked the sacred city of Troy.
Many were the men whose cities he saw, and learnt their minds,
many the sufferings on the open sea he endured in his heart,
struggling for his own life and his companions' homecoming.   5
Even so he could not protect them, though he desired it,
since they perished by reason of their own recklessness,
the fools, because they ate the cattle of the Sun, Hyperion,
and he took away the day of their homecoming. Tell us, too,
goddess daughter of Zeus,* starting from where you will.   10
　　All the others, those who had escaped sheer destruction,
had reached home, now delivered from war and the sea;
one man alone, longing to return to his home and his wife, was
detained by Calypso, revered nymph, bright among goddesses,
in her hollow caverns, desiring him to be her husband.   15
But when in the course of circling seasons the year came
in which the gods had spun the thread for his return home
to Ithaca, not even then was he clear of trials or back
among his own dear ones. All the gods had pity for him
except Poseidon, who raged unrelentingly against   20
godlike Odysseus until the time he reached his homeland.
But Poseidon was visiting the Ethiopians who live far away—
the Ethiopians, most remote of men, who live in two places,
some at the setting of Hyperion and some at his rising.*
He was to receive from them a hecatomb* of bulls and rams,   25
and there he sat among them and enjoyed the feast. Meanwhile
the other gods had gathered in the halls of Olympian Zeus, and
among them the father of men and gods was the first to speak;
he had been brooding in his mind over excellent Aegisthus,*
whom far-famed Orestes, Agamemnon's son, had killed.   30
With this man in mind he addressed the immortals:
'This is not good! See how mortals find fault with us gods!
They say it is from us that all evil things come, yet it is by their
own recklessness that they suffer hardship beyond their destiny;
as only now Aegisthus courted the wedded wife of Atreus' son   35

beyond his destiny, and murdered him on his return home, knowing
it would be his sheer destruction, since we had forewarned him,
and had sent to him Hermes, the keen-eyed slayer of Argus,*
telling him not to court Agamemnon's wife nor to kill him, for
vengeance would come at the hands of Orestes, Atreus' grandson,   40
when he should reach manhood and long for his own country.
That is what Hermes said, but his kindly counsel did not persuade
the mind of Aegisthus, who now has paid the penalty in full.'
    Then the goddess grey-eyed Athena answered him:
'Our father, son of Cronus, supreme among rulers,   45
Aegisthus indeed lies dead, killed exactly as he deserved;
so may any other man perish who commits such acts.
But it is for wise Odysseus that my heart is on fire, ill-
fated man, who has long been suffering hardship, far from
his friends, on a sea-girt island at the navel-point of the sea*—   50
an island full of trees, and a goddess has her dwelling on it,
daughter of murderous-minded Atlas,* who knows the deeps
of the whole sea and by himself holds up the tall pillars
that keep the earth and the high sky asunder.
It is his daughter who delays this unhappy, grieving man,   55
all the time bewitching him with soft, winning words,
hoping to make him forget Ithaca. But Odysseus, yearning
only to catch sight of the smoke curling up from his own land,
longs only to die. Despite this, Olympian, your heart has not
changed towards him in any way. Did not Odysseus win your   60
favour, offering sacrifices to you by the ships of the Argives
in broad Troy? Zeus, why are you so odious to Odysseus?'*
    Then in answer Zeus the cloud-gatherer addressed her:
'My child, what a word has escaped the barrier of your teeth!
How could I ever forget godlike Odysseus, who is beyond   65
all mortals in understanding, and has made offerings beyond
others to the gods who dwell in the broad high sky?
No, it is Poseidon, encircler of the earth, who persists in
stubborn anger because of the Cyclops, godlike Polyphemus,
who rules supreme over all the Cyclopes, and was robbed of   70
his one eye by Odysseus. His mother was the nymph Thoösa,
daughter of Phorcys, who holds sway over the restless sea,
and she had lain with Poseidon in his hollow caverns.
It is for this reason that Poseidon the earthshaker is driving

Odysseus away from his native land, though he stops short   75
of killing him. Come, let all who are here take thought
as to how he may return home. Poseidon will give up
his anger; he will certainly not be able to go on opposing
us, if he is alone against the will of all the immortal gods.'
    Then the goddess grey-eyed Athena answered him: 80
'Our father, son of Cronus,* supreme among rulers,
if it really is now the desire of the blessed gods, that
Odysseus of many designs should return to his home,
let us now rouse Hermes the guide, the slayer of Argus,
to go to the island of Ogygia, so that he may quickly tell   85
the nymph with lovely hair of your infallible decision,
that Odysseus of the enduring spirit must return home.
As for me, I shall make my way to Ithaca, to urge his son
to greater action; I shall put vigour in his heart to summon
the long-haired Achaeans to an assembly, and to speak   90
out against the suitors for their constant slaughter of his
crowding sheep and crook-horned shambling cattle.
I shall send him to Sparta and sandy Pylos, to ask about his
dear father's return, in the hope that he will hear some news,
and so that he may win noble fame in the eyes of men.'   95
    So she spoke, and bound under her feet her beautiful sandals,
golden and deathless, that carried her over the watery sea
and the boundless earth, keeping pace with the wind's breath.
She took up her stout spear, tipped with sharp bronze, heavy,
thick, and massive, with which she beats down ranks of men,   100
of heroes with whom she, child of a mighty father, is enraged.
Down she went, swooping from the peaks of Olympus, and
alighted in the land of Ithaca by Odysseus' porch, on the
courtyard's threshold, bronze-tipped spear in hand; and in
the likeness of his guest-friend* Mentes, the Taphians'* leader.   105
There she found the proud suitors delighting their hearts
in front of the doors with games of draughts, and sitting
on the hides of oxen that they themselves had slaughtered.
Heralds and diligent attendants were busy about them,
some of them mixing wine and water in large bowls and   110
some wiping down tables with porous sponges and setting
them out, while others served out large portions of meat.
    First to notice Athena was Telemachus, looking like a god;

he was sitting among the suitors, troubled in his heart,
picturing his noble father and wondering if he would ever   115
return home and scatter the suitors in confusion about his house,
winning honour for himself and ownership of his possessions.
He was sitting among them with thoughts like these when he
noticed Athena, and made straight for the porch, angry in his
heart that a stranger should stand so long at the door. He stood   120
beside her, grasped her right hand, and took the bronze-tipped
spear from her and addressed her, using winged words:
   'Greetings, friend; you will find hospitality here with us, and
when you have had your meal you can speak of what you need.'
So he spoke, and led the way, and Pallas Athena followed him.   125
When they were inside the lofty hall, Telemachus took
the spear and leant it against a tall pillar, inside a polished
spear-stand, where many other weapons that belonged to
Odysseus of the enduring spirit were standing; leading her to
a beautiful, finely worked chair he invited her to sit, after   130
spreading a linen cloth upon it; and there was a stool for her feet.
For himself he pulled up an ornate seat, apart from the rest, the
suitors, fearing the stranger might be disturbed by their noise
and, surrounded by insolent men, might lose his desire for food;
and besides, he wanted to ask him about his absent father.   135
A maidservant brought water in a beautiful golden pitcher
and poured it into a silver bowl for them to wash their hands,
and drew up a polished table to stand beside them.
A respected housekeeper fetched bread and set it before them,
and added a heap of delicacies, giving freely from her store,   140
while a carver brought platters of different kinds of meat
and set them before them, and placed golden cups alongside,
and a herald passed to and fro and poured their wine.
   Then the proud suitors entered, and took their seats
in proper order on seats and chairs. Heralds moved   145
among them and poured water over their hands, and
women servants heaped up bread in baskets, while
young men filled mixing-bowls to the brim with wine.
The suitors reached out for the good things that lay before them,
and when they had put away the desire for food and drink   150
their minds turned to thoughts of other things—singing
and dancing, which are the accompaniments of feasts.

A herald put a beautifully made lyre into the hands of
Phemius, the one who sang for the suitors under compulsion,*
and he struck up on his lyre the prelude to a splendid song;   155
but Telemachus spoke to grey-eyed Athena, holding his
head close to hers, so that the others should not hear:
'Dear guest, I hope you will not be indignant with what I say?
This is all that these men care about, the lyre and the song—
easy pleasures, for they pay nothing to consume another man's   160
livelihood, a man whose white bones are rotting somewhere
in the rain, lying on the mainland or rolled in the salt sea's swell.
If they were to see him coming back to his home on Ithaca
they would all of them pray for greater swiftness of foot,
instead of further enrichment in gold and in clothing.   165
But that cannot be; he has perished in an evil doom, and
there is no comfort for us, even if some earth-dwelling man
says he will come; his day of homecoming has gone for ever.
But come, tell me this and give me a full and true account:
Who among men are you? Where are you from? Where are your city   170
and parents? What kind of ship did you arrive in? How did sailors
bring you to Ithaca? What kind of men did they claim to be,
for I do not suppose for a moment you arrived here on foot?
So tell me this truly, so that I may know clearly whether
this is the first time you have come here, or if you are also   175
a guest-friend of my father's; there were many who came to
our house at the time when he was going about among men.'
   Then the goddess grey-eyed Athena addressed him:
'I will indeed give you a full account of all you ask:
I am proud to name myself Mentes, son of wise Anchialus,   180
and I rule over the Taphians who take delight in rowing.
I am here now after putting in with my ship and companions,
sailing over the wine-dark sea in search of men of alien tongues,
to Temese* in pursuit of bronze; and my cargo is gleaming iron.
My ship is moored out there near open country, away from   185
the city, in the harbour of Rheithrum, under wooded Neion.
We can claim to be ancestral guest-friends of each other
from long ago—as you would find if you were to go and ask
the hero Laertes, who men say no longer comes to the city,
but lives a life of hardship far from here in the country,   190
with an old woman servant who provides him with food

and drink whenever weariness seizes his joints after
painful toil in the sloping plot of his vine-bearing earth.
So here I am. People did say he was here in his homeland,
I mean your father, but clearly the gods are thwarting his return.   195
Glorious Odysseus cannot yet be dead on this earth,
but must be detained somewhere out in the broad sea,
on a sea-girt island. Hard-hearted men confine him there,
savages, who must be holding him back against his will.
Now I shall speak to you as a prophet, just as the immortals   200
put it into my mind, and as I believe it will be fulfilled,
though I am by no means a seer, nor have any skill in bird-lore.
I tell you, he will not be absent from his dear native land
for much longer, not even if iron chains should hold him;
he is a man of many schemes, and will be planning his return.   205
But come, tell me this and give me a full and true account:
you are a grown man—so are you really Odysseus' son?
You are startlingly like him in your head and your fine eyes.
We were very often in each other's company, at any rate
before he embarked for Troy, to which others too, the best   210
of the Argives, sailed in their hollow ships. But since that
time I have never set eyes on Odysseus, nor he on me.'
    Then in turn thoughtful Telemachus spoke to her in reply:
'I shall indeed, guest-friend, give you a true account.
My mother maintains that I am her son, though for my part   215
I do not know, since no one ever really knows his parentage.
How I wish I were the son of some fortunate man, one whom
old age has come upon in the enjoyment of his possessions!
But as it is—since you ask me this question—they say I am
the son of one who was born the unluckiest of all mortal men.'   220
    Then in turn the goddess grey-eyed Athena addressed him:
'The gods have not given you a family that will be without
fame in time to come, since Penelope has borne a son like you.
But come, tell me this and give me a full and true account.
What feast is this? What is this crowd? What is it to do with you?   225
A feast or a wedding? It is clearly not a contribution dinner.*
How arrogantly and insolently they feast in your house, or
so it seems to me; any sensible-minded man in their company
would be indignant at the sight of such shameless behaviour.'
    Then in turn thoughtful Telemachus answered her: 230

'Guest-friend, since you ask me this, and seek to know:
this house was once most likely to be rich and thriving,
while that man was still at home here among his people;
but now the gods, with evil intent, have wished it otherwise,
causing him to vanish completely, beyond the fate of all men.   235
I would not be grieving for him in this way if he had died
beaten down in the Trojans' land with his companions, or
in the arms of his friends, having spun out the thread of war.
Then all the Achaeans would have made him a burial-mound,
and he would have won great fame for his son in time to come.   240
But as it is, storm winds have swept him to obscurity;
he has gone, unseen, unknown, and has left behind for me
anguish and lamentation. Nor is it for him alone that I mourn
and grieve; the gods have devised further sorrows for me.
All those chieftains who exercise rule over the islands,   245
Dulichium and Same and wooded Zacynthus,* and all
those who are lords throughout rocky Ithaca, are every one
courting my mother and grinding down my house's wealth.
She neither refuses them a marriage hateful to her, nor is able to
bring things to a head; meanwhile they devour my household   250
and waste it away. Soon they will prove to be my ruin too.'
     Then in deep indignation Pallas Athena addressed him:
'A terrible thing! How much you must miss the absent Odysseus,
who would lay his hands on these shameless suitors.
How I wish he could come now and take his stand at the   255
outer doors, with his helmet and shield and his two spears,
looking as he did when I saw him for the first time in my
house, drinking wine and taking his pleasure, on his way
home from Ephyre,* from the house of Ilus, Mermerus' son.
You see, Odysseus had gone to that place on his swift   260
ship in search of a man-slaying drug, so that he could
smear it on his bronze-tipped arrows.* Ilus did not give it
to him, because he had regard for the indignation of the
immortal gods, but my father did, for he loved him greatly.
I wish Odysseus as he then was might come among the suitors—   265
that would mean quick deaths and bitter marriage-hopes
for them all. But this of course lies on the knees of the gods,
whether he returns home and takes vengeance in his own
halls, or not. As for you, I advise you to take thought

as to how you can drive the suitors out of your house.   270
So listen carefully, and pay attention to my words:
tomorrow, summon all the Achaean heroes to an assembly
and address them all; and let the gods be your witnesses.
Order the suitors to leave, each man to his own home; and
as for your mother, if her heart urges her to be married,   275
let her go back to the house of her powerful father, and
the people there will arrange the marriage and prepare
plentiful bride-gifts, such as go with a loved daughter.
As for you, I shall give you shrewd advice, and I hope you
will listen. Fit out a ship with twenty rowers, the best you can,   280
and set off to learn about your long-absent father, to see if
any mortal has word for you, or if you will hear a rumour
from Zeus, which is above all how reports reach men.
First go to Pylos and question glorious Nestor, and from
there to Sparta, to meet fair-haired Menelaus, since he was   285
the very last of the bronze-shirted Achaeans to come home.
If you hear that your father is still alive and on his way home
then, though worn down, you can still endure for even a year;
but if you learn that he is now dead, and no longer living,
you must come back to your dear native land and heap up   290
a grave-mound for him and perform all the funeral rites
due to him, and then give your mother to a new husband.
When you have done all this and brought it to an end,
then you must weigh up in your mind and in your heart
how you may kill the suitors who are in your halls,   295
either by tricking them or in open fight; it is time for you
to give up childish ways, because you are no longer a child.*
Have you not heard of the fame glorious Orestes won in the
eyes of all men by killing the man who slew his father,
Aegisthus the crafty schemer, butcher of his famous father?   300
My friend, I can see that you are a fine, strapping fellow;
you must be brave too, so that future generations will praise you.
As for me, I shall now go back to my swift ship and my
companions, who are doubtless waiting for me with impatience.
Keep your mind fixed on all this, and take my words to heart.'   305
     Then in turn thoughtful Telemachus answered her:
'Guest-friend, what you say is surely done with kind intent,
like a father talking to his son; I shall never forget your words.

But come now, stay a while, eager though you are to leave,
so that you may bathe and let your heart take its ease;　　　310
and then, glad in spirit, go back to your ship with a gift,
a precious, splendid gift, such as close guest-friends
exchange; it will be a valued possession for you from me.'

　　Then the goddess grey-eyed Athena answered him:
'Do not try to detain me longer; I am eager to leave.　　　315
As for the gift, whatever your heart urges you to give me,
give it to me when I come back, to take to my home; choose
a very good one, and you will receive its equal in return.'

　　So the goddess grey-eyed Athena spoke, and at once departed,
shooting upwards in flight like a bird; and into Telemachus' heart　320
she thrust vigour and daring, and made him think of his father,
more than before. In his mind he grasped what had happened,
and was amazed in his heart, for he suspected it was a god.
At once he made his way back to the suitors, a man like a god.

　　The renowned singer was singing to them, and they sat and　325
listened in silence as he sang of the Achaeans' return home,
a bitter ordeal, sent them by Pallas Athena after they left Troy.
In her upstairs room the daughter of Icarius, circumspect
Penelope, heard and understood his divinely inspired song,
and came down the tall staircase from her part of the house,　330
not on her own, but attended by two women servants.
When she, glorious among women, reached the suitors
she stood next to a pillar supporting the strongly built
roof, holding her shining veil in front of her face, and
a devoted woman servant stood on either side of her.　335
Through tears she addressed the god-inspired singer:
'Phemius, you know many other songs to charm mortals—
the deeds of men and gods, such as singers often celebrate.
Sing one of these as you sit among these men, and let them
drink their wine in silence, but leave off this gloomy song,　340
which always bears heavily on the heart in my breast; a
singular grief, one that I cannot forget, comes over me as I
yearn for someone whom I think of constantly, a man whose
fame spreads widely through Hellas and the heart of Argos.'

　　Then in turn thoughtful Telemachus answered her:　345
'Mother, why do you grudge the trusty singer the chance
to give pleasure just as his mind bids him? It is not singers

who are to blame, but Zeus must be to blame, who hands out
their destiny to bread-eating mankind, to each as he pleases.
We should not be indignant if this man sings of the Danaans'*   350
wretched fate, since men always give most praise to the
song that is the latest to reach the ears of its audience.
So let your heart and spirit be strong to listen; Odysseus
is not the only man at Troy to lose the day of his return
home, since many other men perished there as well.   355
Go back to your rooms and take charge of your own tasks,
the loom and the distaff, and order your women servants
to go about their work. Talk must be men's concern, all of
them, and mine especially, for the power in the house is mine.'

Penelope was amazed, and went back again into her rooms,   360
and stored the discerning words of her son in her heart.
She went up into the rooms with her women servants and
there wept for Odysseus, her dear husband, until Athena
the grey-eyed let fall sweet sleep upon her eyes.

Meanwhile the suitors were creating an uproar in the shadowy   365
halls, all praying to be the one to lie in her bed with her.
And now thoughtful Telemachus began to speak among them:
'Suitors of my mother, you are men of violent insolence!
Let us now feast and take our pleasure, and let there be no
shouting, since it is a good thing to listen to a singer such as   370
this one, a man whose voice resembles that of the gods.
But in the morning let us take our seats in the meeting-place,
all of us, and I shall make my demands to you, in all directness.
You must leave my halls, and think of feasting elsewhere,
eating up your own possessions and taking turns in your houses.   375
If, however, you think it is a better thing and more profitable
to exhaust the substance of one man without payment,
then go on consuming it, and I shall cry out to the immortals
in the hope that Zeus may some day grant me redress; and
then you would perish in my house, with no restitution given.'   380
So he spoke, and they all bit hard on their lips and were
amazed at Telemachus, because he had spoken out so boldly.

Then in turn Antinous, the son of Eupeithes, addressed him:
'Telemachus, only the gods themselves can have taught you
to be such an assembly loudmouth, and to speak so boldly!   385
I hope the son of Cronus never makes you king here in

sea-girt Ithaca, though that is admittedly your right by birth.'*
  Then in turn thoughtful Telemachus answered him:
'Antinous, you may well be surprised at what I say, but
I would be ready to accept the kingship, if Zeus granted it.   390
Do you think this is the worst that can happen to a man?
It is certainly no bad thing to be a king; a man's house
quickly becomes wealthy, and he himself gains more honour.
There are however other princes of the Achaeans on sea-girt
Ithaca, many of them, both young and old; let one of them   395
possess this honour, now that glorious Odysseus is dead.
For myself, I shall be the lord of my house and my servants,
those whom glorious Odysseus won by plunder and left to me.'
  Then in turn Eurymachus, the son of Polybus, answered him:
'Telemachus, this matter surely lies on the knees of the gods,   400
which of the Achaeans will be king on sea-girt Ithaca; still,
I hope you keep your possessions, and rule your household,
and that no one will come and wrest them from you by force
against your will, so long as there are men living on Ithaca.
But, my good sir, I want to ask you about this stranger: 405
where is he from, what country does he claim as his own,
where is his family, and where his ancestral ploughlands?
Does he bring some news about your father's coming, or
has he come this way to settle some business of his own?
How quickly he leapt up and vanished, and did not stay to be   410
known! He certainly did not have the look of a low-born man.'
  Then in turn thoughtful Telemachus answered him:
'Eurymachus, I am sure my father's homecoming is lost,
so I can no longer believe messages that come from anywhere;
nor do I pay any heed to divine revelations that my mother   415
may seek to understand by inviting seers into this hall.
This stranger is a guest-friend of my father's from Taphos;
he declares himself to be Mentes, the son of wise Anchialus,
and he rules over the Taphians who delight in rowing.'
  So Telemachus spoke, but he knew in his heart the immortal   420
goddess. The suitors returned to the dance and the charming
song, enjoying themselves and waiting for evening to come.
In the midst of their pleasures black night came down,
and then at last they left for bed, each one to his own house.
But Telemachus headed for where a high room had been   425

built for him in a sheltered part of the splendid courtyard, and
there went to his bed, turning over many things in his mind.
A devoted servant brought blazing torches for him; she was
Eurycleia, the daughter of Ops who was the son of Peisenor,
and Laertes had bought her long ago with his own wealth,   430
in her first youth, and he gave twenty oxen's worth for her,
and honoured her in his halls as much as his devoted wife;
but he never took her to bed, wishing to avoid his wife's anger.
She now brought Telemachus blazing torches; of all the servants
she loved him the most, and had nursed him when he was small.   435
He opened the doors of the strongly built room and sat
down on his bed and took off his soft tunic, and put it
into the hands of the sharp-witted old woman; and she
then folded the tunic, treating it with great care, and
hung it on a peg next to the fretted bed. Then she made   440
her way out of the room and pulled the door to by its
silver handle, drawing home the bolt with its leather strap.
There Telemachus lay all night, wrapped in a woollen blanket,
planning in his mind the journey that Athena had proposed.

BOOK TWO

When early-born Dawn with her rosy fingers appeared,
the dear son of Odysseus rose from his bed and put on
his clothes, and slung his sharp sword from his shoulder;
and under his shining feet he bound his fine sandals, and
made his way from the chamber, in presence like a god.   5
Without delay he commanded his clear-voiced heralds to
summon the flowing-haired Achaeans to an assembly.
So they made the summons, and the men gathered very swiftly.
When they had assembled and were gathered together
he set off for the meeting-place, bronze sword in hand,   10
not alone, but two swift-footed dogs went along with him;
and Athena poured down astounding grace over him.
As he approached all the people gazed in amazement at him;
he took his seat in his father's place, and the elders fell back.

   The first to speak among them was the hero Aegyptius,   15
who was bent with old age and a man of great experience.
His dear son had gone with godlike Odysseus in his hollow
ships to Troy, rich in horses; this was the spearman
Antiphus, and the cruel Cyclops had killed him in his hollow
cave, and served him up last of all to make his supper.   20
Aegyptius had three other sons: one, Euronymus, kept company
with the suitors, and two stayed tending their family farmlands.
Yet Aegyptius never forgot Antiphus, lamenting and grieving
over him. Weeping tears for him now he spoke out among them:
'Listen to me now, men of Ithaca, to what I have to say: 25
we have never yet held a meeting here, nor any session,
since the time that glorious Odysseus left in his hollow ships.
Who has now called this one? Who is he, one of the young
men, or one of the elders? What great need has visited him?
Has he heard a report of some army drawing near, and being   30
the first to find out wishes to give us clear intelligence?
Or is there some public matter he will announce and unfold?
A good man he seems to me, and blessed; I pray that Zeus
may bring whatever he desires in his heart to a good fulfilment.'

   So he spoke, and Odysseus' dear son was glad at the omen;   35

eager to speak out, he did not stay seated for long, but took
his stand in the middle of the assembly. The herald Peisenor,
a man of discerning counsel, put the staff into his hand, and
he first turned to the old man Aegyptius and addressed him:
'Old man, that man is not far away, as you will soon find out: 40
it was I who summoned the people, being sorely touched by grief.
I have heard no report of an army drawing near, about which
I wish to give you clear intelligence, being the first to find out,
nor is there any public matter that I shall announce and unfold.
No, the need is mine alone. Disaster has fallen upon my house,   45
in two ways: I have lost my noble father, who once was king over
you who are gathered here, and was like a kindly father to you;
and now here is a far greater calamity, which will soon utterly
shatter my whole house, and completely ruin my livelihood:
much against her will my mother is assailed by suitors,   50
the dear sons of, yes, those who are the best men here,
but who shrink from approaching the house of her father
Icarius, to persuade him to give his daughter a dowry
and offer her to the man he wishes and favours the most.
Day after day, these people keep coming to my house,   55
slaughtering my oxen and sheep and fat goats, holding
revels and drinking my gleaming wine, in utter heedlessness;
and most of my substance is now wasted. No more is there
a man to keep ruin from the house, such as Odysseus was;
we ourselves are not strong enough to defend it, and will   60
surely prove to be pitiful creatures, quite without courage.
And yet if I had the power, I would stand up for myself;
these deeds are no longer to be borne, and my house's
ruin has become a disgrace; even you should be outraged,
and feel shame before the people who live round about,   65
our neighbours; you should fear the gods' vengeful anger,
lest, affronted by these vile deeds, they turn against you.
I entreat you, in the name of Olympian Zeus, and of Themis,
who both initiates the assemblies of men and breaks them up,
stop, my friends, and leave me alone to be worn down by my   70
wretched sorrow—unless of course my father noble Odysseus
once did some wrong to the well-greaved Achaeans out of ill-will,
in return for which you, out of ill-will, are wronging me in revenge,
by inciting these men. For me, it would be better if you Ithacans

were simply eating up my possessions and flocks of sheep;   75
if it were just your greed, there might one day be recompense,
for then we could confront you all over the city with claims
and demand our property back, until everything was returned.
As it is, you are cramming pain into my heart that I cannot relieve.'

    So he spoke in great anger, and with a sudden burst of tears   80
hurled the staff to the ground, and pity gripped all the people.
All the others stayed silent, and no one was bold enough
to answer Telemachus with angry words equal to his;
and only Antinous addressed him in reply: 'Telemachus,
you intemperate public loudmouth, how your words   85
seek to shame us! You want to fasten the blame on us!
With you the Achaean suitors have no quarrel; no, it is your
mother, that exceedingly cunning woman, who is at fault.
It is now the third year, and a fourth will soon be here, since
she began to deceive the hearts of the Achaeans in their breasts.   90
She holds out hope to all, and promises herself to each man,
sending messages to him, but her mind has another purpose.
And here is a new deception she has devised in her mind.
She set up a great loom in her halls and began to weave
on it, using fine, very long thread, and then said to us: 95
"Young princes, my suitors! Glorious Odysseus is dead; but
eager though you are for this marriage, wait until I finish
this robe, so that my weaving is not wasted, all in vain. It is
a burial shroud* for the hero Laertes, meant for when the cruel
fate of death, bringer of long misery, takes him away, so that   100
no Achaean woman in our people will be indignant with me
because he who amassed great wealth is lying without a shroud."
That is what she said, and our proud hearts were persuaded.
From that time she would weave at the great loom by day, but
at night torches were set beside her and she unravelled her work.   105
So for three years her guile went unnoticed and she fooled the
Achaeans; but when with the seasons' round the fourth year arrived,
then at last one of her women, who knew the deceit well, told us,
and we found her in the act of undoing the bright weaving; and so
the robe was brought forcibly to completion, albeit against her will.   110
This then is the suitors' answer, that you may know the truth
in your own heart, and that all the Achaeans too may know it.
Send your mother away, and tell her to marry whichever

man her father orders her to wed, and who is to her liking.
But if she means to weary the sons of the Achaeans for long,   115
plotting with the many talents that Athena has given her—
her skill in beautiful handiwork, her excellent character and
her cleverness—qualities we do not hear about now, not even
among the lovely-haired Achaean women of long ago, such
as Tyro and Alcmene and Mycene of the beautiful crown;*   120
not one of these was Penelope's equal in shrewdness of mind
(though in this one instance her thoughts have not been seemly);
if she does, your livelihood and possessions will be devoured
as long as she keeps to that purpose, whatever it is that the gods
have now put into her breast. She may be winning great fame   125
for herself, but for you it means much loss of livelihood.
As for us, we will not go back to our estates or anywhere else
until she agrees to marry whichever Achaean she chooses.'
    Then in turn thoughtful Telemachus answered him:
'Antinous, I cannot drive her unwilling from my house,   130
she who bore and nurtured me. My father, alive or dead,
is elsewhere in the world; it will be hard to pay Icarius
a large sum if of my own free will I send my mother away.
I shall suffer some hurt from him, her father, and a god will
send me more trouble, since my mother will call down hateful   135
furies when she leaves the house, and the people's anger
will fall upon me. So I shall never say that word to her.
As for all of you, if your spirits are outraged by my words,
leave my halls and turn your minds to feasting elsewhere,
eating up your own possessions and taking turns in your houses.   140
But if you think it is a better thing and more to your benefit
to exhaust the substance of one man without payment,
then go on consuming it, and I shall cry out to the immortals
in the hope that Zeus may somehow grant me redress;
then you would perish in my house, with no restitution given.'   145
    So Telemachus spoke, and in answer wide-thundering Zeus
sent two eagles swooping down from a high mountain peak.
These for a while flew along on gusts of wind, driving
onwards with their wings close to each other; but when
they were over the middle of the assembly, place of many   150
speeches, they turned and wheeled, wings beating rapidly,
and hovered over the heads of all with destruction in their eyes.

With their talons they tore at each other's cheeks and necks, and
then darted away to the right, over the Ithacans' city and houses.
When they saw these birds before their eyes the people were   155
amazed, and wondered in their hearts what would happen next.
At last the aged hero Halitherses, son of Mastor, spoke out
among them; alone of all his generation he excelled in
the knowledge of birds and interpretation of their omens.
With generous intent he spoke out and addressed them: 160
    'Listen to me now, men of Ithaca, to what I have to say:
to the suitors most of all I make this pronouncement, since
a huge disaster will soon overwhelm them: Odysseus will not
be long away from his loved ones, but is even now somewhere
nearby, planting the seed of slaughter and doom for these men,   165
all of them; and ruin will come upon many others too, on us
who live on clear-seen Ithaca. Long before this happens let us
consider how we may make them stop—or better, let them
stop themselves, because this is surely their better course.
This is no unskilled prophecy; I know well what I am saying.   170
I declare that for Odysseus everything has been fulfilled just
as I prophesied when the Argives took ship on their way to
to Troy, and Odysseus, man of many wiles, went with them.
I said he would suffer greatly and lose all his companions,
and in the twentieth year* would come back to his home,   175
unrecognized by everyone; and now all this is coming to pass.'
    Then in turn Eurymachus, son of Polybus, answered him:
'Enough, old man! Go home now, and prophesy to your
children, for fear they may suffer some harm in the future.
In these matters I am a far better prophet than you. There are   180
many birds flying this way and that in the rays of the sun,
but they do not all signify something. As for Odysseus,
he is dead, far away; and I wish you too had died along with
him, for then you would not be delivering so many predictions,
nor would you be exciting Telemachus to anger like this,   185
hoping that he might give you some gift for your household.
I tell you this plainly, and I believe it will be fulfilled:
if ever you, with all your ancient knowledge and skill,
beguile a younger man with words and so stir him to anger,
first of all it will be the worse for him, because in any case   190
he will not be able to achieve anything because of these men,

and also we shall lay a fine on you, old man, which you will
find painful to pay; and that will be a heavy misery for you.
As for Telemachus, I advise him in the presence of you all:
let him order his mother to return to her father's house, and   195
his people there will arrange the marriage and prepare a
plentiful dowry, such as is proper to go with a loved daughter.
I do not believe the sons of the Achaeans will give up their
unwished-for suit, since despite what men say, we fear no one,
no, not Telemachus, for all that he has become a big talker.   200
Nor do we care for the divine revelation that you, old man, tell
us about; it will come to nothing, and you will be the more hated.
Telemachus' wealth will be brutally eaten away, without any
compensation, so long as she puts off her marriage to us
Achaeans; meanwhile we, waiting expectantly day by day,   205
quarrel with each other over her excellence, and do not pursue
other women whom we might each of us be expected to marry.'

   Then in turn thoughtful Telemachus answered him:
'Eurymachus, and all you other lordly suitors, on this
matter I no longer entreat you, and I have no more to say,   210
since it is now known to the gods, and to all the Achaeans.
So now, grant me a swift ship and twenty companions to
go with me on a voyage, and to come back here afterwards.
I am going to Sparta and to sandy Pylos, in order to learn
about the return of my father who has been gone so long,   215
to see if any mortal has word for me, or if I can hear a rumour
coming from Zeus, which is above all how news reaches men.
If I hear that my father is alive and on his way home,
then, though worn down, I can still endure for even a year;
but if I learn that he is now dead, and no longer living,   220
I shall come back to my dear native land and heap up
a grave-mound for him and perform all the funeral rites
due to him, and then give my mother to a new husband.'

   So he spoke, and took his seat again, and among them stood up
Mentor, a man who had been a companion of excellent Odysseus;   225
when Odysseus took ship he had entrusted his whole household to
this old man to keep everything secure; and all were to obey him.
He with generous intent spoke out and addressed them:
'Listen to me now, men of Ithaca, to what I have to say:
let no staff-holding king ever feel the need to be gentle   230

and kindly again, nor to have right thoughts in his mind;
but let him be always harsh and unjust in his acts, seeing that
no one now remembers godlike Odysseus among the people
he used to rule; yet he was like a gentle father to them.
I say to you that I have no quarrel with the proud suitors,   235
at the violent deeds they commit in their minds' evil scheming,
for by riotously devouring Odysseus' household, thinking that
he will never return, they are putting their own lives at risk.
No, it is you other people I am indignant with, to see how you
all sit in silence and do not speak out and challenge the suitors—   240
they are few and you are many, and you do not restrain them.'

      Then Leocritus the son of Euenor spoke to him in answer:
'Wretched Mentor, your wits are crazed; what a thing to say,
urging them to stop us! It would be hard for them, even with
greater numbers, to fight against us, all for the sake of a feast.   245
Even if Odysseus lord of Ithaca himself were to come upon
the proud suitors feasting in his own house, and his heart was
raging to drive them from his hall, his wife would have no joy
in his coming, much though she had longed for him; but there
and then he would meet a shameful doom, fighting against   250
superior numbers. What you say makes no sense at all.
And now, let the people disperse, each to his own estate, and
Mentor and Halitherses will prepare this man's voyage for him;
they are his friends, as they have always been to his father.
For all that, I think he will sit here in Ithaca for a long time,   255
waiting for news, and will never complete this expedition.'

      So he spoke, and abruptly broke up the assembly, and
the people scattered, each man to his own house, and
the suitors went back into the house of godlike Odysseus.

      But Telemachus made his way apart, to the shore of the sea,   260
and washed his hands in the grey salt sea and prayed to Athena:
'Hear me, you who yesterday came to our house as a god
and ordered me to take ship over the misty sea, to learn
about the homecoming of my father, absent for so long.
But this is all being delayed by the Achaeans, and above   265
all by the suitors, in their wicked, arrogant behaviour.'

      So he spoke in prayer, and Athena came and stood by him,
taking on the likeness of Mentor in both form and voice,
and addressed him, speaking with winged words:

'Telemachus, you will not in future prove cowardly or foolish   270
if you have truly inherited your father's strong vigour—
and what a man he was for carrying out his word and deed—
and so your journey will surely not be unfulfilled or in vain.
If however you are not the offspring of him and of Penelope,
I have no hope that you will ever accomplish what you desire.   275
It is a truth that few sons are the equal of their fathers;
most are inferior to their father, and few surpass them.
Still—since you will not in future prove cowardly or
foolish, nor is Odysseus' cleverness wholly lacking in you—
there is hope that you will one day be successful in this.   280
So pay no attention to the suitors' plots and schemes, for
they are out of their minds, witless and given to wrongdoing,
nor do they know that death and black doom are even now
close to them, and that they will all perish on a single day.
As for you, the voyage you desire will not be long coming now;   285
such is my support for you as your father's companion that
I shall fit out a swift ship for you, and accompany you myself.
Go now to your house and join the company of suitors, and
get your provisions ready, and stow everything in containers,
the wine in two-handled jars and the grain, marrow of men,   290
in tightly fastened skins. I shall go among the people and
collect some volunteers to be your companions. There are
many ships in sea-girt Ithaca, both new and old, and these I
shall inspect and choose the one that is the best; then we shall
quickly fit it out and launch it on to the wide, open sea.'   295

   So spoke Athena, daughter of Zeus, and when Telemachus
had heard the goddess' voice he did not delay long.
He made his way towards his house, troubled in heart,
and there he found the proud suitors still in his halls,
skinning goats and singeing fatted swine in the courtyard.   300
Bursting into laughter Antinous made straight for Telemachus,
and grasping him firmly by the hand addressed him:
'Telemachus; you are an intemperate assembly loudmouth,
but do not let hard words or deeds trouble your heart;
come, please, eat and drink with us as in the past, and   305
the Achaeans will make all these things happen for you:
a ship and chosen oarsmen, so that you may quickly reach
sacred Pylos and search out news of your lordly father.'

Then in turn thoughtful Telemachus answered him:
'Antinous, there is no way that I can dine in silence and　　310
enjoy myself at ease among such arrogant men as you.
Is it not enough that in the past you wasted much of my
splendid property, you suitors, while I was still a child?
But now that I am full-grown, and can learn the true tale from
others, and indeed the spirit within me is growing stronger,　　315
I shall do my utmost to send grim death your way, whether
I sail to Pylos or stay behind here among this people.
But go I certainly shall, and the voyage I speak of will not
be in vain—though as a passenger, since I own neither ship
nor oarsman, which, I suppose, suits your purpose better.'　　320
So he spoke, and coolly pulled his hand away from Antinous'.
Now the suitors were busy with the feast about the house,
and in their talk began to mock and taunt Telemachus;
and this is what one of the arrogant young men would say:
'It must be that Telemachus is planning to murder us;　　325
either he will bring some men to help him from sandy Pylos,
or even from Sparta, since he is so fiercely set on his plan.
Or perhaps he means to visit Ephyre,* that country of rich
ploughland, to fetch back life-destroying poisons, and will
drop them into our mixing-bowl, and kill us every one.'　　330
And another of the arrogant young men would break in:
'Who knows if, sailing far from friends in his hollow ship,
he too will perish in his wanderings, just like Odysseus?
But that would make our task even greater, since we would
have to divide all his property between us, and give his house　　335
to his mother to keep, together with the man who marries her.'
So they spoke; but he went down into his father's high-roofed
storeroom, a wide chamber, where gold and bronze lay piled high,
and clothing stored in chests, and fragrant olive oil in plenty.
There stood jars of vintage wine that was sweet to drink,　　340
jars that held in them a divine drink, unmixed with water,
packed close in a line along the wall, against the time
Odysseus would come home, though after much suffering.
Bolts secured the tightly fitting double doors, made of two
leaves; and a woman housekeeper had charge of the room　　345
day and night, guarding everything with shrewd intelligence—
Eurycleia, daughter of Ops who was the son of Peisenor.

Telemachus now summoned her to the room and said:
'Look sharp, nanny, and draw me off some wine into jars,
sweet wine, the finest you have in your care after what you   350
are saving for that ill-fated man, hoping that Zeus-sprung
Odysseus will one day escape grim death and come home.
Fill twelve jars, and fit stoppers to them all. Then pour
some barley into well-stitched leather bags for me; I shall
need twenty measures in all of mill-crushed barley meal.   355
Keep this knowledge to yourself. Let it all be stacked up
together, since this very evening I shall collect it as soon as
my mother goes to her upper rooms and prepares for sleep.
You see, I am going to Sparta and to sandy Pylos, to ask
about my dear father's return, hoping I might hear some news.'   360
   So he spoke, and his dear nurse Eurycleia shrieked aloud,
and addressed him in winged words of lamentation:
'Dear child, how has this thought come into your mind?
How can you want to journey all over the wide world,
you, a beloved only son? Zeus-sprung Odysseus must be   365
lying dead in some foreign land, far from his own country.
As soon as you go these suitors will plan some wickedness
against you, to outwit you by guile and then share all this out.
Stay here, I beg you, and look after what you own. You have
no need to endure the misery of wandering over the restless sea.'   370
   Then in turn thoughtful Telemachus answered her:
'Do not despair, nanny; this plan is not without a god's making.
Come, swear that you will not report this to my dear mother
until the eleventh day from this has come, or the twelfth, or
until she misses me herself, or hears that I have set sail;   375
I would not want her to mar her lovely skin with weeping.'
   So he spoke, and the old woman swore a great oath by the
gods not to tell. When she had sworn, and brought her oath
to an end, she quickly drew off the wine for him into jars, and
poured the barley into strongly stitched leather bags; then   380
he went back to the palace and joined the suitors' company.
But then the goddess grey-eyed Athena had different plans:
she took on the likeness of Telemachus and went through the
whole city; she stood next to each man and spoke to him,
telling them to gather together that evening by the swift ship.   385
Next she sought out Noëmon, Phronius' renowned son,

and begged him for a swift ship; and he gladly promised it.
    The sun went down, and all the ways grew dark; and now
Athena dragged the swift ship down to the sea, and stowed
in it all the tackle that a well-benched ship carries.   390
She moored it at the harbour's far edge, and around it the good
crew gathered in a crowd, each man urged on by the goddess.
    But then the goddess grey-eyed Athena had still more plans.
She made her way to the palace of godlike Odysseus,
and there set about pouring sweet sleep over the suitors, dazing   395
them as they drank and knocking the cups from their hands.
Not one of them stayed sitting for long, and they rose and went
to their rest in the city, for sleep was dropping on to their eyes.
Then grey-eyed Athena addressed Telemachus, having first
summoned him from his well-situated halls, and taken on   400
herself the likeness of Mentor in both form and voice:
'Telemachus, your well-greaved companions are already
seated at their oars, waiting for you, for the order to sail.
So let us go; we must not delay our journey any longer.'
    So spoke Pallas Athena, and swiftly led the way, and   405
Telemachus followed, walking in the goddess' footsteps.
When they had come down to the ship and the sea they
found their flowing-haired companions on the shore;
and Telemachus, a man of divine might, spoke among them:
'Here, my friends, let us fetch our provisions; they are already   410
stacked up in my hall, and my mother knows nothing about it,
nor do the woman servants, except that one alone has been told.'
    So he spoke, and led the way, and the men went with him,
and fetched everything and stowed it in the well-benched
ship, just as the dear son of Odysseus had instructed them.   415
Then Telemachus boarded the ship, but Athena went first
and sat down in the ship's stern. Telemachus took his seat
next to her, and the others slipped the stern-cables and then
boarded themselves and took their seats at their oarlocks.
Grey-eyed Athena sent them a following breeze, the fresh-   420
blowing westerly, whistling over the wine-dark sea.
Telemachus urged on his companions, and told them to
set their hands to the tackle, and they obeyed his orders:
they stepped the fir-tree mast, making it fast inside its
hollow socket, and then secured it with forestays, and   425

hauled up the white sail, using tight-twisted oxhide ropes.
The wind filled the belly of the sail, and a dark wave
hissed loudly about the stem as the ship sailed on,
speeding over the waves and keeping close to its course.
When the men had made the rigging fast in the black ship,   430
they set up mixing-bowls and filled them to the brim, and
made drink-offerings to the immortal gods who live for
ever, but most of all to Zeus' grey-eyed daughter. And all
night long and into the dawning day the ship cut her way.

BOOK THREE

The sun leapt up into the brazen sky, leaving Ocean's
lovely waters behind, to shine on immortals and mortal
men, spreading its light over grain-giving ploughland;
and they came to Pylos, Neleus' well-established citadel.
There on the sea shore the people were making a sacrifice   5
of all-black bulls to the earthshaker, the god with dark-blue hair.
There were nine stations, and at each of them were seated
five hundred men; and every company presented nine bulls.
They had just tasted the entrails and burnt the thigh-bones
for the god when the Ithacans landed, brailed up the sail and   10
stowed it, moored the well-balanced ship, and came ashore.
Telemachus disembarked, but the grey-eyed goddess
Athena led the way, and she spoke first, addressing him:
'Telemachus, now there is no need to hold back, not even a little;
you have sailed over the sea with this one purpose, to learn about   15
your father: what kind of death he met, and where the earth
hides his body. So now go straight up to Nestor, breaker of horses;
let us find out what shrewd advice he keeps hidden in his breast.
Entreat him in person, so that he will speak the plain truth;
he will not lie to you, for he is a man of sound understanding.'   20
    Then in turn thoughtful Telemachus answered her:
'Mentor, how should I approach him, and how speak to him?
I have no skill yet in closely argued words; and then again,
it is embarrassing for a young man to question an older one.'
    Then in turn the goddess grey-eyed Athena addressed him: 25
'Telemachus, some words you will think of yourself in your mind,
and others some divinity will prompt you to—for I do not think
it was without the gods' purpose that you were born and raised.'
    So spoke Pallas Athena, and swiftly led the way, and
he followed, walking in the footsteps of the goddess, and   30
they came to where the Pylians were seated in assembly.
There Nestor sat with his sons, and around them their men were
cooking meat for the feast, and threading more on skewers.
When they saw the strangers the Pylians all came up together,
greeted them with handclasps, and invited them to be seated.   35

The first to reach them was Peisistratus, son of Nestor;
he grasped both by the hand and seated them on soft fleeces
that were spread on the sands of the shore, near the feast and
next to his brother Thrasymachus and his father. He then
gave them portions of entrails to eat, and poured wine   40
into a golden cup for them, and in welcome addressed
Pallas Athena, the daughter of Zeus who wields the aegis:*
'Make a prayer now, stranger, to the lord Poseidon;* his is
the feast that you have chanced upon in your coming here.
When you have made your offering and prayed, as is right,   45
then give a cup of honey-sweet wine to this man too, for him
to make an offering of drink; I think that he also will pray
to the immortals, since all men have need of the gods. But
this man is younger than you, and of the same age as myself,
and that is why I shall give you the golden cup before him.'   50
    So he spoke, and put the cup of sweet wine in her hand,
and Athena was delighted with the thoughtful, right-thinking
man, because he had given her the golden cup first.
At once she made an earnest prayer to lord Poseidon:
'Hear me, Poseidon, holder of the earth, and do not refuse   55
to bring to fulfilment what we shall now pray for.
First of all, grant lasting fame to Nestor and to his sons,
and next, give to the rest, to all the men of Pylos,
a pleasing return for their splendid hecatomb; lastly,
grant that Telemachus and I may return after completing   60
the business for which we came here in our black ship.'
    So she prayed, and herself made sure it would all be fulfilled.
She handed the beautiful, two-handled cup to Telemachus,
and in the same way Odysseus' dear son prayed. Then, when
they had cooked the outer meat and drawn it off the skewers,   65
they shared out portions and feasted on the magnificent meal.
When they had put away their desire for food and drink,
Nestor the Gerenian horseman was the first to speak:
'Now is a better time, when they have enjoyed their meal,
to seek news from the strangers and ask them who they are.   70
Strangers, who are you? Where have you sailed from, over the
watery pathways? Do you seek some business, or do you
roam on chance, like pirates who range over the sea, risking
their lives and bringing ruin to people in foreign lands?'

Then in turn thoughtful Telemachus answered him— 75
confidently, for Athena had put boldness into his heart,
so that he might question him about his absent father,
and so that he might win noble fame in the eyes of men:
'Nestor son of Neleus, great glory of the Achaeans,
you ask where we are from, so I shall give you a full account. 80
We have come from Ithaca, that lies under Mount Neion,
and the business I tell you of is not public but private: I am
seeking for news from abroad of my father, hoping somewhere
to hear about glorious Odysseus of enduring spirit, who they say
once fought with you when you sacked the city of the Trojans. 85
Of the others, all those went to war against the Trojans,
we have heard where each of them died his miserable death;
but even the death of this man has been concealed from us by
Cronus' son, and no one can say with certainty when he died—
whether he was beaten down by men in battle on the mainland, 90
or if he perished on the open sea in the waters of Amphitrite.*
That is why I now entreat you at your knees, hoping that you
can tell me about his unhappy death; perhaps you saw it with
your own eyes, or heard the tale of his wanderings from another.
More than other men, his mother bore him for wretchedness. 95
Do not let respect or pity for me soften your words,
but tell me exactly how you chanced to see him.
I entreat you: if ever my father, noble Odysseus, made any
promise in word or deed to you and then fulfilled it, in the
land of the Trojans where you Achaeans were hard pressed, 100
call it now to mind and tell me—and tell me the plain truth.'
Then Nestor, the Gerenian horseman, answered him:
'My friend, you remind me of all the misery we suffered
in that country, we the sons of the Achaeans of unbounded
vigour, both with our ships on the mist-shrouded open sea, 105
roving in search of booty wherever Achilles directed us,
and in all that we endured as we fought around the great
city of lord Priam. There all the best of us were killed;
there lies Ajax,* a man of Ares, there Achilles, and there
lies Patroclus,* a match for the gods in counsel; there 110
lies my own dear son, a man both mighty and blameless,
Antilochus,* who surpassed all men in running and fighting.
Many besides were the miseries we suffered there; no one among

death-doomed men could tell you the tale of them all, not even
if you were to stay with him for five years or six, questioning him   115
about the terrible sufferings the glorious Achaeans there endured;
for by that time you would have become weary and gone back home.
For nine years we wove ruin for the Trojans, busily plotting
all kinds of stratagems, and only after much labour did Cronus'
son end the war. There at Troy no one ever dared rank himself   120
against glorious Odysseus in scheming, since he far excelled
everyone in all kinds of cunning—your father, if you really
are his son. Indeed, amazement grips me as I look at you;
certainly you speak just as he did, and no one would think it
likely that a younger man's speech would so resemble his.   125
For as long as I and glorious Odysseus were there we never
spoke against each other in assembly or in council, but since
we were always of one mind we gave thoughtful advice to the
Argives, scheming how things might be ordered for the best.
But once we had sacked the sheer city of Priam, and had   130
embarked on our ships, and a god had scattered the Achaeans,
Zeus in his mind planned a sorry homecoming for the Argives,
since not all of them were upright in thought and deed; and
for that reason many of them met an evil doom, resulting from
the deadly anger* of the grey-eyed daughter of a mighty father.   135
It was she who caused strife between the two sons of Atreus:*
they summoned all the Achaeans to an assembly, without
due thought and in no proper order, towards the sun's setting.
The sons of the Achaeans came, heavy with wine, and Atreus'
sons announced why they had brought the people together.   140
First Menelaus told all the Achaeans that they should think
about returning home on the broad back of the sea; but
this was not at all to Agamemnon's liking, for he preferred
to hold the people back and to sacrifice sacred hecatombs,
hoping to appease the terrible anger of Athena—fool that he was,   145
because he did not know that she would not listen to him;
the minds of the gods who live for ever are not easily moved.
So the two of them stood there, exchanging hard words, and
the well-greaved Achaeans rose to their feet, making an
astonishing clamour, persuaded by one plan or the other.   150
So we passed the night, turning over hard thoughts in our minds
against each other, for Zeus was plotting dreadful suffering for us.

At dawn, some of us began to drag our ships down to the bright
sea and to stow in them our goods and deep-girdled women;
but half the army was being held back, waiting there with   155
Agamemnon, son of Atreus, shepherd of the people, while we,
the other half, embarked and made haste away. Our ships sailed
very swiftly, and a god calmed the monster-infested deep.
When we reached Tenedos we made holy offerings to the gods,
longing for home; but Zeus did not yet purpose our return,   160
hard god, and once again stirred up wretched strife among us.
Some, those who followed the wise lord Odysseus, cunning
counsellor, turned their well-balanced ships round and sailed back,
wishing to ingratiate themselves with Atreus' son Agamemnon;
but I fled on with the full number of ships that had come with me, 165
since I knew too well what miseries the god was planning.
With me sailed the son of Tydeus,* a son of Ares, urging on his
companions; and late in the day fair-haired Menelaus joined us,
catching up with us at Lesbos as we debated over our long voyage:
whether we should make our course north of rocky Chios,   170
towards the island of Psyria, keeping it to our left side, or should
sail to the south of Chios, keeping alongside windswept Mimas.
We begged the god to reveal a portent, and he sent us a sign,
telling us to cut across the open sea to Euboea, so that
we might make the swiftest possible escape from disaster.   175
A shrill wind began to blow, and the ships ran at speed
over the fish-rich pathways, and brought us by night to
Geraestus.* There we sacrificed thigh-bones of bulls in plenty
to Poseidon, because we had crossed a great expanse of sea.
On the fourth day from then the companions of Tydeus' son,   180
Diomedes, breaker of horses, stood their trim ships in at Argos,
but I held on for Pylos, and the wind never once eased, from
the time that a god had sent it forth to blow. And so I came
back here, dear child, without news, knowing nothing of the
others, which Achaeans had survived and which had died.   185
However, everything I have learned as I sit here in my halls
you shall hear, as is right, and I shall not hide it from you.
Men speak of a safe return for the spear-battling Myrmidons,
who were led by the brilliant son of great-hearted Achilles,
and a safe return is also told for Philoctetes,* Poeas' splendid son. 190
Idomeneus* brought all his companions back to Crete, those,

that is, who escaped the war, and the sea took none of them.
Of Atreus' son you have heard yourselves, though living far away:
how he came back and how Aegisthus planned his wretched death;
but Aegisthus paid a terrible penalty for his deed, showing   195
how good a thing it is for a dead man to leave behind a son;
for Orestes* took vengeance on his father's killer, Aegisthus
the wily schemer, the man who slew his famous father. So too
with you, my friend, for I see you are a handsome, strapping fellow;
be brave too, and future generations will speak well of you.'   200

     Then in turn thoughtful Telemachus answered him:
'Nestor, son of Neleus, great glory of the Achaeans, Orestes
did indeed take full vengeance, and the Achaeans will carry
his fame far and wide, to be a song-theme for men to come.
I wish the gods would clothe me in as great a power,   205
to be revenged on the suitors for their grievous outrages,
for the reckless and violent acts they devise against me.
But no, the gods have not spun this thread of good fortune
for me or for my father; but we must endure it all the same.'

     Then Nestor the Gerenian horseman answered him: 210
'My friend, now that your words remind me of this, men
do say that in your halls a gang of suitors for your mother
are plotting dreadful deeds, contrary to your will.
Tell me, are you willing to be browbeaten, or do the people
in your land hate you, following some prompting from a god?   215
Who knows if Odysseus may not one day return and punish
them for their violence, either alone or with all the Achaeans?
If only the grey-eyed goddess Athena were minded to love you,
as once she took special care of excellent Odysseus in the
Trojans' land, where we Achaeans suffered such hardships!   220
I have never seen gods so openly showing affection to a man
as when Pallas Athena took her stand at his side, for all to see;*
if she were so minded to love and care for you in her heart
then many a suitor would quite forget his hopes of marriage.'

     Then in turn thoughtful Telemachus answered him: 225
'Aged sir, I do not think these words of yours will be fulfilled.
What you say goes beyond my hopes, and confusion grips me;
I cannot hope that this will be, not even if the gods should wish it.'

     Then in turn the goddess grey-eyed Athena addressed him:
'Telemachus, what a word has escaped the barrier of your teeth!   230

It is easy for a god to protect a man, even from far away, if he so
wills it. For my part, I would rather endure great suffering and only
then reach home and see the day of my return, instead of coming
straight back to be cut down at my hearth, as Agamemnon
was slain by the treachery of Aegisthus and of his own wife.   235
But for all that, death comes alike to all, and not even the gods
can shield a man from it, however loved he is, once the
cruel fate of death that brings long misery has taken him.'

   Then in turn thoughtful Telemachus answered her: 'Mentor,
let us talk no more of such things, troubled though we are.   240
Odysseus' homecoming is no longer certain; already the
immortal gods have planned death and dark fate for him. But
now I want to question Nestor, and ask him about another tale,
since he knows what is just and wise better than other men;
they say he has ruled over three generations of men, and   245
indeed, as I look at him he has the appearance of an immortal.
Nestor, son of Neleus, give me a true account of this story:
How did the son of Atreus, wide-ruling Agamemnon, die?
Where was Menelaus? And what kind of death did the wily
counsellor Aegisthus plan for him, to kill a far better man?   250
Or was Menelaus not in Achaean Argos, but wandering abroad
among men, and so Aegisthus grew in courage to do the killing?'

   Then Nestor the Gerenian horseman answered him:
'Very well, my boy, I will tell you the whole tale, truly.
It would indeed have happened as you yourself guessed   255
if Menelaus, the fair-haired son of Atreus, had on his return
from Troy caught Aegisthus in the palace, still alive. For
then men would not have heaped up a burial-mound for him,
even in death, but dogs and vultures would surely have eaten him
lying on the plain, far from the city, and not one Achaean woman   260
would have wept for him, so monstrous was the deed he planned.
We had labours in plenty to perform, sitting it out there at Troy,
while Aegisthus took his ease in a corner of horse-rearing Argos,
busy practising speeches to beguile the wife of Agamemnon.
At first glorious Clytemnestra refused to take part in this   265
ugly deed, because she was endowed with good sense; and
there was too in the palace a man, a singer,* whom Atreus' son
on leaving for Troy had strictly charged to watch over his wife;
but when her god-sent destiny fixed its shackles on her, and

she yielded, Aegisthus took the singer off to a desolate isle   270
and left him there, to become the spoil and prey of vultures,
and carried her away to his house; and she wished it as he did.
Many were the thigh-bones he burnt on the gods' sacred altars,
and many the bright offerings he hung up, woven stuff and gold,
in return for this monstrous deed, one never hoped for in his heart. 275
Now, we were sailing together on our way back from Troy,
Atreus' son and I, joined by feelings of mutual friendship;
but when we reached sacred Sunium, the furthest cape of Athens,
there Phoebus Apollo came at the helmsman of Menelaus
with his gentle shafts and killed him, his hands still gripping   280
the steering-oar of the swiftly running ship. He was Phrontis,
the son of Onetor, who surpassed all sorts of men in
steering a ship whenever storm blasts were driving it along.
So Menelaus was detained there, though anxious to press on,
in order to bury his companion and perform the proper rites.   285
But when he too was again crossing the wine-dark sea in
his hollow ships, and in his rapid course had reached the
steep cliff of Malea,* wide-thundering Zeus planned to make
his voyage a disaster, and loosed blasts of howling winds at
him, and huge swollen waves, as big as mountains. Menelaus   290
then split his fleet in two and with half drew near to Crete,
where the Cydonians lived around the waters of Iardanus.
There is at the furthest point of Gortyn a smooth cliff out in the
misty sea, falling sheer to the water, where southerly gales
drive huge waves against a westward cape, in the direction of   295
Phaestus, and this small rock protects it from the mighty surge.
There some ships put in, and the crews only just escaped
destruction, but the waves splintered their ships on the reefs.
The five dark-prowed ships that remained were carried
away by wind and water, and forced to sail towards Egypt.   300
And so it was that Menelaus amassed quantities of gold and
goods as he roved with his ships among men of alien tongue,
while back at home Aegisthus was planning this grim deed.
For seven years after murdering Atreus' son he ruled over
Mycenae, rich in gold, and under him the people were crushed;   305
but when the eighth year came, glorious Orestes, his bane,
returned home from Athens and slew the slayer of his father,
Aegisthus the wily schemer, the killer of his famous father.

When Orestes had killed him he gave a funeral feast to the
Argives for his hateful mother and the coward Aegisthus; and   310
on that very day Menelaus, master of the war-cry, came home,
bringing much treasure with him, all that his ships could carry.
So you too, my friend, must not wander long, far from home,
abandoning your possessions and leaving men in your house,
these arrogant men, for fear they share out all your wealth and   315
consume it entirely, and you will have come on a fruitless voyage.
I do, however, urge and instruct you to travel on to Menelaus,
because he has recently returned from foreign parts, from
men whose land no one would expect in his heart to escape,
once storm winds have blown him off course on to the huge   320
expanse of the open sea, from where the very birds cannot
find their way back within a year, so vast and terrible it is.
So come, leave now with your ship and your companions,
or, if you wish it, travel by land; there are chariot and horses
here for you, and my sons are at your service, to be your guides   325
to glorious Lacedaemon,* where fair-haired Menelaus lives.
Entreat him in person, so that he will speak the plain truth;
he will not lie to you, for he is a man of sound understanding.'
   So he spoke; and the sun went down, and darkness came over.
Then the goddess grey-eyed Athena spoke among them: 330
'Aged man, what you have said is indeed right and proper.
Come now, cut out the victims' tongues and mix the wine,
so that we may pour drink-offerings to Poseidon and the other
gods, and then turn our thoughts to sleep, for it is time;
already the light has gone into the gloom, and it is not proper   335
to sit here any longer at the gods' feast. It is time to depart.'
   So spoke the daughter of Zeus, and they listened to her words.
Heralds moved among them and poured water over their hands,
and young men brimmed the mixing-bowls with wine and
distributed it to all, after pouring the first drops into their cups.   340
They threw the tongues into the fire, then rose and poured drink-
offerings over them; when they had done this, and drunk as
much as their hearts desired, Athena and godlike Telemachus
revealed their wish to go together to their hollow ship; but
Nestor made to restrain them, addressing them in these words: 345
'May Zeus and the other immortal gods not permit that you
should leave my presence and go to your swift ship, as if

from a man stricken with poverty and quite destitute in
blankets, with no store of coverlets and rugs in his house,
either for himself or his guests to sleep on in comfort!   350
No; I do possess coverlets and fine rugs; and the dear
son of Odysseus, the man we speak of, will certainly not
have to lie down to sleep on a ship's decking, not while
I live, and while there are sons left to me in my halls who
will entertain any guest who happens to come to my palace.'   355
     Then in turn the goddess grey-eyed Athena addressed him:
'Well said indeed, my aged friend! It is right and proper that
Telemachus should be persuaded, since it is much better thus.
He will now go with you as you propose, and will sleep in
your palace, but I shall return to my black ship, to rally   360
my companions and tell them all that has happened. I am
the only one of them who can speak of myself as an older man;
they are young men who have come with great-hearted
Telemachus out of friendship, all of them about the same age.
There I shall lie down to sleep beside the hollow black ship,   365
tonight; but at daybreak I shall be away to the great-hearted
Caucones,* where there is a debt owing to me, by no means recent
or small. You must send this man on his way, with a chariot and
a son of yours, since he has come to your house; give him horses,
the swiftest runners there are, possessed of the greatest strength.'   370
     So spoke grey-eyed Athena and left them, likening herself
to a vulture; and amazement gripped all the Achaeans, and
the old man was astonished at the sight before his eyes.
He took Telemachus by the hand, and addressed him:
'My friend, I do not think you will prove to be a coward or   375
spiritless, if, young though you are, the gods escort you thus.
Of all those whose home is on Olympus, this was none other
than the daughter of Zeus, renowned Tritogeneia,* who
always honoured your noble father too among the Argives.
I beg you, queen, be propitious, and grant me noble fame,   380
myself and to my sons, and my revered wife, and in return
I will sacrifice to you a broad-browed heifer, one year old,
unbroken, whom no man has yet led under the yoke;
I shall cover its horns with gold and then sacrifice it to you.'
     So he spoke in prayer, and Pallas Athena heard him.   385
Then the horseman, Gerenian Nestor, conducted the rest,

his sons and his daughters' husbands, towards his fine palace.
When they reached the splendid palace of this lord
they took their places in order on chairs and on seats,
and as they came in the old man mixed for them a bowl   390
of wine, sweet to the taste, that his housekeeper had opened
ten years after its making, undoing the stopper upon it. This
wine the old man mixed in a bowl, and after pouring an offering
he prayed fervently to Athena, daughter of aegis-wielding Zeus.
     When they had all poured and drunk as much as their hearts   395
desired, the others departed to sleep, each to his own home;
but Nestor the Gerenian horseman offered Telemachus, the
dear son of godlike Odysseus, a place to sleep in the palace,
on a fretted couch under a far-echoing colonnade; and next
to him slept Peisistratus of the fine ash spear, captain of men,   400
who alone of Nestor's sons in his halls was not married.
Nestor himself slept in the inner part of his lofty house, and
beside him his wife, mistress of the house, served the marital bed.
     When early-born Dawn with her rosy fingers appeared,
Nestor the Gerenian horseman rose from his bed and   405
went out and took his seat on a polished stone bench
that was his, in front of his lofty doors; it was white,
and gleamed with oil,* and in former times Neleus,
a counsellor equal to the gods, would sit there; but he
had gone to Hades, brought down by death, and now   410
in his turn Gerenian Nestor, protector of the Achaeans,
sat there, staff in hand. His sons left their rooms and
gathered round him in a body: Echephron and Stratius,
Perseus and Aretus, and Thrasymedes, equal to a god;
and the sixth to join them was the hero Peisistratus.   415
Then they brought out godlike Telemachus, and seated him.
Nestor the Gerenian horseman was the first to speak to them:
'Be quick, my dear sons, and do this for me, so that
first of all gods I may win the favour of Athena, who
came to me at the god's rich feast, clear for all to see.   420
Let one of you go out to the plain for a heifer, to be brought
here without delay, and let one of the oxherds drive her.
And let another go to great-hearted Telemachus' black ship
and fetch all his companions, leaving only two behind.
And let another order the gold-worker Laerces to come here,   425

for him to cover the heifer's horns with gold. The rest of you
stay here in a group, and tell the serving-women inside the
house to busy themselves preparing a magnificent feast, and
set chairs out all around, and bring firewood and bright water.'

So he spoke, and they all began bustling about. The heifer came   430
from the plain, the companions of great-hearted Telemachus
came from his well-balanced ship, and the smith came with
bronze tools in his hands, the implements of his craft:
anvil and hammer, and well-made fire-tongs, which he used
to work the gold. And Athena came too, to be present at   435
her sacred rites. The old horseman Nestor gave the smith gold
with which he gilded the heifer's horns, working with skill,
that the goddess might be glad when she saw her offering.
Stratius and splendid Echephron led in the heifer by the horns,
and from an inner room came Aretus, carrying water for their   440
hands in a flower-patterned bowl, and in the other hand
barley-grains in a basket. Thrasymedes, steadfast in war, stood
by the heifer with a sharp axe, ready to deliver the blow, and
Perseus held the blood-bowl. Then the old horseman Nestor
began the rite with water and barley-grains, and prayed fervently   445
to Athena, first throwing hairs from the beast's head into the fire.
When they had prayed, and sprinkled the barley-grains,
straightaway the son of Nestor, high-hearted Thrasymedes,
stood by the beast and struck it, and the axe sheared through
its neck tendons and loosened the heifer's strength. Nestor's   450
daughters and his sons' wives set up a ritual cry, as did his
respected wife Eurydice, the eldest of Clymenus' daughters.
Then they lifted the heifer up from the broad-wayed earth and
held it firmly, and Peisistratus, captain of men, cut its throat.
When the dark blood had all run out and the spirit had left its   455
bones, they at once chopped it into joints, and quickly cut out
the thigh-bones, all in the proper way, and wrapped them in fat,
making a double layer, and laid raw hunks of meat on top.
The old man burnt these over billets of wood, and poured gleaming
wine over them; and by him young men held five-pronged forks.   460
When the thigh-bones were quite burnt, and they had tasted the
entrails, they chopped the rest into pieces and threaded them on to
sharp skewers, and holding these in their hands cooked the meat.

Meanwhile Telemachus was being bathed by lovely Polycaste,

eldest daughter of Nestor the son of Neleus. When she had   465
bathed him and rubbed him richly with olive oil, she gave
him a tunic and a fine robe to wear, and he rose from
the bath, looking like the immortals in stature, and then
went and took his seat next to Nestor, shepherd of the people.

Now when they had cooked the outer meat and drawn it off,   470
they took their seats and feasted, and well-born men rose
to their feet and poured wine for them into golden cups.
When they had put away their desire for food and drink,
the first to speak to them was the Gerenian horseman Nestor:
'Now, my sons, bring out fine-maned horses for Telemachus,   475
and yoke them under the chariot, so he can pursue his journey.'

So he spoke, and they listened carefully and did as he said,
and without delay yoked swift horses under a chariot; and
a woman housekeeper stowed in it bread and wine and
cooked meats, of the kind that Zeus-nurtured kings eat.   480
Telemachus stepped up into the magnificent chariot, and
beside him Nestor's son Peisistratus, captain of men,
climbed into it and took the reins in his hands. He touched
the pair with a whip to start them, and they flew willingly
on to the plain, leaving the steep city of Pylos behind them.   485
All day long the horses set the yoke rocking, pulling side by
side. The sun went down, and all the ways grew dark, and
they came to Pherae,* to the house of Diocles, who was the
son of Ortilochus, whom the river Alpheus had once sired.
There they slept the night, and he gave them gifts of hospitality.   490
When early-born Dawn with her rosy fingers appeared,
they yoked the horses and climbed into the decorated chariot,
and drove through the echoing courtyard and out of the gate.
Peisestratus touched the pair with a whip to start them, and they
flew willingly on. They came to wheat-bearing plains, and hastened   495
on to complete their journey's end, so quickly did the swift horses
convey them. And the sun went down, and all the ways grew dark.

BOOK FOUR

When they reached the deep hollow of Lacedaemon, land of
many ravines, they drove up to the palace of renowned Menelaus.
They found him giving a wedding-feast in his house to his
many clansmen, in honour of his son and beautiful daughter.
He was sending his daughter to the son of Achilles the rank-breaker,   5
for back in Troy he had promised and agreed to give her to him,
and now the gods were bringing the marriage to fulfilment;
and he was about to send her off with chariot and horses to go to
the far-famed city of the Myrmidons, whom the young man ruled.
As bride for his son, mighty Megapenthes,* Menelaus was bringing   10
a girl from Sparta, Alector's daughter; he was the last of his
children and born of a slave-woman, for the gods granted Helen
no more offspring once she had given birth to her daughter,
lovely Hermione, who had her beauty from golden Aphrodite.

So these men, neighbours and clansmen of renowned Menelaus,   15
were feasting in the great, high-roofed house, and making
merry; and among them a god-inspired singer sang to his
lyre, and through the midst of the company two tumblers
went spinning, taking the lead in the dance and the song.
The two men, hero Telemachus and Nestor's splendid son,   20
brought their chariot to a halt by the house's outer porch,
and waited. Lord Eteoneus saw them and came forward,
he who was the diligent attendant of renowned Menelaus,
and set off through the palace to report to the shepherd of
the people; standing next to him he spoke in winged words: 25
'Menelaus, nurtured by Zeus, look, here are two strangers,
two men who look like the offspring of great Zeus.
Instruct me: should we unyoke the swift horses for them,
or send them on to some other person, to entertain them?'

Then, deeply vexed, fair-haired Menelaus addressed him: 30
'Eteoneus, son of Boëthus, you were never known to be a fool,
but now you are talking nonsense, just like a child.
We two ate many hospitable meals in other men's houses
before we reached home, hoping that Zeus would free us
from misery in the days to come; so quick, unyoke the   35

strangers' horses, and bring them in here, to join our feast.'

So he spoke, and Eteoneus hurried back through the hall,
and called to other diligent attendants to go with him.
They freed the sweating horses from under the yoke, and
tethered them at their own horses' mangers, and threw   40
emmer wheat before them, mixing it with white barley;
they leaned the chariot body against the shining courtyard
wall, and conducted the men into the wonderful house.
When the pair saw it they marvelled at the house of the king,
nurtured by Zeus; for like the brightness of the sun or moon   45
was the high-roofed palace of renowned Menelaus.
When they had had their pleasurable fill of gazing at the sight,
they stepped into well-polished baths and bathed there;
maidservants washed and rubbed them with olive oil, and
clothed them in tunics and thick woollen cloaks; then they   50
conducted them to seats next to Menelaus, son of Atreus.
A woman servant brought water in a beautiful golden pitcher,
and poured it over a silver bowl for them to wash their hands,
and drew up a polished table to stand beside them.
A respected housekeeper brought bread and set it before them,   55
and added a heap of delicacies, giving freely from her store.
Then a carver brought platters of different kinds of meat, which
he set before them, and put golden cups beside them. And now,
with a welcoming gesture, fair-haired Menelaus addressed them:
'Welcome! Set your hands to the food, and when you have   60
eaten your meal we shall ask you who among men you are.
Clearly, your parents' lineage has not gone to waste in you;
you must be of the stock of staff-holding kings, nurtured by
Zeus, for no one of lowly station could have sired men like you.'

So he spoke, and picked up the fat chine of an ox, cooked   65
and served to him as his special portion, and put it before them.
They reached out for the good things that lay before them, and
when they had put away the desire for food and drink,
Telemachus spoke to the son of Nestor, leaning his head
close to his, so that none of the others should hear: 70
'Son of Nestor, delight of my heart, look around at this
echoing palace: at the flashing brilliance of bronze, of
gold and amber, of silver and of ivory! It must be like this
inside the court of Zeus on Olympus, such is the amazing

abundance of it all. Astonishment grips me as I look at it.'   75
    Fair-haired Menelaus heard what he was saying, and
addressed the two of them, speaking with winged words:
'My dear boys, no mortal would dare to contend with Zeus,
for his houses and wealth are immortal; but as for men,
few, if any, can rival me in the matter of possessions.   80
Much I endured, and wandered far, before I brought
them home in my ships, returning only in the eighth year.
I roamed as far as Cyprus and Phoenicia and Egypt, and
reached the Ethiopians, the Sidonians,* and the Erembi,*
and I visited Libya, where lambs grow horns from birth;   85
ewes there lamb three times in the course of each year.
In that land neither lord nor shepherd goes without meat
and cheese, nor is in want of sweet milk, since the ewes
yield milk all the year round for their lambs to suck.
But during the time that I was wandering in those parts,   90
amassing great wealth, a man killed my brother by stealth,
catching him unawares, through the guile of his accursed wife.
So lording it over these riches gives me no pleasure. You are
likely to have heard this from your fathers, whoever they are,
since I suffered much, and have lost one household that was   95
very well ordered and contained many splendid possessions.
I would rather I lived in this house owning only a third part of
all this wealth, and that they were still alive, the men who in
those days died in broad Troy, far from Argos, rearer of horses.
And yet, though there are many occasions when I lament   100
and grieve for them all as I sit here in my halls, times when
I give my heart pleasure with weeping—and then others
when I cease, for chill lamentation quickly leads to surfeit—
yet, grieved though I am, I do not mourn for them all as much
as I do for one man, remembrance of whom makes sleep and   105
food hateful to me; for of all the Achaeans no man toiled as hard
and achieved as much as Odysseus did. But for him this was to
bring sorrow, and for me pain for his sake that never leaves me;
such a long time has he been gone, and we know nothing of him,
whether he is alive or dead. Others must surely mourn for him   110
as well: old Laertes, and Penelope, that faithful woman,
and Telemachus, whom he left, a new-born baby, in his house.'
    So he spoke, and quietly stirred in Telemachus a desire

to weep; hearing his father named he let fall a tear from
his eyes to the ground, and with both hands held his purple   115
cloak in front of his face. Menelaus noticed him,
and pondered in his mind and in his heart whether
he should wait until Telemachus might mention his father,
or if he should first ask questions and test him in detail.

While he was weighing this in his mind and in his heart,   120
Helen appeared from her high-roofed, fragrant room,
looking like Artemis, goddess of the golden distaff.
With her came Adreste, who set a well-made chair for her,
and Alcippe brought a coverlet of soft wool. Phylo
carried a silver basket, a gift from Alcandre, wife of   125
Polybus, whose home was in Egyptian Thebes, where
people keep huge amounts of treasure in their houses.
Polybus had given Menelaus two baths made of silver,
two tripods, and ten talents of gold; and apart from these
his wife had presented Helen with some very beautiful gifts: 130
she gave her a golden spindle and a basket made of silver
that ran on wheels, and its rims were rounded off with gold.
It was this basket that Helen's attendant Phylo brought and
put before her, piled high with artfully spun yarn; and
on top of it was laid a distaff, with violet-dark wool.   135
Helen sat on the chair, with a footstool under her feet,
and at once began to speak, questioning her husband closely:
'Menelaus nurtured by Zeus, do we know who these men
who have come to our house profess themselves to be?
Shall I lie, or shall I speak the truth? Well, my heart tells me: 140
I do not believe I have ever seen such a resemblance in
either man or woman, and amazement grips me as I gaze.
This man is so much like the son of great-hearted Odysseus,
Telemachus, whom he left as a new-born babe in his house
when the Achaeans arrived under Troy's walls for my sake,   145
shameless bitch that I am, and set in motion wild war.'

Then in answer fair-haired Menelaus addressed her:
'Lady, now I too can see the likeness, just as you do.
Odysseus' feet and hands were the same; so too
the glance of his eyes, his head and his hair.   150
And indeed, just now when I was speaking of Odysseus,
calling to mind all the hardships he had undergone

on my behalf, he let fall streams of tears from his eyes,
and held up his purple cloak in front of his face.'
Then in turn Peisistratus, son of Nestor, answered him: 155
'Zeus-nurtured Menelaus, Atreus' son, captain of the people,
this man is in truth the son of Odysseus, as you say;
but he is modest and restrained, and in his heart he thinks
it unseemly, coming into your presence for the first time,
to rush into speech in front of you, whose voice we two   160
delight in as if you were a god. The Gerenian horseman Nestor
sent me with him as an escort, because he was longing to
see you, hoping you could offer him help in word or deed.
The son whose father has gone away has many trials in his
halls if he has no one to support him, as now is the case   165
with Telemachus: his father has disappeared, and there is
no one among his people to protect him from ill-treatment.'
Then in answer fair-haired Menelaus addressed him:
'Well! It is indeed a dear man's son who has come to my
house, one who tackled many heavy challenges in my cause.   170
I had thought to entertain him above all other Argives when
he returned, if only wide-thundering Olympian Zeus had
granted us both a homecoming over the sea in our swift ships.
I would have founded a city for him in Argos, and built him a
palace, bringing him over from Ithaca with his possessions,   175
his son, and all his people; I would have cleared out one of the
cities under my rule that are established round here, and we would
have lived here together, our peoples continuously intermingling,
and nothing would have hindered our mutual friendship and
pleasure, at least until the black cloud of death enveloped us.   180
But, I suppose, the god must have become jealous, and made
sure that this ill-fated man should be the only one not to return.'
So he spoke, and aroused in them all the desire to lament.
Argive Helen, offspring of Zeus, began to shed tears,
Telemachus began to weep, as did Atreus' son Menelaus;   185
nor were the eyes of Nestor's son without tears, for
he remembered in his heart excellent Antilochus,*
whom the resplendent Dawn's brilliant son had killed.
Calling Antilochus to mind, he spoke winged works:
'Son of Atreus, aged Nestor used to say you were by far   190
the wisest of mortals, whenever the talk in our halls turned

to you, and we asked one another about you. So now, if
you can, be persuaded by me; I myself take no pleasure in
weeping over supper, and early-born Dawn will soon be here.
It is not that I think it unseemly to weep on behalf of any   195
mortal man who has died and met his destiny, for that
is the only tribute one can offer to pitiable mortals,
to cut one's hair and to let a tear fall down one's cheek.
I too had someone who died, my brother, by no means the
worst of the Argives. You would have known him, though   200
for my part I never met or saw him. But men say Antilochus
excelled all others, both at running and as a fighting man.'
    Then in answer fair-haired Menelaus addressed him:
'My friend, in all this you have spoken as a thoughtful
man would speak and do, even one older than you are.   205
In this you resemble your father, because you speak so wisely.
It is easy to discern the breeding of a man into whose life
Cronus' son has woven prosperity at his marriage and
fathering, as in our time he has granted Nestor for all his days—
to grow old himself in his halls in sleek comfort, with   210
sons of both good sense and excellence in spear-work.
So we should leave off the weeping that came on us just now;
let people pour water over our hands and let us turn our
thoughts again to supper. As for stories, Telemachus and I
can wait until dawn to recount them to each other at length.'   215
    So he spoke, and Asphalion poured water over his hands,
he who was one of renowned Menelaus' diligent attendants,
and they reached out for the good things that lay before them.
    But Helen, offspring of Zeus, had other plans: she threw
into the bowl from which they were drinking a drug that   220
banished grief and anger, causing forgetfulness of all troubles.
No one who swallowed this when dissolved in the wine-
bowl would shed a tear down his cheek on that day,
not even if his mother and father had died, nor even
if men had cut down his brother or his dear son with   225
the bronze, and he had witnessed it before his very eyes.
Such were the benign and subtle drugs that Zeus' daughter
possessed, given her by Polydamna, wife of Thon, in Egypt,
where more than anywhere the grain-giving land produces
medicines, many benign when mixed, and many harmful.   230

In that country everyone is a healer skilled beyond all
other men, and they are truly the descendants of Paieon.*

   When she had thrown this drug into the bowl and ordered
the wine to be poured, she once again spoke to Menelaus:
'Atreus' son Menelaus, nurtured of Zeus, and all you sons of   235
noble men here! The god Zeus allots good and evil to men,
sometimes to one and sometimes another, for he can do anything.
Now it is time to take your seats in the hall and to feast, and to
find pleasure in stories; I shall tell one that suits the occasion.
Now, I could not describe or recount the many exploits that   240
Odysseus of the enduring spirit accomplished; but I can relate
one feat that this mighty man was bold enough to perform
in the land of Trojans, where you Achaeans were hard pressed.

   'He scarred himself with ugly, shameful whip-blows, and
threw round his shoulders a rough garment like a slave's,   245
and then slipped secretly into the enemy's city of wide ways.
Disguising his own appearance, he looked like someone else—
a beggar, quite unlike the man he was by the Achaean ships.
In this form he stole into the Trojans' city, and they were
deceived by him, all of them. I alone realized who he was,   250
and questioned him at length, but his cunning deceived me.
But after I had bathed him and rubbed him with olive oil,
and given him clothes to wear, and sworn a mighty oath
that I would not reveal to the Trojans that he was Odysseus
until he had made his way back to the swift ships and huts,   255
then at last he gave me a full account of the Achaeans' plans.
So after killing many Trojans with the sharp-bladed bronze
he rejoined the Argives, taking much information with him.
The other Trojan women set up a shrill wail, but my heart was
delighted since it had now shifted to returning to my home again;   260
I looked back with grief* on the blind delusion sent me by Aphrodite
when she took me away to Troy from my dear homeland, and
when I abandoned my daughter and bridal-room and husband,
who was inferior to no man, in either understanding or beauty.'

   Then in answer fair-haired Menelaus addressed her: 265
'Everything you have said, lady, is right and proper. Many
are the heroes whose mind and counsel I have come to know
before this, and wide is the expanse of earth I have travelled;
but never have I set eyes on a man such as Odysseus was,

a man in whose heart there was such an enduring spirit.   270
Let me tell you another feat of that mighty, daring man.
We were all sitting inside the wooden horse, the best of
the Argives, ready to bring death and doom to the Trojans.
You approached it, Helen; it was likely that some divinity
who wished to give glory to the Trojans directed you;   275
and indeed godlike Deiphobus* came with you on your way.
Three times you circled the hollow ambush, feeling along it
with your hands, calling out to the Danaan chieftains name
by name and imitating the voice of all the Argives' wives.
Now, I and the son of Tydeus and glorious Odysseus were   280
sitting in the midst of them, and we heard you calling out;
both of us started up, full of eagerness either to leap out
or to give an immediate answer from inside, but Odysseus
held us back and stopped us, for all our impatience.
Then all the rest of the sons of the Achaeans sat in silence,   285
and only Anticlus was prepared to give you an answer;
but Odysseus clamped his mighty hands over his mouth
with brutal force, and so saved all the Achaeans, holding
him there all the time until Pallas Athena took you away.'

     Then in turn thoughtful Telemachus answered him: 'Son of   290
Atreus, Menelaus nurtured of Zeus, captain of the people:
it is the more painful that this did not save him from miserable
death, nor would it have, even if his heart had been of iron.
But now, please, release us to our beds, so that we may
prepare ourselves for rest and take pleasure in sweet sleep.'   295

     So he spoke, and Argive Helen ordered her women servants
to lay out beds for them under a colonnade, to throw on fine
purple blankets and to lay coverlets on top,
and over them all to spread fleecy woollen cloaks.
They went out of the hall with torches in their hands and   300
laid out the beds; and a herald led the strangers from the hall,
and they settled to their rest there in the forecourt of the house,
the hero Telemachus and the splendid son of Nestor; but
Atreus' son slept in the innermost part of his lofty house, and
beside him lay Helen of the long robe, bright among women.   305

     When early-born Dawn with her rosy fingers appeared
Menelaus, master of the war-cry, rose from his bed and
put on his clothes, and slung a sharp sword from his shoulder,

and under his feet he bound his shining sandals, and set off
from his bedroom, looking like a god to those who met   310
him, and sat beside Telemachus, and addressed him by name:
'Hero Telemachus, what pressing need has brought you here
to glorious Lacedaemon, over the broad back of the sea?
Is it a public or a private matter? Give me a true answer to this.'

    Then in turn thoughtful Telemachus answered him: 315
'Zeus-nurtured Menelaus, Atreus' son, captain of the people,
I have come hoping you can give me news of my father.
My household is being eaten away, my rich farmland is ruined,
and my home is full of men who hate me, who all the time
slaughter my crowding sheep and crook-horned shambling cattle;   320
such are the suitors of my mother, arrogant and violent men.
It is for this reason that I now entreat you at your knees, hoping
you can tell me about his unhappy death; perhaps you saw it with
your own eyes, or heard the tale of his wanderings from another.
More than any other man his mother bore him for wretchedness.   325
Do not let respect or pity for me soften your words,
but tell me exactly how you chanced to see him.
I entreat you: if ever my father, noble Odysseus, made any
promise in word or deed to you and then fulfilled it, in the
land of the Trojans, where you Achaeans were hard pressed,   330
call it now to mind and tell me—and tell me the plain truth.'

    Then, deeply troubled, fair-haired Menelaus addressed him:
'How dreadful! For sure it was a strong-hearted man whose
bed they hoped to sleep in, though they themselves are cowards.
As when a hind settles her newly born fawns who are still   335
drinking her milk to sleep in the woodland den of a mighty lion,
and herself goes out to scour the foothills and grassy hollows
in search of grazing—but the lion returns to his lair
and unleashes an ugly death on both hind and fawns—
so will Odysseus unleash an ugly death on those men.   340
Father Zeus and Athena and Apollo, I wish he could now be
the same man who once on well-founded Lesbos stood up
and wrestled Philomeleides* for a challenge, and threw
him violently down, and all the Achaeans were delighted!
I wish Odysseus could come like that among the suitors; it   345
would mean quick deaths and bitter marriage-hopes for them all.
As for your question and entreaty, I will not sidestep

the matter and answer you crookedly, nor will I deceive you.
And the tale the truth-telling Old Man of the Sea told me—
I shall keep nothing of that story back or conceal it from you.   350
    'I was in Egypt, impatient to sail home but held back there
by the gods, for not sacrificing perfect hecatombs to them;
it is always their wish that we remember their commands.
There is there an island, set in the ever-surging deep,
off the coast of Egypt, and men call it Pharos; it is as   355
far out to sea as a hollow ship can run in a full day,
if a shrill stern wind is blowing it along. There is on it
a harbour, well-sheltered, where men can draw dark water
and launch their trim ships again on to the open sea.
Here the gods detained me for twenty days, and never   360
did an offshore breeze spring up and blow, one of those
that commonly escort ships over the broad back of the sea.
Indeed, all our victuals and the men's vigour would have failed
had not one of the gods shown compassion and taken pity on
me—the daughter of Proteus, the powerful Old Man of the Sea,   365
Eidotheë. Her heart was profoundly stirred when she met me
wandering miserably alone away from my companions,
who every day would roam over the island, angling for fish
with bent hooks, since hunger was tormenting their bellies.
She stood close and addressed me in these words: 370
"Are you a complete fool, stranger, and slack-witted too,
or have you chosen to give up and enjoy your torment,
that you are confined so long on this island, and cannot
find a means of escape, while your men's hearts waste away?"
So she spoke, and I addressed her by way of answer: 375
"I will tell you plainly, whoever of the goddesses you are:
it is not by choice that I am confined here, but I must have
offended the immortal gods whose home is the broad high sky.
So tell me—for the gods know everything—which of the
immortals is tying me down in shackles, preventing my   380
going. How I can make my way home over the fish-rich sea?"
So I spoke, and she, bright among goddesses, at once said:
"I will indeed, stranger, give you a true account.
This place is the haunt of the truth-telling Old Man of the
Sea, immortal Proteus, an Egyptian, who knows the deep   385
places of the entire sea; he is the servant of Poseidon, and

they say that he is also my father, and that he sired me.
If you could somehow lie in ambush and hold him fast,
he would tell you your route and the stages of your voyage,
and how to make your way home over the fish-rich sea.   390
And also, man nurtured of Zeus, if you wanted him to, he could
tell you what has been going on in your halls for good or for ill
while you have been away on your long and wearisome travels."
So she spoke, and I addressed her by way of answer:
"Explain to me now how I can ambush this aged god; I am   395
afraid he may see me first, or guess my intent and avoid me.
It is a hard thing for a mortal man to overcome a god."
So I spoke, and she, bright among goddesses, at once said:
"I will indeed, stranger, tell you truly what will happen.
When the sun bestrides the middle of the high sky, then the   400
truth-telling Old Man of the Sea rises from his salt element,
hidden in dark ripples blown by the West Wind's breath,
and after emerging he goes to sleep in a sheltering cavern;
and around him seals, brood of a lovely sea-goddess,
come out of the salt sea and sleep in a crowd together,   405
giving off the sour smell of the sea's deep gulfs.
There, at break of day, I shall take you, and settle you
down in good order; you must be careful to choose three
companions, the best there are in your well-benched ships.
Now I shall explain to you all the old man's cunning devices.   410
First, you must know, he will do his rounds of the seals and
number them; then, when he has reviewed and counted them,
he will lie down among them like a shepherd in his flock.
As soon as you see he has settled himself for sleep, then
you must call upon all your strength and might to hold him   415
fast there, for all his raging and striving to break free.
And try he will, turning himself into every kind of creature
that moves on the earth, into water and awesome fire, but you
must all hold on to him doggedly, and grip him the more tightly.
When he resumes his own shape and starts to question you,   420
becoming as he was when you saw him settling for sleep,
then, hero, you should relax your grip and let the old man go,
and ask him which of the gods it is who persecutes you,
and how you will make your way home over the fish-rich sea."

    'So she spoke, and plunged beneath the surging sea.   425

I went back to my ships, to where they were beached
on the sands, and my heart was darkly troubled as I went.
But when I came back down to the ship and the sea
we prepared our supper, and deathless night came over us,
and we laid ourselves down for sleep at the breakers' edge.   430
Then, when early-born Dawn with her rosy fingers appeared,
I made my way along the shore of the broad-wayed sea,
with many prayers to the gods; and I took with me three
companions, those whom I especially trusted in any venture.

'Eidotheë had plunged into the sea's broad trough, but now   435
she emerged from it, bringing the skins of four seals, all
newly flayed; this was the trick she was planning on her father.
She had scooped out hiding-places in the sands of the seashore
and sat there waiting for us, and we came up close to her;
she settled us down in order, and threw a skin over each man.   440
It might have been a truly repellent ambush, because the
dreadful stench of the sea-bred seals tormented us terribly—
for who would choose to bed down with a sea-monster?
But the goddess devised an excellent solution and saved us:
she brought ambrosia and dabbed it under the nose of each   445
man; it smelled very sweet, and so killed off the seals' reek.
All through the morning we waited there with steadfast hearts,
and then the seals came up out of the sea in a great mass,
and lay down to sleep in rows at the breakers' edge.
At midday the old man emerged from the sea, and found his   450
well-fed seals, and went round them all and counted them.
We were the first of the seals he counted, not suspecting
in his heart that it was a trick, and after this he too lay down.
Then we gave a shout and rushed at him, and threw our arms
around him; but the old man did not forget his artful trickery,   455
and first of all changed himself into a thickly maned lion,
and then into a snake and a panther and a giant boar,
and then became running water and a tree with lofty leaves.
But we held on to him doggedly, with steadfast hearts;
and only when the old man, master of cunning, began to   460
grow weary did he address me, questioning me in these words:
"Which of the gods, Atreus' son, helped you devise this plan,
to lie in ambush and catch me unawares? What do you want?"

'So he spoke, and I addressed him by way of answer:

"Old man, you know already; why try to distract me like this?   465
You know full well that I am trapped on this island, and cannot
find out how to escape, and the heart within me wastes away.
So tell me—for the gods know everything—which of the
immortals ties me down in shackles, preventing my going.
How can I make my way home over the fish-rich sea?"   470
    'So I spoke, and he immediately addressed me in answer:
"Before embarking, you should have offered splendid sacrifices
to Zeus and the other gods, and then you might have quickly
reached your native land, sailing over the wine-dark sea.
You must know that it is not your destiny to see your friends   475
and reach your well-established house and your native land
until you have sailed once more into the waters of Egyptian
Nile, that Zeus-fed river, and have sacrificed sacred hecatombs
to the immortal gods whose home is the broad high sky;
only then will the gods grant you the voyage you long for."   480
    'So he spoke, and the heart within me was shattered,
because he had ordered me to sail once again over the
misty deep to Egypt, a long and wearisome journey.
Even so, I answered him, addressing him in these words:
"All this I shall perform, old man, just as you instruct me.   485
But now, tell me this and give me a full and true account:
did all the Achaeans return home in their ships without mishap,
all those whom Nestor and I left behind when we sailed from
Troy, or did some perish by a cruel death in their ships, or in
their friends' arms, after they had spun out the thread of war?"   490
    'So I spoke, and he immediately addressed his answer to me:
"Son of Atreus, why probe me like this? You do not need
to know this, nor to understand my mind. I think you will not
restrain your tears for long once you have learnt everything.
Many of these men were beaten down, and many survived.   495
Two alone of the bronze-shirted Achaeans' leaders died on
their way home. As for the fighting, you yourself were there.
And one man is still alive, confined somewhere on the wide
deep. Ajax* was wrecked, and his long-oared ships with him;
Poseidon first drove him against the huge rocks of Gyrae,*   500
yet he then saved him from the sea—and he would have escaped
grim death, though hated by Athena, had he not been
mightily deluded and flung out an arrogant boast: he said he

had escaped the sea's great gulf in defiance of the gods' will.
Poseidon heard him when he made this noisy boast, and   505
straightaway picked up his trident in his sturdy hands and
struck the rock of Gyrae and split it into two; one part
stayed where it was, but the other fragment, on which Ajax
was perched when mighty delusion struck him, fell into
the sea, and carried him down into its limitless surging deep.   510
And so he drank down salty water, and perished there.
Your brother somehow eluded grim death, and got away
in his hollow ships; it was revered Hera who saved him.
But when he was on the point of making the steep rock
of Cape Malea,* a storm caught him and carried him away,   515
groaning deeply, over the fish-rich open sea, to the edge
of the land where formerly Thyestes had his palace, but
at this time was lived in by Aegisthus, Thyestes' son. But
even from there he was granted a trouble-free homecoming;
the gods made the wind veer round, and they reached home,   520
and Agamemnon set foot joyfully on his native ground, and
touched his own soil, and kissed it many times. Many warm tears
flowed down his face, so glad he was to see his country again.
But from his lookout a watchman saw him; Aegisthus the crafty
schemer had stationed him there, and had promised a reward   525
of two gold talents. This man had been watching for a year,
in case Agamemnon, calling up his surging courage, should slip
by undetected. He set off for the palace, to report to the people's
shepherd, and Aegisthus at once devised a crafty stratagem:
choosing twenty of the best men from the people, he laid an   530
ambush, and in another part ordered a feast to be prepared.
He set off to welcome Agamemnon, shepherd of the people,
riding in his horse-drawn chariot, with ugly thoughts in his mind.
Up from the shore he brought him, unaware of impending death,
and killed him at the feast, as a man slaughters an ox at the manger.   535
Not one of the companions accompanying Atreus' son survived,
nor any one of Aegisthus' men; they were all killed in the halls."

'So he spoke, and the heart within me was shattered,
and I wept, sitting there on the sands, and my heart
had no more desire to live and to see the light of the sun.   540
But when I had had my fill of weeping and rolling on the
ground, the truth-telling Old Man of the Sea addressed me:

"Son of Atreus, you have wept much; do not persist so
unrelentingly, for we shall achieve nothing by it. Rather
do your best to get back as fast as you can to your native land.   545
Either you will find Aegisthus alive, or else Orestes will have
killed him first, and you will be in time for the funeral feast."

   'So he spoke, and my heart and the proud spirit in my
breast were once again warmed, for all that I was grieving,
and I addressed him, speaking in winged words: 550
"So these two men I know about; now name me the third,
whoever it is, the one imprisoned alive on the wide sea,
or else dead. I want to know, though it may cause me sorrow."

   'So I spoke, and he at once addressed me in answer:
"This is the son of Laertes, whose home is in Ithaca.   555
I saw him on an island, and he was weeping huge tears,
in the halls of the nymph Calypso, who holds him there
by compulsion; he is not able to return to his native land,
because he has no oared ships nor any companions
who might convey him over the broad back of the sea.   560

   '"For you, Zeus-nurtured Menelaus, it is not divinely decreed
that you will die and meet your doom in horse-rearing Argos;
no, the immortals will send you to the plain of Elysium* at the
ends of the earth, where fair-haired Rhadamanthys dwells,
and where life for mortal men is most full of ease; where   565
no snow falls, nor great storms blow, nor is there ever rain,
but always Ocean sends up the West Wind's shrill-blowing
breezes, to refresh men's spirits. This is because Helen is
your wife, and in the gods' eyes you are son-in-law to Zeus."

   'So he spoke, and sank back into the deep billowing sea;   570
and I returned to my ships together with my godlike
companions, and as I went my heart was darkly troubled.
When we arrived back at our ship, beside the sea,
we prepared our supper, and deathless night came over us;
and we prepared ourselves for sleep at the breakers' edge.   575
When early-born Dawn with her rosy fingers appeared,
we first of all dragged our ships down to the bright salt sea,
and stepped the masts with their sails in our well-balanced ships.
Then the men embarked, and took their places at the oarlocks,
and sitting in rows struck the grey sea with their oars.   580
I sailed the ships back to the Egyptian Nile, river fed by Zeus'

rains, moored them and made a sacrifice of perfect hecatombs.
When I had placated the anger of the gods who live for ever
I heaped up a burial-mound for Agamemnon, so that his fame
might never be quenched. Our task finished I set sail, and the   585
gods sent a following wind and sped us back to our dear homeland.
    'But now; stay for a while in my halls, until the eleventh
or the twelfth day has come. After that I shall send you with
due honour on your way: I shall give you splendid gifts, three
horses and a well-polished chariot, and as well I shall give   590
you a beautiful cup, so that when you make drink-offerings
to the immortal gods you will remember me for all your days.'
    Then in turn thoughtful Telemachus answered him:
'Son of Atreus, do not make me stay here any longer.
Truly, I could endure to remain with you for a whole year,   595
and not be seized by a longing for my house and parents,
so strongly do I take delight in hearing your tales and
their telling. But already, while you prolong my visit here,
my companions in sandy Pylos grow impatient with me.
As for the gift you give me, let it be something to treasure;   600
horses I shall not take with me to Ithaca, but will leave them
here for you to delight in; you rule over a wide plain,
where clover grows in abundance, and galingale and
wheat and millet and broad-eared white barley, while on
Ithaca there are neither broad rides nor meadows; goats are   605
what it feeds, but to me it is dearer than any horse-rearing land.
None of the islands which slope down to the sea are good for
chariot-driving, nor rich in meadows, Ithaca least of all.'
    So he spoke, and Menelaus, master of the war-cry, smiled,
and stroking him with his hand spoke to him directly: 610
'Your words show you are from a good bloodline, dear boy,
and therefore I shall change my gift, for it is in my power.
Of all the treasures that lie stored up in my house
I shall give you the one that is finest and most prized:
I shall give you a well-wrought mixing-bowl, made of   615
solid silver, and finished off around its lip with gold.
It is the work of Hephaestus, and was given to me by the hero
Phaedimus, king of the Sidonians, when his house received me
on my homeward journey. This is what I wish to give you.'
    While these two conversed with each other on these matters,   620

guests began to arrive at the palace of the godlike king.
They drove up their own sheep, and brought man-cheering wine,
and their wives who wore lovely veils sent in bread for them.
So they busied themselves over the meal in Menelaus' halls.

Meanwhile, on a level space before Odysseus' palace the suitors 625
were amusing themselves, throwing discuses and spears,
full of the same arrogance that they had shown before.
There sat Antinous, and Eurymachus who looked like a god;
they were the suitors' leaders, and in manliness by far the best.
Noëmon, the son of Phronius, came and stood next to them 630
and addressed a question to Antinous, using these words:
'Antinous, do we have any idea in our minds or do we not,
when Telemachus will come back from sandy Pylos?
He went off with my ship, and now I have need of it, to
cross over to Elis of the wide dancing-places, where I have 635
twelve brood mares, which are suckling hard-working mules,
not yet tamed; I wish to drive off one of these and break it in.'

So he spoke, and the others' hearts were amazed; they had not
thought he had gone to Neleus' Pylos, but was at home,
somewhere on his estate, with his flocks or his swineherd. 640
Then in turn Antinous, the son of Eupeithes, addressed him:
'Tell me this truly: when did he leave, and which young men
went with him? Were they choice men of Ithaca, or were they
his own serfs and servants? He might well have done even this.
And tell me this in addition, truly, so that I may know it well: 645
did he take your black ship by force, without your permission,
or did you give it to him willingly, when he asked you for it?'

Then Noëmon, the son of Phronius, spoke to him in reply:
'I myself gave it to him willingly. Would not anyone do the
same, when a man like this, with anxieties in his heart, asks him 650
for a favour? It would be very hard to refuse him the giving.
As for the young men who went with him, they are the best men
in the people, next to us. Their leader, whom I saw embarking,
was Mentor—or else some god who resembled him in every way.
But this I am surprised at: I saw splendid Mentor here, yesterday 655
at dawn, and yet he boarded the ship for Pylos at the time I said.'

So he spoke, and went back to his father's house, and the two
men were indignant in their proud hearts. They called an end
to the other suitors' games and made them sit all together,

and among them Antinous the son of Eupeithes spoke out,   660
deeply troubled; his heart was full to overflowing with
black rage, and his two eyes looked like flashing fire.
'Outrageous! What an insolent thing this voyage of Telemachus
has turned out to be! And we thought he would not bring it off.
Despite all of us, this lad, just a boy, has simply gone off and   665
launched a ship, choosing the best men from among the people.
What he has begun now will lead to further trouble; may Zeus
destroy his strength before he reaches the measure of manhood!
Quick, now; give me a swift ship and twenty companions,
and I will lay an ambush for when he returns, catching him   670
in the narrows between Ithaca and rocky Samos. This voyage
in search of his father will bring him nothing but misery.'
     So he spoke, and they all approved, and said he should do this;
and at once they rose and made for the house of Odysseus.
     It was not long before Penelope became aware of the plans   675
that the suitors were plotting deep in their minds. The herald
Medon had told her, for he had heard them scheming; he was
outside in the courtyard, while they wove their intrigue inside.
He set off through the palace to bring the news to Penelope,
and as he set foot on the threshold Penelope addressed him: 680
'Herald, what errand have the lordly suitors sent you on?
Was it to tell godlike Odysseus' servants to stop working
at their tasks and busy themselves with a banquet for them?
I wish this could be the end of their meeting here all the time
and courting me—I wish this could be their very last meal!   685
Day after day you suitors gather here and exhaust the bulk of
our livelihood, wise Telemachus' property. You did not listen
in the past when you were children and your fathers told you
what kind of a man Odysseus was towards your parents,
how he was never arbitrary in word or deed with any man of   690
his people—though this is the way of godlike kings, that they
hate one man among mortals and show favour to another—
but he never committed a wrongful act against any man.
No, the spirit in all of you and your ugly actions are all too
plain, and there is no gratitude for good deeds in time past.'   695
     Then in turn Medon, a man of sound good sense, addressed her:
'I wish, my queen, that all this was the worst of your troubles;
but now the suitors are planning something much worse, and

harder to bear; may the son of Cronus not bring it to fruition!
They are determined to cut Telemachus down with the sharp   700
bronze as he returns home; he has gone to find news of his
father, sailing to sacred Pylos and to splendid Lacedaemon.'
     So he spoke, and Penelope's knees and heart at once went
slack; for a long time she was gripped by speechlessness,
both eyes filled with tears, and her rich voice was choked.   705
At length she answered him, addressing him in these words:
'Herald, why has my son gone away? There was no need
for him to embark in swift-sailing ships, which are for men
as chariots of the sea, and cross vast expanses of water.
Was it so that his very name should be forgotten among men?'   710
     Then in turn Medon, a man of sound good sense, addressed her:
'I do not know if it was some god that impelled him, or if
his own heart was stirred to go to Pylos, to find out about his
father's homecoming, or to learn what kind of death he has met.'
     So he spoke, and went back through the house of Odysseus.   715
Spirit-devouring grief enveloped Penelope; she could no longer
bear to sit on a chair, though there were many in the house,
but sank down on the threshold of her richly decorated room,
piteously lamenting; and around her women servants wept
quietly, all who lived in the palace, both young and old.   720
Groaning ceaselessly, Penelope addressed them:
'Listen to me, my friends: the Olympian has given me
sorrows beyond all other women born and raised in my time.
First, I have lost my noble, lion-hearted husband, one supreme
among the Danaans in all kinds of manliness, a good man   725
whose fame spreads widely through Hellas and Argos' heart.
And now storm-winds have torn my beloved son from his
halls, without a trace; I did not even hear of his departure.
Women, you are hard; you did not think, not even you,
to rouse me from my bed, when you must have known well   730
when that son of mine departed in his black, hollow ship.
If I had found out he was planning this voyage he would
most certainly have stayed here, eager though he was
to leave—or else he would have left me dead in these halls.
Let someone go quickly and summon the aged Dolius,   735
my servant, whom my father gave me when I came here,
and who tends an orchard full of trees for me, and order

him to go quickly and sit by Laertes, and tell him all this,
in the hope that he can weave some scheme in his mind,
and leave his farm and appeal to the people, who are determined   740
to extinguish his own line and that of godlike Odysseus.'

Then in turn her dear nurse Eurycleia addressed her:
'Dear girl, you may kill me with the pitiless bronze, or let me
live on in your hall; but I shall not hide the truth from you.
I knew all of this, and I supplied him with all the provisions   745
he demanded, bread and sweet wine; he bound me with a
great oath not to tell you until the twelfth day came, or when
you yourself noticed his absence and heard he had set sail,
so that you would not mar your lovely skin with weeping.
Come now, wash yourself and put on clean clothes, and   750
go up into the rooms above with your women servants,
and pray to Athena, daughter of Zeus who wields the aegis,
and she will perhaps keep Telemachus safe, even from death.
But do not trouble a troubled old man. I do not think that
the line of Arceisius' son is wholly hated by the blessed   755
gods; there will doubtless be someone to come after him
and inherit his high-roofed palace and his rich lands beyond.'

So she spoke, and stilled Penelope's groans and checked her
eyes' weeping. So she washed herself and put on clean clothes,
and went up to her rooms with some serving-women, and   760
put grains of barley in a basket and prayed to Athena:
'Hear me, daughter of Zeus who wields the aegis,* Atrytone!*
If ever Odysseus, man of many wiles, burnt for you
in his halls the fat thigh-bones of oxen or of sheep,
remember that now, and rescue my dear son for me;   765
save him from the evil schemes of these arrogant suitors.'

So she spoke, and cried out, and the goddess heard her prayer.
But in the shadowy halls the suitors broke into a great uproar,
and this is what one of the arrogant young men would say:
'For sure, this much-courted queen is preparing a wedding   770
for us, and knows nothing of the death planned for her son.'

That is what they said, not knowing what had happened.
Among them Antinous spoke out and addressed them:
'You are all mad! Give up this wild, arrogant talk, all
of it, in case someone goes inside and carries tales there.   775
Now, let us all get up and say nothing, and put that plan

into action, the one that we all devised and agreed upon.'

So he spoke, and picked out twenty of the best men, and
set off towards his swift ship and the shore of the sea.
First they dragged the ship down to the salt sea's waters,   780
and stepped the mast with its sail in the black ship,
and then fitted the oars into their leather straps, all in
their proper order, and then spread the white sail; and
high-spirited attendants brought their war-gear for them.
They moored the ship well out in the water, disembarked,   785
ate their supper, and waited for the evening to come.

Meanwhile wise Penelope was lying in her upper room
without nourishment, refusing to touch food or drink,
brooding on whether her excellent son would escape
death, or if he would be laid low by the arrogant suitors.   790
As a lion ponders when it is cornered by a gang of men,
terrified as it sees the circle being drawn stealthily round it,
so Penelope brooded, until refreshing sleep came over her;
she sank back and fell asleep, and all her joints were eased.

But now the goddess grey-eyed Athena had different plans: 795
she formed a phantom, making it in shape like a woman
called Iphthime, daughter of great-hearted Icarius, whom
Eumelus had taken to wife, he who had his house in Pherae.*
She sent this phantom to the palace of godlike Odysseus
so that Penelope, still lamenting and groaning, would   800
cease from her weeping and tearful wailing.
It entered her bedchamber by pulling the strap on the
door-bolt, and standing above her head addressed her:
'Are you asleep, Penelope, troubled in your heart?
It surely cannot be that the gods who live a life of ease   805
intend to let you weep and grieve while your son is even now
on his way home; in their eyes he has done nothing wrong.'

Circumspect Penelope answered her, though she was
still deep in sweet slumber, and at the gate of dreams:
'Sister, why are you here? You never visited us much   810
before, for you live in a palace that is very far distant.
You tell me to forget my misery and the many pangs
that afflict me in my heart and mind—I who, first, have
lost a noble, lion-hearted husband, one supreme among
the Danaans in all kinds of manliness, a good man, whose   815

fame spreads widely through Hellas and the heart of Argos.
And now my beloved son has gone away in a hollow ship—
still a child, knowing nothing of hard toil or public debate.
It is for him that I lament more than for his father, it is
for him I tremble, fearing what may befall him, either   820
in the country where he has gone or on the open sea;
he has many enemies who are making plots against him,
desperate to kill him before he returns to his native land.'

　　The shadowy phantom then answered and addressed her:
'Do not despair, and do not let your heart be over-fearful.   825
An escort goes with him, one that other men have prayed
to come and stand by them, for she has the power; this is
Pallas Athena, who has pity on you in your lamentations,
and it is she who sent me here to bring this message to you.'

　　Circumspect Penelope in turn answered and addressed her: 830
'If you are indeed divine and have heard a goddess' voice,
give me now a true account also of that other, pitiable man:
is he still alive somewhere, and does he look on the light of
the sun, or is he by now dead, and in the house of Hades?'

　　The shadowy phantom then answered and addressed her: 835
'I cannot speak to you with any truth about him, whether
he is alive or dead; and idle talk is a dangerous thing.'

　　So it spoke, and slipped away past the bolt in the doorpost,
into the winds' breath. Icarius' daughter started up from
sleep, and her heart was warmed by the unmistakable   840
dream that had sped to her in the darkness of the night.

　　Meanwhile the suitors had embarked and were sailing over
the watery pathways, bent on sudden death for Telemachus.
There is a rocky island, set in the middle of the strait, not large,
halfway between Ithaca and rugged Samos, called Asteris;   845
it has a harbour with two mouths that offers shelter to ships,
and there the Achaeans waited in ambush for Telemachus.

BOOK FIVE

Now Dawn rose from the bed she shared with lordly Tithonus,*
to bring light to immortals and to mortals alike, and
the gods took their seats for an assembly; among them
was Zeus the high-thunderer, whose power is supreme.
Athena spoke first, recalling Odysseus' many troubles,   5
concerned that he was still in the house of the nymph:
'Father Zeus and all you other blessed gods who live for ever,
let no staff-holding king ever feel the need to be gentle
and kindly ever again, or to have right thoughts in his mind,
but let him be always harsh, unjust in his acts, seeing that   10
no one now remembers godlike Odysseus among the people
he used to rule; yet he was like a gentle father to them.
Now he lies on an island, suffering cruel anguish,
in the halls of the nymph Calypso, who holds him there
by constraint; he cannot reach his native land, because   15
he has no oared ships at hand, nor any companions
who might accompany him over the broad back of the sea.
Now, to add to this, men are determined to kill his beloved son
as he returns home; he has gone to find news of his father,
sailing to sacred Pylos and to splendid Lacedaemon.'   20
    Zeus who gathers the clouds answered and addressed her:
'My child, what words have escaped the barrier of your teeth!
Did you not devise this plan yourself, intending that
Odysseus should return and take vengeance on these men?
As for Telemachus, use your art to send him back (for you can   25
do this), so that he reaches his native land quite unharmed, and
the suitors sail back in their ship without achieving their aim.'
    So he spoke, and addressed his dear son Hermes:
'Hermes, you are my messenger in other matters, so now
go and tell the nymph with lovely hair of my unerring plan,   30
that Odysseus of the enduring spirit must return home.
He will go without the safe-conduct of gods or mortals,
but sailing on a raft which he has lashed together; after much
hardship, on the twentieth day he will reach fertile Scheria,*
land of the Phaeacians, who are close in kin to the gods.   35

They will honour him in their hearts as if he were a god,
and will convey him in a ship back to his native land,
giving him much bronze and gold and clothing, more than
he could ever have won for himself from Troy as his due
share of the booty, if he had returned without mishap.   40
In this way it is his destiny to see his dear ones, and again
come to the land of his fathers and his high-roofed house.'
   So he spoke, and the guide, slayer of Argus,* did not disobey.
Immediately he bound under his feet his beautiful sandals,
golden and deathless, that carried him over the watery deep   45
and the boundless earth, keeping pace with the wind's blasts.
He picked up the wand with which he charms the eyes of
those he chooses, while others he rouses from their sleep.
With this in hand, the mighty slayer of Argus flew off;
dropping from the upper air he landed on Pieria,* then   50
swooped down to the sea, speeding over the waves like the
bird that wets its fast-beating wings with brine as it hunts
after fish, ranging over dangerous gulfs of the restless sea.
Just like this bird, Hermes rode over wave after wave;
and when he had made his way to the faraway island,   55
he stepped out of the violet-tinged sea on to land, and
walked until he reached the great cavern where the nymph
with lovely hair lived; and he found her at home.
A great fire was ablaze on her hearth, and the scent of
burning cedar-wood and juniper logs drifted far across   60
the island. She was inside, singing in her lovely voice,
as she went to and fro at her loom, weaving with a
golden shuttle. Around the cavern there grew a luxuriant wood,
alder and black poplar and sweet-smelling cypress,
and in the trees were the roosts of long-winged birds: 65
owls and hawks and cormorants with long tongues,
birds of the deep, whose business is with the sea.
Around the hollow cavern was trained a flourishing
garden-vine, heavily loaded with grapes; and by it
four springs flowed with bright water, channelled close   70
to each other but directed to run on differing courses.
Around these, soft meadows of violets and wild celery
grew in abundance; even an immortal who chanced to
visit might wonder at the sight, and delight his heart.

The guide, slayer of Argus, stood and marvelled; and when   75
he had gazed at everything and admired it in his heart he
went at once into the wide cave. Calypso, bright among
goddesses, did not fail to recognize him in front of her,
for the immortal gods are not unknown to each other,
even if one of them has his home far from the rest.   80
But Hermes did not find great-hearted Odysseus within;
he was sitting on the seashore and weeping as was his custom,
tearing at his heart with tears and groans and anguish, and
all the time as he wept looking out over the restless sea.
Calypso, bright among goddesses, seated Hermes on   85
a lustrous, shining chair, and began to question him:
'Hermes of the golden wand, what brings you here to me?
You are a welcome and honoured guest, but you have not
come often before this. Speak what is in your mind; my heart
tells me to fulfil it—if I can, that is, and if it may be fulfilled.   90
But follow me in, so I may put gifts of hospitality before you.'

   So the goddess spoke, and set a table beside Hermes and
loaded it with ambrosia, and mixed red nectar* for him; and
the guide, slayer of Argus, set about eating and drinking.
When he had finished eating, and satisfied his heart with   95
food, he answered Calypso, addressing her in these words:
'You ask me, goddess to god, why I have come. Well,
I will give you a true account, since that is what you ask.
It was Zeus who sent me here, though I had no wish to—
who would willingly cross such an indescribably vast tract   100
of salt water? There is no city of mortals hereabouts, men
who make holy offerings and perfect hecatombs to the gods.
But there is no way that another god can secretly frustrate
the intention of aegis-wielding Zeus, or cause it to fail.
He says there is a man living here with you, the most pitiable   105
of all those who fought for nine years around the city of
Priam, and in the tenth sacked it and set out for home.
But during their homecoming they caused affront to Athena,*
who stirred up a terrible storm and huge waves against them.
All the rest of them, his excellent companions, perished,   110
but the wind and waves bore him away and brought him here.
It is this man that Zeus now orders you to send on his way
without delay; it is not his destiny to die here, far from his

loved ones, but it is still his fate to see his people again and
to return to the land of his fathers and his high-roofed house.'   115
   So he spoke, and Calypso, bright among goddesses,
shuddered and addressed him in winged words:
'You are hard, you gods, and envious beyond all others,
bearing a grudge against any goddess who takes a man
openly to her bed, if she desires to make him her husband.   120
It was so when Dawn with the rosy fingers chose Orion;*
the gods who live an easy life bore a grudge against her*
until finally chaste Artemis of the golden throne pursued
him in Ortygia and killed him with her gentle shafts.
It was so when Demeter of the lovely hair yielded to   125
passion and coupled in love with Iasion,* in a thrice-
ploughed field. It was not long before Zeus found out
and killed him with a cast of his flashing thunderbolt.
And now it is my turn; you gods begrudge me that I have a
mortal here, a man I rescued as he bestrode his ship's keel,   130
alone, after Zeus had hurled a flashing thunderbolt at his
swift ship and shattered it far out on the wine-dark sea.
Then all the rest of them, his good companions, perished,
but the wind and waves bore him away and brought him here.
I made him welcome and cared for him, and I promised   135
to make him immortal and ageless for all his days.
But since there is no way a god can secretly frustrate
the intention of aegis-wielding Zeus or cause it to fail,
well, let him come to grief, if Zeus so urges and orders,
on the restless sea. Yet I will not help him go, I will not,   140
for I have no oared ships at hand, nor any companions
who might convey him over the broad back of the sea.
But I will gladly give him advice, and not hide anything,
so that, completely unharmed, he may reach his native land.'
   Then in turn the guide, slayer of Argus, addressed her: 145
'Very well, send him now on his way; and beware of Zeus'
anger, lest he grow resentful hereafter and bear hard on you.'
   So the mighty slayer of Argus spoke, and went on his way,
and the revered nymph went in search of great-hearted
Odysseus, now that she had heard the message from Zeus.   150
She found him sitting on the seashore; his eyes were never
without tears, and his sweet life drained away as he grieved

for a way home, since the nymph no longer pleased him.
He spent his nights in her hollow cavern, but by constraint,
since she desired him, while he had no love for her.   155
All his days he passed sitting on rocks on the seashore,
tearing at his heart with tears and groans and anguish,
forever weeping and looking out over the restless sea.
Standing beside him she, bright among goddesses, spoke:
'Ill-fated man, please do not grieve forever, and do not let your life   160
wither here, for now I am willing* to send you on your way.
So come, cut down some long timbers with a bronze axe
and shape them into a wide raft, and then fix decking on top
of them, so that it may carry you across the misty open sea.
To satisfy your needs I shall stow on board bread and water   165
and red wine, such as will keep hunger away; and I shall
provide you with clothing, and send you a following breeze,
so that you may reach your native land quite unharmed—
if the gods who inhabit the broad high sky will it, they who
have more power than I in making plans and carrying them out.'   170

So she spoke, and much-enduring glorious Odysseus
shuddered, and addressed her in winged words: 'Goddess,
it is not my safe passage you are planning but something else
when you tell me to cross the great gulf of the sea on a raft—
a dangerous and difficult enterprise. Not even swift-running   175
trim ships, exulting in a wind from Zeus, are able to cross it.
No; without your goodwill I cannot set sail on a raft,
unless you bring yourself, goddess, to swear a great oath
that you are plotting no more arduous troubles for me.'

So he spoke, and Calypso, bright among goddesses, smiled,   180
and stroking him with her hand she spoke to him, saying:
'You are a real scoundrel, and crafty-witted as well,
to think of something like this and then to say it!
Let the earth be my witness in this, and the high sky above,
and the waters of Styx* that flow below, which is the   185
greatest and most terrible oath for the blessed gods,
that I shall not plot any more arduous troubles for you;
I am thinking and planning only that which I would
devise for myself if a need as great as yours came upon me.
You must know that my mind is fair and just, and the heart   190
in my breast is not made of iron but is disposed to pity.'

So she, bright among goddesses, spoke, and led the way,
swiftly, and he followed, walking in the goddess' footsteps.
So they came to the hollow cavern, the goddess and the man,
and Odysseus sat down on the chair from which Hermes   195
had risen, and the nymph put before him all kinds of fare
for him to eat and drink, of the kind that mortals consume.
She herself sat opposite, facing godlike Odysseus, and
handmaids set out ambrosia and nectar before her.
So they reached out for the good things that lay before them;   200
and when they had taken their pleasure in food and drink
the first to speak was Calypso, bright among goddesses:
'Zeus-sprung son of Laertes, Odysseus of many wiles,
are you resolved to return home to your dear land, now,
this moment? May you fare well, in spite of everything!   205
If you knew in your heart the many hardships it is your fate
to suffer in full measure before you reach your native land,
you would stay here and watch over this house with me,
and would become immortal, however much you long
to look on the wife for whom you yearn, day after day.   210
And yet I claim to be in no way her inferior, either in
stature or in form, since it is not at all fitting for mortal
women to compete with immortals in stature or in beauty.'

Then in answer Odysseus of many wiles addressed her:
'Revered goddess, do not be angry with me for this; I too   215
know well that circumspect Penelope is of less account
than you in beauty and in stature to look upon, for
she is a mortal, and you are immortal and do not age.
But for all that I desire and long all my days to go back
home and to see the day of my return. Furthermore, if   220
one of the gods wrecks me on the wine-dark sea, I shall
endure it, since the spirit in my breast can bear suffering;
already I have borne much hardship and many labours
on sea and in war; so let this too come on, after all the rest.'

So he spoke, and the sun went down and darkness came over   225
them, and they went into an inner part of the hollow cave
and took their pleasure in lovemaking, lying side by side.

When early-born Dawn with her rosy fingers appeared,
Odysseus quickly clothed himself in a tunic and a cloak,
while she, the nymph, put on a long, silvery robe,   230

finely spun and becoming, and round her waist she tied
a beautiful golden girdle, and covered her head with a scarf.
Then she planned the home-sending of great-hearted Odysseus.
She gave him a great axe, one that suited his grip well,
made of bronze, and sharp-edged on both its sides, and into   235
it was fitted a fine handle of olive-wood, snugly embedded.
Then she gave him a well-honed adze, and set off, leading
the way to the island's furthest part, where trees grew tall:
alder and black poplar, and fir that reached to the high sky,
but long-dried and seasoned, to make his craft run lightly.   240
When Calypso had shown him where the tall trees grew,
she, bright among goddesses, set off back to her home.
Meanwhile Odysseus began to cut his timber, and quickly
finished his task; twenty trees in all he felled and trimmed
with his bronze axe, smoothed them skilfully and trued them   245
against a line. Calypso, bright among goddesses, brought him
augers, and he bored through all the planks and matched the
joints to each other, making them fast with pegs and dowels.
As a shipwright, skilled in his trade, rounds out the hull
of a ship, a broad-bottomed merchantman, to a certain width,   250
so Odysseus built his broad raft to the same dimensions.
So he worked away, fixing a platform on to it, jointed
into close-set ribs, and finished it off with long gunwales.
In the vessel he set a mast, with a yard-arm fitted to it, and
after that made a steering-oar with which to guide the raft.   255
All down its length he fenced it with osier mat-work, as a
defence against waves, backed by a mass of brushwood.
Then Calypso, bright among goddesses, brought cloth
for him to make a sail, and this too he fashioned with skill.
On the raft he made fast the stays and halyards and sheets,   260
and then levered it with crowbars down to the bright sea.

   The fourth day came and all his work was finished, and
on the fifth glorious Calypso saw him off from the island,
first bathing him and clothing him in fragrant garments.
She stowed on board for him one skin of dark wine and   265
another of water, a large one, and also provisions in a bag,
putting in it plenty of cooked meat, to satisfy his heart;
and she sent forth a warm and constant breeze for him.
Cheered by this breeze glorious Odysseus spread his sail,

and sitting next to the steering oar kept the raft skilfully   270
on course; nor did sleep ever fall on his eyelids, but he
held his gaze on the Pleiades* and late-setting Boötes,*
and the Bear that men also call the Wain,* which turns
always in the same place and keeps close watch on Orion,
and alone has no share in the baths of Ocean;* for indeed   275
Calypso, bright among goddesses, had instructed him
to keep this star on his left as he sailed across the sea.
For seventeen days on end he sailed across the open sea,
and on the eighteenth day the shadowy mountains of the
Phaeacians' land showed, where it jutted out nearest to him;   280
and it seemed to him like a shield lying on the misty sea.

    But now the lord earthshaker, returning from the Ethiopians,
saw him from afar from the mountains of the Solymi.* When he
spotted him sailing over the open sea he was exceedingly angry
within, and with a shake of his head spoke to his heart: 285
'What is this? The gods must foolishly have changed their
minds about Odysseus while I was away with the Ethiopians;
and now here he is near the Phaeacians' land, where it is
his destiny to escape the great snare of misery that holds him.
Nevertheless I think I can even now fill him full of torment.'   290

    So he spoke, and massed the clouds; taking his trident in his
hand he heaved the sea into confusion and roused storm-
blasts of all the winds there are, and hid earth and sea alike in
clouds; and night rushed down from the high sky. The East and
South Winds and the hard-blowing West Wind crashed together,   295
and the sky-born North Wind rolled a huge wave before it.
Then indeed Odysseus' knees and his heart went slack,
and, deeply troubled, he spoke to his great-hearted spirit:
'How unlucky I am! What is there left that can happen to me
now? I fear that all the goddess told me will turn out to be true: 300
she said before I reached my ancestral land I would have my full
measure of agonies on the sea; and now it has all been fulfilled,
with Zeus wrapping the high sky in clouds like these and churning
the sea into confusion; and storm-blasts of all the winds there are
come raging furiously together. Now my sheer destruction is certain.   305
O three times blessed, four times even, were those Danaans who
died long ago in broad Troy, performing a service to Atreus' sons!
How I wish that I too had perished and met my death on the

day that Trojans in great numbers hurled their bronze-tipped
spears at me over Peleus' dead son!* I would have had my   310
due burial rites, and the Achaeans would have spread my fame
abroad; but now my fate is to be taken in a miserable death.'

As he said this a huge wave smashed down from above,
striking him with a terrible force, and spun the raft shuddering
in a circle. He was flung from the raft, and his hands slipped   315
from the steering-oar; the winds crashed together, and a
fearful storm-blast swept down and shattered his mast in
two, and the sail and yard were flung far off into the sea.
For a long time he was trapped under water, and could not
swim upwards, thwarted as he was by the huge wave's swell,   320
and cumbered by the clothes given him by bright Calypso.
But at last he broke the surface, and spat from his mouth the
bitter brine that streamed down in torrents from his head.
For all that, though battered, he did not forget about his raft,
but heaving himself up in the waves he seized hold of it,   325
and sitting in the middle escaped the final end of death.
The huge swell carried the raft with the current this way and that:
as at the time of harvest the North Wind blows thistledowns
that cling one to another in clusters all over a plain,
so the winds blew the raft here and there over the sea;   330
now the South Wind would fling it to the North to carry off,
and now the East Wind would leave it to the West to pursue.

But now Cadmus' daughter, Ino of the lovely ankles, saw him:
Leucotheë, who once spoke with a human voice, but now
lives in the deep sea, sharing in the honour paid to the gods.   335
She took pity on storm-tossed Odysseus in his misery;
like a gull she rose in flight from the water,
and perching on his raft addressed him in these words:
'Ill-fated man, how can it be that earthshaker Poseidon is
so violently at odds with you, to cause you all this suffering?   340
For all that, he will not kill you, great though his rage is. Now—
you do not seem a foolish man to me—do exactly as I say:
take off all your clothes and leave the raft to be carried away
by the winds, and then swim with your arms and strive for
landfall on the Phaeacians' land, where your fate is to be saved.   345
Here, take this scarf and fasten it below your chest; it is
immortal, and so you need have no fear of injury or death.

Then, when you feel the dry land under your hands, untie
the scarf and throw it back into the wine-dark sea, a long
way from the shore, and turn your face away as you do it.' 350
    So the goddess spoke, and handed him the scarf, and
plunged once again into the wave-swollen sea like
a gull, and the dark waters closed over her.
Glorious much-enduring Odysseus pondered what to do,
and, deeply troubled, spoke to his great-hearted spirit: 355
'Ah! I am afraid that yet again one of the immortals
is weaving a snare for me, telling me to abandon my raft.
No—I shall not obey her, not yet, since with my own eyes
I saw the land far off where she told me I would find refuge.
This is what I shall do, since it seems to me the best course: 360
as long as the planks hold together at their joints I shall
remain where I am and endure whatever hardship comes,
and only when the waves shatter my raft in pieces shall I
take to swimming, since I cannot think of any better plan.'
    While he was pondering this in his heart and in his mind, 365
Poseidon the earthshaker heaved up a huge wave, grim and
terrifying, which towered over and then crashed down on him.
As when a hard-blowing wind disturbs a heap of parched
chaff and scatters it in all directions, so this wave
scattered the raft's long planks; it left Odysseus sitting 370
astride one timber, like a man riding on horseback, and
stripped of the clothes that bright Calypso had given him.
At once he coiled the scarf around his chest and dived head-
first into the sea, striking out with his arms, and swimming
as hard as he could; but the lord earthshaker saw him, and 375
with a shake of his head spoke to his heart: 'Go on, then!
Now drift across the open sea in terrible suffering until
you fall in with men who are favoured by the gods. But
even then I do not think you will find fault with your ordeal.'
    So he spoke, and touched the whip on his fine-maned horses, 380
and arrived at Aegae,* where his famous palace stands.
    But now Athena, daughter of Zeus, had different plans:
she tied back the paths of three of the winds, and ordered
them all to stop blowing and go to sleep, and then roused
the blustering North Wind to beat down the waves in his way, 385
until Zeus-sprung Odysseus should fall in with the Phaeacians

who delight in rowing, and so escape death and destruction.
    For two days and two nights Odysseus drifted, driven by the
heavy swell, and often his heart saw death looming over him;
but when lovely-haired Dawn brought in the third day,   390
then at last the wind stopped blowing and a breathless calm
broke out. Odysseus, keeping a sharp lookout, was lifted up
on the crest of a huge wave and caught sight of the land nearby.
As when his children see welcome signs of life in their father
who lies ailing in bed, wasting away in the grip of a long   395
and painful illness—for some hateful divinity has assailed him—
and then the gods send him a welcome release from his anguish,
so the land and its woods came as a welcome sight to Odysseus,
and he swam on, impatient to set foot upon dry land. But
when he was as near as a man's voice carries when he shouts,   400
and indeed could hear the sea crashing against the rocky coast—
for the huge rollers kept breaking against the hard land with a
fearful roar, and everything was obscured in salt spray, since
here there were no roadsteads to offer shelter to ships, nor any
place to anchor, but only jutting headlands, reefs, and sea-cliffs—   405
then indeed Odysseus' limbs and heart went slack, and,
deeply troubled, he spoke to his great-hearted spirit:
'Ah! Against expectation I managed to cleave my way
across this watery expanse, and Zeus granted me to see land;
but now I cannot see any way to escape from the grey sea.   410
Offshore there are sharp-edged reefs; about them the swell
crashes and roars, and behind them a cliff runs sheer upwards,
there is deep water near the shore, and there is nowhere
I can stand firm on both my feet and so escape from danger.
If I do reach land, I am afraid a great wave may lift and   415
dash me against the jagged cliff, and my efforts will all be
in vain; but if I swim on along the coast, in the hope of finding
a landspit jutting aslant to offer me a haven from the sea,
I am afraid that a squall will once again lift me up and
carry me, groaning deeply, out on to the fish-rich sea;   420
or else some god will let loose a huge sea-monster at me,
one of the many that renowned Amphitrite* nurtures;
I know how the famous earthshaker is at odds with me.'
    While he was pondering this in his mind and in his heart,
a huge wave carried him on to the jagged shore; and here the   425

skin would have been torn from him and his bones smashed,
had not the goddess grey-eyed Athena put a thought in his mind:
as he was swept in he caught the rock in both his hands
and clung on to it, groaning, until the great wave passed.
So he escaped from this wave, but the backwash once again   430
battered him with great force and flung him far out to sea.
As when an octopus is dragged from its hiding-place, and
pebbles cling in thick clusters to its suckers, in the same way
pieces of skin were stripped from Odysseus' bold hands and
stuck to the rock; and a huge wave hid him from view. Then   435
wretched Odysseus would surely have died before his time,
had not the goddess grey-eyed Athena given him another idea:
he got clear of the surf where it heaved on to the shore and kept
swimming outside it, looking towards the land, and hoping to find
a landspit jutting aslant to offer him a haven from the sea.   440
And as he swam he came to the mouth of a clear-flowing river,
and it seemed to him to be the best place; it was clear of rocks,
and there was somewhere to shelter from the wind. He knew
the river-god as he came flowing out, and prayed in his heart:
'Hear me, lord, whoever you are! I come to you with prayers,   445
as many do, fleeing from the sea and the threats of Poseidon.
Anyone who comes as a wandering suppliant deserves respect,
especially from the immortal gods; I am such, and I come
now to your stream and to your knees, after great suffering.
Pity me, lord, I beg you; I claim to be your suppliant.'   450

So he spoke, and the river at once checked his current and stayed
his waves, calming the water in front of him, and carried him
safely to his outflow. There Odysseus' knees gave way, and his
brawny arms hung slack, for his heart was crushed by the sea.
His flesh was swollen all over, and streams of sea-water gushed   455
from his mouth and nostrils. Without breath or speech, he lay
with little life in him, for terrible weariness had overcome him.
But when he had recovered his breath and his spirit had
gathered inside him, then at last he untied the goddess' scarf;
he let it fall into the river as it flowed towards the sea, and   460
a great wave carried it along with the current, and Ino took it
straight back into her hands. Odysseus turned away from the
river and collapsed on to a bed of reeds, and kissed the grain-
giving earth; deeply troubled, he spoke to his great-hearted spirit:

'What will become of me now? What is left to happen to me?   465
If I stay awake for a comfortless night beside the river, I am
afraid that bitter frost and soaking dew will between them
defeat me, weakened as I am and ready to gasp out my spirit,
since before dawn a chilly wind can blow up from the river.
If, however, I climb up the bank into shady woodland and   470
settle to sleep in some dense thicket, hoping that cold and
weariness may loosen their grip and sweet sleep come upon me,
I fear I shall become the prey and victim of wild beasts.'
    And as he pondered this seemed to him the better plan:
he set off for the woodland, and found it near the water,   475
next to a clearing; and here he stole under a pair of bushes
growing from one stock, one of wild, one of cultivated olive.
The blustering winds' damp force never blew through these,
nor could the rays of the bright sun ever penetrate them,
nor did rain ever pass completely through, so close-set they   480
grew, and interlaced with one another. It was under these
that Odysseus crept, and with his own hands quickly heaped
up a wide bed, for there was a great pile of leaves there,
enough to make a covering for two or even three men in
the winter season, however severe the weather might be.   485
Much-enduring glorious Odysseus was glad to see this bed,
and lay down in the middle, and heaped leaves over himself.
As when a man living on the edge of worked land, one who
has no neighbours, hides a firebrand under dark ashes,
to preserve the seed of fire, and to save looking for a light   490
elsewhere, so Odysseus hid himself under the leaves; and
Athena poured sleep over his eyes, drawing down his lids,
so that he could put the swiftest end to his weariness and misery.

BOOK SIX

So much-enduring glorious Odysseus slept on in this place,
worn out by sleep and exhaustion. Meanwhile Athena
made her way to the city and land of the Phaeacians, who
in former times had lived in Hypereia* of the wide dancing-
places, near the Cyclopes: men of great arrogance, who   5
continually plagued them, because they were much stronger.
From there Nausithous who looked like a god uprooted them
and led them to settle in Scheria,* far from grain-eating people.
He drove a wall round their city, and built houses, and
erected temples for the gods, and shared out the ploughland.   10
But he was long gone to Hades, overcome by death, and
now Alcinous, whose counsel came from the gods, ruled.
It was to his house that the goddess grey-eyed Athena now
went, devising the homecoming of great-hearted Odysseus.
She made her way into a richly decorated chamber, in which   15
there slept a girl equal to the gods in stature and beauty:
Nausicaa, daughter of great-hearted Alcinous. Beside her,
on either side of the doorposts, slept two maids whose
beauty came from the Graces; and the shining doors were shut.
Like a breath of wind, Athena sped to the girl's bedside,   20
and stood above her head and spoke to her, making
herself look like the daughter of famed Dymas the seafarer,
who was the same age as her, and very dear to her heart.
Resembling this girl, grey-eyed Athena addressed Nausicaa:
'Nausicaa, how could your mother have such a careless daughter?   25
You have shining garments lying here neglected, and yet your
marriage is impending, when you must have fine clothes both
to wear yourself, and to provide for those who will escort you.
From such things, you know, a good reputation goes about
among men, and brings delight to your father and revered mother.   30
Let us go, then, as soon as dawn comes, and do some washing.
I shall come along to help you, so you can quickly get it done,
because, as you know, you will not be a maid for long;
already all the best men among the whole Phaeacian people,
where your family too belongs, are wanting to marry you.   35

Come, then, and early in the morning urge your renowned
father to make ready some mules and a wagon, to carry the
sashes and women's dresses and shining blankets for you.
It will be much better for you too to go like this than on foot,
because the washing-pools are a long way from the city.'   40

   So grey-eyed Athena spoke, and departed for Olympus,
where men say is the unchanging home of the gods.
It is never shaken by winds or drenched by rains, nor does
snow ever penetrate there, but a bright sky, clear and cloudless,
is spread over all, and a white radiance plays round it;   45
and there for all time the blessed gods take their pleasure.
There the grey-eyed one went, when she had spoken to the girl.

   Very soon Dawn on her splendid throne arrived, and woke
the fine-gowned Nausicaa, who marvelled at her dream,
and made her way through the palace to tell her parents,   50
her dear father and mother; and she found them indoors.
Her mother was sitting by the hearth with her women servants,
spinning sea-purple yarn; and she met her father as he was
on his way out to join the renowned lords in a council
to which the lordly Phaeacians had as usual invited him.   55
Standing very close to him, Nausicaa spoke to her dear father:
'Dear papa, could you please have a wagon prepared for me,
high-sided with strong wheels, so I can take our fine clothes to
wash in the river? They are lying dirty, and I must see to them.
And indeed it is proper for you too to have clean garments   60
to wear when you deliberate in council with the leading men.
And then you have five sons who were born in your halls,
two of them married men and three lively bachelors;
they are always wanting newly washed clothes to
wear at the dance—and all this is a concern for me.'   65

   She spoke like this because she felt awe at naming her fruitful
marriage to her father, but he understood it all and answered:
'I do not grudge you the mules, my child, or anything else.
Away you go; servants will prepare a wagon for you, high-
sided with strong wheels, and fitted with an upper carriage.'   70

   So he spoke, and summoned his servants, and they obeyed.
They prepared a strong-wheeled wagon outside, drawn by
mules, and led the animals under the cart and yoked them up,
and the girl brought the shining clothes from the inner room.

These she stowed in the well-polished wagon, and her mother   75
packed in a box all kinds of food that please the heart,
putting in plenty of cooked meat, and poured some wine
into a goatskin bag; and the girl climbed onto the wagon.
Her mother gave her smooth olive oil in a golden flask
for her and her maidservants to rub themselves down.   80
Nausicaa took up the whip and the shining reins, and flicked
the mules to make them go, and they clattered away,
straining unflaggingly, carrying the clothing and the girl along.
She was not alone, for maidservants went with her.

When they reached the river and its beautiful flowing waters,   85
where the ever-replenished washing-pools were, with plenty of
water always welling up, enough to clean even the dirtiest
garments, there they freed the mules from the wagon's yoke.
They chased them away to the whirling river's bank, to graze on
sweet dogstooth grass, and lifted the clothes from the wagon   90
in their arms and carried them into the dark water, and set to
treading them in the pools, in quick rivalry with each other.
When they had washed all the clothes and rinsed away the dirt,
they spread them out in a line along the shore, just
where the sea beating on the land washed the pebbles clean.   95
Then they bathed and rubbed themselves richly with olive oil
and took their meal beside the banks of the river, and
waited for the clothes to dry in the shining of the sun.
When the maids and Nausicaa had enjoyed their meal,
they threw aside their headscarves and began to play at ball,   100
and among them white-armed Nausicaa led their games.
Like Artemis, shooter of arrows, when she moves down
the mountains, striding along lofty Taygetus or Erymanthus,*
taking delight in the chase of boars or swift deer; and
country-haunting nymphs, daughters of aegis-wielding Zeus,   105
sport with her as she goes—and Leto's* heart is gladdened
because Artemis holds her head and brow higher than them
all, and she is easily marked out, though all are beautiful—
just so the unwed girl stood out among her maidservants.

But when she was on the point of returning home,   110
and had yoked the mules and folded the fine clothes,
then the goddess grey-eyed Athena had a different plan:
that Odysseus should wake and see the beautiful girl, and

that she should escort him to the city of the Phaeacians.
And so the princess threw the ball to one of her maids,   115
but it missed her and fell into the deep swirling water;
the girls gave a loud shriek, and glorious Odysseus woke
and sat up, and pondered in his mind and in his heart:
'What shall I do? What mortals' land have I reached this time?
Are they violent and uncivilized, and given to wrongdoing, or   120
are they hospitable, and there is in them a god-fearing temper?
Around me there echoed the sound of shrieking, of girls—
of nymphs perhaps, who haunt sheer crags of mountains,
and springs that give rise to rivers, and grassy meadows.
Or perhaps I am near people who speak with a human voice?   125
Up, then; I must try to find out, and see who they are.'
    So glorious Odysseus spoke, and came from under the thicket.
With his brawny hand he broke off a branch of dense brushwood,
a leafy one, to hold before his body and hide his man's parts.
He set off like a mountain-nurtured lion that trusts in its strength,   130
advancing buffeted by wind and rain, and the eyes in it are
blazing; now it goes hunting among cattle or sheep, now after
deer in the wild, and now its belly drives it on to make an attack
on a strongly built farmyard and to fall upon the sheep there.
Just so Odysseus made ready to join the lovely-haired girls,   135
naked though he was, because necessity had come upon him.
A fearful sight he presented to them, disfigured by brine, and
they fled in terror, this way and that along the jutting sand-spits.
Only the daughter of Alcinous stood firm, for Athena had
put boldness in her heart and taken the fear from her limbs.   140
So she stood, resolutely facing him, and Odysseus considered
whether he should grasp the lovely girl's knees and entreat her,
or if he should stand away, just where he was, and entreat her
with soft words to give him clothing and direct him to the city.
And as he pondered this seemed to him the better plan, to keep   145
his distance and entreat her with soft words, in case the girl
should become angry in her heart if he grasped her by the knees.
And so he spoke to her at once with soft, cunning words:
'Lady, I come to your knees; are you a goddess, or mortal?
If you are one of the gods who live in the broad high sky,   150
then it is most nearly to Artemis, daughter of great Zeus,
that I compare you in beauty and in stature and in form.

But if you belong to the race of mortals who live on earth,
three times blessed are your father and your revered mother,
and three times blessed your brothers! How their hearts must　　155
grow warm with pleasure because of you, every time they
see you, such a lovely slip of a girl, going to join the dance!
But that man's heart must be blessed beyond all others who
prevails with wedding gifts and takes you home as his bride.
Never yet have I set eyes on anyone who resembles you,　　160
neither man nor woman; I am seized by awe as I gaze.
In Delos once, next to the altar of Apollo, I did see the like—
the youthful shoot of a palm tree, reaching upwards;
I had gone there, and a large company went with me,
on that journey which was to bring me hardship and grief.　　165
And just as when I saw it I wondered for a long time in my
heart, for never yet had such a shoot sprung up from the earth,
so I marvel and wonder at you, lady, and I am terribly afraid
to touch your knees, even though hard sorrow is upon me.
Yesterday, after nineteen days, I escaped from the wine-dark　　170
sea; until then the surge and blustering storms carried me from
the island of Ogygia, and now some god has cast me up here,
so that here too, I suppose, I should be tormented. I do not think
this will stop; before then the gods have plenty in store for me.
I beg you, princess, have pity on me; after my many travails　　175
you are the first person I have met, and I do not know a
single one among the people who dwell in this land and city.
Direct me to the city, and give me some rags to cover myself,
perhaps a wrapping-cloth you brought when you came here.
Then may the gods grant you all that you desire in your heart,　　180
and may they bestow on you a husband, a house, and good
harmony of minds;* there is nothing better or more powerful
than this, when a man and his wife keep house in sympathy
of mind—a great grief to their enemies, but a joy to those who
wish them well; and they themselves are highly esteemed.'　　185

　　Then in turn Nausicaa of the white arms answered him:
'Stranger, you do not strike me as either a rogue or a fool.
It is Olympian Zeus himself who dispenses prosperity to men,
to both good and bad, to each as he wishes; he must surely
have sent you these troubles, and you must bear them as you may.　　190
But now, since you have arrived here at our city and land,

you will not go without clothing or anything else that it is right
for a sorely tried suppliant to receive from those he meets.
I will direct you to the city, and tell you our people's name:
it is the Phaeacians who dwell in this city and this land,   195
and I myself am the daughter of great-hearted Alcinous,
on whom hangs the authority and might of the Phaeacians.'
    So she spoke, and gave orders to her lovely-haired maids:
'Stop there, maids! Where are you running, just at the sight
of a man? You cannot think he is some enemy of ours;   200
that mortal creature does not exist, nor could ever be born,
who could bring war and fighting with him to the land of the
Phaeacians, because they are close friends of the immortals.
We live in a remote place, in the midst of the surging sea, on
the edge of things, and no other mortals have dealings with us.   205
No, this man who has fetched up here is some unlucky wanderer;
we must now look after him, because all strangers and beggars
are under Zeus' protection, and any gift, though small, is welcome.
So come here, maids; give the stranger some food and drink,
and bathe him in the river where there is shelter from the wind.'   210
    So she spoke, and they stood still and urged each other on.
They sat Odysseus down in a sheltered place, as instructed
by Nausicaa, the daughter of great-hearted Alcinous,
and laid out clothes beside him: a tunic and a cloak,
and gave him soft olive oil in a jar made of gold, and   215
told him to wash himself in the river's running waters.
Then glorious Odysseus addressed the maidservants:
'Stand over there, you maids, a little away from me, so that
I can wash the brine from my shoulders and rub my body
with oil; it has been a long time since oil touched my skin.   220
I will not bathe myself in front of you, for I am ashamed
to go naked in the company of lovely-haired young women.'
    So he spoke, and they fell back and reported to the young girl.
Meanwhile glorious Odysseus was washing off with river
water the brine that lay thick on his back and broad shoulders,   225
and sluicing from his head the salt scurf of the restless sea.
When he had washed all over and rubbed himself with oil,
he put on the clothes which the unwed girl had given him;
and Athena, daughter of Zeus, made him taller and more
thickset to look at, and from his head she made the locks   230

of his hair hang thickly down, like the hyacinth flower.
As when a skilled man, one whom Hephaestus and Pallas
Athena have taught all manner of crafts, overlays gold on silver,
and graceful are the works of art he creates,
so she poured grace down over his head and shoulders.   235
He withdrew a little way and sat on the seashore, gleaming
with beauty and grace; and the girl, admiring, watched him.
Then Nausicaa addressed her lovely-haired maidservants:
'Listen to me, white-armed servants, to what I shall say:
it is not without the will of all the gods who dwell on Olympus   240
that this man has come among the godlike Phaeacians;
before this he looked to me like a man of mean appearance,
but now he resembles the gods who live in the broad high sky.
How I wish such a man could live here and be acknowledged
as my husband—if only it pleased him to stay among us!   245
But hurry, maids, and give the stranger food and drink.'

   So she spoke, and they listened carefully and did as she said,
and set food and drink near him; and glorious Odysseus,
he who had endured so much, ate and drank voraciously,
for it had been a long time since he had tasted food.   250

   Meanwhile white-armed Nausicaa had another plan: after
folding the clothes she stowed them in the fine wagon,
and yoked the strong-hoofed mules, and herself climbed in.
Then she roused Odysseus, speaking directly to him:

   'Up with you now, stranger, and make for the city; I mean   255
to send you to the house of my wise father, where I believe
all the very best men among the Phaeacians will meet you.
Now—for you do not strike me as a foolish man—do exactly
as I say: as long as we are passing through the worked fields
of men, for that time you must walk quickly with my maids   260
behind the mules and the wagon, and I will lead the way.
But as soon as we reach the city, which has high walls
around it, and there is a fine harbour on either side of it,
and the way in is narrow; well-balanced ships are drawn up
on the road, and there is a slipway for each and every man.   265
There they have their assembly-place, next to the splendid
precinct of Poseidon, set with deep-bedded quarried stones.
It is there that the men look after their black ships' gear,
their cables and sails, and there they shape their oar-blades;

for the Phaeacians care nothing for bows and quivers, but   270
concern themselves only with masts and oars and balanced
ships, in which they take delight, crossing over the grey sea.
I wish to avoid these people's sour gossip, in case someone
hereafter finds fault with me; there are insolent men among
them, and one of the lower sort might say when meeting us: 275
"Who is this handsome, well-set-up stranger with Nausicaa?
Where did she find him? Her future husband, I would guess!
No doubt she rescued him, some rover, from his ship, a man
from a far-off people, since there are none such around here.
Or else he is some god, come down from the high sky in answer   280
to her insistent prayers, and he will have her for all his days.
Better so, that she herself should go about and find a husband
from somewhere else, since she clearly despises the many
noble Phaeacians here among the people who are courting her."
This is what they would say, and it would be my disgrace; and   285
indeed I would be indignant with any other girl who acted thus,
who against her father's and mother's wishes, while they were
still alive, associated with men before being decently married.
Now, stranger, you must quickly mark my words, if you
want to obtain a swift safe passage home from my father.   290
    'You will come to a fine poplar grove beside the road, sacred
to Athena, with a spring flowing through it, and a meadow
around; this is my father's estate and flourishing orchard,
as far from the city as a man's voice carries when he shouts.
Sit there and wait for a while, until such time as we reach   295
the city and arrive at the palace of my father. Then,
when you think we have reached the palace, you must
make your way straight to the Phaeacians' city and ask for
the palace of my father, great-hearted Alcinous. It is easy
to recognize, and even a little child could show you the way;   300
for the houses that are built for the Phaeacians do not in
any way resemble the house of the hero Alcinous. Now,
as soon as the courtyard and the house have hidden you
from view, go very quickly through the hall, to reach
my mother, who sits by the hearth in the fire's brightness,   305
spinning sea-purple yarn—a wonder to look at—her chair
leaning against a pillar; and her women servants sit behind.
And there is my father's chair, set next to her, on which

he sits and drinks his wine, as if he were an immortal god.
You must pass him by, and grasp the knees of my mother   310
in your arms; you must do this if you soon wish to see the
happy day of your homecoming, however far away you live.
If she has kindly thoughts toward you in her heart, there is
some hope that you will once again see your dear ones
and return to your well-built house and ancestral land.'   315
     So she spoke, and flicked the mules with her shining whip,
and they quickly left the river's flowing waters, and trotted
briskly along, their feet weaving patterns as they went.
She drove with care, so that those on foot, the maids and
Odysseus, could keep up, and she handled the whip with   320
judgement. The sun went down, and they came to the famous
grove sacred to Athena, and there glorious Odysseus sat
down. At once he began a prayer to the daughter of great Zeus:
'Hear me, child of Zeus who wields the aegis, Atrytone,* and
listen to me this time; you did not hear me before, when I was   325
storm-tossed, when the renowned earthshaker shipwrecked me.
Grant that I may come to the Phaeacians as a friend, worthy of pity.'
     So he spoke in prayer, and Pallas Athena heard him; but she
did not yet appear before him face to face, for she felt shame
before her father's brother, who would still rage furiously   330
against godlike Odysseus until he reached his own country.

BOOK SEVEN

So much-enduring glorious Odysseus prayed in that place,
while the powerful mules carried the girl on to the city.
When she reached her father's splendid palace she reined in
the mules at the outer porch, and her brothers, men like
the immortals, gathered round her and unyoked them   5
from the wagon and carried the clothes indoors.
She herself went to her room, and an old woman of
Apeira, the chamber-servant Eurymedusa, lit a fire for her.
Well-balanced ships had long ago brought her from Apeira,*
and the people had chosen her as a gift for Alcinous, since   10
he ruled over all the Phaeacians, who obeyed him like a god.
This woman had been Nausicaa's nurse in his halls, and it
was she who now lit a fire and prepared a meal in her room.

  Now Odysseus started out towards the city; and Athena,
showing goodwill to him, poured a thick mist around him,   15
in case one of the great-spirited Phaeacians should meet him
and challenge him with jeering words and ask him who he was.
But when he was on the point of entering the beautiful city,
there the goddess grey-eyed Athena came to meet him,
likening herself to a young unwed girl, carrying a pitcher.   20
She stood before him, and glorious Odysseus questioned her:
'Child, could you show me the way to the house of a man
called Alcinous, who rules over the people in this place?
You see, I have come here from far away, a stranger from a
distant land, a sorely tried man, and I do not know anyone   25
among the people who live in this city and the land around it.'
  Then in turn the goddess grey-eyed Athena addressed him:
'Father stranger, I can certainly show you the house that you
ask me about, since it lies near that of my excellent father.
But you must walk in silence, and I shall lead the way,   30
and you must not look straight at any man, or question him;
people here do not take at all kindly to strangers, and do not
readily entertain any man who comes from other lands.
They put their trust in the speed of their fast ships, in which
they cross the sea's great expanse; this is the earthshaker's gift   35

to them, and their ships are as swift as a bird, or as thought.'

So Pallas Athena spoke, and without more ado led the way,
and Odysseus followed in the footsteps of the goddess; but the
Phaeacians, famed for their seamanship, did not see him as he
passed through their city, because Athena of the lovely hair,   40
the terrible goddess, prevented it, shedding an astonishing mist
around him, since her heart was kindly disposed towards him.
Odysseus marvelled at the sight of the harbours and trim ships,
at the meeting-places of the heroes themselves, and the high,
soaring walls, topped with stakes—a wonder to behold.   45
When at last they reached the king's magnificent palace,
the goddess grey-eyed Athena was the first to speak:
'Here it is, father stranger, the house that you asked me to
show you. You will find princes nurtured by Zeus there,
enjoying their feast. Go in, and have no fear in your heart;   50
in every kind of action the dauntless man always proves
the better, even if he hails from some distant country.
The first person you will find in these halls is the mistress;
she is called Arete, and she is descended from the same
forebears as those who in fact founded King Alcinous' line.   55
Nausithous was the first, son of Poseidon, shaker of the
earth, and of Periboea, the most beautiful of women;
she was the youngest daughter of great-hearted Eurymedon,
who long ago was king of the over-proud Giants;
but he ruined that reckless people, and ruined himself.   60
Poseidon then lay with Periboea, and she bore him a son,
great-spirited Nausithous, who ruled over the Phaeacians.
Now Nausithous was the father of Rhexenor and Alcinous;
Rhexenor had just married, and had no sons, when Apollo
of the silver bow shot him down in his halls; he left only   65
one daughter, Arete, and Alcinous made her his wife,* and
honoured her as no other woman on earth is honoured, of all
those today who keep a household under their husbands' charge.
In this heartfelt way has Arete been honoured, and still is so,
both by her dear children and by Alcinous himself; and by   70
the people, who look on her as if she were a goddess, and
greet her with respectful words when she walks about the city.
She too is by no means lacking in good judgement, and she
solves disputes for those she favours, even when they are men.

If Arete herself is well disposed towards you in her heart   75
there is hope that you will in time see your loved ones,
and reach your high-roofed house and your native land.'
    So grey-eyed Athena spoke and departed, leaving lovely
Scheria behind, and crossed the restless open sea, and
came to Marathon and Athens of the wide streets, and   80
entered the strongly built house of Erechtheus.* Meanwhile
Odysseus went on to Alcinous' famed palace, stopping and
pondering much in his heart before reaching its bronze threshold.
A brilliance like that of the sun or moon shone over the
high-roofed palace of great-hearted Alcinous. Brazen walls   85
ran in both directions, from the threshold to the inner
part, and round them was a frieze of dark blue enamel; and
golden were the doors that secured the strongly built house;
silver doorposts were embedded in a brazen threshold, and
silver was the lintel above, and the handle was made of gold.   90
On either side of the doors stood golden and silver dogs,
which Hephaestus in his cunning craftsmanship had forged
to be the guardians of the house of great-hearted Alcinous;
they were immortal, and ageless for all time. Inside, chairs
were set firmly on both sides round the wall, right through   95
from the threshold to the innermost part, and over them
were thrown fine-woven delicate cloths, the work of women.
There it was the custom of the chief Phaeacian men to sit,
eating and drinking, for they had a never-failing supply.
Golden statues of young men stood on solid plinths,   100
holding in their hands blazing torches, which gave light
all night long for the men feasting throughout the house.
Alcinous had fifty women to serve in his palace:
some of them grind apple-yellow grain at the mills,
while others weave at their looms, or sit spinning yarn,   105
their hands fluttering like the leaves of a tall poplar-tree;
and from close-woven fabrics there drips soft olive oil.
Just as the Phaeacians are skilled beyond all other men
in steering swift ships over the open sea, so their women
are equally proficient at the loom, for Athena has given them   110
supreme skill in beautiful works, and fine understanding.
Beyond the yard and next to the entrance there is a large
orchard of four acres, and all the way around it runs a wall.

In it there are tall trees growing, laden with produce:
pear and pomegranate and apple trees with glossy fruit,   115
sweet fig trees and olives in abundance; they never fail
to bear, nor do they ever give less than their usual yield
in winter or summer, year after year, but the West Wind
blows unceasingly, nourishing some and ripening others.
Pear upon pear mellows into ripeness, apple upon apple,   120
grape-cluster upon grape-cluster, and fig upon fig.
There too Alcinous has a vineyard planted, rich with fruit:
in one part, on level ground, there is a sun-warmed patch
where grapes dry, and in another they are gathered, and
others are trodden. In front are unripe grapes shedding   125
their blossom, and others starting to show a purple tinge.
There too, along the last row, all kinds of vegetables grow
in neat order, in full ripeness all the year round. In this
garden there are two springs: one is channelled to every part,
while the other flows opposite under the yard entrance to   130
the lofty house, and from this the citizens draw their water.
Such were the gods' magnificent gifts in Alcinous' palace.
    Standing there, much-enduring glorious Odysseus was amazed.
When he had admired everything to his heart's content, he
stepped quickly over the threshold and entered the house,   135
and found there the chief men and leaders of the Phaeacians
pouring offerings from their cups to the keen-sighted Argus-slayer,
their custom being to pour last to him, when their minds turned to bed.
Much-enduring glorious Odysseus passed through the house,
enveloped in the dense mist that Athena had poured round him,   140
until he came to Arete and Alcinous the king. Odysseus
threw his arms around the knees of Arete, and immediately
the mist that the goddess had sent rolled back from him.
When all those in the house saw the man they fell silent, and
wondered as they gazed; and Odysseus began to make his prayer: 145
'Arete, daughter of Rhexenor who was equal to the gods, I come
after many hardships to your knees as a suppliant, to your husband,
and to these feasters here—may the gods grant them prosperity in
their lives, and may each one hand on to his sons the possessions
in his halls, and such privileges as the people have granted him.   150
But my plea is for you to arrange an escort to my ancestral land,
and quickly; my troubles have kept me too long from my friends.'

So he spoke, and sat down by the hearth, in the ashes and
next to the fire; and they all remained silent and still.
Then at last the aged hero Echeneus spoke among them,   155
he who was an elder among the men of Phaeacia, skilled in
speaking, and deeply wise in the wisdom of the past.
With generous intent he spoke out and addressed them:
'Alcinous, it is not a good thing for you, nor is it seemly,
that a stranger should sit on the ground, in ashes at the hearth.   160
Those here are holding themselves back, waiting for your word;
so come, raise the stranger up and give him a seat on a chair
studded with silver, and order the heralds to mix wine for us,
so that we may pour a libation to thunder-delighting Zeus;
he is the protector of suppliants who deserve men's respect.   165
And let a housekeeper bring him a meal from her inner store.'
    When Alcinous, a man of divine vigour, heard this, he took
Odysseus the shrewd, cunning counsellor by the hand and
raised him up from the hearth and seated him on a shining
chair, having moved his son, courteous Laomedon, from it;   170
he was sitting next to Alcinous, and was the one he loved most.
A maidservant brought water in a beautiful golden pitcher and
poured it out over a silver bowl for Odysseus to wash his
hands, and drew up a polished table to stand beside him.
A respected housekeeper brought bread and set it before him,   175
and added a heap of delicacies, giving freely from her store.
Much-enduring glorious Odysseus began to eat and drink,
and now the powerful Alcinous addressed his herald:
'Pontonous, mix a bowl of wine and hand it round to all in
the hall, so that we may pour a libation to Zeus who delights   180
in thunder, protector of suppliants who deserve men's respect.'
    So he spoke, and Pontonous mixed mind-cheering wine, and
distributed it to all, after pouring the first drops into their
cups. When they had made offerings and drunk to their hearts'
content, then Alcinous spoke out and addressed them all: 185
'Listen to me, chief men and leaders of the Phaeacians,
and I shall tell you what the spirit in my breast urges me.
For the moment, now you have feasted, go home to sleep,
and in the morning we shall summon more of the elders
and offer the stranger hospitality in my halls, and make fine   190
offerings to the gods. After that we shall give thought to an

escort, so that this stranger may without trouble and distress
come to his native land under our protection, in comfort
and speedily, even if his country lies a great distance away.
He must not suffer any calamity or hardship on his way,   195
until he sets foot on his own land; after that he will have to
endure whatever his destiny and the grim Fates span for him
with their thread at his birth, on the day his mother bore him.
But if he is one of the immortals, come down from the high sky,
then this must be some deceit that the gods are contriving;   200
for in time past the gods have appeared quite clearly to us
whenever we offered them magnificent hecatombs; and
they feast at our side, taking their seats wherever we are.
Even if one of them meets us on the road as a solitary traveller,
they do not conceal themselves, since we are close to them,   205
just as the Cyclopes are, and the savage tribes of the Giants.'

  Then in answer Odysseus, man of many wiles, addressed him:
'Alcinous, you need not trouble your mind on that account;
I am nothing like the immortals who dwell in the broad
high sky, either in form or in stature, but only like mortal men.   210
If you can think of any among men who have borne the
worst of miseries, I could match them in my troubles;
indeed, I could tell you of even worse afflictions, were I to
describe all that I have suffered through the will of the gods.
But leave me now to eat my supper, distressed though I am;   215
there is nothing more shameless than a man's wretched belly,
which lays him under necessity to be mindful of it even
when he is sorely troubled and nursing grief in his heart.
This is now my case: I am nursing grief in my heart, and
yet it is forever urging me to eat and drink, making me   220
forget all that I have suffered, always telling me to eat my fill.
But as for you—as soon as dawn breaks stir yourselves to help
this unlucky man to set foot on his own land, after so much
suffering. Once I have seen my estates again, my servants,
and my great high-roofed house, I shall be happy to die.'   225

  So he spoke, and they all approved and said that the stranger
should have an escort, since what he said was right and proper.
When they had poured offerings and drunk to their hearts'
content they went each to his own house to sleep, and
glorious Odysseus was left behind in the hall; beside him   230

were seated Arete and Alcinous who looked like a god,
while the maidservants began to clear away the dinner-things.
Among them white-armed Arete was the first to speak,
for when she saw the fine clothes she recognized the cloak
and tunic that she herself and her women servants had made.   235
Speaking winged words she addressed Odysseus:
'Stranger, this first question I shall ask of you myself:
Who are you? Where are you from? Who gave you these clothes?
Did you not say that you came here after drifting across the sea?'
     Then in answer Odysseus, man of many wiles, addressed her: 240
'Queen, it would be a painful task to describe all my troubles
at length, for the gods in the high sky have sent me them in plenty;
but this I will tell you, since you question and inquire of me.
There is an island, Ogygia, lying in the sea far from here,
and on it lives a daughter of Atlas, subtle Calypso of the   245
lovely hair, an awesome goddess. No one, either of the gods
or of mortal men, has any dealings with her, though
some divine force compelled me to be her unhappy guest.
I was on my own, since Zeus had hurled a flashing thunderbolt
and shattered my swift ship out on the wine-dark sea, and   250
after that all my excellent companions perished. For nine
days I was borne along, clinging with arms wrapped round the
keel of my well-balanced ship, and on the tenth day, in the
dark of night, the gods landed me on the island Ogygia, where
Calypso of the lovely hair, an awesome goddess, lives. She took   255
me in, treated me kindly and looked after me, and declared
she would make me immortal and ageless for all my days;
but she was never able to win over the heart within my breast.
For seven full years I remained there, all the time drenching
with tears the immortal clothes that Calypso had given me;   260
but when the eighth year came round in its circling course,
she stirred me into action and urged me to leave, either
obeying a message from Zeus, or she may have changed
her mind. She sent me off on a tightly bound raft with many
provisions, bread and sweet wine, and gave me immortal clothes   265
to wear, and sent a warm and constant breeze to blow for me.
For seventeen days I sailed, traversing the open sea,
and on the eighteenth the shadowy mountains of your land
hove into sight, and my heart was glad; but ill luck stayed

with me, for I was fated to live with more of the misery   270
that Poseidon, shaker of the earth, had in store for me.
He stirred up the winds and headed me off my course,
and caused an astonishing sea to swell up, and the waves
would not allow me, groaning constantly, to be borne onward
on my raft. A squall now smashed it to pieces, and I began   275
to swim, cleaving my way through the expanse of sea, until
the wind and water lifted me and drove me close to your land.
There, as I tried to land, the swell would have thrown me
violently on to the shore, hurling me at a grim place of huge cliffs,
but I pulled back and began to swim again, until I came upon   280
a river, which seemed to me the best place to land; it was clear
of rocks, and there was somewhere to shelter from the wind.
There I collapsed, fighting to stay alive, and immortal night
came on. I got out of the river fed by rains from Zeus,
and lay down to sleep some way away in a thicket under a   285
heap of leaves; and some god poured boundless sleep over me.
There, covered with leaves and troubled in my heart,
I slept all night, right through morning until the noonday.
The sun was westering, and sweet sleep had released me,
when I became aware of your daughter's maidservants playing   290
on the seashore, and she among them looking like a goddess.
I entreated her, and she did not fail to show excellent good
sense, such as you would not expect to meet in a young
person, for the young are generally given to thoughtlessness.
She gave me a large meal of bread and gleaming wine,   295
and made me bathe in the river, and gave me these clothes.
Though it causes me grief, I have told you the exact truth.'

     Then in turn Alcinous answered and spoke to him:
'Stranger, my daughter's judgement was certainly not correct
in one thing, that she did not bring you to our house with her   300
attendants, though you came to her as a suppliant first of all.'

     Then in answer Odysseus, man of many wiles, addressed him:
'Hero, do not reproach your blameless daughter because of me;
she did tell me to follow her with the maidservants, but I was
reluctant, being both fearful and moved by feelings of shame   305
in case your heart should take offence when you saw me.
We people on this earth are apt to suspect the worst in others.'

     Then in turn Alcinous answered and addressed him:

'Stranger, it is not the habit of the heart in my breast to
become angry to no purpose; in all things moderation is best.   310
Father Zeus and Athena and Apollo, how I wish that
someone like you, with the same cast of mind as I have,
could marry my daughter and stay here and be called my
son-in-law! I would give you a house and property—but only
if you wanted to stay. Even so, no Phaeacian will detain you against   315
your will—may father Zeus never look kindly on that!
And as for your escort home, to reassure you I appoint
it for tomorrow; then you will lie, overcome by sleep, while
they row you over calm seas, until you arrive at your
native land and your house, or anywhere else you wish—   320
even if it is very far away, more remote than Euboea,
which those of our people who have seen it declare to be
the world's most distant place; they were then taking
fair-haired Rhadamanthys to visit Tityus, Gaia's son,* and
they went there and performed their task and returned home   325
successfully on the same day, all without becoming wearied.
You too will find out how far my ships are the best, and
how my young men excel at churning the sea with their oars.'

   So he spoke, and much-enduring glorious Odysseus was
glad, and he made a prayer, calling on the god by name: 330
'Father Zeus, may it be that Alcinous brings to fulfilment
all that he has said! Then his fame will never die out over
the grain-giving earth, and I will come to my native land.'

   While these two were conversing with each other in this way
white-armed Arete gave orders to her servants to lay   335
out a bed under the colonnade, and to throw fine purple
blankets on top of it and spread rugs over them, and
to add fleecy woollen cloaks to be a covering over all.
They went out of the hall holding torches in their hands, and
quickly set to work laying the strongly made bed; then they   340
came and stood by Odysseus and roused him with these words:
'Rise, guest, and go to your rest; your bed is ready for you.'

   So they spoke, and the thought of rest was welcome to him.
And so much-enduring glorious Odysseus slept there on
a fretted couch, under the far-echoing colonnade, while   345
Alcinous went to his rest in the inner part of his high palace,
and beside him his wife, lady of the house, served his bed.

BOOK EIGHT

When early-born Dawn with her rosy fingers appeared,
Alcinous, a man of divine vigour, rose from his bed,
and Odysseus, Zeus-nurtured sacker of cities, rose too.
Alcinous, a man of divine vigour, led the way to the
Phaeacians' meeting-place, built for them near their ships.   5
There they went and sat on polished stones, side by
side, while Pallas Athena went searching about the city,
taking on the appearance of a herald of wise Alcinous;
she was planning the return of great-hearted Odysseus,
and standing next to each man she told her story: 10
'Chief men and leaders of the Phaeacians, come with me
to the meeting-place, to learn about the stranger who has
just now arrived at the palace of wise Alcinous, after being
driven over the open sea; in stature he is like the immortals.'
  So she spoke, and stirred the ardour and spirit of every man;   15
quickly all parts and seats in the meeting-place were filled with
men gathered there, and many gazed with admiration when
they saw Laertes' shrewd son. Over him Athena had poured
a godlike grace, down over his head and shoulders,
and had made him taller and more thickset to look upon,   20
so that he might win the friendship of all the Phaeacians,
and deserve their awe and respect, and might be successful
in the many contests by which they later made trial of him.
When they were assembled and gathered together,
Alcinous gave voice publicly and addressed them: 25
'Listen to me, chief men and leaders of the Phaeacians,
and I shall tell you what the spirit in my breast urges me.
This stranger—I do not know who he is, or if from eastern
or western people—has come in his wanderings to my house.
He presses us for a safe passage, and entreats our assurance.   30
Let us then, as we have done before, speed his despatch;
for no one, not one man, who has come to my palace has
ever stayed here too long, grieving for want of an escort.
So come, let us drag a black ship down to the bright sea for
her maiden voyage, and let fifty-two young men be chosen   35

from the town, those who before have proved to be the best.
When you have fitted your oars securely to their oarlocks,
come ashore and make your way to my house to join in
a quickly taken meal; I shall provide amply for everyone.
These are my orders for the young men. As for you others   40
who are staff-holding princes, come to my splendid palace
so that we may entertain this guest-stranger in my halls;
and let no one refuse. And summon our god-inspired bard,
Demodocus; a god has given him matchless powers of song
to delight us, on whatever pathway his spirit moves him to sing.'   45

So he spoke, and led the way, and the staff-holding princes
followed; and a herald went to fetch the god-inspired bard.
The fifty-two chosen young men went off as he had
directed to the shore of the restless salt sea;
and when they had come down to the ship and the sea,   50
they dragged the black ship into the sea's deep waters,
and stepped the mast with its sail in the black ship,
and then fitted the oars into their leather straps, all
in their proper order, and then spread the white sail.
They moored her well out in the water, and then   55
set off to return to the great house of wise Alcinous.
The colonnades and courts and rooms were filled with
people gathered there, many young men as well as old.
For them Alcinous had made a sacrifice of twelve sheep,
eight white-tusked boars, and two oxen with shambling gait.   60
These they flayed and dressed, and so made a pleasing feast.

A herald drew near, guiding the worthy bard,* whom
the Muse loved above others, but had given him both bad
and good, taking away his sight, but giving him sweet song.
The herald Pontonous drew up a silver-studded chair for him   65
in the midst of the feasters, leaning it against a tall pillar.
He then hung Demodocus' clear-voiced lyre on a peg
above his head, and showed him how to put his hand to it;
by him he placed a fine table with a basket of bread, and
a cup of wine to drink from when the spirit urged him.   70
They all reached out for the good things that lay before them,
and when they had put away the desire for food and drink
the Muse prompted the bard to sing the glorious deeds of men,
choosing from that song known then as far as the broad high

sky—the dispute between Odysseus and Peleus' son Achilles: 75
how they had once quarrelled with violent words at a gods'
rich feast, though the lord of men Agamemnon was secretly
glad because the best of the Achaeans* were wrangling, and
this fulfilled what Phoebus Apollo had revealed to him in an
oracle at holy Pytho, when he had crossed the stone threshold   80
in search of a response. This was the first of the calamities
that rolled over Trojans and Danaans, by the plan of great Zeus.
     This was the tale that the renowned bard sang; but Odysseus
took hold of his great purple cloak in his brawny hands
and drew it down over his head, and hid his handsome face,   85
for he felt shame that the Phaeacians should see his eyes wet
with tears. Each time the god-inspired bard stopped singing
he would pull the cloak from his head and wipe the tears away,
and pick up his two-handled cup and make the gods an offering;
but whenever the bard began again, and the Phaeacian nobles   90
encouraged him to sing—because they were enjoying the story—
then once again Odysseus would cover his head and groan.
All the others were unaware of the tears he was shedding,
but Alcinous alone observed it and took note, sitting as
he was close by Odysseus and hearing his heavy sighs.   95
At once he addressed the Phaeacians who delight in rowing:
'Listen to me, chief men and leaders of the Phaeacians!
Our hearts have now had their fill of the fairly apportioned
meal, and of the lyre, which is the companion of a rich feast.
Now let us go outside and compete in all kinds of contests,   100
so that the stranger may be able to tell his friends, when
he returns home, how far we are superior to other men
in boxing and in wrestling, and in leaping and running.'
     So he spoke, and led the way, and they went with him.
The herald hung the clear-voiced lyre back on its peg,   105
and took Demodocus' hand and began to lead him from
the hall, going before him on the same route that the rest,
the Phaeacian nobles, were taking to witness the contests.
They made their way to the meeting-place, followed by a
huge crowd. Many fine young men stood up to compete: 110
Acroneos* rose to his feet, as did Ocyalus and Elatreus,
Nauteus and Prymneus and Anchialus and Eretmeus,
Ponteus and Proreus, Thoön and Anabesineos,

Amphialus the son of Polyneus who was Tecton's son,
and Euryalus too, the equal of Ares, bane of mortals;   115
he was Naubolus' son, and after blameless Laodamas was
the most handsome of all the Phaeacians in form and beauty.
There stood up too the three sons of blameless Alcinous,
Laodamas and Halius and Clytoneus who looked like a god.

  The first of their competitions was a race on foot, and   120
right from the starting-line the running was intense, all
flying swiftly together over the plain, kicking up the dust.
By far the best runner was blameless Clytoneus: as far as
is the day-range of two mules ploughing a field, so far he
shot ahead and reached the spectators, leaving the rest behind.   125
After that they competed with each other in painful wrestling,
and in this Euryalus in his turn excelled all the best men.
In leaping Amphialus surpassed all others, and when it
came to the discus Elatreus was by far the best; and in
the boxing Laodamas, Alcinous' excellent son, prevailed.   130
When everyone had delighted their hearts with the contests,
Laodamas, the son of Alcinous, spoke out among them:
'Friends! Let us ask the stranger if he has experience
and skill in any kind of contest! He has a good build:
stout thighs and legs, a fine pair of arms, and a powerful   135
neck—a man of great strength. He is not far from the
prime of life, but is broken down by his many troubles;
in my opinion there is nothing worse than the sea at
crushing a man, however great his strength may be.'

  Then in turn Euryalus answered and addressed him: 140
'Laodamas, what you have said is right and proper.
Go now and speak to him yourself, and make a challenge.'

  So when the noble son of Alcinous heard him he went
and stood in the middle ground and addressed Odysseus:
'Come, father guest, you too must join in the contests, if you   145
have any gift for them. You should certainly have that skill,
since there is no greater glory for a man as long as he lives
than what he can achieve by the exercise of his feet or hands.
So come, make your challenge, and scatter your spirit's cares.
It is not long till your voyage home; already a ship has been   150
dragged down to the sea for you, and your companions are ready.'

  Then in answer Odysseus, man of many wiles, addressed him:

'Laodamas, why do you all taunt me with this challenge?
The cares in my heart mean more to me than mere contests.
I have before this borne much hardship and many labours,   155
and now I sit with you in your meeting-place, desiring only
my return, and entreating your king and all the people for it.'

    Then in turn Euryalus answered, provoking him to his face:
'I knew it, stranger, for I was wrong to liken you to an
athlete skilled in the many contests that men engage in.   160
You look more like one who plies his trade in a many-benched
ship, a master of sailors who buy and sell, always watchful
of his cargo, and keeping a keen eye on his merchandise,
his greedily sought profit. No, you do not look like an athlete.'

    Looking darkly, Odysseus of many wiles addressed him: 165
'Friend, that was not well said; you seem a reckless man to me.
The gods, we see, do not bestow pleasing gifts on all men,
in the way of a handsome form or intellect or eloquence.
One man may be less striking than others in appearance,
but a god crowns his eloquence with charm, and men derive   170
pleasure from looking at him; he speaks with a confidence
that arouses gentle respect, and stands out in company, and
as he goes about the city people look on him like a god.
Then again, another man may resemble the gods in beauty,
but there is no charm surrounding his words. This is the way   175
with you too: you have outstanding beauty, such as not even
a god could improve upon, and yet your mind is feeble.
When you spoke in such an unseemly way you stirred my
breast to anger. I am no novice at athletic contests, as you
foolishly claim; always, I think, I was among the best, as   180
long as I could rely on my youthful prime and my hands.
But now I am gripped by painful affliction, and have endured
much, fighting through wars of men and troublesome seas.
For all that, though I have suffered greatly, I will try my hand
at these contests. Your words bite at my heart, and drive me on.'   185

    So he spoke, and sprang up, still with his cloak on, and seized
a discus that was bigger and thicker and much heavier than
the one used by Phaeacians when throwing against each other.
With a swing he flung it from his brawny hand, and the stone
discus hummed as it flew. Under the stone's flight the Phaeacians,   190
men of the long oar and famed for their seamanship, ducked

to the ground; speeding lightly from his hand, it flew beyond
the marks of all the others. Athena, likening herself to a man,
marked its distance and then spoke out, addressing him:
'Stranger, even a blind man could tell your mark apart from   195
the rest by feeling for it, for it does not lie jumbled with them,
but is far in front. In this event at least you may be encouraged;
no one of the Phaeaecians will reach it, let alone throw beyond.'

   So she spoke, and much-enduring glorious Odysseus was glad,
delighted to have seen one kind friend in the company.   200
With lifted spirits he addressed the Phaeacians again:
'Now match that, you youngsters! My next throw, I think,
will travel every bit as far as this one, or even farther.
As for the rest of you, since you have angered me so much,
if anyone's heart and spirit urge him, let him step up and   205
try me at boxing or wrestling or running; it matters not
which of all the Phaeacians, except Laodamas himself, for
he is entertaining me—and who would fight with his host?
That man is a worthless fool who, when he finds himself
among alien people, brashly challenges his host to a contest,   210
for by that he completely damages his own interests. As for
the rest of you, I do not scorn or refuse to meet any man,
and I am ready to look him in the eye and challenge him,
since I am by no means the worst performer among athletes:
I know well how to handle a well-polished bow, and would   215
be the first to bring down a man in the mass of the enemy's
soldiery, even when there are large numbers of fellow-fighters
standing at my side and aiming their shafts at the enemy.
Indeed, in archery only Philoctetes* surpassed me when
we Achaeans used our bows in the land of the Trojans;   220
and as for other mortals who are alive now and eat bread
on the earth, I claim to be better than all of them by far.
With men of the past, however, I should not want to compete,
not with Heracles, nor Eurytus who hailed from Oechalia,
men who challenged the immortal gods in the art of archery.   225
This was why great Eurytus died suddenly, and old age
did not come upon him in his halls; Apollo killed him
in anger, because he had challenged him to a bow-contest.
With the spear I can throw farther than a man can shoot
an arrow. It is only in the foot-race that I fear a Phaeacian   230

may outstrip me, for I have been shamefully battered
by heavy seas; I could not look after myself on my long
raft voyage, and so the strength of my legs has been undone.'

So he spoke, and they all remained still and silent,
and only Alcinous answered and addressed him: 235
'What you have said here to us, guest, is not graceless:
you wish only to display the mettle that is inborn in you,
angered because this man came up and provoked you in
our assembly; no mortal man who knew in his heart
how to speak fittingly could disparage your manliness.   240
So listen to me, and understand what I say; and one day
you may repeat it to another hero as you feast in your
halls with your wife and children beside you, recalling
our manly virtues, and the pursuits Zeus has laid down
for us, for all time, from the days of our fathers until now.   245
We are not distinguished fist-fighters, nor yet wrestlers,
but we are fast racers on foot, and champion sailors, and
have always been lovers of the feast, the lyre, and the dance;
lovers of changes of clothing, and warm baths and beds.
So come, you who are the best of the Phaeacian dancers,   250
show off your steps, so that when he returns home our
guest may tell his loved ones how far we excel all other
men in seamanship and running, in dancing and in song.
Let someone go at once and fetch his clear-voiced lyre
for Demodocus; it must be lying somewhere in my house.'   255

So spoke Alcinous who looked like a god, and a herald
rose to fetch the hollow lyre from the palace of the king.
Stewards then stood up, nine judges in all chosen from the
people, whose customary task it was to manage all such events;
they smoothed the dancing-floor and cleared a good wide space.   260
Then the herald approached, carrying the clear-voiced lyre for
Demodocus, who went into the middle ground, and about him
young men in youth's first bloom, skilled in the dance, took
their places and stamped their feet in the divine measure; and
Odysseus watched their flashing feet and marvelled in his heart.   265

Next, Demodocus struck up on his lyre the prelude to a fine
song, the love affair of Ares and fair-crowned Aphrodite,
telling how they first lay together in the house of Hephaestus,
in secret; how Ares gave her many gifts, and shamed lord

Hephaestus' marriage bed; but soon a messenger came to him,   270
the Sun, who had seen them coupling in mutual desire.
When Hephaestus heard the heart-wounding tale he set off
for his forge, turning over evil schemes deep in his mind;
he set up his great anvil on its stand and hammered out chains
that could not be broken or undone, to hold the lovers fast.   275
Then, when in his anger at Ares he had fashioned this trap,
he set off for the room where his marriage-bed stood and
wrapped the chains around the bedposts, entirely encircling
them, and hung many more bonds from the roof-beams, like a
delicate spider's web, such that no one was able to see them,   280
not even one of the blessed gods, so cunning was their making.
When he had spread the trap completely around his bed
he pretended to go off to Lemnos, that well-founded city,
which of all places on the earth is the one that he loves most.
Now Ares of the golden reins was not keeping blind watch,   285
and he saw Hephaestus the famed craftsman departing,
and made his way to the house of the renowned smith-god,
filled with passionate desire for the fair-crowned Cytherean.*
She had just come from the house of her father, Cronus' mighty
son, and had gone in and sat down. Ares entered the house   290
and took her hand firmly in his and spoke to her, saying:
'Come, my darling, let us go to bed and make love, because
Hephaestus is no longer at home; he has just gone, I think,
to Lemnos, to visit the Sintians who speak a harsh tongue.'*

So he spoke, and she was clearly eager to sleep with him.   295
So they both went to the bed and lay down; but about them
dropped the chains artfully fashioned by cunning Hephaestus,
and it was impossible for them to move or lift a limb. Then
at last they knew the truth, that there was now no escape.
And now the far-famed god, lame in both legs, drew near,   300
having turned back before reaching the land of Lemnos, for
the Sun had been keeping watch, and had told him the news.
He made his way towards his house, troubled in heart,
and stood at the outer door, and wild anger gripped him.
He gave a terrible shout, and called out to all the gods: 305
'Father Zeus, and all you other blessed gods who live for ever,
come here and see a ridiculous thing, and unendurable too!
Aphrodite Zeus' daughter always treats me with disrespect

because I am lame, and she dotes on this murderous Ares,
because he is handsome and sound of foot, while I was born   310
limping—but I reckon the blame for this lies squarely
with my two parents. I wish they had never given me birth!
But look at these two; see where they have got into my bed
and are sleeping as lovers. It breaks my heart to see them.
Still, I do not think they will go on lying like this, even for   315
a short time, much as they desire each other. Both will soon
tire of sleeping; but my cunning chains will keep them here,
until her father gives me back every single one of the bride-
gifts I made over to him, to win this shameless trollop; she
may be his lovely daughter, but she cannot control her lusts.'   320
    So he spoke, and the gods gathered at the brazen-floored house:
up came Poseidon, holder of the earth, up came Hermes the
swift runner, up came lord Apollo who shoots from afar;
but the goddesses modestly stayed behind, each in her home.
So the gods, givers of good things, stood at the outer doors,   325
and unquenchable laughter arose among the blessed immortals
when they saw the contrivance of ingenious Hephaestus.
And one of them would say, looking at his neighbour:
'Bad deeds do not thrive! The sluggard catches the speedy,
as now ponderous Hephaestus has caught Ares by his craft,   330
lame though he is, and Ares is the swiftest of the gods who
dwell on Olympus. So he must pay the adulterer's penalty.'
    So they conversed, one with another, in this way,
and lord Apollo, son of Zeus, addressed Hermes:
'Hermes, son of Zeus, guide, giver of good things,   335
would you like, even if loaded with mighty chains,
to lie in bed by the side of golden Aphrodite?'
    Then the guide, slayer of Argus, answered him:
'Lord Apollo, shooter from afar, if only this could be!
The chains holding me could be three times as many, and   340
endless, and all you gods and goddesses could be watching;
but I would still be sleeping next to golden Aphrodite.'
    So he spoke, and laughter broke out among the immortals;
but laughter did not take hold of Poseidon, who kept
entreating Hephaestus, famed for his craft, to set Ares free.   345
Speaking in winged words he addressed him:
'Let him go; and I promise that he will pay you all that is

proper, as you ask, in the presence of the immortal gods.'
   Then in turn the far-famed limping god addressed him:
'Poseidon, holder of the earth, do not ask this of me;   350
worthless are the pledges pledged for the worthless.
How could I keep you bound before the immortal gods
if Ares were to get away, evading both debt and chains?'
   Then in turn Poseidon, shaker of the earth, addressed him:
'Hephaestus, if indeed Ares avoids paying his debt   355
and gets away scot-free, I myself will pay it to you.'
   Then the far-famed limping god addressed him:
'It is neither possible nor proper for me to deny your request.'
   So powerful Hephaestus spoke, and unfastened the chain;
and when the pair were set free, strong though it was,   360
they straightaway sprang up and fled—Ares to Thrace,
while Aphrodite, lover of laughter, went to Cyprus,
to Paphos, where she has her precinct and smoking altar.
There the Graces bathed and anointed her with immortal
oil of the kind that covers the skin of the ever-living gods;   365
and they dressed her in beautiful clothes, a wonder to behold.
   This then was the tale the famous singer sang, and Odysseus
was glad in his heart as he listened to it, as were the others,
the Phaeacian men of the long oar, famed for their seamanship.
   Next Alcinous gave orders for Halius and Laodamas   370
to dance on their own, since no one was a match for them.
In their hands they held a beautiful ball, coloured
purple, that skilful Polybus had made for them; one of
them, bending over backwards, would throw it up towards
the shadowing clouds, and then the other would spring up from   375
the ground and catch it easily before his feet touched earth.
When they had tested their skill by throwing it straight up,
they danced on the earth that nourishes many, passing the
ball to each other many times; and the other young men
standing around the arena beat time, and a great din arose.   380
Then indeed glorious Odysseus addressed Alcinous:
'Lord Alcinous, distinguished among all peoples,
you boasted that your dancers were the best, and here
is the proof that it is so. Amazement grips me as I watch.'
   So he spoke, and Alcinous, a man of divine vigour, was glad.   385
At once he addressed the Phaeacians who delight in rowing:

'Listen to me, chieftains and leading men of the Phaeacians!
Our guest here seems to me to be a man of great good sense;
so come, let us give him gifts of friendship, as is fitting.
Now, there are twelve lords in our people, men of note,   390
who rule with power, and I myself am the thirteenth.
Let each of you donate a well-washed cloak for him, and
a tunic, and also a talent* of precious gold. Let us bring all
these gifts together, quickly, so that our guest may have them
in his hands and be glad in his heart when he goes to supper.   395
But Euryalus must make amends to him personally, with
words and a gift; what he said was in no way right and proper.'
     So he spoke, and they all approved and said it should be
done, and each man sent his herald away to bring the gifts.
Then in his turn Euryalus spoke in answer to Alcinous: 400
'Lord Alcinous, distinguished among all peoples, I shall
indeed make amends to our guest, as you instruct me;
I shall give him this sword, made of bronze throughout,
which has a silver hilt on it; and its case is a scabbard of
fresh-sawn ivory, and it will be worth a great deal to him.'   405
     So he spoke, and put the silver-studded sword in Odysseus'
hands, and addressed him in winged words: 'Fare well,
father guest! If any ill-timed word has been spoken,
may storm-winds at once catch it up and carry it away;
may the gods grant you reach your homeland and see your wife,   410
for your troubles have kept you too long from your loved ones.'
     Then in answer Odysseus, man of many wiles, addressed him:
'And may you fare well, too, friend; may the gods grant you
prosperity, and may you not in time to come miss this sword
which you have here given me, with words that make amends.'   415
     So he spoke, and slung the silver-studded sword from his
shoulder. The sun went down, and the splendid gifts for him
appeared, brought by lordly heralds to the house of Alcinous;
the sons of blameless Alcinous received them, and laid
these beautiful presents out next to their respected mother.   420
Meanwhile Alcinous, a man of divine power, led the others
into the house, and they took their seats on high-backed chairs.
Then Alcinous, a man of power, addressed Arete:
'Now, wife, bring a splendid chest, the best we have, and lay
in it a well-washed cloak and a tunic, to be from you. Heat a   425

bronze cauldron over the fire for him, and warm some water,
so that when he has bathed he may see that all the gifts which
the excellent Phaeacians have brought for him are well packed,
and that he may enjoy the feast and listen to a song sung.
Look, I will also give him this very fine cup, made of gold,   430
so that when he pours drink-offerings to Zeus and to the
other gods in his hall he may remember me for all his days.'

    So he spoke, and Arete instructed her women to make
haste and stand a great three-legged cauldron over the fire.
They set the cauldron for bath-water on the glowing embers   435
and poured water into it, and fetched kindling for the fire;
flames began to lick round the cauldron's belly, and the water
grew hot. Meanwhile Arete brought a beautiful chest from a
storeroom for her guest and laid the fine presents in it,
the clothing and gold which the Phaeacians had given him.   440
Then she herself laid in it a cloak and a fine tunic, and
speaking in winged words she addressed Odysseus:
'Now see to this lid yourself, and tie a knot on it now,
so that on your voyage no one may rob you when later
you fall into sweet sleep, sailing along in our black ship.'   445

    When much-enduring glorious Odysseus heard this he
at once shut the lid and quickly tied the fastening on it
with a subtle knot that revered Circe had once taught him.
Straightaway a housekeeper invited him to step into a tub
for his bath; and the hot water was a welcome sight to his   450
spirit, for he had not often been so cared for since the
time he had left lovely-haired Calypso's house—though
while there her care for him had been constant, as for a god.
When the maidservants had washed and rubbed him with oil
they clothed him in a tunic and a fine cloak, and he stepped   455
out of the bath and went to join the others at their wine-
drinking. Now Nausicaa, whose beauty came from the gods,
was standing by a pillar supporting the strongly built roof,
filling her eyes with wonder at the sight of Odysseus.
Speaking with winged words she addressed him: 'Fare well,   460
guest! And when you are in your own land think of me
sometimes, for to me first you owe the debt for your life.'

    Then in answer Odysseus of many wiles addressed her:
'Nausicaa, daughter of great-hearted Alcinous; even so

may Zeus, Hera's loud-thundering husband, grant that   465
I may come to my home and so see the day of my return.
There too, every day of my life, I will pray to you as to a
goddess, for it was you, dear girl, who gave me back my life.'
   So he spoke, and went to sit on a chair by King Alcinous, for
they were now serving round food and mixing wine. A herald   470
came up to them, leading the esteemed singer, Demodocus, a
man honoured by the people; he made a seat for him among
those feasting, where he could lean against a tall pillar.
And now Odysseus of many wiles addressed the herald,
having cut a slice from the chine of a white-tusked boar—   475
the larger part was left over—with the fat rich around it:
'Here, herald, take this meat to Demodocus, so that he may
eat, and so that I may salute him, troubled though I am.
In the eyes of all earth-dwelling men singers deserve
respect and honour, because the Muse has taught them   480
pathways of song,* and she loves the company of singers.'
   So he spoke, and the herald took the meat and put it into the
hero Demodocus' hands; he took it and his heart was glad.
They reached out for the good things that lay before them,
and when they had put away the desire for food and drink   485
Odysseus, man of many wiles, addressed Demodocus:
'Demodocus, I commend you indeed above all other men;
either the Muse, Zeus' daughter, or Apollo has taught you,
for you sang the doom of the Achaeans in exact due order,
all that they accomplished and endured, and their struggles,   490
as if you had somehow been there yourself, or heard it from
one who was. But now change your theme, and sing of the
wooden horse's making, that Epeius built with Athena's help,
and glorious Odysseus had them take one day into the citadel,
as a trap, having filled it with men who then sacked Ilium.   495
If you can tell me this story in full and proper order I shall
lose no time in telling all other men how generously a god
has bestowed on you the gift of divinely inspired song.'
   So he spoke, and Demodocus began, starting with the goddess,
and unfolded his song, from the point when the Argives fired   500
their huts, boarded their well-benched ships, and sailed away.
Meanwhile the others, with famed Odysseus, were already
sitting concealed in the horse, in the Trojans' assembly-place;

for the Trojans themselves had dragged it into the citadel.
So the horse stood there, while the Trojans sat around it   505
and held a long and endless debate. Three plans appealed
to them: either to cut through the hollow timber with pitiless
bronze, or to drag it to the edge of a cliff and throw it over,
or to leave it there as a great offering to win the gods' favour;
and this last was how things came to a conclusion, for it was   510
their destiny to be destroyed when the city took into its midst
the huge wooden horse, in which were sitting all the best
of the Achaeans, bringing death and doom to the Trojans.
He sang how the sons of the Achaeans left their hollow ambush
and streamed out of the horse, and went on to sack the city.   515
He sang how they fanned out in all directions and plundered
the steep city, and Odysseus, looking like Ares, went to the
house of Deiphobus together with godlike Menelaus; and
there, he said, Odysseus boldly fought his most terrible battle,
and was finally victorious, with the help of great-hearted Athena.   520

    This, then, was the famed singer's tale; and as he sang
Odysseus melted, and tears fell from his eyes, wetting his
cheeks. As when a woman weeps, throwing herself on her
dear husband, who has fallen in battle in front of his city and
people while warding off the pitiless day from the town and   525
its children; she finds him dying, gasping for breath, and
throws her arms about him with a shrill cry of keening; but
the enemy follow up and beat her back and shoulders with
their spears and drag her off into slavery, to endure toil and
misery, and her cheeks are ravaged by her piteous anguish;   530
so Odysseus let fall a flood of piteous tears from his eyes.
All the others were unaware of the tears he was shedding,
but Alcinous alone observed it and took note, sitting as
he was close by Odysseus and hearing his heavy sighs.

    At once he addressed the Phaeacians who delight in rowing: 535
'Listen to me, chief men and leaders of the Phaeacians!
Let Demodocus now restrain his clear-voiced lyre, for
it may be that this song of his does not please everyone.
From the moment we started our meal and the god-inspired
singer began, our guest has never stopped weeping dolefully;   540
some great grief must surely be compassing his senses about.
So let the singer hold back, and then we all may enjoy ourselves,

hosts and guest alike; it is far better this way, since it is on
our respected guest's behalf that all this has been arranged—
safe-conduct home, and the friendly gifts we give him as hosts.   545
Guests and suppliants should be treated like brothers—at least
in the opinion of any man who has a shred of good sense in him.

'So you too should not with crafty intention hide the answers
to my questions; it is a better thing for you to speak out.
Tell me the name your mother and father called you by at home,   550
and those who live in your city and in the country around,
because no one among men is altogether nameless,
whether low-born or noble, from the moment he is born,
and all children are given a name at birth by their parents.
Tell me your country, your people and your city, so that   555
our ships may plot their course to it and take you there.
There are no helmsmen, you see, among the Phaeacians,
nor any steering-oars, as is the way with other vessels,
but the ships themselves have the thoughts and minds of men,
and they know the cities of all men and their fertile lands,   560
and they cross the wide expanse of the sea at great speed,
shrouded in mist and cloud; nor is there ever any fear in them
that they will suffer damage or be wrecked. And yet, long ago
I heard from my father Nausithous the tale I shall now tell you.
He always said that Poseidon would hold a grudge against us,   565
because we, remaining unharmed, give safe-conduct to all men.
He said that one day he will smash a fine ship of the Phaeacians
as it returns from an escort mission on the mist-shrouded sea,
and will then hide our city behind a huge encircling mountain.
This was what the old man said; and the god will either   570
make it happen or leave it undone, as his spirit pleases him.
So now, tell me, and give me a full and true account of where
your wanderings drove you and what lands of men you visited;
tell me their inhabitants and their well-established cities, which
of them are cruel and uncivilized and given to wrongdoing, and   575
which hospitable, and there is in them a god-fearing disposition.
Tell me what causes you to weep and your heart to lament
when you hear the doom of the Argive Danaans and of Ilium.
The gods shaped this doom, weaving destruction for men, so
that they might become the stuff of songs for future generations.   580
Perhaps some marriage-kinsman of yours died before Troy,

a good man, a son-in-law or wife's father, one of those who
are especially close to us after our own blood and family.
Or then, could it have been some companion, a like-minded
fellow and a good man? A companion who is wise and   585
understanding is surely of no less account than a brother.'

BOOK NINE

Then in answer Odysseus of many wiles addressed him:
'Lord Alcinous, distinguished among all peoples,
it is indeed a good thing to listen to a singer such as
this man here, who is like the gods in his singing.
To my mind, there is no more perfect enjoyment   5
than when good cheer prevails among a whole people,
and feasters in the palace, sitting in due order,
listen to a singer, and the tables beside them are laden
with bread and meat, and a steward draws off wine from
the mixing-bowl, brings it round, and pours it into cups.   10
This seems to my mind to be the finest of all things.
But your heart has moved you to ask about my woeful
troubles, so I shall have to lament and groan all the more.
Where shall I begin my tale to you, and where end it?
The gods of the high sky have sent me miseries in plenty.   15
Still, I shall first tell you my name, so that you all may
know, and so that if hereafter I escape the pitiless day
I may be your guest-friend, though my home is far away.

   'I am Odysseus, Laertes' son, known to all men for my
cleverness; and my fame reaches as far as the high sky.   20
My home is in Ithaca, an island that is clear to discern.
There is a mountain there, Neriton, easily seen, with shivering
leaves, and nearby lie many islands close to one another:
Dulichium and Same and Zacynthos, covered in woods.
Ithaca itself lies low in the sea, furthest out to the west,   25
away from the others, which face the east and the sun's rising.*
It is a rough land, but a good nurse of young men; I tell you,
I can think of no sight sweeter to a man than his own country.
Calypso, bright among goddesses, tried to keep me with her,
there in her hollow caverns, desiring me to be her husband;   30
and in the same way Circe, the cunning woman of Aeaea,
sought to imprison me in her halls, desiring me to be her
husband; but she never persuaded the heart in my breast,
for there is nothing sweeter to a man than his own land
and parents, even if he lives in a wealthy house far away   35

in a foreign country, separated from his father and mother.
So listen, and I will tell you of my troubled homecoming,
inflicted on me by Zeus as I was returning from Troy.

'From Troy a wind bore me to the region of the Cicones,*
to Ismarus; and there we sacked their city and killed its men.   40
From the city I took their wives and much treasure and
divided it, so that no one to my knowledge should go without
his share. Then I gave orders that we should make haste
and leave, but they, great fools, would not listen, and stayed
there on the shore, drinking great quantities of wine and   45
slaughtering many sheep and crook-horned shambling cattle.
Meanwhile some Cicones went off and raised the alarm to
their neighbours who lived inland, and were moreover more
numerous and braver, skilled both at fighting against men
from chariots and also when they had to do battle on foot.   50
They came at dawn, as many as leaves or flowers that appear
in season; and then an evil fate from Zeus stood close to us,
ill-fated as we were, and caused us to suffer many torments.
Both sides stood and fought a pitched battle by the swift ships,
hurling volleys of bronze-tipped spears at one another.   55
As long as it was morning and the sacred day was growing,
we stood firm and, though outnumbered, kept them at bay;
but when the sun sloped towards the time for unyoking oxen,
the Cicones overpowered the Achaeans and put them to flight.
Six of my well-greaved companions out of each ship   60
perished, but the rest of us fled, escaping death and fate.

'From there we sailed on, grieving in our hearts, glad
to have escaped death but having lost our dear companions;
even so, I would not let our well-balanced ships sail until
we had made three ritual calls to each of our poor friends   65
who had died on the plain, cut down by the Cicones.
Zeus the cloud-gatherer now roused the North Wind against
our ships with an astonishing blast, and hid earth and sea
alike in clouds; and night swept down from the high sky.
The ships were now pitching wildly, their sails torn   70
into three or four pieces by the violence of the wind;
fearing destruction, we struck the sails down into the
ships, and taking to the oars rowed vigorously towards
land. There for two nights and two days on end we lay

at rest, eating our hearts out with anguish and weariness. 75
When Dawn with her lovely hair brought the third day
we stepped the masts, hauled the white sails up, and sat
still; and the wind and the steersmen held us on our course.
And indeed I would have come unharmed to my own land,
had not the swell, the current, and the North Wind driven me 80
off course as I rounded Malea, and sent me drifting past Cythera.*

'For nine days after this I was borne along by deadly winds
over the fish-rich deep; and on the tenth day we reached
the land of the Lotus-eaters, who feed on a flowery food.
There we went ashore and drew water, and my companions 85
lost no time in making their supper beside the swift ships.
When we had had our fill of eating and drinking I sent
some of my companions to go and find out what kind
of men, what eaters of bread, lived in this land, choosing
two and sending a third to accompany them as herald. 90
Without more ado they set off, and found themselves among
the Lotus-eaters. So far from plotting destruction for our
companions, these people gave them some lotus to taste;
and whoever of them ate the honey-sweet fruit of the lotus,
no longer wished to come back and to bring us a report, 95
but preferred to remain there with the Lotus-eaters,
browsing on the fruit and forgetting their journey home.*
These I forcibly brought back, weeping, to the hollow ships,
dragged them aboard, and tied them up under the benches.
Then I gave orders to the rest of my trusty companions 100
to make haste and go on board the swift ships, in case
anyone else should eat the lotus and forget his homecoming.
They quickly embarked and took their seats at their oarlocks,
and sitting in rows they struck the grey sea with their oars.

'From there we sailed on, grieving in our hearts, and came 105
to the land of the Cyclopes,* arrogant and lawless beings,
who, leaving all responsibility to the immortal gods,
do not set their hands to planting crops or to ploughing.
Everything grows unsown, from fields that are untilled:
wheat and barley and vines that give wine in rich grape- 110
clusters, and the rain from Zeus swells the fruit for them.
The Cyclopes have no counsel-forming assemblies, nor
any established laws, but live in hollow caverns on high

mountain peaks, and each man makes laws for his women
and children; and they have no interest at all in one another.   115

  'Now, there is a low island lying off the harbour of
the Cyclopes' land, neither near nor far away from it,
and wooded. It is the home of countless goats, wild
ones, for the footsteps of men do not trouble them,
nor do hunters visit it—hunters who live a hard life,   120
pursuing their quarry over woods and mountain peaks.
The island is not given over to flocks or to arable land,
and for all time remains unsown and unploughed, free
from men's presence and feeding only its bleating goats.
The Cyclopes, you see, have no crimson-cheeked ships,   125
nor are there shipwrights among them, men who could
build strong-benched vessels so as to reach other men's
cities and answer all the needs for which people often
cross the sea in ships, to meet one another. Men such as
these could have made this island a good place to settle,   130
for it is by no means a poor land, and could bear everything
in season. There are meadows along the shore of the grey
sea, soft and well-watered, where grapes would never fail.
There is level land for ploughing; one could reap a good crop
every year in season, for there is a rich tilth below the surface.   135
There is a good harbour, with no need for mooring-cables,
nor to drop anchor-stones or make fast with stern-ropes,
for a man has simply to beach his ship and wait until
the sailors' spirit moves them and favourable breezes blow.
At the head of the harbour a stream of bright water flows,   140
running from a spring deep in a cave; and around it grow
poplars. It was there that we stood in, and some god guided us
through the murky night, for there was no light to see;
a thick mist surrounded the ship, and there was no moon
shining from the high sky, for it was enveloped in clouds.   145
There was no one whose eyes could make out the island,
nor were we able to see the long breakers rolling on to
the beach, until we ran our strongly benched ships ashore.
When we had beached them we lowered all the sails,
and disembarked at the place where the breakers reached.   150
There we fell asleep and waited for the bright Dawn.

  'When early-born Dawn with her rosy fingers appeared

we ranged all over the island, amazed at what we saw.
Nymphs, daughters of Zeus who wields the aegis, started
some mountain goats so that my companions might eat;   155
at once we fetched our curved bows and long-socketed hunting-
spears from the ships, and dividing ourselves into three parties,
we began to shoot; and a god soon sent us an abundant bag.
Twelve ships had accompanied me, and to each one nine goats
fell as their portion; but for me alone they picked out ten.   160
And so, all day long until the setting of the sun, we sat there,
feasting on boundless quantities of meat and sweet wine;
the red wine in our ships had not yet given out, and there
was still some remaining, for each ship had drawn off
plenty in jars when we sacked the sacred city of the Cicones.   165
We looked out at the land of the Cyclopes lying nearby,
and saw smoke and heard the bleating of sheep and goats.
When the sun went down and darkness came over us we
settled ourselves for sleep where the sea's breakers reach.

'When early-born Dawn with her rosy fingers appeared,   170
then I called an assembly and addressed everyone:
"My trusty companions; the rest of you now stay here,
while I go in my ship, together with my companions,
and find out about these men, to see who they are,
if they are violent and uncivilized, and given to wrongdoing,   175
or are hospitable, and there is in them a god-fearing disposition."

'So I spoke, and boarded my ship, and gave orders to my
companions to embark as well and cast off the stern-ropes.
Without more ado they went on board and sat at their oarlocks,
and sitting in rows they struck the grey sea with their oars.   180
When we reached the agreed place, which lay close by,
there on a promontory we saw a cave next to the sea,
high up and overhung with bay-trees; here great flocks of
sheep and goats would spend the night, and around the cave
a high-walled yard was constructed with deep-bedded   185
stones, the trunks of tall pine-trees, and high-leaved oaks.
Here a monstrous man spent his nights, one who pastured
his flocks on his own, away from everyone else; he had no
dealings with others, but lived apart with his lawless thoughts.
And indeed he was a monstrous, amazing sight, not at all   190
like men who eat bread, but more like a wooded peak that

stands out alone on lofty mountains, distant from the rest.
  'At this point I ordered the rest of my trusty companions
to wait there beside the ship and mount guard over it,
while I chose the twelve who were the best of them, and   195
set off. I had with me a goatskin filled with dark, sweet
wine which Maron, the son of Euanthes, priest of
Apollo who stands guard over Ismarus,* had given me
because we had protected him with his son and wife,
out of respect, for he lived in a grove of trees sacred to   200
Phoebus Apollo. He presented me with splendid gifts:
seven talents of skilfully worked gold he gave me,
and a mixing-bowl that was made of solid silver,
and then he drew off sweet, unmixed wine into jars,
twelve in all; it was a divine drink. Not a single servant   205
in his house, man or woman, knew of this wine, but
only he himself knew, his wife, and one housekeeper.
When he drank this red, honey-sweet wine, he would
fill one cup and add twenty measures of water;* and when
he poured it an amazingly sweet fragrance rose from   210
the mixing-bowl; and then no one wanted to hold back.
I filled a great wineskin with this drink, and also put
provisions in a bag, for my proud spirit had a foreboding
that we were going to meet a man clothed in huge strength,
a savage with no understanding of either justice or laws.   215
  'Quickly we reached the cave, but did not find him at home,
because he was tending his fat flocks out in his pastures.
We went into the cave, and looked wonderingly at everything.
There were baskets heavy with cheeses, and folds crowded
with lambs and kids; each kind was penned separately, the   220
firstlings on their own, the later-born on their own, and the
newly weaned on their own; and all his well-made vessels,
the pails and bowls he used for milking into, were brimming
with whey. At first, my companions begged me to take
some of the cheeses and then go back and waste no   225
time in driving some lambs and kids from their pens down
to the swift ship, and after that to set sail over the salt sea.
I was not persuaded—though it would have been much better—
as I wanted to see him, hoping he might give me presents; but
when he did appear my crew found him anything but pleasant.   230

'We lit a fire and made an offering, helped ourselves to some
cheeses and ate; then we sat down in the cave and waited.
When he came back, driving his flocks, he was carrying a
huge load of dry wood to serve him at supper time, and
after entering the cave he threw this down with a crash.   235
We were terrified, and scuttled away into the cave's recesses.
After this he drove all those of his fat flocks he was milking
into the wide cave, while he left the males—the rams and
billy-goats—beyond the door, outside in the high-walled yard.
Then he heaved up a huge rock and used it to block the door: 240
a massy thing, one that not even twenty-two good four-
wheeled carts could have shifted it from the ground, so
massive was the steepling rock he set over the doorway.
Then he sat and began to milk his ewes and bleating goats,
all in due order, and under each mother he put her young.   245
Half of the white milk he curdled straightaway, and then
collected the whey and set it aside in woven baskets;
and half he left to stand where it was in the pails, so that
it might be there for him to drink when he ate his supper.
When he had finished busying himself with his tasks   250
he lit the fire and caught sight of us, and demanded:
"Strangers, who are you? Where have you sailed from, over
the watery ways? Are you after some business, or do you
roam on chance, like pirates who range over the sea, risking
their lives and bringing ruin to people in foreign lands?"   255

'So he spoke, and the hearts in us were shattered, terrified
as we were by the huge size of the man and his rumbling voice.
Even so, I answered him, addressing him in these words:

'"We are Achaeans, on our way from Troy, driven off course
by all the winds there are over the great gulf of the deep.   260
We are making for home, but have taken the wrong way
and the wrong course; this I suppose was Zeus' favoured plan.
We claim to be the war-band of Agamemnon, Atreus' son,
whose fame is now the greatest there is under the high sky,
because he sacked that great city and killed many people.   265
And now in turn we chance to come as suppliants at your
knees, hoping you will offer us hospitality, or else give us
the kind of present that is customary between host and guest.
So, master, show the gods respect; we are your suppliants,

and Zeus is the protector of suppliants and strangers, the   270
guest-champion who attends strangers; they deserve respect."
    'So I spoke, and he at once answered me from his ruthless heart:
"You are a fool, stranger, or you have come from very far away,
if you tell me to fear the gods or seek to avoid their anger.
We Cyclopes care not one jot for Zeus who wields the aegis,   275
nor for the blessed gods, since we are much stronger than them;
for my part, I would spare neither you nor your companions
just to escape Zeus' enmity, unless I was so inclined. But
tell me where you moored your well-made ship when you came;
was it somewhere far away, or nearby? I should like to know."   280
    'So he spoke, testing me, but I am a wise fellow and he did not
fool me, and I returned an answer to him in cunning words:
"As for my ship, Poseidon shaker of the earth has shattered it;
the wind drove us from the sea, and forced it against a headland,
hurling it onto rocks at the far limit of your country.   285
But I and these men here managed to escape sheer destruction."
    'So I spoke, and he in his pitiless heart made no reply, but
started up and, stretching out his hands towards my companions,
seized two of them as if they were puppies and beat their heads
on the ground; and their brains ran out and drenched the earth.   290
He then tore them limb from limb, and so prepared his supper;
he ate like a lion bred in the mountains, leaving nothing
behind, neither flesh nor entrails nor marrow-filled bones.
Meanwhile we, weeping, held up our hands to Zeus at the
sight of such cruel deeds; but helplessness gripped our hearts.   295
When the Cyclops had filled his vast belly with this meal
of human flesh, washing it down with unwatered milk,
he lay down in his cave, sprawled out among his flocks.
Then I pondered in my great-spirited heart whether I should
draw the sharp sword from beside my thigh and approach him,   300
feeling with my hand for where the midriff lies next to the liver,
and stab him in the chest. But a second thought restrained me;
we too would then have died a dreadful death in the cave,
since we would have been unable to use our hands to shift
the huge stone with which he had blocked the high doorway.   305
So, groaning, we resolved to wait for the bright Dawn to come.
    'When early-born Dawn with her rosy fingers appeared, the
Cyclops stirred up the fire and set about milking his famed

flocks, all in due order, and under each mother he put her
young. When he had finished busying himself with his tasks   310
he once again seized two of my men and prepared his meal;
and when he had eaten he drove his fat flocks out of the cave,
easily pushing aside the huge door-stone; but then he set it
back in place, just like a man putting the lid on to a quiver.
Whistling loudly, he drove his fat flocks towards the mountain,   315
and I was left behind, plotting evil deeds deep in my mind,
how I might pay him back, if Athena answered my prayer.
And this seemed to my mind to be the best plan: beside
the Cyclops' fold there lay a massive club of green
olive-wood, which he had cut down to carry when it was   320
seasoned. As we looked at it, we guessed it to be as tall
as the mast of a twenty-oared black ship, a broad-bottomed
merchantman, of the kind that crosses the sea's great deep;
so prodigious was its length and thickness as we gazed at it.
I went and stood beside this and cut off about a fathom's   325
length and gave it to my companions, with orders to trim it.
They made it smooth, and I stood by them and sharpened
it to a point, which I then hardened in the fire's embers.
This done, I hid it with great care, concealing it under the
dung that was spread in vast quantities throughout the cave.   330
Next, I ordered the others to cast lots to see which of them
would have the courage to lift the stake up with me and grind
it in the Cyclops' eye when sweet sleep had come upon him.
And the lots fell to the very men I myself would have
chosen; four of them, and I with them made up the fifth.   335

   'Evening came and the Cyclops with it, herding his fleecy
flocks; he quickly drove the fat beasts into the wide cave,
all of them, leaving not one outside in the high-walled yard—
either suspecting something, or a god might have warned him.
Then he picked up the huge door-stone and put it back, and   340
sitting down set about milking his ewes and bleating she-goats,
all in due order, and under each mother he put her young.
When he had finished busying himself with his tasks,
he once again seized two of my men and prepared his meal.
This time I stood next to the Cyclops and addressed him,   345
holding in my hands an ivy-patterned bowl full of dark wine:
"Here, Cyclops, you have eaten human meat; now drink some

wine, and learn what kind of drink we have stored in our ship.
I brought it for you as an offering, hoping you would have
pity and send me home; but your cruel madness is intolerable.   350
Hard man! How can you expect anyone else to visit you
after this? What you have done is against all that is right."

'So I spoke, and he took the wine and drank it down, greatly
pleased with the sweet wine, and asked for a second bowlful:
"Be good enough to give me some more, and tell me your   355
name, now, so that I may give you a gift that will please you.
I must tell you, the grain-giving soil bears full-bodied wine
for the Cyclopes, and the rain from Zeus swells the grapes;
but this drink is an outpouring of nectar and ambrosia."

'So he spoke, and I gave him a second cup of gleaming wine.   360
Three times I fetched and gave it, and three times in his folly
he drained the bowl. Only when the wine had stolen round
his wits did I address him, speaking in beguiling words:
"Do you ask me my name, Cyclops? Well, I shall tell you,
and then you must give me the present that you promised.   365
No-man is my name, and No-man is what my mother
and father call me, and all my companions as well."

'So I spoke, and at once he answered from his ruthless heart:
"Then I shall eat No-man last of all his comrades, and
the others first. That shall be my guest-present for you."   370

'So he spoke, and falling backwards lay there on his back,
his thick neck twisted to one side; and sleep, tamer of all,
overpowered him. Heavy with wine, he vomited, and from his
throat poured a stream of wine and gobbets of human flesh.

'Then it was that I drove the stake under a great heap of ash   375
to make it hot, and spoke encouragingly to all my men,
to make sure that no one would hold back through fear.
When the olive-wood stake was on the point of catching fire
in the embers, green though it was, and was glowing fiercely,
I went up and pulled it from the fire, while my companions   380
stood round me. Some god breathed great daring into them:
they lifted up the olive-stake, sharpened to a point, and
thrust it into his eye, while I, leaning my weight from above,
kept twisting it. As when a man bores ship-timber with a
drill, and those below him keep it turning with a leather   385
strap, held at both ends, and it runs without ceasing;

so we set our hands to the fire-hardened stake, twisting it
to and fro in his eye, and the hot blood flowed round it.
The fierce heat scorched the eyelids and brows around
his burning eyeball, and its roots crackled in the fire.   390
As when a blacksmith plunges a great axe or an adze
into cold water to temper it, causing it to hiss loudly—
for this is the treatment that gives the iron its strength—
so the Cyclops' eye sizzled around the olive-wood stake.
He let out a terrible howl, and the rock echoed around,   395
and we scuttled back in terror. The Cyclops seized
the stake, befouled with copious gouts of blood, and tore
it out of his eye, and in a frenzy flung it away from him.
He gave a great roar, calling out to the other Cyclopes
who lived round about in caves along the windy heights,   400
and they heard his shouts and arrived from all directions.
Standing round his cave they asked what troubled him:
"What on earth afflicts you, Polyphemus, to make you bawl
like this through the immortal night, interrupting our sleep?
Surely no mortal* is driving off your flocks against your will?   405
Surely no one is trying to kill you, by trickery or by force?"
Then the mighty Polyphemus answered them from his cave:
"My friends, No-man is killing me—by trickery, not by force."
    'Then in turn they answered him, speaking in winged words:
"Well, if no man is using force on you, and you are alone,   410
the sickness that comes from great Zeus cannot be avoided.
Your best course now is to pray to your father, lord Poseidon."
    'So they spoke and departed, and I laughed in my heart, because
the excellent ruse of my "No-man" name had deceived him.
    'Now the Cyclops was groaning in agonized torment; feeling   415
for the rock with his hands, he pushed it from the doorway
and then sat down in the opening and stretched out both arms,
to see if he could catch anyone getting out with his sheep;
I suppose he thought in his heart that I would be so foolish.
Meanwhile I was weighing up how to find the best course,   420
to see if I could discover some escape from death, for myself
and for my companions. I kept weaving all kinds of trickery
and scheming, for great danger loomed and our lives were
at stake. This seemed to me in my heart to be the best plan:
there were some well-fed rams with thick fleeces, splendid   425

large creatures, whose wool was violet-dark; these I tied
together in silence with the well-twisted withies on which
the monstrous, lawless-minded Cyclops used to sleep.
I chose them in threes: the one in the middle carried a man,
and the other two sheltered my companions on either side.   430
So each man was carried by three rams. When it came
to my turn, there was a ram which was by far the best in
all his flocks. I grasped its back, and curling up beneath
its shaggy belly I lay there; turned face up, without letting
go, I held on with persevering spirit to its amazing fleece.   435
And so, groaning, we all waited for the bright Dawn.

'When early-born Dawn with her rosy fingers appeared, the
male beasts began to push out towards the pasture, while
the ewes and nannies bleated, unmilked, about the pens,
their udders ready to burst. Their master, worn out by his   440
bitter pangs, kept feeling along the backs of all the sheep
when they stopped—not realizing, the fool, that men were
lashed under the bellies of his thick-fleeced sheep. The last
of his flock to pass through the door was my ram, cumbered
by its woolly fleece and me with my cunning stratagem.   445
Mighty Polyphemus felt along its back and spoke to it:
"My favourite ram! Why are you the last of my flocks to
leave the cave? Never in the past have you lagged behind
the others, but were easily the first to stride boldly off to feed
on tender shoots of grass, first to reach the river's streams,   450
and first to make your way back eagerly to the fold of an
evening; but now you are the last. Can you be grieving for
your master's eye, that a cowardly man and his vile friends
have robbed of its sight, after fuddling my wits with wine?
I mean No-man, who I declare has not yet escaped ruin.   455
If only you could think as I do, and had the power of speech,
to tell me where that man is now skulking from my anger!
I would give him such a beating! His brains would splash all
over my cave's floor, and my heart would find some relief
from the travails which that worthless No-man has brought me!"   460
So he spoke, and sent the ram on its way through the door.

'When we had gone a little way from the cave and the yard,
I first freed myself from the ram, and then untied my friends.
Then, with many a backward glance, we quickly drove on the

long-striding flocks, rich with fat, until we reached our ship.　465
We who had escaped death were a welcome sight to our dear
companions, though they began to weep and wail for the rest; but
I stopped their lamenting, with a gesture of my head and brows
to each man. Instead, I told them to be quick to load the flock
of fine-fleeced beasts into the ship and set sail on the salt sea.　470
Without more ado they went on board and sat at their oarlocks,
and sitting in rows they struck the grey sea with their oars.
When we were as far away as a man's voice can carry when
he shouts, I addressed the Cyclops with jeering words:
"Cyclops, he was not after all a spiritless man whose friends　475
you meant to beat down and eat in your hollow cave!
Hard man, your wicked deeds were all too likely to catch up
with you, because you did not scruple to dine on guests in your
own house. And so Zeus and the other gods have punished you."

'So I spoke, and his heart now became even more enraged.　480
He broke off the peak of a huge mountain and hurled it at us,
so that it fell in front of our dark-prowed ship, missing by just
a little distance, and nearly reaching the tip of the steering-oar;
and as the rock plunged in, the sea was churned up around it.
The backwash from this wave, rolling in from the open sea,　485
carried the ship towards land and drove us close to the shore;
but I seized a long pole in my hands and shoved us off, and
urging on my companions with nods of my head, I ordered them
to bend to their oars and so make sure that we would escape
destruction; and they leaned into their task and began to row.　490
When we had covered twice the distance over the sea that we
had gone before, I was going to hail the Cyclops, but from all
over the ship my crew tried to restrain me with calming words:
"Hard man, why would you want to provoke this savage?
He has only just thrown a rock into the sea and forced our　495
ship back to land, and we really thought it was all up with us.
If he had heard any of us crying out or speaking he would have
flung another jagged boulder, and smashed our heads and
our ship's timbers to smithereens; he has a very long throw."

'So they spoke, but they did not persuade my great-hearted spirit.　500
Once again I addressed him, with a heart full of bitter rage:
"Cyclops, if anyone among men who are doomed to die
questions you about the shameful blinding of your eye, tell

him it was Odysseus, sacker of cities, who took your sight—
Odysseus, son of Laertes, who has his home in Ithaca."   505

'So I spoke, and he groaned and answered in these words:
"Ah, so that ancient prophecy has now come true for me!
There was once a prophet in our land, a valiant and mighty man,
Telemus, the son of Eurymus, a man supreme in seercraft,
who grew old among the Cyclopes in the exercise of prophecy.   510
This man told me that all this would one day be fulfilled,
that I would be robbed of my sight at the hands of Odysseus.
I had always expected it would be some big, handsome man
who would come here, someone clothed in great courage;
but it turned out to be a puny, insignificant weakling who   515
deprived me of my sight, after overpowering me with wine.
So come here, Odysseus, so that I can give you your presents,
and also urge the famed earthshaker to send you safely home.
I am his son, you know, and he is proud to be called my father.
He alone, and no one else, will heal me, if he so wishes;   520
it will not be another of the blessed gods, nor any mortal man."

'So he spoke, and I addressed him in answer: "I wish
I had the power to deprive you of your life and breath
and send you down to Hades, as surely as there is no one
who will heal your eye, no, not even the shaker of the earth."   525

'So I spoke, and straightaway he prayed to lord Poseidon,
stretching out both his hands to the starry high sky:
"Hear me, Poseidon, earth-encircler, dark-haired god!
If I really am your son, and you are proud to be my father,
grant that Odysseus, son of Laertes, sacker of cities,   530
whose home is in Ithaca, may never reach his homeland.
But if it is his fate to come to his well-founded house in his
own land, and see his loved ones again, may he arrive there
late, and in a wretched state, after losing all his companions,
in a foreigner's ship; and may he find disorder in his house."   535

'So he spoke in prayer, and the dark-haired god heard him.
Once again the Cyclops hefted a rock, an even bigger one;
whirling round he flung it, forcing enormous strength into
the throw, so that it fell short of our dark-prowed ship
by just a little, nearly reaching the tip of the steering-oar.   540
As the rock fell the sea was churned up around it, and the
swell carried the ship onward, driving it on to the shore ahead.

When we reached the island, where our other well-benched
ships were waiting gathered together, and round them our
companions were sitting desolate, watching constantly for us,   545
we guided our ship in and beached it on the sands; then we
disembarked at the place where the sea's breakers reach, and
drove the Cyclops' sheep ashore from the hollow ship, and
apportioned them; and I made sure that no one lacked his share.
As for the ram, when the sheep were being shared out my well-   550
greaved crew presented it to me as a special gift. I sacrificed
it on the seashore to Cronus' son, Zeus of the dark clouds,
ruler of all men, and burnt the thigh-bones; but he did not
receive the offering, musing instead how to wreck my well-
benched ships, every one, and my trusty companions with them.   555
And so, all day long until the setting of the sun, we sat there,
feasting on boundless quantities of meat and sweet wine.
When the sun went down and darkness came over us we
settled ourselves for sleep where the sea's breakers reach;
and when early-born Dawn with her rosy fingers appeared,   560
then I roused my companions and gave them orders
to embark in the ships and cast off their stern-cables.
Without more ado they went on board and sat at their oarlocks,
and sitting in rows struck the grey salt sea with their oars.

   'From there we sailed on, grieving in our hearts, glad   565
to have escaped death but having lost our dear companions.

BOOK TEN

'Next we came to the island of Aeolia, the home of Aeolus
son of Hippotas, who is beloved of the immortal gods;
this is a floating island, and all around it extends a wall
of bronze, unbroken, and sheer cliffs run up to meet it.
Aeolus has twelve children born to him in his halls,   5
six daughters, and six sons in their youthful prime; and
he has given his daughters to his sons to be their wives.
These feast continually with their dear father and devoted
mother, on the countless delicacies that are laid before them;
by day the house is filled with the savour of cooking,   10
and the courtyard echoes all around, and at night they sleep
beside their respected wives, under coverlets on fretted beds.
It was to these people's city and fine palace that we came.
For a full month Aeolus entertained and questioned me closely
about everything—Ilium, the Argive ships, the Achaeans'   15
return—and I told him the whole story, in detail and due order.
When I came to request a route home, asking him to send
me on my way, he did not refuse, and arranged my passage.
He gave me a bag, made from the hide of a nine-year-old ox,
in which he had tied up the pathways of the blustering winds;   20
Cronus' son, you see, had made him steward of the winds,
either to still or to rouse them, in any way that he wished.
This he stowed in my hollow ship, secured with a shining silver
cord, so that not a breath, however insubstantial, should escape.
Then he released a breeze to blow from the west for me, to   25
drive my ships and their crews onward; but, as it turned out,
this was not to be, for we perished by our own reckless folly.

  'For nine days then we sailed on, by day and night alike,
and on the tenth day my ancestral ploughland hove into sight;
we could actually see men not far away, tending their fires.   30
But at this point sweet sleep came over me, wearied as I was
with continuously handling the ship's sheet; I would not give it
to any of my companions, so that we might more quickly reach
our homeland. They started a discussion among themselves,
saying that I was bringing home gold and silver for myself,   35

gifts from Aeolus the great-hearted son of Hippotas; and
this is what one of them would say, looking at his neighbour:
"For shame! This man is welcomed and held in high regard
by everyone, whoever's city and land he comes to. He is
bringing back masses of fine treasure for himself from Troy　　40
as his share of booty, while we who have made exactly
the same journey are returning home with empty hands.
And now Aeolus has given him this, showing him kindness
out of their friendship. Quick, let us find out what is here,
how much gold and silver there is inside this leather bag."　　45
　'This is what they said, and their wicked counsel prevailed.
They undid the bag, and all the winds rushed out; and
a squall seized and bore them off, wailing, out to the
open sea, away from the land of their fathers. Meanwhile
I awoke, and pondered in my excellent mind whether　　50
to throw myself off the ship and so perish in the deep,
or to endure in silence and so remain among the living.
Well, I endured and remained, and lay down in the ship,
covering my face; and the ships, along with my groaning men,
were blown by terrible storm-blasts back to Aeolus' island.　　55
Once there we went ashore and drew water, and my
companions made a hurried meal beside the swift ships.
When we had had our fill of eating and drinking, then
I chose a herald to go with me, and one companion, and I
set off for Aeolus' famous palace. We found him at home,　　60
enjoying a feast with his wife and children, and went into
the house and sat down on the threshold, by the doorposts.
They were amazed in their hearts, and began to question me:
"Here again, Odysseus? What evil spirit has done you this hurt?
Did we not send you on your way with kind intent, to help you　　65
reach your house and land, or anywhere else you wished?"
So they spoke, and I addressed them, grieved in my heart:
"My wretched companions were my undoing, and cruel sleep
as well. Set this right, my friends, please; it is in your power."
　'So I spoke, trying to win them round with calming words;　　70
but they remained silent, and their father answered me:
"Most contemptible of creatures, get off my island at once!
It is not right for me to provide for or to send safely on
his way any man who is so hated by the blessed gods.

Get out! Coming here proves that the immortals hate you."   75
So he spoke, and dismissed me, groaning heavily, from his house.
From there we sailed onward, grieving in our hearts; and
my men's spirits were worn down by the hard rowing, for
thanks to our own folly there was now no breeze to speed us on.
   'For six days we sailed on, through night and day alike,   80
and on the seventh we reached the steep citadel of Lamus,*
Telepylus of the Laestrygonians, where one herdsman bringing
his flock home calls out to another, who answers as he drives
his out. There a man who could do without sleep could earn
two wages, one minding cattle and the other tending white sheep;   85
so close to each other do the paths of night and of day lie.
There we found a splendid harbour, with a sheer cliff running
round it and stretching without a break in both directions;
two headlands thrust outward, opposite each other, forming
the harbour's mouth, and there is only a narrow entrance.   90
Through this my men all steered their well-balanced ships,
and moored them inside the curve of the harbour, alongside
one another; for there the sea never lifted itself to a swell,
neither steep nor slight, but a bright calm is spread over all.
I alone made my black ship fast outside the harbour,   95
there at its outermost edge, tying the mooring-ropes to a rock.
Then I climbed up to a rocky lookout place, and stood there.
There were no signs of cattle to be seen, or of cultivation by men,
and all we could make out was smoke rising from the land.
So I despatched some of my companions to go and find out   100
what kind of earth-dwelling, bread-eating men were living here,
choosing two and sending a third to go with them as herald.
They left the ships, and set off along a smooth road, on which
wagons brought wood down from the high mountains to the city.
There outside the city they fell in with a girl fetching water—   105
the strapping daughter of Antiphates the Laestrygonian;
she had come down to the clear-flowing spring called Artacië,
for it was from this that they used to fetch water for the city.
My men went up and addressed her, and inquired who
the king of this people might be, and who were his subjects;   110
and she promptly pointed out her father's high-roofed house.
When they entered this splendid palace they found his wife,
huge as a mountain peak; and they were aghast at the sight.

She immediately summoned her husband, famed Antiphates,
from their meeting-place, and he at once devised a cruel death   115
for them. He seized one of my companions to serve as his supper,
but the other two scurried away in flight, and returned to the ships.
Meanwhile Antiphates raised a hue and cry throughout the city,
and the mighty Laestrygonians heard, and came from all around
in great numbers, looking more like giants than ordinary men.   120
From the cliff-top they began to throw boulders at us, as heavy
as a man could just lift; about the ships a fearful din arose,
of men dying and the splintering of ships. They speared my
crews like fish, and carried them off to make their gruesome
feast. But while they were slaughtering them in the deep   125
harbour I drew my sharp sword from beside my thigh and
with it cut the cable that was mooring my dark-prowed ship.
Hastily I shouted exhortations to my companions, telling them
to bend to their oars and make sure we escaped destruction,
and they all, fearing they would be killed, churned up the sea.   130
My one ship was glad to get clear of those beetling cliffs
to the open sea, but the rest, crammed together, perished there.
From there we sailed onward, grieving in our hearts; glad
to have escaped death, but having lost our dear companions.

   'After this we came to the island of Aeaea; here lived   135
Circe of the beautiful hair, an awesome goddess who spoke
with a mortal's voice, sister of murderous-minded Aeëtes.*
They are both children of the Sun who gives light to mortals,
and their mother was Perse, who was Oceanus' daughter.
At this place we made landfall, and beached silently in   140
a secure harbour; and some god guided us in. Here we
disembarked, and for two days and two nights lay there,
worn down by weariness and eating out our hearts with grief.
But when Dawn with the lovely hair brought in the third day,
then I picked up my spear and my sharp sword, and quickly   145
made my way inland from the ship to a vantage-point, hoping
to see signs of land worked by men or to hear their voices.
I climbed up and stood on a rocky place from where I could
see, and in the broad-wayed land glimpsed smoke rising
through dense scrub and woodland from the house of Circe.   150
As soon as I saw this ruddy smoke I considered in my mind
and in my heart whether I should go farther and investigate;

and as I pondered this seemed to me to be the better plan,
to return first to my swift ship and the shore of the sea, give
my crew their supper, and then send men out to explore.   155
And when on my way back I was near my well-balanced ship,
one of the gods took pity on me in my lonely state and
sent a huge high-antlered stag right across my path.
He was coming down from his wooded pasture to the river
to drink, for the fierce strength of the sun held him in its grip.   160
As he stood up from the water I hit him on the spine, in the
middle of his back; the bronze-tipped spear passed clean through,
and he fell bellowing in the dust, and life flew away from him.
Setting my foot on the beast I wrenched the bronze-tipped
weapon from the wound and laid it on the ground, leaving it   165
to lie there; I then pulled up some brushwood and withies, and
twisted them into a rope about a fathom long, plaiting both
strands tightly together, and tied the huge beast's feet together.
Slinging him round my neck, I made my way to my black ship;
I propped the weight on my spear, for it was impossible to hold   170
him on my shoulder with one hand; he truly was an enormous beast.
I threw the stag down in front of the ship, and with gentle words
approached each one of my companions and roused his spirits:
"My friends, grief-stricken though we are, we shall not yet
go down to the house of Hades—not until our fated day arrives.   175
Come; as long as there is food and drink in our swift ship, let us
turn our minds to food; we do not need to be worn down by hunger."

'So I spoke, and they quickly obeyed my words. There on the
shore of the restless sea they uncovered their faces and stared
in amazement at the stag; he truly was an enormous beast.   180
When they had gladdened their eyes at the sight they washed
their hands and set about preparing a magnificent feast.
And so, all day long until the setting of the sun, we sat there,
feasting on boundless quantities of meat and sweet wine.
But when the sun went down and darkness came over us,   185
we settled ourselves for sleep where the sea's breakers reach.
And when early-born Dawn with her rosy fingers appeared,
then I called an assembly and spoke to all my companions:
"You have suffered much, comrades, but hear what I have to say.
Friends, we do not know where the darkness lies, nor the dawn,   190
nor where the sun that brings light to mortals sinks below the

earth, nor where he rises. Even so, let us without more ado consider
if we have any plan left to us—though I do not think we have,
for when I climbed to a rocky lookout place I saw that this is
an island, ringed about with a boundless expanse of sea.   195
The island itself is low-lying, and through the dense scrub
and woodland I glimpsed smoke rising from the middle of it."

   'So I spoke, and their hearts were shattered as they remembered
the deeds of Antiphates the Laestrygonian, and also
the savagery of the great-hearted Cyclops, eater of men.   200
They began to weep loudly, shedding copious tears—
but all in vain, for no good came from their lamentations.

   'Then I divided all my well-greaved companions into two
parties, and detailed a leader for each band: one to be led
by me, and the other by Eurylochus who looked like a god.   205
Without more ado we shook lots in a bronze helmet,
and out of it leapt the lot of great-hearted Eurylochus.
He set off, and with him went twenty-two companions,
weeping; and we were weeping too as they left us behind.
In a wooded valley they came upon the palace of Circe,   210
built of polished stone, set in a sheltered position; and
around it were prowling mountain wolves and lions, men
to whom Circe had fed noxious drugs and so bewitched.
These did not charge at my men, but actually reared up on
their hind legs and fawned on them, wagging their long tails.   215
As when dogs fawn on their master when he comes from
a feast, because he always brings scraps to please them,
so these wolves and strong-clawed lions fawned about my
men; but when they saw these grim beasts they were afraid.
They stood at the outer doors of the lovely-haired goddess,   220
and could hear Circe indoors, singing in her sweet voice and
moving back and forth at her great, immortal loom, weaving
the kind of delicate, bright, and graceful stuff that goddesses make.
The first of them to speak was Polites, captain of men,
who of all my companions was nearest and dearest to me.   225
"My friends, there is someone indoors working at a great loom,
singing sweetly, and the whole floor echoes to her voice—
it is either a goddess or a woman; let us call out to her at once."

   'So he spoke, and they raised their voices and called out.
Straightaway Circe opened the shining doors and came out   230

and invited them in; and they all in their folly went with her.
She led them inside and seated them on chairs and seats—
though Eurylochus alone hung back, suspecting some trickery—
and prepared a mixture of cheese, barley, and yellow honey,
blended with Pramnian* wine. Into this she stirred some   235
noxious drugs, to make them lose all thought of their homeland.
When she had given them this and they had drunk it down, she
tapped them with her stick and drove them into her pigsties,
for now they had the heads and bodies and bristles of pigs, and
grunted like pigs, though their minds were unchanged from before. 240
And so they were shut inside weeping; and Circe threw before
them acorns and oak nuts and cornel-tree berries for them to
eat, the kind of thing that earth-wallowing pigs always feed on.

   'Meanwhile Eurylochus had come back to the swift black ship,
to bring the news of his companions and their unpleasant fate;   245
but though impatient to speak he could not utter a single word,
so overwhelmed was he by his huge grief; his eyes were
filled with tears, and the only thought in his heart was to weep.
We were all dumbfounded, and kept asking him questions,
and at last he told us the full story of his companions' doom: 250
"We went, illustrious Odysseus, through the scrub as you ordered,
and in a wooded valley we found a beautiful palace, built of
polished stones and set in a sheltered position. Inside there was
someone moving to and fro at a great loom and singing in a clear
voice—either a goddess or a woman. The others called out loudly, 255
and she at once opened the shining doors and came out and
invited them in; and they all in their folly went with her.
Only I hung back, because I suspected some trickery; and then
they vanished, the whole crowd of them, and not a single one
reappeared; I sat there for a long time, watching out for them." 260

   'So he spoke; and I slung my great bronze sword, studded with
silver, from my shoulder, and then my bow and arrows,
and told him to lead me back on the way that he had come.
But he grasped my knees with both arms and entreated me,
and weeping loudly addressed winged words to me: 265
"Zeus-nurtured man, do not force me to go back there! Leave
me behind! I know that you too will not come back, nor will
you rescue any of your crew. No, let us quickly escape, with
these men here, and in that way we may yet avoid the evil day."

So he spoke, but I answered him and said: "Eurylochus,　　270
as for you, you may certainly stay behind where you are,
eating and drinking next to our hollow black ship;
for my part, I shall go, for a strong necessity is upon me."
　'So I spoke, and started inland, up from the ship and the sea.
But when on my way through the sacred valleys I had nearly　　275
reached the great house of Circe, skilled in many drugs,
Hermes of the golden rod fell in with me as I was walking
towards the house, in the likeness of a young man whose beard
is just coming, which is the most charming time of youth.
He gripped my hand firmly in his and spoke directly to me:　　280
"Where are you off to now, poor fellow, alone on these
uplands, ignorant of the country, while your companions
are penned like pigs here in crowded sties? Have you really
come here to free them? I do not think you will now reach
your home, but will stay here yourself just like them. Still,　　285
I will save you and set you free from your troubles. Look,
here is a drug of great power; take it and then go to Circe's
palace, and it will preserve your life against the day of evil.
Furthermore, I will reveal to you all Circe's malignant wiles.
She will make you a potion, and drop drugs into the mixture,　　290
but even so she will not be able to bewitch you, because this
benign drug that I shall give you will stop her. Now I shall tell you
exactly what will happen. Circe will strike you with her long stick,
and that is when you must draw the sharp sword from beside
your thigh and rush at her as if in a frenzy to kill her.　　295
She will cower in terror before you, and invite you into her bed.
Now, you must not hold out against the goddess's offer of bed,
if you want her to set your companions free and to treat you well,
but you must order her to swear the blessed gods' great oath
that she will not plot any other kind of harm against you,　　300
nor unman and make a coward of you once you are naked."
　'So the Argus-slayer spoke, and gave me a plant he had
pulled out of the ground, and showed me its nature:
it had a black root, but its flower was the colour of milk,
and the gods call it moly. It is difficult to dig up, at least　　305
for mortal men; but the gods, as ever, can do anything.
　'Hermes then departed through the wooded island, heading
for far Olympus, and I went on towards Circe's palace;

and as I went my heart brooded darkly on many things.
At the doors of the goddess with beautiful hair I stopped   310
and shouted from where I stood, and she heard my voice.
At once she opened the shining doors and came out and
invited me in, and I followed her, troubled in my heart.
She led me in and seated me on a silver-studded chair, fine
and intricately worked, and there was a footstool for my feet.   315
Next she prepared a potion in a golden cup for me to drink,
and into it, with evil thoughts in her heart, dropped a drug.
She offered it to me, and I took and drained it, but she did
not bewitch me; she tapped me with her stick, saying:
"Off to the pigsty with you now, and lie with your comrades!"   320
    'So she spoke, but I drew the sharp sword from beside my
thigh and rushed at Circe, as if in a frenzy to kill her. She
shrieked aloud, ducked under my sword and grasped my knees,
and in grief-laden tones addressed me with winged words:
    '"Who are you? Where are you from? Where is your city, and your   325
parents? I am amazed you were not bewitched when you drank.
No other man, no one at all, has been able to resist this potion
once it has passed the barrier of his teeth and he has drained it—
you have a heart in your breast that is proof against sorcery.
Surely you must be Odysseus, man of many turns, the one who   330
the Argus-slayer, god of the golden rod, has always told me
would come in his swift black ship on his way back from Troy.
So come, put your sword back in its scabbard, and then
let us both go up to my bed, so that when we have slept
together in the bed of love we may come to trust one another."   335
    'So she spoke, but I answered and addressed her:
"Circe, how can you tell me to be gentle towards you when
you have turned my companions into swine in your halls?
And now you have me here you invite me, with deceit in
your heart, to go to your bedroom and into your bed, so that   340
when I am naked you can unman and make a coward of me.
I certainly have no intention of going to your bed, goddess,
unless you can bring yourself to swear a great oath to me
that you will not plot any kind of harm against me after this."
So I spoke, and she without more ado swore as I had ordered her;   345
and only when she had sworn not to harm me, and ended her oath,
did I go up into the wonderfully beautiful bed of Circe.

'All this time maidservants were busying themselves in the
hall, four of them, who worked for Circe about her house.
Now these were the offspring of springs and of groves,   350
and of sacred rivers that run down into the salt sea.
One of them was busy throwing fine purple coverings
over chairs, while underneath them she spread linen cloths.
The second maid drew up tables made of silver in front of
these chairs, and on them she arranged golden baskets.   355
The third set about preparing sweet mind-cheering wine
in a silver mixing-bowl, and set out golden cups.
The fourth maid brought water and kindled a great fire
under a huge tripod-cauldron; and the water grew hot.
When the water in the flashing bronze vessel had boiled, she   360
sat me in a bath and washed me from the huge basin, pouring
the water, now mixed to a pleasing warmth, down over my
head and shoulders, until she had taken the heart-breaking
weariness from my limbs. When she had washed and rubbed
me richly with olive oil, she clothed me in a tunic and a fine   365
cloak and conducted me to sit on a fine silver-studded chair,
cunningly made; and there was a stool to go under my feet.
Another maid brought water in a beautiful golden pitcher
and poured it into a silver bowl for me to wash my hands,
and then drew up a polished table to stand beside me.   370
A respected housekeeper fetched bread and set it before me,
and added a heap of delicacies, giving freely from her store.
Circe then invited me to eat; but my spirit could find no joy,
and I sat thinking of other things, my heart brooding on evil.

'When Circe saw me simply sitting there, not reaching out   375
my hands for the food, but nursing a mighty grief within me,
she stood next to me and addressed me in winged words:
"Why on earth do you sit here, Odysseus, as if you were dumb,
eating your heart out and holding back from food and drink?
Do you perhaps suspect some further trickery? You should not   380
be fearful; I have already sworn a mighty oath not to harm you."

'So she spoke, and I answered and addressed her:
"O Circe, how could any man who has right thoughts in his
mind bring himself to taste food and drink before he had
rescued his companions and seen them before his own eyes?   385
Come now; if you are honestly inviting me to eat and drink,

release them, so that I can set my eyes on my trusty companions."

'So I spoke, and Circe strode straight out through her hall,
holding her stick in her hand, and opened the pigsty gates
and drove my men out, looking like nine-year-old hogs. 390
They stood in front of her, and she went among them
and smeared every one of them with another ointment.
The bristles which the noxious drug given them by revered
Circe had caused to grow on them fell from their limbs,
and they became men once again, younger than they were 395
before, and far more handsome, and taller to look upon.
They recognized me, and each man grasped my hand, and
into the hearts of all there stole tender lamentation, and a loud
echo went all around the house; even the goddess pitied them.
Then she, bright among goddesses, stood close and spoke: 400
"Son of Laertes, sprung from Zeus, Odysseus of many wiles,
now you must go to your swift ship and the shore of the sea.
First of all you must drag your ship on to the land, and
store your treasure and all your ship's gear in caves. Then
come back here, bringing your trusty companions with you." 405
'So she spoke, and my proud spirit was persuaded.
I set off for my swift ship and the shore of the sea, and
after a time I found my trusty companions beside the swift
ship, lamenting piteously and shedding floods of tears.
As when calves in a farmyard all frisk about together 410
to meet a herd of cows when they return full of
fodder to the dung-strewn fold; the pens can no longer
contain them, and they run around their mothers, lowing
continually; so my men, when they saw me, streamed
out about me, weeping, and the feeling in their hearts 415
was as if they had reached their homeland and the very city
in rugged Ithaca where they had been born and raised.
Full of lamentation they addressed me with winged words:
"Zeus-nurtured man, we are as full of joy to see you returning
to us as if we had come back to rugged Ithaca, our homeland. 420
But now, tell us the full tale of the death of our companions."
So they spoke, and I answered them with soothing words:
"The first thing we must do is to drag our ship on to land, and
then store our treasure and all the ship's gear in some caves.
After that you must all make haste to come with me to 425

see your companions in Circe's sacred palace, eating and
drinking; they have enough there to last them a long time."

'So I spoke, and they quickly obeyed my orders; only
Eurylochus resisted and tried to restrain his companions,
and spoke to them, addressing them in winged words: 430
"You poor wretches! Where are we going now? Why seek
trouble by going down to Circe's hall, where she will likely
change us all into pigs or wolves or lions, to be compelled
to stand guard over her great house for her—just as when
the Cyclops trapped our companions after they got into   435
his inner yard, and this reckless Odysseus with them.
It was because of his reckless folly that those men perished."

'So he spoke, and I pondered in my heart, whether I should
draw my long-bladed sword from beside my sturdy thigh
and with it cut off his head to roll on the ground, though   440
he was my kinsman, and a close one at that; but my friends
stood around, and tried to restrain me with soft words:
"Zeus-born hero, if you so order it, we will leave this man
to stay behind here with the ship and mount guard over it.
But as for us, lead us on to the sacred palace of Circe!"   445
So they spoke, and set off inland from the ship and the sea.
Even so, Eurylochus was not left beside the hollow ship,
but came with us, because he was afraid of my terrible rebuke.

'Meanwhile Circe had hospitably bathed the rest of my crew
in her palace and rubbed them richly with olive oil, and   450
had given them all clothes, tunics and woollen cloaks; and
they were feasting happily when we found them in her halls.
When my men came face to face and recognized them, they
set up a tearful lamentation, and the house echoed to its sound.
Then Circe, bright among goddesses, stood close and
          addressed me: 455
"Son of Laertes, sprung from Zeus, Odysseus of many wiles,
you must now make an end of this outburst of sorrow; I too
know of the great hardships you have endured on the fish-rich
sea, and also the cruelties hostile men have done to you on land.
So come now, eat your food and drink your wine, until   460
such time as you recover that same spirit in your breasts
which you had when you first left your native land of rugged
Ithaca. Now you are exhausted and without spirit, always

thinking of your painful wanderings, nor are your hearts
ever given to pleasure, for you have surely suffered much."   465

'So she spoke, and our proud hearts were persuaded. And so,
day after day until one year had completed its round, we sat
there, feasting on boundless quantities of meat and sweet wine.
But when a year had gone, as the seasons turned and the
months passed and the long tale of days was completed,   470
then my trusty companions called me to a meeting and said:
"Are you mad? Now is the time to remember your ancestral land,
if indeed it is divinely ordained for you to survive and to reach
the country of your fathers and your well-established house."

'So they spoke, and the proud heart in me was persuaded.   475
All day long until the setting of the sun we sat there,
feasting on boundless quantities of meat and sweet wine.
But when the sun went down and darkness came over us,
my men settled down to sleep throughout the shadowy palace,
while I went up to the beautifully fashioned bed of Circe   480
and clasped her knees in entreaty, and the goddess listened to
my voice; speaking in winged words I addressed her:
"Circe, now fulfil that promise you made to me, to see me
on my way home. The spirit in me is now impatient to go, and
it is the same with my companions; they are wearing my heart   485
out with their constant lamentations whenever you are not here."

'So I spoke, and she, bright among goddesses, at once replied:
"Son of Laertes, sprung from Zeus, Odysseus of many wiles;
let none of you stay any longer in my house against your will.
But first you must all complete another journey, and visit   490
the dwelling-place of Hades and of dread Persephone,
in order to consult the shade of Theban Teiresias,
the blind prophet, whose senses are still secure in him;
to him alone, even after death, Persephone has granted
intelligence, while all the others are but flitting phantoms."   495

'So she spoke, and the heart within me was shattered.
Sitting there on the bed I wept, and my heart no longer had
any desire to live and to look on the light of the sun. But
when I had had my fill of weeping and rolling on the ground,
I gave her my answer, addressing her in these words: 500
"Circe, how can I do this? Who will be my guide on this
journey? No man has ever yet sailed his black ship into Hades."

'So I spoke, and she, bright among goddesses, at once replied:
"Son of Laertes, sprung from Zeus, Odysseus of many wiles,
do not let the lack of a guide for your ship trouble you;   505
simply step the mast, spread the white sail, and take your
seats, and the North Wind's blasts will carry her onward.
When you have crossed the Ocean in your ship, you will
come to a low-lying shore and the groves of Persephone,
where tall poplars grow, and willows that shed their fruit early;   510
beach your ship there, on the margin of deep-eddying Ocean,
and yourself make your way into the dank house of Hades.
There the waters of Pyriphlegethon and Cocytus, which is
a branch of the river Styx, flow together into Acheron,
the two rivers meeting at a rock with a thunderous roar.   515
Next, hero, you must do as I tell you: come close to this place
and dig a trench about a cubit's length* in each direction,
and round its edge pour a drink-offering to all the dead,
first of honey and milk, then of sweet wine, and thirdly of
water; then sprinkle white barley over them. Pray at length   520
to the powerless shades of the dead, promising when you reach
Ithaca to sacrifice in your halls a cow that has not yet calved,
the best you have, and to pile the pyre high with treasures;
and to Teiresias alone, apart from the rest, promise to offer
a sheep that is black all over, the finest there is in your flocks.   525
After this, when you have prayed in entreaty to the famous
company of the dead, sacrifice a ram and a black ewe,
twisting their heads towards Erebus;* but you must turn
yours away, looking toward Ocean's streams. Now the
shades of the departed dead will come up in great numbers.   530
At this point urge on your companions, and tell them to
flay the sheep that are lying there, throats cut by the pitiless
bronze, and to burn them and make prayers to the gods,
to powerful Hades and to dread Persephone. Meanwhile,
draw your sharp sword from beside your thigh and sit   535
there, and do not allow the powerless shades of the dead to
come closer to the blood until you have consulted Teiresias.
The prophet will soon come to you, captain of the people,
and tell you your route and the stages of your voyage, and
how you will make your way home over the fish-rich sea."   540
'So she spoke, and soon Dawn on her golden throne appeared.

The nymph Circe then gave me clothes to wear, a tunic
and a cloak, and she herself put on a long, silvery robe,
finely-woven and becoming, and round her waist she tied
a beautiful golden girdle, and fastened a scarf on her head.   545
Then I went through her palace rousing my companions,
and standing by each man addressed him in winning words:
"No more lying in bed now, enjoying the pleasure of sweet
sleep! It is time to go; revered Circe has given me directions."

'So I spoke, and they obeyed me in their proud hearts.   550
But even then I did not lead them away without adversity.
There was a man called Elpenor, the youngest of us, not
very brave in battle nor quite secure in his wits. This man
was, I think, drunk; longing for cool air he had left his friends
and had gone to sleep on the roof of Circe's sacred palace.   555
When he heard the din and clatter of my companions making
ready to depart he leapt up suddenly, and, not thinking,
forgot to look for the long ladder and descend that way,
and so tumbled headlong from the roof. His neck was broken,
sheared from his spine, and his shade went down to Hades.   560

'When the others came to meet me I said to them:
"No doubt you think you are going home to your dear
native land; but Circe has mapped out a different journey,
taking us to the house of Hades and of dread Persephone,
where I have to consult the shade of Theban Teiresias."   565

'So I spoke, and their hearts were shattered within them.
There and then they sat down and wept and tore their hair—
but all in vain, for no good came of their lamentations.

'So, grieving, we made our way down to the ship
and the seashore, weeping copious tears. Meanwhile   570
Circe had gone before us and had tethered a ram and
a black ewe beside the black ship, slipping past us
with ease; for when a god does not wish to be observed
who can cast an eye upon his going back and forth?

BOOK ELEVEN

'When we had made our way back to the ship and the sea,
we first of all dragged it down to the bright salt water,
then stepped the mast and set the sail in the black ship.
We collected the sheep and drove them on board, and
embarked ourselves, troubled and shedding copious tears.   5
Lovely-haired Circe, the awesome goddess speaking with
a mortal voice, sent us a following breeze to fill our sail, a
good friend, which blew astern of our dark-prowed ship.
We secured the tackle all along the ship and sat still,
and the wind and the steersman held her on course.   10
All day long the sail was stretched taut as she sped over
the deep; and the sun went down, and all the ways grew dark.

   'The ship reached the limit formed by deep-flowing Ocean,
where there is the city and people of the Cimmerians,*
who are enveloped in mist and cloud. Never does Helios,   15
the blazing god, look down on them with his rays,
either when he climbs up to the high sky, set with stars,
or when he turns back from there towards the earth;
but grim night extends over these wretched mortals.

   'Here we put in and beached our ship and took the sheep   20
ashore; then we made our way along the stream of Ocean,
until we came to the place that Circe had described to us.
Here Perimedes and Eurylochus held the sacrificial victims
fast, and I drew my sharp sword from beside my thigh
and dug a trench about a cubit's length in each direction,   25
and round its edge I poured a drink-offering to all the dead,
first of honey and milk, after that of sweet wine, and
thirdly of water; then over these I sprinkled white barley.

   'I prayed at length to the powerless shades of the dead, vowing
when I reached Ithaca to sacrifice in my halls a cow that had not   30
calved, the best I had, and to pile the pyre high with treasure;
and for Teiresias alone, quite separately, that I would offer
a sheep that was black all over, the finest in my flocks.
When I had made my supplications and vows to the company
of the dead, I seized the sheep and cut their throats over the   35

trench, and dark-clouded blood ran into it. And now the shades
of the departed dead came crowding round, up from Erebus:
brides and unwed young men, old men who had endured much,
and tender young women, bearing fresh grief in their hearts;
and many who had been pierced with bronze-tipped spears,   40
battle-slain men still wearing their blood-spattered armour.
They came from all around, swarming in multitudes about the
trench, with an astonishing clamour; and pale fear gripped me.
At last, with much urging, I ordered my companions to flay
the sheep that lay slaughtered by the pitiless bronze, and   45
to burn them, and then to make prayers to the gods, to
mighty Hades and dread Persephone; meanwhile I drew
the sharp sword from beside my thigh and sat there, and
I would not allow the powerless shades of the dead to
come any closer to the blood until I had consulted Teiresias.   50
   'The first shade to approach was of my companion Elpenor.
He had not yet been buried in the broad-wayed earth,
because we had left his body behind in Circe's palace,
unwept and unburied, since a new task pressed us urgently.
When I saw him I burst into tears, pitying him in my heart,   55
and I addressed him, speaking with winged words:
"Elpenor, how did you come here, under the misty darkness?
You got here faster on your feet than I did in my black ship."
   'So I spoke, and he groaned and answered me in these words:
"Son of Laertes, sprung from Zeus, Odysseus of many wiles;   60
it was a god-sent evil destiny that ruined me, and too much wine.
I had lain down to sleep on the roof of Circe's palace, and
did not think to make for the long ladder to go back down,
and I tumbled headlong from the roof; my neck was broken,
sheared from my spine, and my shade came down to Hades.   65
So now I beseech you, by those we left behind, no longer here,
by your wife, by your father who reared you as a child, and by
Telemachus your only son whom you left behind in your halls.
I know that when you go from here, from the realm of Hades,
you will again put in your well-built ship at the isle of Aeaea;   70
once there I beg you, lord, to remember me: do not sail away
and leave me behind, for ever after unwept, abandoned, and
unburied, lest I bring the gods' just anger down on you;
but burn me there with all the war-gear that is mine, and heap

up a burial-mound for me on the grey sea's shore, to mark   75
an ill-fated man, so that men yet to come may learn about me.
Do all this for me, and on the burial-mound plant the oar I
used to pull while I was alive and among my companions."

'So he spoke, and I answered and addressed him: "All
this, ill-fated man, I shall perform for you; it will be done."   80

'So we two sat, conversing with each other in mournful words,
I on my side of the trench, holding my sword over the blood,
while on the other my companion's phantom told his long tale.

'Next to approach was the shade of my departed mother,
Anticleia the daughter of great-hearted Autolycus, who was   85
still living when I left her behind on my way to sacred Ilium.
When I saw her I burst into tears, pitying her in my heart;
but for all that, despite my thick grief, I would not let her
come any closer to the blood until I had consulted Teiresias.

'And then there came up the shade of Teiresias the Theban,   90
holding a staff made of gold; he recognized me and spoke:
"Son of Laertes, sprung from Zeus, Odysseus of many wiles,
ill-fated man! How can it be that you have left the sun's light
to come here, to look on dead men in this joyless place?
Draw back from the trench, and hold your sharp sword away,   95
so that I may drink the blood and speak the truth to you."

'So he spoke, and I retreated and pushed my silver-studded
sword back into its scabbard. Then Teiresias drank the dark
blood, and, blameless prophet that he was, addressed me:

'"Brilliant Odysseus, you hope for a pleasant homecoming;   100
but a god is about to make it painful for you. I do not think
you will go unnoticed by the earthshaker, who holds resentment
in his heart against you, angry because you blinded his dear son.
Still, though you all have hardships to endure, you may yet arrive
safely, if you are prepared to restrain your and your men's greed,   105
once you have escaped from the violet-tinged sea in your
well-built ship and made landfall on the island of Thrinacia,
where you will find the oxen and sturdy sheep of Helios
grazing—Helios who observes all and hears all things.
If you think only of your return and leave them unharmed,   110
you may all reach Ithaca, though suffering much on the way;
but if you harm them I predict destruction for you, your ship,
and your companions. Even if you yourself escape, you will

reach home late, in a sorry state, after losing all your men,
and on a foreign ship. In your house you will find trouble—   115
men of arrogance, who even now are devouring your livelihood,
paying court to your godlike wife and offering marriage-gifts.
When you return you will punish these men for their
violence; but when you have killed them all in your halls, these
suitors, either by trickery or openly with the sharp bronze,   120
you must then take your well-shaped oar and go on a journey
until such time as you encounter men who are ignorant of
the sea, and who eat food that is not seasoned with salt.
They will know nothing of ships with crimson prows, or
of well-shaped oars, which serve as the wings of ships.   125
Now, I shall give you a clear sign, which you cannot miss:
when you fall in with another traveller, who tells you that
you are carrying a winnowing-fan on your bright shoulder,
then at last you must plant your well-shaped oar in the
ground and make a splendid offering to lord Poseidon,   130
of a ram, a bull, and a boar-pig that is a mounter of sows.
Then you should return home and offer holy hecatombs
to the immortal gods whose dwelling is in the high sky,
all of them in due order. As for you, death will come to you
far from the sea, such a gentle death, taking you when   135
you are now worn out, in sleek old age and surrounded by
your prosperous people. All this that I say is the exact truth."

    'So he spoke, and I answered and addressed him: "Teiresias,
doubtless this is the fate that the gods themselves have spun.
But come, tell me this and give me a full and true account: 140
over there I can see the shade of my departed mother,
sitting in silence near the blood; but she cannot bring herself
to look directly at her son or to address a word to him.
Tell me, lord, how can she recognize me for what I am?"

    'So I spoke, and he immediately answered and addressed me: 145
"It is easy for me to explain this and fix it into your mind:
any of the dead who have passed away whom you allow to
come near the blood will speak the truth to you, but those
to whom you refuse this will go back whence they came."

    'So spoke the shade of lord Teiresias, and went back into the   150
house of Hades, now that he had delivered his clear prophecy.
    'Meanwhile I stayed resolutely where I was, until my mother

approached and drank the dark-clouded blood. She knew me
at once, and in melancholy tones addressed winged words to me:
"My child, how did you come here, under the misty darkness,   155
and you alive? It is hard for mortals to look on these things.
In between lie great rivers and dreadful torrents: first of all
the river Ocean, which is impossible for a traveller to cross
on foot, and can only be done if he possesses a well-built ship.
Have you come here now on your way from Troy, after long   160
wandering in your ship with your companions? Have you not
yet been to Ithaca, or seen your wife in your halls?"
    'So she spoke, and I answered and addressed her:
"Mother, a pressing need has brought me to Hades' realm:
I needed to consult the shade of Teiresias the Theban.   165
I have not yet been anywhere near Achaea, nor set foot
on my own land; always I have been wandering miserably,
from the very first moment I followed glorious Agamemnon
to Troy, home of fine horses, to fight against the Trojans.
But tell me this, and give me a full and true account: 170
what deadly doom, dealer in long suffering, laid you low?
Was it some lingering illness? Or did Artemis, shooter of
arrows, come at you with her gentle shafts and so slay you?
Tell me too about my father, and the son I left behind: do
they still enjoy my princely position, or does some other man   175
now possess it, because people say that I will never return?
Tell me about my wedded wife's intentions, and her resolve:
is she still with our son, keeping all our property safe,
or is she now married to the best man of the Achaeans?"
    'So I spoke, and my revered mother immediately answered: 180
"Constant she certainly is as she waits in your halls, her
heart patient and steadfast; she weeps unceasingly, and
her nights and days as they come and go are full of misery.
But no one yet enjoys your princely status. Telemachus
controls your allotted lands untroubled, and dines out at   185
equally appointed feasts, as befits a judgement-giving man,
for everyone invites him. But your father stays where he is
on his farm, and never comes down to the city. He has no
proper bed or bedding, neither cloaks nor shining blankets,
but in winter he sleeps in the same house as his servants,   190
in the ashes by the fire; and his clothes are poor stuff.

And when the summer and fruitful harvest-time come round,
everywhere along the slope of his vineyard-plot there are
piles of fallen leaves on the ground which serve him for a bed.
There he lies grieving, and the sorrow grows big in his heart,   195
yearning for your return; painful old age has come upon him.
This too was the reason I died and met my doom: it was
not that the keen-eyed shooter of arrows* came after me
and overcame me in our halls with her gentle shafts,
nor did any illness attack me, of the kind that most often   200
comes with painful wasting and takes the life from the limbs.
No, brilliant Odysseus, it was yearning for you and your
cleverness and your gentle spirit that took away my sweet life."

   'So she spoke; and I pondered in my heart and longed
to take the shade of my departed mother in my embrace.   205
Three times I started forward, my heart urging me to hold her,
and three times she fluttered through my arms, like a shadow
or a dream; and the grief in my heart grew even keener,
and I addressed her, speaking in winged words:
"Mother, why do you avoid me when I ache to hold you,   210
hoping even in Hades' realm we may throw our loving arms
around each other and so enjoy our fill of chill weeping?
Or is this a mere phantom that proud Persephone has
sent me, to make me lament and groan all the more?"

   'So I spoke, and my revered mother answered me at once: 215
"Ah my child, ill-fated beyond all men! It is not that
Persephone, daughter of Zeus, is deceiving you, but it is
the law that touches all mortal beings when they die:
no longer do they have sinews that bind flesh and bone
together, for as soon as the spirit* departs from their white   220
bones the fierce heat of the blazing fire destroys everything,
and their shade flies off, fluttering like a dream. Hurry now,
and make for the light as quickly as you can, and remember
all this, so that some day you will be able to tell your wife."

   'While we were conversing with each other in this way,   225
there came up to us, sent by proud Persephone, all those
women who had been the wives or daughters of great men.
They swarmed around the dark blood in a crowd,
and I considered how I might put questions to each one.
And this seemed to me in my heart to be the best plan: 230

drawing my long-bladed sword from beside my sturdy thigh,
I would not let them drink the dark blood at the same time;
so they approached one after the other, each one proclaiming
her own ancestry; and in this way I questioned them all.

'The first woman I saw was Tyro, daughter of a noble father;   235
she said she was the daughter of excellent Salmoneus,
and became the wife of Cretheus, the son of Aeolus.
She fell in love with a river, the god Enipeus,* who was
by far the handsomest of rivers to send his waters flowing
over the earth, and she used to haunt his lovely streams.   240
The earthshaker, holder of the world, took on Enipeus'
likeness, and lay with Tyro at the whirling river's mouth;
a dark wave, high-arching and mountain-huge, enfolded
them, and concealed both the god and the mortal woman.
He loosed her maiden girdle, and poured sleep over her.   245
When the god had finished with his act of passion,
he took Tyro firmly by the hand and spoke directly to her:
"Be happy, lady, in this act of love! In the course of this year
you will bear splendid children (an immortal's bedding is not
without fruit), and you must bring up your sons with great care.   250
Go home now, restrain yourself, and never speak my name;
but I tell you I am Poseidon, the one who shakes the earth."
So he spoke, and plunged beneath the sea's heaving surge.
Tyro did conceive, and gave birth to Pelias* and Neleus,*
both of whom later became mighty attendants of great Zeus.   255
Pelias, rich in sheep-flocks, had his home in Iolcus of the
wide dancing-places, while Neleus dwelt in sandy Pylos.
This queen among women had other sons, by Cretheus: Aeson,
Pheres, and Amythaon, whose delight was in the chariot-fight.

'The next woman I saw was Antiope, daughter of Asopus,   260
who boasted she had spent a night in the arms of Zeus.
She gave birth to two sons, Amphion and Zethus,
the original founders of the city of seven-gated Thebes;
they built its walls, since, mighty though they were, they
could not live in Thebes' wide spaces if it had no walls.   265

'After her I saw Alcmene, Amphitryon's wife, the one
who lay in the passionate embrace of great Zeus and gave
birth to daring-spirited Heracles, who had a lion's heart;
and I also saw Megara, daughter of high-hearted Creon,

who was wed to Amphitryon's son, a man of tireless vigour.   270

   'My eyes then fell on the mother of Oedipus, lovely Epicaste,*
who committed a monstrous act in her mind's ignorance,
marrying her own son; he had killed his own father and made
her his wife, but the gods soon made this public knowledge.
Oedipus, for all his troubles, continued by the gods' cruel   275
scheming to hold sway over the Cadmeians in lovely Thebes,
but she went down to the realm of mighty Hades the gatekeeper:
possessed by grief, she had knotted a fatal noose to a high
roof-beam in her house. To Oedipus she bequeathed all the
countless miseries that a mother's Furies can bring into being.   280

   'Next I saw the surpassingly lovely Chloris, whom Neleus wed
for her beauty, after paying countless marriage-gifts for her.
She was the youngest daughter of Amphion, son of Iasus,
who long ago ruled by might over Minyan Orchomenus;
she was queen in Pylos, and bore splendid children to Neleus,   285
Nestor and Chromius and illustrious Periclymenus.
Besides these she bore beautiful Pero, a wonder among mortals,
who was courted by all who lived around Pylos; but Neleus
would only give her to a man who could drive the crook-horned,
broad-browed cattle of mighty Iphiclus out of Phylace. This   290
was a difficult task, and the only one to undertake it was the
excellent seer;* but cruel destiny, sent from a god, shackled him,
and he was bound in painful chains by rough peasant oxherds.
But when the months and days had completed their course,
and when with the year's full circling the seasons returned,   295
mighty Iphiclus set him free again because he divulged all
that the gods had decreed; and the plan of Zeus was fulfilled.

   'Next I saw Leda, who was the wedded wife of Tyndareus,
and who bore to him two stout-hearted sons, Castor the
breaker of horses and Polydeuces the skilful boxer. The life-   300
giving earth now holds them, though they are both alive;
even under the ground they enjoy honour from Zeus,
for on one day they are alive, while on the next they are
dead;* in the honour they receive they are equal to the gods.

   'After Leda I caught sight of Iphimedeia, the wife of   305
Aloeus, who boldly claimed she had lain with Poseidon,
and then gave birth to two sons, who lived but for a short time:
godlike Otus, and Ephialtes whose fame spread far abroad,

the tallest men ever nourished by the grain-giving earth,
and by far the most handsome, after far-famed Orion: 310
in their ninth year they measured nine cubits in breadth,
and had reached a height of nine fathoms. These two
even made threats to the immortals that they would
rouse the noise of violent war against them on Olympus.
They strove to pile Ossa on Olympus, and leaf-shivering   315
Pelion on Ossa, to make a stairway to the high sky, and
would surely have succeeded had they reached manhood's
prime, but they were slain by Zeus' son, whom lovely-haired
Leto bore*—both of them, before the curly hair had flowered
below their temples and covered their chins with thick down. 320

    'Next I saw Phaedra and Procris and beautiful Ariadne,
daughter of murderous-minded Minos, she whom Theseus
once tried to carry off from Crete to the hill of sacred Athens;
but he had no joy of her, for before he could, Artemis
slew her on sea-girt Dia, on the testimony of Dionysus.*   325

    'And I saw Maera and Clymene and loathsome Eriphyle,
she who took precious gold in return for her husband's life.*

    'I could not tell the tale or give a name to all the many
heroes' wives I saw, or their daughters; immortal night
would fade before I reached my story's end. But now it is   320
time to sleep, whether I join the men on my swift ship, or
stay here. My journey home is the gods' concern, and yours.'

    So he spoke, and they all remained silent and still, gripped
throughout the shadowy halls by the magic of his tale.
The first among them to speak was white-armed Arete: 335
'Phaeacians, what do you think of this man among us—
his form, his stature, and the evenly balanced mind in him?
He is my guest, but every man shares that honour with me.
Do not then be in a hurry to send him away, nor stint
the gifts he is in such need of, for thanks to the favour of 340
the gods you have much treasure lying stored in your halls.'

    Then there spoke among them the aged hero Echeneus,
he who was the oldest man among the Phaeacians:
'My friends, what our wise queen says is surely not wide
of the mark, nor does it conflict with our thoughts. So do as 345
she says—though both deed and word depend on Alcinous.'

    Then in turn Alcinous answered and addressed him:

'It shall indeed be as you say, as long as I live and rule
over the Phaeacians who take delight in their oars. But as for
our guest, much though he longs for his homecoming, let him   350
be patient, and wait at least until tomorrow, when we shall give
him gifts in full measure. His escort will be all men's concern,
but especially mine, for I hold the power among this people.'
   Then in answer Odysseus of many wiles addressed him:
'Lord Alcinous, distinguished among all peoples,   355
if you were to persuade me to stay here even for a year, and
still hastened my journey home and gave me splendid gifts,
that would be even more to my liking; and I would profit
more by reaching my dear native land with a fuller hand,
and I would meet with more respect and friendship on the   360
part of all those men who saw me on my return to Ithaca.'
   Then in turn Alcinous answered and addressed him:
'Odysseus, when we look at you we do not in any way
see you as a cheat or a swindler, of the kind that the
black earth nurtures in great numbers all over the world,   365
fashioning lies out of things that no one can disprove.
There is in you both eloquence and fine judgement, and
when you recount your and the Argives' dreadful sufferings
your tale is skilful and detailed, as if it were a singer's.
But now tell me this, and give me a full and true account: 370
did you set eyes on any of those godlike heroes who
went with you to Troy and met their doom in that land?
This night is long, infinitely so; it is not yet time for us to
sleep in the palace. Tell me more of those marvellous events;
I could wait until the bright dawn, if you could bring yourself,   375
here in the hall, to continue the story of your troubles.'
   Then in answer Odysseus of many wiles answered him:
'Lord Alcinous, distinguished among all peoples,
there is a time for long tales, and there is a time for sleep;
but if you are keen to hear more, I would certainly not   380
refuse to continue my tale with an even more pitiable story
about the miseries of my comrades, who died later on.
They escaped the grief-laden war with the Trojans, but
died after reaching home, by the will of an evil woman.
   'Holy Persephone finally drove the shades of the women   385
away, scattering them in all directions, and then there

came up the shade of Agamemnon the son of Atreus,
grieving; and other shades gathered round him, those who
had died with him and met their doom in Aegisthus' house.
He knew me at once, as soon as he drank the dark blood,   390
and began to weep loudly, shedding tears in abundance,
and reached out his hands in his longing to embrace me;
but he could not, for there was no longer any strength or vigour
left in his supple limbs, such as there had been in time gone by.
When I saw him I burst into tears, pitying him in my heart,   395
and I addressed him, speaking in winged words:
"Most glorious son of Atreus, Agamemnon lord of men,
what deadly doom, dealer in long suffering, laid you low?
Did Poseidon stir up some terrible tempest, rousing
dreadful storm-blasts to overwhelm you in your ships?   400
Or did some cruel men take your life on dry land while you
were driving off their cattle and their fine flocks of sheep, or
fighting with them for the prize of their city and womenfolk?"
    'So I spoke, and he at once answered and addressed me:
"Son of Laertes, sprung from Zeus, Odysseus of many wiles,   405
it was not that Poseidon stirred up a terrible tempest, rousing
dreadful storm-blasts to overwhelm me in my ships,
nor did any cruel band of men take my life on dry land;
it was Aegisthus who brought about my death and doom.
With my accursed wife's help he invited me into the palace,   410
feasted me, and then cut me down like an ox at its stall.
So I died a most wretched death; and all around me my men
were killed in relentless succession, like white-tusked boars
slaughtered in the house of some rich and powerful man,
for a wedding or a shared feast or a lavish private banquet.   415
You have in the past witnessed the deaths of many men,
slain either in single combat or in the fierce crush of battle;
but at these deaths your heart would have grieved most deeply,
seeing us sprawled in the hall next to the mixing-bowl and
the loaded tables, and the whole floor swimming with blood.   420
But the most pitiable thing I heard was the shriek of Cassandra,
Priam's daughter, whom that crafty schemer Clytemnestra slew
over me. Crumpled round the sword in death, I lifted my hands
and beat them on the ground; but the brazen bitch turned her back,
and though I was on my way to Hades' realm she could not bring   425

herself to shut my eyes with her hand or close my mouth.
There is nothing more terrible, nor anything more shameless,
than a woman who can plan deeds like this in her heart, deeds
like this ugly crime that Clytemnestra plotted: the murder of
her lawful wedded husband. Surely, I thought, when I returned   430
home I would be given a warm welcome by my children
and my household; but she, the most depraved of schemers,
has poured shame not only over herself but also over all
women yet to be born, even those who live upright lives.”

'So he spoke, and I answered and addressed him: “Dreadful!   435
Clearly wide-thundering Zeus has long nursed a terrible hatred
for Atreus' family, working through the schemes of women,
right from the start: many of us died for Helen's sake, and
Clytemnestra set this trap for you while you were still far away.”

'So I spoke, and he immediately answered and addressed me: 440
“For this reason you too should never be indulgent to your wife,
nor give her a full account of everything that is in your mind;
you should tell her some of it and keep the rest concealed.
Still, Odysseus, your wife is certainly not likely to murder you;
she is utterly loyal, circumspect Penelope, Icarius' daughter,   445
and the thoughts in her heart are always right and proper.
She was but a young married woman when we left her on
our way to the war, and her son was still a baby at the breast;
I suppose he is now taking his seat in the company of men,
fortunate fellow that he is—and his dear father will return and   450
see him, and he will embrace his father, as is right and proper.
But in my case, my wife did not even allow me to have my
fill of gazing upon my son, but killed me before I could.
I tell you another thing, and you should store it in your mind:
when you return to your dear native land, bring your ship to   455
land secretly, not openly; women are no longer to be trusted.
Now tell me this, and give me a full and true account: have you
and your men heard any news of my son? Is he still living?
Is he perhaps in Orchomenus, or in sandy Pylos, or might
he be with Menelaus in the broad land of Sparta?   460
Glorious Orestes has not yet died up there on the earth.”

'So he spoke, and I answered and addressed him:
“Son of Atreus, why do you ask me these questions? I do not
know if he is alive or dead—and idle talk is dangerous.”

'So the two of us conversed in this way in cheerless words,   465
standing there miserably and shedding copious tears;
and there approached the shade of Achilles, son of Peleus,
and the shades of Patroclus, of excellent Antilochus,
and of Ajax, who was the finest man in form and beauty
of all the Danaans, after the excellent son of Peleus.   470
The shade of Aeacus' swift-footed grandson knew me,
and in melancholy tones addressed winged words to me:
"Son of Laertes, sprung from Zeus, Odysseus of many wiles;
hard man, what greater feat than this could your mind devise?
How did you find the daring to descend to Hades, where   475
bodies without sense dwell, mere phantoms of dead mortals?"
  'So he spoke, and I answered and addressed him:
"Achilles, Peleus' son, by far the greatest of the Achaeans,
I came to consult Teiresias, hoping that he could give me
some stratagem to find my way back to rocky Ithaca.   480
I have not yet been anywhere near Achaea, nor yet set foot
on my own land, but always run into misfortune. But you,
Achilles—no man has been more blessed than you, nor will
ever be. While you were alive, we honoured you like a god,
and now you have come down here you hold supreme power   485
among the dead; so do not grieve over your death, Achilles."
  'So I spoke, and he immediately answered and addressed me:
"Do not try to comfort me about death, splendid Odysseus.
I would rather be a land-labourer, bonded to another man,
one who owns no land, and with little enough to keep him   490
alive, than to be king over all the dead who have passed away.
But now; tell me some news about that lordly son of mine—
did he follow me to the war, to be a champion there, or not?
Tell me too if you have heard any report of excellent Peleus,
if he still enjoys honour among the numerous Myrmidons,   495
or if in Hellas and Phthia they now treat him without respect
because old age binds his hands and feet fast in its grip.
I cannot now be his protector under the light of the sun—
the kind of man I once was in Troy's wide lands, when I
defended the Argives and killed the best of Troy's fighters.   500
If I could go back to my father's house as I was, even for
a moment, I would make those who browbeat him and keep
due honour from him shudder at my fury and irresistible hands."

'So he spoke, and I answered and addressed him:
"Of the excellent Peleus I have heard no report at all;   505
but about your dear son Neoptolemus I can tell you the
whole true story, just as you have asked me, because
it was I who brought him in my hollow, well-balanced ship
from Scyros to join the well-greaved Achaeans. Indeed,
whenever we used to debate tactics around Troy's city,   510
he was always the first to speak, and never gave bad advice.
Only godlike Nestor and I excelled him in this. And again,
whenever we Achaeans fought with the Trojans on the plain,
he never hung back in the mass of soldiery or in the crowd,
but always ran out ahead of all, yielding to none in his fighting   515
spirit. Many were the men he killed in the grim conflict;
I could not relate the number of these, nor give them names,
all the many fighters he slew while supporting the Argives.
I will mention only the hero Eurypylus, son of Telephus,
slain with the bronze; and with him many Cetaean* companions   520
were cut down, all because of presents given to a woman;
he was the handsomest man I have seen, after glorious Memnon.*
Again, when we, the best of the Argives, had climbed into
the horse that Epeius built, and I had the authority either to
open the doors on our cunning ambush or else to close them,   525
all the rest of the Danaan captains and chieftains were wiping
away tears, and every man's legs were trembling beneath him;
but not for one moment did I see your son's handsome features
grow pale, nor notice him wiping away a tear from his cheek.
On the contrary, he kept begging me to let him jump from   530
the horse, his hand for ever on the hilt of his sword and his
bronze-heavy spear; he was raging to loose ruin on the Trojans.
When we finally sacked the steep city of Priam, he embarked
in his ship with a choice prize as his fair share of the booty,
quite unharmed: neither wounded by the sharp bronze spear   535
nor sword-stabbed in close combat, as often happens in
battle; for it is always Ares' way to rage blindly, at random."

'So I spoke, and the shade of swift-footed Achilles stalked
away, making long strides through the meadow of asphodel,
happy because I had told him of the renown his son had won.   540

'Then other shades of the dead who had passed away stood
around me sorrowing, and each asked about their own concerns.

Only the shade of Ajax son of Telamon stood apart, keeping
his distance, bitter because of the victory I had won over him
by the ships when I defended my cause over the arms of   545
Achilles; his goddess mother had put them forward as a prize,
and the judges were the sons of the Trojans and Pallas Athena.
How I wish I had not won in a contest like this! It was thanks
to this armour that the earth now holds such a splendid man,
Ajax, who surpassed all the rest of the Danaans in beauty   550
and accomplishments, save for the excellent son of Peleus.
So I addressed him, trying to win him over with my words:
   ' "Ajax, son of blameless Telamon! You were not destined, then,
even in death, to forget your anger against me because of
those cursed arms? It was the gods who made them a bane for   555
the Argives. Such a strong tower they lost by your death,
and we Achaeans grieve ceaselessly for you now you are dead,
as much as we do for hero Achilles, Peleus' son. No one else
is to blame but Zeus, who nursed a long and violent hatred for
the army of Danaan spearmen, and brought you to your doom.   560
Come nearer, lord, please, and listen to the tale I have to tell;
restrain your fury and hold your proud spirit in check."

   'So I spoke, but he gave me no answer, and turned away
into Erebus to join the other shades of the departed dead.
Yet for all his bitterness, he might have spoken to me   565
there, or I to him; but the heart in my breast was longing
to see the shades of others who had finished with life.

   'And indeed I did see Minos,* the splendid son of Zeus
sitting there, holding his golden staff and giving judgements
to the dead; and they stood or sat around him in wide-gated   570
Hades' realm, asking their lord for decisions on their pleas.

   'Next to him I caught sight of monstrous Orion,* rounding
up wild beasts through the asphodel meadow, the same
beasts he had killed before on remote mountains, carrying
in his hands a solid bronze club, indestructible for ever.   575

   'I saw Tityus* too, who was the son of illustrious Earth,
sprawled over the ground. Nine measures of land he covered,
and two vultures, perched on either side of him, were tearing
his liver, ripping through the caul; but he could not use his hands
to fend them off. He had raped Leto, Zeus' famous consort,   580
as she passed through spacious Panopeus on her way to Pytho.

'There too I saw Tantalus,* enduring dreadful agonies,
standing upright in a lake whose water reached his chin.
Thirsting, he strained to drink the water, but could not catch it,
for as many times as the old man stooped in his desire to drink,   585
so often the water disappeared, swallowed up by the earth, and
around his feet black soil appeared and a god kept drying it up.
Over his head, tall leaf-clad trees dangled their fruit in plenty—
pear trees and pomegranates, apple trees with shining fruit,
and trees of sweet figs and ripe olives. But every time   590
the old man stretched out his hands, hoping to grasp them,
a wind would whisk them off towards the shadowy clouds.

'And look, there too I saw Sisyphus,* suffering cruel agonies,
using both his hands to heave at a monstrous boulder.
Time after time he would brace himself with hands and feet   595
to push the stone upwards towards a hill's crest, but when
he was about to shove it over the top, its mass turned it back,
and at once the pitiless stone bounded back to the plain.
Then, once again, he would heave and strain at it; sweat
ran down over his limbs, and dust swirled about his head.   600

'After him I caught sight of the mighty Heracles—or his
phantom,* for he now enjoys feasting among the immortal
gods, and he has Hebe of the lovely ankles to wife, she,
the daughter of great Zeus and Hera of the golden sandals.
Around him there was a clamour of the dead, like birds,   605
flying everywhere in panic; and he, looking like dark night,
held his bow uncased, with an arrow on the string, looking
keenly around with a fierce gaze, always as if about to shoot.
There was a terrifying belt about his breast, worn as a
baldric; it was golden, and on it were worked many marvels—   610
bears and wild boars and lions with glittering eyes,
battle-clashes and combats, deaths and the slayings of men.
I wish the man who created that belt with his skill had
never done it; and may he never create another like it!
The moment he set eyes on me Heracles knew who I was,   615
and touched by my plight addressed winged words to me:
"Zeus-sprung son of Laertes, Odysseus of many wiles;
poor wretch, you too must be working out some evil doom,
such as I carried all the time that I was in the sun's light.
My father was Zeus, Cronus' son, and yet I had to suffer   620

misery without bounds: I was bound subject to a man far
inferior to me,* who gave me harsh labours to perform, and
once even sent me down here to fetch the dog Cerberus, for
he thought there could be no more dangerous task than this.
But I did capture him and bring him up from Hades' realm;   625
I was helped on my way by Hermes and grey-eyed Athena."

  'So he spoke, and went back into the realm of Hades;
but I stayed rooted to the spot, hoping that some other hero,
one of those who had died in the past, might still approach.
And indeed I might yet have seen still earlier men whom I   630
wanted to see, Theseus and Peirithoüs, illustrious sons of gods;
but before I could the tribes of the dead swarmed round in
great numbers, making an astonishing clamour; and pale fear
gripped me, for I was afraid that proud Persephone might send
up the gorgon-head of some ghastly monster to confront me.   635
Quickly I made my way back to my ship, and ordered my
crew to get themselves on board and cast off the stern-cables;
and without more ado they embarked and sat at their oarlocks.
The stream's current carried the ship down the river Ocean;
first we rowed, and after that came a fair-blowing wind.   640

BOOK TWELVE

'Now when the ship had left the waters of Ocean behind,
she came to the surging wide open sea, and reached
the island of Aeaea, where early-born Dawn has her
house and her dancing-floors, and the Sun his place of rising;
and there we put in and beached our ship on the sands,   5
and went ashore at the place where the sea's waves broke.
There we fell asleep and waited for the bright Dawn.

'When early-born Dawn with her rosy fingers appeared,
I first sent some of my companions to the palace of Circe,
to bring back the body of the dead Elpenor. Quickly   10
we chopped some logs, and, full of grief and shedding
copious tears, we duly buried him on the furthest point of a
jutting promontory. When the dead man and his battle-gear
were burnt, we heaped up a mound, and dragged up a stone to
mark it; and on top of the mound we fixed his well-made oar.   15

'So we duly conducted each rite. Meanwhile Circe was well
aware that we had returned from Hades; she quickly made
herself ready, and came up attended by maidservants carrying
bread and quantities of meat, and red gleaming wine.
She, bright among goddesses, stood in our midst and spoke: 20
"You are hard men, going down alive to the realms of Hades!
You will now die twice, while all other men only die once!
Come, eat this food and drink this wine, and stay here for
the rest of today; and tomorrow as soon as Dawn appears
you shall set sail. I will show you the route, and give you   25
exact advice, so that on both sea and on land you may
avoid painful suffering rising from others' wicked designs."

'So she spoke, and our proud hearts were persuaded.
And so, all day long until the setting of the sun we sat,
feasting on boundless quantities of meat and sweet wine.   30
When the sun went down and darkness came over us,
my companions settled down to sleep by the stern-cables;
but Circe took my hand and led me away from them, and
invited me to sit. Reclining by my side she questioned
me, and I told her the whole story in detail and due order.   35

Then revered Circe addressed me in winged words:
   ' "Very well; all that has been done, as you say. Now listen
to what I shall say, though a god himself will remind you.
The next beings you meet will be the Sirens, who cast a
spell on all men who chance to approach them. Whoever   40
in his ignorance sails close to the Sirens and hears their
voice, for him there will be no wife to greet him, nor little
children brightening at their father's return to his home.
The Sirens will enchant him with their clear singing as
they sit in their meadow, surrounded by great heaps of   45
men's mouldering bones, with the skin on them rotting away.
Sail quickly past this place, having first softened some sweet
beeswax and stopped your companions' ears with it, so that
none of them may hear; but if you yourself wish to listen,
let the men in your swift ship tie you hand and foot, upright   50
on the mast-box, with the ropes' ends lashed round the mast,
so that you may hear and enjoy the voice of the two Sirens.
And if you entreat your companions and order them to release
you, they must bind you with even more ropes than before.
   ' "When your companions have driven you past the Sirens,   55
I cannot tell you exactly which of the two routes you
should then go on to take; you yourself will have to
decide in your own mind, but I will describe both.
In one direction lie overhanging rocks, and against them
beats and roars the huge swell of dark-eyed Amphitrite;   60
the Wanderers is the name the blessed gods give them.
No bird can easily fly past this place, not even the timid
doves that fetch and carry ambrosia for father Zeus, but
every time the sheer rock snatches one of them away—
though the Father sends another to make their number up.   65
No ship of men that came this way has yet escaped them;
there is only a confusion of ships' planks and men's bodies,
tossed about by the sea's surge or blasts of deadly fire.
Only one sea-traversing ship has passed by these rocks,
and that was storied Argo, sailing home from Aeëtes; and   70
waves would have flung even her against the great rocks,
had not Hera sped her past, because Jason was her favourite.
   ' "In the other direction are two rocks, one with a sharp peak
reaching up into the broad high sky; it is enveloped in a

dark cloud that never leaves it, nor does clear air ever touch   75
its summit, either in summer or in the time of harvest.
No mortal man could ever climb to its top, still less
set foot on it, not even if he had twenty feet and hands,
because the rock is smooth, and seemingly polished.
In the middle of this cliff there is a shadowy cavern,   80
facing west towards Erebus and the dark places; past
this, splendid Odysseus, you will steer your hollow ship.
Not even a strong young man aiming his bow from
a hollow ship could shoot his arrow as far as this cave.
It is the home of Scylla, a beast with a fearful bark; her   85
howling may be no louder than that of a new-born whelp,
but she herself is an evil monster, and no one meeting her
would be glad at the sight, not even if he were a god.
She has twelve feet, all of them waving in the air,
and six enormously long necks, on each of which sits   90
a ghastly head; and in these there are three rows of teeth,
crammed in close-set ranks, packed with black death.
She is sunk waist-deep inside her hollow cavern, but
holds her heads outside this terrible abyss; and from
here she fishes, peering around the rock to see what she   95
can catch—dolphins or sharks, or perhaps some bigger
monster, such as loud-roaring Amphitrite rears in profusion.
No sailors have ever yet boasted of passing her unscathed
in their ship, for from every dark-prowed vessel she seizes
and carries off one man with each of her heads.   100
  ' "The other rock is lower, Odysseus, as you will see; the two
lie close to each other, and you could shoot an arrow across.
On it there is a huge fig tree, covered thickly with leaves,
and beneath it bright Charybdis sucks the black water down.
Three times a day she vomits it out, and three times she gulps   105
it back with a fearful noise; do not be there when she swallows,
for not even the earthshaker could then save you from ruin.
Rather, be sure to hug Scylla's rock and drive your ship
swiftly past it, since it is far better to lose six of your
companions from your ship than all of them at one blow."   110
  'So she spoke, and I answered and addressed her:
"Now, goddess, tell me truthfully: is there any way I could
somehow get clear from deadly Charybdis and sail on, and

then fight off Scylla when she tries to carry off my men?"

'So I spoke, and she, bright among goddesses, at once answered: 115
"Stubborn man! Here you are again, looking for fighting
and trouble! Will you not yield even to the immortal gods?
I tell you, Scylla is not human, but an immortal affliction,
a terrible thing, obdurate, savage, and impossible to fight.
There is no defence; flight from her is the best course.   120
If you waste time near her rock putting on your armour
I am afraid she will burst out and attack you again, and
grab men from the ship to match the number of her heads.
No; you must drive on with full power, and call on Crataïs,
Scylla's mother, who bore her to be a torment to mortals,   125
and she will then prevent her from darting out at you again.

'"Next you will come to is the isle of Thrinacia, where many
cattle and fat sheep belonging to Helios the Sun-god graze:
seven herds of cattle, and as many again of fine fleecy sheep,
with fifty head in each. No births take place in these flocks, 130
nor do any of them ever die; their shepherds are goddesses,
nymphs with beautiful hair—Phaëthusa and Lampetië,
whom bright Neaera bore to Hyperion* the Sun-god.
When their revered mother had given birth and raised them
she sent them to a new home on the far-off isle of Thrinacia   135
to watch over their father's sheep and crook-horned cattle.
If you fix your mind on home and leave them unharmed,
you may all still reach Ithaca, though after much suffering;
but if you harm them, I predict destruction for you, your ship,
and your companions. If you yourself escape, you will reach   140
your home late, in a sorry state, after losing all your men."

'So she spoke, and Dawn appeared on her golden throne.
The bright goddess departed, directing her steps inland;
and I made my way back to my ship, and ordered my
crew to get themselves on board and slip the stern-cables,   145
and without more ado they embarked and sat at their oarlocks,
and sitting in rows they struck the grey salt sea with their oars.
Then lovely-haired Circe, the awesome goddess speaking with
a mortal voice, sent us a following breeze to fill our sail, a
good friend, which blew astern of our dark-prowed ship.   150
We secured the tackle all along the ship and sat still,
and the wind and the steersman held her on course.

Only then did I address my companions, troubled at heart:
  '"Friends, it is not right that only one or two should know
the prophecies that Circe, bright among goddesses, has   155
given me; so I shall tell you, and then we shall all know,
whether we die, or escape, evading death and destruction.
The first thing she said was that we must keep clear of the
divine Sirens' song as they sit in their flowery meadow.
Only I, she said, should hear their voice; you must bind me   160
painfully tight with ropes, so that I stay immobile in place,
upright on the mast-box, with the ropes' ends lashed round
the mast. And if I entreat you and order you to release me,
you must bind me more tightly, using even more ropes."
  'So I explained everything to my companions, in detail.   165
For a while the well-built ship sailed swiftly on its way
towards the Sirens' island, sped on by the favourable breeze.
But then the wind dropped suddenly, and there followed a
still, airless calm; some divine power had hushed the waves.
My companions stood up, and lowering the sail stowed it in   170
the hollow part of the ship, and then, sitting at their oars, they
beat the water into white foam with their polished pine blades.
Meanwhile I fetched a great wheel of wax and with the sharp
bronze cut it into small pieces, which I set about kneading in
my brawny hands; and the wax quickly grew warm under my   175
great strength and the rays of the Sun-god, Hyperion's son.
With this I blocked the ears of all my crew, one after the other,
and they bound me hand and foot where I stood, upright
on the mast-box, and lashed the ropes' ends to the mast; then
they took their seats and struck the grey sea with their oars.   180
When we were as far away in our rapid course as a man's voice
carries when he shouts, the Sirens did not fail to notice our
swift ship drawing close, and they began their clear-voiced song:
"Odysseus of many tales, great glory of the Achaeans, draw near;
bring your ship into land, and listen to our twofold song!   185
No man has ever sailed past this place in his black ship without
hearing the honey-toned voice that issues from our lips, and
then, full of delight, going on his way a much wiser man.
You see, we know everything that both Trojans and Argives
endured on Troy's wide plain, by the will of the gods; and we   190
know too all that happens on the earth that nourishes many."

'So they sang, in their ravishing voices. My heart longed to
listen, and I kept signing with my eyebrows, trying to tell
my men to release me; but they bent to their oars and rowed on.
Straightaway Perimedes and Eurylochus rose to their feet and   195
set about binding me with more ropes, tying them more tightly.
Only when they had driven the ship well past the Sirens, and
we could no longer hear their voices or the words of their song,
did my trusty companions quickly remove the wax with which
I had blocked their ears, and set me free from my bonds.   200
'When we had left the island behind us, I soon saw a cloud
of spray and a heavy swell, and heard a booming noise. My
companions were terrified; the oars all flew from their hands
and fell with a splash into the water, and the ship stopped still,
since they could no longer wield the long oars to drive it on.   205
I went up and down the ship, stopping beside each of
my companions and encouraging them with gentle words:
"Friends, there are horrors ahead which we must undergo;
but what is coming our way is no worse than the time when
the Cyclops imprisoned us in his hollow cave by violent force;   210
yet we escaped even from there, by my courage, scheming, and
forethought, and I think we shall one day remember this too.
So listen now, and let us all be resolved to do as I say;
you must all take your seats at your oarlocks, and beat the
salt sea's deep surf with your oars, in the hope that Zeus will   215
somehow grant that we escape unscathed from this danger too.
My orders for you, steersman, are these, and you must store them
in your mind, since you handle the hollow ship's steering-oar:
hold the ship well away from that cloud of spray and swell,
and head for this rock, in case she veers the other way   220
without your noticing, and so you pitch us into disaster."
'So I spoke, and they without more ado obeyed my words.
I said no more about Scylla, the inescapable danger,
in case my crew should be terrified at my words and
forget to row, and huddle together in the ship's bilge.   225
But then I forgot the galling command that Circe
had given me, telling me not to arm myself in any way.
I arrayed myself in my famed armour and picked up two
long spears in my hands, and set off for the foredeck,
because from there I expected to catch my first sight of   230

rock-dwelling Scylla, who was to bring misery to my men;
but I could not see her anywhere, even though my eyes grew
weary with peering everywhere on the mist-covered rock.

'So, wailing, we sailed on through the narrow passage.
On one beam was Scylla, and on the other bright Charybdis   235
made a hideous noise as she gulped the salt water down.
Whenever she spewed it out she churned up the whole sea,
seething like a cauldron on a great fire, and the spray
was flung upwards to fall on the rocky crags on both sides;
but every time she sucked the sea's salt water back down,   240
the whole of her boiling inner gulf was revealed, and the
rock roared terribly around, exposing the seabed far below,
dark with sand; and pale terror gripped my companions.
We gazed at Charybdis, fearing destruction; and while we
looked, Scylla snatched six of my crew from the hollow   245
ship, the best of my men in the strength of their hands.
When I looked back at the swift ship and my companions,
I saw their arms and legs flailing above me, high in the air—
screaming, and in their hearts' agony calling on me by
name, though this was the last time they were to do so.   250
As a fisherman on a jutting rock with a long rod scatters
his bait to lure little fishes, and casts into the sea his
line with its horn tube,* made from a field-reared ox,
and he hooks one, pulling it gasping from the water;
so my men were lifted aloft towards the rocks, gasping,   255
and Scylla at her cave entrance gobbled them up, shrieking
and stretching out their hands to me in their dreadful agony.
This was the most pitiable sight my eyes endured, of all the
hardships I suffered while exploring the pathways of the sea.

'When we had escaped from the rocks, and from terrible   260
Charybdis and Scylla, we soon came to the god's splendid
island, where lived the fine, broad-browed cattle of Hyperion
the Sun-god, and also numerous flocks of his sturdy sheep.
Even though our black ship was still out on the open sea,
I could hear the lowing of cattle being driven to stalls   265
for the night, and the sheep's bleating; and there came into
my mind the words of the blind seer, Teiresias the Theban,
and of Circe the Aeaean, who time and again had told me to
steer clear of the island of the Sun who brings joy to mortals.

So then, troubled at heart, I addressed my companions: 270
"You have endured much, comrades, but you must listen to my
words, and I will tell you the prophecy spoken by Teiresias,
and by Circe the Aeaean, who time and again told me to
steer clear of the island of the Sun who brings joy to mortals.
Both said many times that our most terrible danger lay there.   275
So look sharp, and drive our black ship well past the island."
    'So I spoke, and their hearts were shattered within them,
and immediately Eurylochus answered me with bitter words:
"You are a hard man, Odysseus! Your energy never flags,
and your limbs never weary; you must be made all of iron,   280
if you are going to forbid men exhausted by toil and lack
of sleep to set foot on dry land, on to this sea-girt island
where we could once again make ourselves a welcome supper.
You are telling us instead to keep drifting on through the
fast-dropping night, and go wandering from this island over   285
the mist-shrouded sea. At night fierce winds, ship-wreckers,
spring up; and where could a man escape sheer destruction
if a sudden stormy squall should chance to blow up, from either
the South Wind or the evil-gusting West, which can especially
smash a ship to pieces, despite the will of our lords the gods?   290
No, I tell you—let us now give way to black night, and stay
by our swift ship and prepare ourselves a meal; and at dawn
we shall embark and launch our ship on to the broad deep."
    'So spoke Eurylochus, and the rest of my crew agreed
with him. It was then I realized some god was planning evil   295
for us, and I addressed him, speaking in winged words:
"Eurylochus, I am but one man, and you force me to it.
But listen, all of you; you must swear a mighty oath to me,
that if we chance to find a herd of cattle or a grand flock
of sheep, no one will in any way yield to fatal recklessness   300
and kill a single ox or sheep; instead you must be patient, and
content to eat the food that the immortal Circe has given us."
    'So I spoke, and they without more ado swore as I had ordered them.
When they had sworn to hold back, and ended their oath,
we anchored our well-built ship in a harbour with a curving shore,   305
with a sweet-water spring nearby; my companions went ashore
and then set about preparing our supper in their skilful way.
When they had put away their desire for eating and drinking

they called to mind their dear comrades and wept for them,
those whom Scylla had seized from the hollow ship and eaten;   310
and as they lamented sweet sleep came over them. When
it was the third part of the night, and the stars had crossed
their zenith, Zeus who gathers the clouds roused a wind
with an astonishing blast against us, and hid the earth and
sea alike in clouds; and night rushed down from the high sky.   315
But when early-born Dawn with her rosy fingers appeared
we beached our ship and then hauled her into a hollow cave,
where lovely nymphs had their dancing-floors and gatherings.
Then I called an assembly, and addressed my companions:
"My friends, since there is food and drink in our swift ship   320
let us keep clear of the cattle, in case we suffer some mishap;
these cattle and sturdy sheep are the property of an awesome
god, Helios the Sun, who observes all and hears all things."
    'So I spoke, and their proud hearts were persuaded.
But for a full month the South Wind blew ceaselessly, and   325
then the only winds that sprang up were the East and South.
For as long as my men had victuals and red wine they kept
away from the cattle, since they were eager to save their
lives; but when the ship's provisions gave out altogether,
they were compelled to range far afield in search of prey,   330
hunting with bent hooks for fish or birds, anything
that came to hand; for hunger kept tormenting their bellies.
So I went off through the island on my own, to pray to
the gods, hoping that one of them might show me my way.
When I had gone far enough in the island to avoid my men,   335
to a place sheltered from the wind, I washed my hands
and prayed to all the gods who live on Olympus; and they
then poured a sweet sleep over my eyelids. Meanwhile
Eurylochus was setting out a wicked plan before his friends:
    ' "We have suffered much, comrades, but you must listen to   340
my words. All ways of dying are hateful to wretched mortals,
but the most miserable way to meet one's doom is by hunger.
So come, let us drive off the best of the Sun-god's cattle, and
sacrifice them to the gods who dwell in the wide high sky.
Then, if we ever manage to reach Ithaca, our native land,   345
we shall before anything else build a rich temple to Hyperion
the Sun-god, and deposit many splendid offerings in it.

But if the god is angry because of his straight-horned cattle
and wishes to wreck our ship, and the other gods follow him,
then I would rather lose my life with one last gulp of sea-water   350
than have it slowly squeezed out of me on some desolate island."
　　'So spoke Eurylochus, and his companions agreed with him.
Without more ado they rounded up the best of the Sun-god's cattle;
these were nearby, for the crook-horned beasts with their broad
foreheads were grazing not far from the dark-prowed ship.   355
My men then surrounded the cattle and prayed to the gods,
and picked some fresh leaves from a high-branched oak tree,
since they had no white barley* in the well-benched ship.
When they had prayed and slaughtered the beasts and flayed
them, they cut out the thigh-bones and wrapped them in fat,   360
making a double layer, and laid raw hunks of meat on top.
Then, since they had no wine to pour over the blazing sacrifice,
they made libations with water while cooking all the entrails.
When the thigh-bones were quite burnt and they had tasted the guts,
they chopped the rest into pieces and threaded them onto skewers.   365
　　'It was at this point that sweet sleep suddenly left my eyelids,
and I set off for the swift ship and the shore of the sea.
When I had reached a place not far from the well-balanced ship,
the sweet savour of cooking meat came drifting around me;
I let out a cry of misery, and shouted aloud to the immortal gods: 370
"Father Zeus, and you other blessed gods who live for ever!
So it was to drive me into delusion that you lulled me into that
cruel sleep, while my men planned this monstrous deed back here!"
　　'Swiftly a messenger, Lampetië of the long robe, came to the
Sun-god Hyperion, with the news that we had killed his cattle.   375
Straightaway he addressed the immortals, furious in his heart:
"Father Zeus, and you other blessed gods who live for ever!
You must punish the companions of Odysseus Laertes' son,
who have wantonly killed my cattle, in whom I always
took delight whenever I climbed up to the starry high sky,   380
and every time I turned back from the sky down to the earth.
If they do not pay me a fitting recompense for these cattle,
I shall go down to Hades' realm and shine among the dead."
　　'Then in answer Zeus who gathers the clouds addressed him:
"Sun-god, of course you must continue to shine on the immortals,   385
and on mortal men who live on the grain-giving ploughland.

As for these men, I shall at once hurl a shining thunderbolt at
their swift ship, and smash it in pieces out on the wine-dark sea."

'All this I heard later from Calypso of the beautiful hair, and
she told me she herself had heard it from Hermes the guide.   390

'When I returned to the ship and to the seashore, I confronted
each of my men in turn and rebuked them at length; but we
could find no way out, because the cattle were now dead.
Very soon the gods began to reveal portents to them: the hides
began to crawl about, and the skewered meat, both cooked   395
and raw, bellowed, and a sound as of cattle lowing was heard.

'For six days after this my trusty companions feasted on
the best of the Sun-god's cattle that they had rounded up;
but when Zeus the son of Cronus brought the seventh day,
then the wind dropped its furious blowing, and we quickly   400
set about embarking and launching the ship on to the wide
deep, stepping the mast and hauling the white sail on to it.

'So we left the island and sailed on, and there was no other
land to be seen, only the high sky and the sea; and it was
now that the son of Cronus caused a black cloud to hang   405
above the hollow ship, and the sea grew dark underneath it.
The ship sped on, but not for much longer, for suddenly the
West Wind came howling on, rushing at us with a great
blast; the force of its squall snapped both forestays, the
mast toppled backwards, and the whole rig fell aft in a   410
tangled heap into the ship's bilge. The mast crashed on
to the stern and struck the steersman's head, smashing
all the bones in his skull; he plunged from the deck like
a diver, and his proud spirit departed from his bones.
At the same time Zeus thundered and hurled a bolt into   415
the ship; she shivered from stem to stern at its impact, and
was filled with the stench of sulphur. My men fell overboard
and were tossed like cormorants on the swell about the
black ship; and the god took away their homecoming.
Meanwhile I kept moving about the ship, until a wave tore   420
her sides from the keel, which, stripped of planking, was
carried along by the swell; it had snapped the mast off at
the keel, but the backstay, made of oxhide, had fallen over
it, and this I used to lash the keel and the mast together.
Sitting astride these I was borne away by deadly winds.   425

'Now the West Wind dropped its furious blasts, only for the
South Wind to spring swiftly up, bringing grief to my heart,
for it made me retrace my course to murderous Charybdis.
All night through I was swept along, until with the sun's
rising I came to the rock of Scylla and terrible Charybdis.   430
Charybdis was at this time sucking down the sea's salt water,
but I swung myself upward towards the tall fig tree, and
held firmly to it, clinging like a bat; but I could nowhere
plant my feet firmly nor climb up it, because its roots were
a long way below and its branches hung far above my head,   435
the enormous, long branches that overshadowed Charybdis.
Still, I hung on grimly, until she should spew up the mast and
keel again. I waited anxiously, and they reappeared, but later,
at the hour when a man, after judging many disputes between
litigious young men, rises from the assembly to go for his supper.   440
So long it took for the timbers to reappear from Charybdis.
I let go with my hands and feet and fell from above with a loud
splash into the middle of her pool, missing the long timbers; but
I climbed on to them and used my hands to paddle myself along.
As for Scylla, the father of men and gods did not this time let her   445
notice me; otherwise I would not have escaped sheer destruction.

'From there I was borne along for nine days, and in the tenth night
the gods brought me to the island of Ogygia, where Calypso of
the beautiful hair lives, an awesome goddess with a mortal voice,
who received me kindly and cared for me. But why go over this   450
story again? It was only yesterday that I related it to you in your
palace, to you and your excellent wife, and I have no stomach
to repeat a long story that has already been plainly told.'

BOOK THIRTEEN

So he spoke, and they all remained silent and still,
gripped through the shadowy halls by the magic of his tale.
But then Alcinous spoke up and addressed him:
'Odysseus, now that you have reached my high-roofed,
brazen-floored house, I am sure you will now return home   5
and not be blown off course, for all your great suffering.
But now I say this as a charge to each man of you here,
all you who are my council of elders, and every day drink
gleaming wine in my halls, and listen to the singer of tales.
There is clothing for our guest stored in his well-polished   10
chest, and also cunningly worked gold, and many more
gifts, brought for him by the Phaeacian counsellors.
Now, let each of us, man by man, give him a great tripod
and a cauldron; we will repay ourselves by a collection from
the people, for it is hard that one man should give without return.'   15
   So spoke Alcinous, and his words were acceptable to them all.
And so they departed to sleep, each to his own house; and
when early-born Dawn with her rosy fingers appeared, they
hurried to the ship, taking with them the welcome bronze gifts.
Alcinous, a man of divine vigour, himself went up and down the   20
ship and stowed them securely under the thwarts, so as not to
impede any of the crew as they sped the ship along with their oars.
They returned to Alcinous' house, and got ready for a feast.
   For them Alcinous, a man of divine vigour, sacrificed an ox
to Cronus' son, Zeus of the dark cloud, who rules over all.   25
When they had burnt the thighs they feasted on the rich meal
with delight; and in their midst sang the god-inspired bard,
Demodocus, a man honoured by the people. But Odysseus
kept turning his head towards the brightness of the blazing sun,
impatient for its going down, because he was eager to go home.   30
As when a man whose pair of wine-red oxen have all day been
dragging the well-jointed ploughshare over his new land longs
for his supper, and is glad to see the bright sun set, and to
return for his meal, because his knees pain him as he walks,
so Odysseus was then glad to see the setting of the bright sun.   35

At once he addressed the Phaeacians who delight in their oars,
but directed the words of his speech especially at Alcinous:
'Lord Alcinous, distinguished among all peoples, make your
drink-offerings and then send me safely on my way; and fare
well to you all! All that my heart desired has been fulfilled—   40
an escort home, and welcome gifts, which I hope the sky-gods will
turn into good fortune for me. When I return, may I find a wife
without reproach in my house, and my loved ones safe and sound.
As for you, may you continue to live here, bringing comfort to
your wedded wives and your children; may the gods grant you   45
every kind of success, and may no misfortune befall your people!'
    So he spoke, and they all approved, and said that their guest
should be sent on his way, for his words were right and proper.
Then Alcinous, a man of vigour, addressed his herald:
'Pontonous, mix us a bowl of wine and hand it to everyone   50
in the hall, so that after making a prayer to father Zeus
we may send our guest on his way to his own native land.'
    So he spoke, and Pontonous mixed the mind-cheering wine,
and served it to everyone, standing by each man in turn, and
they, from where they were sitting, made drink-offerings to the   55
blessed gods who dwell in the broad high sky. But glorious
Odysseus rose to his feet and placed his two-handled cup in
Arete's hands, and spoke up, addressing her in winged words:
'I bid you farewell, O queen, for all time, until old age and
death, which must come to all mankind, visit you. My course   60
lies away from here; may you continue to take pleasure in your
house here, your children, your people, and in King Alcinous.'
    So spoke glorious Odysseus, and stepped over the threshold.
Alcinous, a man of vigour, sent a herald to accompany him,
to show him the way to the swift ship and the sea-shore,   65
and Arete sent some of her serving women to go with them:
one was carrying a freshly washed cloak and a tunic,
and another she sent with them to carry the strong chest,
while a third servant brought food and red wine.
When they had come down to the ship and the sea, the   70
lordly escort crew took charge of the gifts and stowed
them in the hollow ship, and also all the food and drink;
while for Odysseus they spread a coverlet and a linen sheet
on the stern deck of the hollow ship, so that he might enjoy

undisturbed sleep. Then he himself embarked and lay down   75
in silence, and the crew took their seats in order, each at his
oarlock, and untied the stern-cable from its pierced stone.
Leaning into their task they flung the salt sea up with their
blades, while on Odysseus' eyes there gradually fell sweet
sleep, a welcome sleep with no waking, very like death.   80

Now the ship, like a four-horse team of stallions on the plain
who start off all at the same time at the touch of the whip,
and leaping up and forward swiftly travel on their way,
so the ship's stern kept pitching up and down, and left a great
dark wave in her wake in the seething, loud-roaring sea.   85
So she sped on, keeping steadfastly to her course. Not even
a wheeling falcon, swiftest of winged creatures, could have
kept pace with her, as, lightly running, she cut the swell
of the sea, carrying a man equal to the gods in cleverness,
who in time past had endured so much pain in his heart,   90
fighting his way through wars of men and implacable seas,
but now at last was sleeping peacefully, forgetful of all his trials.

At the hour when that most brilliant star* rose high, the one
whose coming more than others heralds the light of early-born
Dawn, then the sea-traversing ship drew near to the island.   95

There is in the land of Ithaca a harbour, named for Phorcys,
Old Man of the Sea. It has two sheer promontories that jut
into the sea, and slant down towards the harbour, keeping
the huge waves roused by stormy winds outside from
breaking in. Inside, well-benched ships may ride without   100
cables when they have come within mooring distance of
the shore. At the harbour's head there is a long-leafed olive
tree, and hard by it is a charming cavern, full of shadows,
a place sacred to the nymphs who are called spring-dwellers.
Inside the cave there are bowls, and two-handled stone jars,   105
and there too it is the custom of bees to store their honey.
In it too there are huge looms of stone where the nymphs
weave their sea-purple stuff, a wonder to look upon; and
through it water flows constantly. It has two openings,
one facing north, by which any man may climb down,   110
while the other, facing south, is used only by gods, and
no man may go in by this, for it is the immortals' way.

Here the Phaeacians put in, knowing about it from former

visits. Their ship, with a burst of speed, ran ashore up to
half its length, so strongly did the rowers' arms drive it on.   115
They disembarked from the well-benched vessel on to dry
land, and their first act was to lift Odysseus from the hollow
ship, and lay him, still wrapped in his linen sheet and shining
coverlet and still overcome by sleep, down on the sandy shore.
Then they lifted out the treasure that the lordly Phaeacians   120
had given him, at the prompting of great-hearted Athena, as
he set out for home. This they piled up beside the olive tree's
trunk, clear of the path, so that no chance passer-by should
stumble on it and make off with it before Odysseus woke.
Then they set off again for home; but the earthshaker was not   125
minded to forget the threats he had made at the start against
godlike Odysseus; and so he asked Zeus to explain his plans:
   'Father Zeus, it seems that I will no more enjoy the immortal
gods' respect, now that mortals do not hold me in esteem—
I mean these Phaeacians, even though they are of my own blood.   130
I have always said that Odysseus would reach home only after
great suffering, but I never robbed him altogether of his return,
once you had promised this and nodded your assent to it.
But now the Phaeacians have conveyed him over the deep in
their swift ship, and have landed him, asleep, on Ithaca. And   135
they have given him gifts beyond telling, bronze and much gold
and woven clothing, far more than he would ever have won from
Troy as his share of the booty, if he had returned without mishap.'
   Then in answer Zeus who gathers the clouds addressed him:
'Come now, earthshaker of wide power—what a thing to say!   140
In no way do the gods refuse you respect; it would be a serious
matter for them to fling insults at the most revered and best among us.
But if any man, giving way to his strength and power, were to
disrespect you, it is your right to punish him, now or later.
So now do just as you please, and as your heart prompts you.'   145
   Then in answer Poseidon who shakes the earth addressed him:
'Lord of the dark cloud, I shall at once do as you say, though
as always I stand in awe of your anger and hope to avoid it.
This time, however, it is my wish to wreck the Phaeacians'
splendid ship as it returns from its mission over the misty deep,   150
so that they may now hold back, and stop giving men an escort.
I mean to hide their city behind a huge encircling mountain.'

Then in answer Zeus who gathers the clouds addressed him:
'My dear brother, this seems in my heart to be the best plan:
when all the people are looking out from their city and see 155
the ship speeding past, turn her into a rock that looks like a
swift ship, lying close offshore, so that all men may marvel at it.
Then hide their city behind a huge encircling mountain.'
    When Poseidon, shaker of the earth, heard these words,
he set off and came to Scheria, where the Phaeacians live, 160
and waited there. The seagoing ship, speeding lightly along,
drew near the shore, and the earthshaker came close to her
and with a blow from the flat of his hand struck and turned her
to stone, rooting her to the seabed. By then he was far away.
    At this the Phaeacians, men of the long oar and famed for their 165
seamanship, began to speak to each other with winged words,
and this is what one of them would say, looking at his neighbour:
'Disaster! Who can have tied our swift ship down out at sea as
she was speeding home? She had only just come fully into view.'
    That is what they said, but they did not know what had happened. 170
But Alcinous spoke out among them and addressed them:
'Ah—my father's ancient prophecy* has now come home to me!
He always said that Poseidon would bear a grudge against us
because we offer safe conduct to all men and yet come to no harm.
One day, he said, Poseidon will wreck a splendid ship of the 175
Phaeacians as it returns from escort duty on the misty deep,
and will hide our city behind a huge encircling mountain.
That is what the old man said, and now it has all been fulfilled.
So listen to me, and let us all be resolved to do what I say:
you must give up pledging an escort to any mortal who happens 180
to come to our city; and as for Poseidon, let us sacrifice to him
twelve specially chosen bulls, in the hope that he will pity us,
and will not hide our city behind a huge encircling mountain.'
    So he spoke, and they were afraid, and made the bulls ready.
And so they began their prayer to lord Poseidon, the leaders 185
and chieftains of the Phaeacian people, standing around his
altar. Meanwhile glorious Odysseus woke from sleep; he was
now in his own land, though he did not realize where he was,
having been away for so long. The goddess Pallas Athena,
Zeus' daughter, had poured a mist everywhere, meaning to 190
make him unrecognizable, and then explain everything to him

exactly, so that his wife and citizens and friends should not
know him, until the suitors had paid for all their wild excesses.
And so to lord Odysseus everything appeared unfamiliar:
the long, winding footpaths, the harbours that gave good   195
anchorage, the steep sheer cliffs, and the tall sturdy trees.
He leapt up and stood there; and as he gazed at his ancestral
land he let out a groan, and beat both thighs with the flat
of his hands, and cried out in a voice full of lamentation:
'What shall I do? What mortals' land have I reached this time?   200
Are they violent and uncivilized, and given to wrongdoing, or
are they hospitable, and there is in them a god-fearing disposition?
Where should I hide all this treasure? And which direction should
I myself set off in? How I wish I had stayed where I was, with
the Phaeacians! I could have continued my travels on to some   205
other mighty king, who would have welcomed me and sent me
on my way. Now I do not know where to store these goods; I
cannot leave them here, in case they fall into the hands of others.
I see it now: those Phaeacian rulers and chieftains were not, after
all, completely fair in their thinking and dealing! They said   210
they would convey me to clear-seen Ithaca, but now they have
landed me in some other country; they have not kept their word.
May Zeus, protector of suppliants, punish them—Zeus who
sees all men's dealings and chastises those who do wrong.
Still, let me now inspect this treasure and count it up, in case   215
they took something of mine when they left in their hollow ship.'
   So he spoke, and set about making a tally of his fine tripods,
his cauldrons, his gold, and his beautiful woven fabrics; and
there was nothing missing. So, weeping for his homeland,
he went limping along the shore of the loud-roaring sea,   220
with many a groan; but now Athena approached him, likening
herself in form to a young man, a herdsman of sheep,
delicately nurtured in the way that the sons of kings are,
with a finely woven cloak over her shoulders, folded double;
on her shining feet she wore sandals, and in her hands was a   225
spear. Odysseus was overjoyed at the sight, and went to
meet her, and spoke, addressing her in winged words:
'Friend, you are the first person I have met in this place!
Greetings! I hope you do not meet me with mischief in mind;
please leave these goods unharmed, and do not harm me. I pray   230

to you as to a god, and come to your knees as a suppliant.
So tell me this truly, so that I may have clear knowledge:
What land is this? What country? And what men live here?
Is this one of those clear-seen islands, or is this coast
that slants to the sea part of the rich-soiled mainland?'   235

Then in answer the goddess grey-eyed Athena spoke to him:
'You are a fool, stranger, or you come from very far away,
if you ask me about this country. It is not wholly without
repute, and is known in fact to a great number of people,
both those who live towards dawn and the sun's rising   240
and those dwelling the other way, towards the darkling west.
It is a rough land, to be sure, and not fit for driving horses,
but not over-poor, even though it has no great breadth.
Corn grows here in abundance, and there is wine as well,
for the rain is constant, and so too is the nourishing dew.   245
It has good grazing for goats and oxen; and there is woodland
of all kinds here, and watering-places that never fail. For this
reason, stranger, the name of Ithaca has reached even to Troy,
though people say that city lies far from the land of Achaea.'*

So she spoke, and much-enduring glorious Odysseus   250
was glad, delighted that Pallas Athena, daughter of Zeus
who wields the aegis, had told him it was his ancestral land.
Speaking with winged words he addressed her; but
he held his story back and left the truth unsaid, being
always ready to put the cunning mind in his breast to use: 255
'I often heard of Ithaca, even in spacious Crete,* far across
the sea; and now I have come here myself, bringing these
goods that you see. I left as much again there for my sons.
I am an exile, you see, having killed the son of Idomeneus*—
Orchilochus of the swift feet—who surpassed all grain-   260
eating men in spacious Crete in the speed of his feet;
he had wanted to rob me of all the booty that I brought
from Troy, for which my heart endured many hardships,
fighting my way through wars of men and implacable seas—
all because I would not oblige his father, nor serve him   265
in the land of Troy, preferring to command my own men.
So, with a friend, I lay in wait by the road and struck him
down with a bronze-tipped spear as he came back from the
fields. A night of deep blackness had obscured the sky;

not a man saw us, and I was able to take his life undetected. 270
But then, when I had killed him with the sharp bronze, I
made straight for a ship belonging to some lordly men of
Phoenicia and appealed to them; I gave them plenty of my
booty, and begged them to take me to Pylos and land me there,
or to the splendid land of Elis where the Epeians hold power. 275
But when we left Crete violent winds forced them off course,
much against their purpose, for they did not wish to cheat me.
After this we sailed aimlessly and reached this place at night,
and rowed as hard as we could into this harbour. No one had
any thought for supper, though we were in sore need of it, 280
but we went ashore and everyone lay down where they were.
I was exhausted, and was soon overcome by sweet sleep,
while the others fetched my goods from the hollow ship
and laid them out where I was sleeping on the sandy shore.
Then they went back on board and set off for Sidon,* that well- 285
established city, and I, troubled in my heart, was left here.'
  So he spoke, and the goddess grey-eyed Athena smiled,
and stroked him with her hand. In appearance she was now
like a tall, beautiful woman, skilled in exquisite crafts;
and she addressed him in winged words: 'It would take 290
a very quick-witted man, one full of cunning, to outwit you
in any kind of trickery, even if it was a god up against you.
You are a stubborn man, crafty and full of guile! Clearly you
are not prepared, even in your own country, to give up those
lying, thievish tales that you love from the bottom of your heart. 295
Come now, let us not talk like this any longer, since we are both
well versed in deception: among mortals you surpass all men in
plotting and tale-spinning, while among all the gods I am well
known for cleverness and cunning. But you did not recognize
Pallas Athena, daughter of Zeus, I who have always stood 300
by you in all your trials and have watched over you;* it was
I who made sure you were welcomed by all the Phaeacians,
and now I am here again, minded to weave some scheme
with you, and to hide the great treasure presented to you by
the lordly Phaeacians on your way home—planned and devised 305
by me—and to explain to you all the troubles you are fated to
endure in your well-constructed palace. Bear them, as indeed
you must, and do not tell anyone, either man or woman, that

you are back from your wanderings; you must suffer many
miseries in silence, and patiently bear the violence of men.'   310

Then in answer Odysseus of many wiles addressed her:
'It is hard, goddess, for a mortal to know when he meets you,
even a very clever one, for you can take on anyone's likeness.
But this I do know well, that you looked kindly on me once,
when we sons of the Achaeans were fighting around Troy.   315
Yet after we sacked the steep city of Priam and embarked
in our ships, and some god scattered the Achaeans, I never
saw you then, daughter of Zeus, nor did I ever notice you
boarding my ship to protect me from disaster. No—
off I went on my wanderings, the heart in my breast for   320
ever torn in two, until the gods released me from my troubles;
and then at last, in the rich land of the Phaeacians, you spoke
encouragingly to me and yourself conducted me to their city.
So now I entreat you, by your father—since I do not believe I
am really here in clear-seen Ithaca, but have drifted off course   325
to some other land; and I think you have told me this tale
by way of provoking me, meaning to lead my wits astray—
tell me if it is true I have come to my dear ancestral land.'

Then in answer the goddess grey-eyed Athena said to him:
'This is always the way that the mind within you works!   330
And that is why I cannot abandon you in your unhappy state,
because you are so shrewd, sagacious, and firm of purpose.
Any other man returning from his wanderings would have been
overjoyed, anxious to set eyes on his wife and children at home;
but it does not yet suit you to question and find things out,   335
until you have made trial of your wife; yet she, as always,
simply sits in her halls, shedding tears, and as they come
and pass away her nights and days are full of misery.
I myself never doubted it, but knew well in my heart, that
you would come home, after losing all your companions;   340
but you must know that I was unwilling to fight with Poseidon,
my father's own brother, who has stored up rancour in his heart
against you, angry because you took away his dear son's sight.

'But look; I will show you this land of Ithaca, and then you will
believe me. This is the harbour of Phorcys, Old Man of the Sea,   345
and here at the harbour's head is the long-leafed olive tree,
and hard by it the charming cave that is full of shadows,

a place sacred to the nymphs who are called spring-dwellers.
Here, you see, is that spacious, arch-roofed cave, where it was
your custom to sacrifice many perfect hecatombs to the nymphs.　　350
And over there is the mountain Neriton, clothed in forests.'
　　So the goddess spoke, and dispersed the mist, and the land showed
clear. Now at last glorious, much-enduring Odysseus was gladdened,
overjoyed to be in his own country, and kissed the grain-giving earth.
At once he lifted up his hands and made a prayer to the nymphs:　　355
'Spring-dwelling nymphs, daughters of Zeus, never did I expect
to set eyes on you again! Now receive my greeting, made in
these courteous prayers. Later I will give you gifts, as I did in
time past, if only Zeus' daughter, war-host leader, graciously
allows me to survive, and my dear son to grow to manhood.'　　360
　　Then in answer the goddess grey-eyed Athena addressed him:
'Take courage, and do not let these things trouble your heart.
Now, before anything else, let us store these goods deep inside
this marvellous cavern, where they may remain safe for you.
Then let us consider how things may be ordered for the best.'　　365
　　So the goddess spoke, and stepped down into the shadowy cave,
looking all around for hiding-places. Meanwhile Odysseus
set about bringing everything in: the gold, the tireless bronze,
and the well-made clothing that the Phaeacians had given him.
All these he stored carefully away, and Pallas Athena, daughter　　370
of Zeus who wields the aegis, set a stone in the doorway.
　　So these two sat against the trunk of the sacred olive tree,
and plotted destruction to come for the arrogant suitors.
The first to speak was the goddess grey-eyed Athena:
'Son of Laertes, sprung from Zeus, Odysseus of many wiles,　　375
think now how you may lay hands on those shameless suitors,
who for three years now have been lording it in your hall,
courting your godlike wife and bringing her marriage-gifts.
Yet she, troubled at heart, longs for your homecoming; she
holds out hope to them all, making promises to each man and　　380
sending them messages; but her mind's intent is quite different.'
　　Then in answer Odysseus, man of many wiles, addressed her:
'Well! I would indeed most likely have been killed in my halls,
meeting the same dreadful destiny as Atreus' son Agamemnon,
if you, goddess, had not explained everything exactly to me.　　385
So now, weave me a scheme to revenge myself on the suitors, and

stand beside me in person, filling me with the spirit of daring,
as once you did when we tore down Troy's shining headdress.*
If, grey-eyed one, you were to stand by me in all your fury as
you did before, then with your help I could take on even three   390
hundred men—if, revered goddess, you support me unstintingly.'
    Then in answer the goddess grey-eyed Athena addressed him:
'I shall indeed be always at your side, and you will not be far
from my mind when we take on this task; and I reckon
that many of those suitors who are eating up your livelihood   395
will spatter your wide floor with their blood and brains.
Now attend: I am going to make you unrecognizable to all men.
I shall shrivel up the handsome flesh on your supple limbs,
and spoil the fair hair on your head; I shall clothe you in the
kind of rags that will disgust any man who sees them on you,   400
and cloud those eyes of yours that were so brilliant before,
so that you will appear shamefully ugly before the suitors,
and before the wife and son you left behind in your halls.
But first of all, you must go out to meet the swineherd
who looks after your pigs, and is as ever loyal towards you,   405
and is devoted to your son and to faithful Penelope.
You will find this man looking after his pigs where they
feed near the rock of Corax, over by Arethusa's spring,
rootling among their favourite acorns and drinking from dark
pools, for both of these help pigs' fat to grow to richness.   410
Stop there, sit down with him, and ask him about everything,
while, Odysseus, I go off to Sparta, home of lovely women, to
summon your beloved son Telemachus; you must know that he
left here to visit Menelaus in Lacedaemon of the wide dancing-
places, hoping to learn news of you, if you were still alive.'   415
    Then in answer Odysseus of many wiles addressed her:
'Why then did you not tell him, you who know everything?
Doubtless it was so that he too should suffer hardship, wandering
over the restless sea, while other men devoured his livelihood.'
    Then the goddess grey-eyed Athena answered him: 420
'Do not let your heart be greatly troubled about him. I myself
was his guide, for I intended he should win noble fame by
his going there; he has encountered no hindrance, but is sitting
at his ease in the palace of Atreus' son, surrounded by plenty.
It is true that young men are lying in wait for him in their black   425

ship, determined to kill him before he reaches his homeland,
but I do not think they will succeed; sooner the earth will close
over many of those suitors who now devour your livelihood.'
  So spoke Athena, and touched him with her rod.
She shrivelled up the handsome flesh on his supple   430
limbs and spoiled the fair hair on his head; over his
entire body she gave him the skin of an ancient, old man,
and clouded his eyes that were so brilliant before, and
clothed him in different garments: a tattered cloak and
tunic, all torn and filthy, besmirched with grimy smoke.   435
Over these she gave him the great, hairless hide of a swift deer
to wear, and handed him a staff and shabby satchel,
full of holes, with a twisted cord as its shoulder-strap.
So these two made their plans and then parted, and Athena
went off to bright Lacedaemon, to fetch Odysseus' son.   440

BOOK FOURTEEN

Meanwhile Odysseus left the harbour and took a rough track
through woods up towards high ground, where Athena had
told him the excellent swineherd would be, who more than
any in Odysseus' household took good care of his property.
    And he found him sitting in front of his hut, where a high-   5
walled enclosure had been built, visible from all sides; a fine,
large yard, with a cleared space round it. The swineherd
had built this yard himself, for the pigs of his absent master,
without the help of his mistress and aged Laertes, with huge
quarried stones, and had capped it with a hedge of wild pear.   10
Outside, running the length and breadth of the yard, he had
driven a stockade of many close-set oaken stakes whose
dark bark he had stripped away. Inside the yard he had built
twelve sties, set close to each other, to be beds for the pigs,
and in each one fifty earth-wallowing swine were penned,   15
sows which had produced litters. The hogs slept outside;
far fewer of them, because the godlike suitors kept eating them
and so reduced their number, since the swineherd would
regularly send them the very best of his carefully nurtured
pigs; and there were in all three hundred and sixty of these.   20
Hard by them dogs like wild beasts kept constant night-watch,
four of them, reared by the swineherd, captain of men.
He himself was engaged in making sandals to fit his feet,
cutting them from a piece of good oxhide, and his men had
gone out in different directions with the droves of swine;   25
there were three of these, and the fourth he had already sent to
the city, being forced by the arrogant suitors to take them
a hog for them to slaughter and satisfy their desire for meat.
    Suddenly the harsh-baying dogs caught sight of Odysseus,
and rushed at him, barking; but Odysseus, crafty man, sat   30
down on the ground and let the staff drop from his hand.
There, in his own farm, he would have suffered a shameful
mauling, had not the swineherd dropped the hide and dashed
on swift feet through the yard gate, chasing the dogs away.
Shouting angrily at them, he drove them off this way and that   35

with a shower of stones; and then he addressed his lord:
'Old man, my dogs were quickly upon you, and came close to
tearing you apart; so you would have poured shame over me—
to add to all the other pain and grief the gods have sent me.
Here I sit, lamenting and grieving for my godlike master,   40
feeding up his fat swine only for other men to devour, while
he, probably without enough to eat, is wandering in some land
or city of men who speak an alien tongue—if, that is, he is
still alive somewhere and looks on the light of the sun.
But follow me, old man. Let us go into my hut, and there with   45
me you may satisfy your desire for food and wine, and tell
me where you are from, and what troubles you have endured.'
   So the good swineherd spoke, and led Odysseus towards his hut.
After showing him in, he heaped up some brushwood, and laid
on top the fleece of a shaggy wild goat, and invited him to sit;   50
the fleece was huge and thick, and he used to sleep on it himself.
Odysseus was delighted with the welcome, and spoke directly to him:
'May Zeus and all the other immortal gods grant you whatever
you most desire, for welcoming me in such a hospitable way!'
   Then in answer you addressed him, swineherd Eumaeus:*   55
'Stranger, it is not right for me to treat a guest dishonourably,
not even one in a worse state than you; all strangers and
beggars are under the protection of Zeus. What I can offer is
small, but you are welcome to it. Such, you see, is the way of
servants who live in fear of their masters—I mean when they   60
are new. As for my old master, the gods have surely thwarted his
homecoming; he would have treated me properly and given me
possessions, the kind of things a generous lord gives to his
servant—a house, a plot of land, and a much-courted wife—
a servant who works hard for him and a god makes his labour   65
prosper, just as the labour that I spend my time on here prospers.
That is why my lord would have rewarded me richly, if he had
grown old here; but he is dead—and I wish Helen's clan too had
perished utterly, for she has weakened the knees of many men.
You see, my lord was one who went to Troy of the fine horses   70
to do battle with the Trojans, all to bring glory to Agamemnon.'
   So he spoke, and quickly hitched up the tunic under his belt and
set off for the pigsties where his stock of young pigs were penned.
From them he chose two, brought them back and slaughtered both,

singed them, then diced the meat and threaded it on skewers.   75
When he had cooked it all he fetched and set it before Odysseus,
still hot, skewers and all, and sprinkled white barley-meal on top.
In an ivy-patterned bowl he mixed some honey-sweet wine,
and took his seat opposite Odysseus and spoke, urging him on:
    'Eat now, stranger. This is the kind of food that servants have   80
to eat, piglet's meat; the fattened swine are devoured by suitors,
who have no thought for the gods' vengeance, nor any pity.
Yet the blessed gods have no love at all for acts of cruelty,
but hold justice in respect, and the righteous deeds of men.
Even men beyond the pale, who invade other men's land and   85
bring conflict into it, and Zeus awards them plunder, and they
fill their ships full and set sail for home—even on the minds
of these there descends a strong fear of the gods' vengeance.
These suitors, believe me, know something; they have heard
some god-sent rumour of that man's wretched death, so have   90
no mind to do their courting fairly, or return to their homes, but
at their ease they arrogantly devour his property, sparing nothing.
As many as are the days and nights that come from Zeus,
on each one they slaughter not one animal, nor stop at two;
and they insolently draw off his wine-stock, and squander it.   95
I tell you, his property used to be beyond telling; no hero ever
possessed as much, either on the black-soiled mainland or
on Ithaca itself. Not even the wealth of twenty men, added
all together, would amount to his. I will list it for you:
on the mainland, twelve cattle herds, and as many flocks of   100
sheep; the same number of swine-droves, and as many ranging
herds of goats, all tended by hireling herdsmen and by his own.
Here on Ithaca wide-ranging herds of goats, eleven in all,
graze on marginal lands, and trusty men watch over them.
Each of these, every day, drives a beast in for the suitors,   105
the one that is obviously the best of his well-nourished goats;
and I tend and stand guard over these swine here, and take
care to choose the best of them and send it in to the suitors.'
    While he spoke Odysseus eagerly ate his meat and drank his
wine, hastily and in silence, while sowing seeds of ruin for the   110
suitors. When he had finished supper and satisfied his hunger,
he filled the cup from which he had been drinking and handed it,
full of wine, to Eumaeus, who took it, rejoicing in his heart.

Odysseus then addressed him, speaking with winged words:
'My friend, who was the man who used his riches to buy you,   115
the one you say was so outstandingly wealthy and powerful?
You say he met his end for the sake of Agamemnon's glory; so
tell me who he was, in case I recognize him from your account.
Zeus knows, I imagine, and the other immortal gods, if I have
seen him and can give you news; I have certainly roved far afield.'   120
    Then in answer the swineherd, captain of men, said:
'Old man, no one who comes here on his travels with
news of that man is going to convince his wife and son.
Vagrants looking for a meal waste our time, telling us
nothing but lies, and have no interest in relating a true story.   125
Every wandering beggar who comes to the land of Ithaca
makes straight for my mistress and babbles a pack of lies;
and she receives him kindly and questions him in detail,
while the tears fall from her grief-stricken eyes, as is the
way with a woman whose husband has died in a far-off land.   130
You too, old fellow, might easily invent some lying tale,
if someone were to give you a cloak and a tunic to wear.
As for him, swift dogs and vultures are already about him,
tearing the skin from his bones, and his spirit has left him;
or else fishes out in the sea have eaten him, and his bones   135
lie on the shore, with the sand heaped high over him.
So has he perished far away, a source of sorrow to come
for his dear ones, but especially for me; never shall I find
another lord as gentle as he was, wherever I may go, not
even if I were to go back to the house of my father and   140
mother, the house where I was born and where they raised
me. I do not grieve deeply for them, even though I yearn
to be in my own land and to set eyes on them, as much as
I am gripped by a yearning for Odysseus, so long gone.
Even though he is not here, stranger, I am reluctant to   145
name him, for he loved me dearly and cared for me
in his heart; though he is far away, I still call him my dear lord.'
    Then in turn much-enduring glorious Odysseus addressed him:
'My friend, clearly you will not listen, thinking that man will
never come back; your heart must ever be full of disbelief.   150
And yet I am about to tell you, not just in words but on oath,
that Odysseus is on his way home. And this will be my reward

for the good news: that as soon as he returns and enters his
house you must give me fine clothes to wear, a tunic and cloak;
until that happens I shall accept nothing, reduced to beggary   155
as I am. For just as I hate the gates of Hades so I hate the man
who is driven by poverty to spout deceitful lies.
May my witness be Zeus, before other gods, and this hospitable
table, and excellent Odysseus' hearth, to which I have come,
that all these things will surely come to pass as I declare.   160
Before this very year reaches its close, Odysseus will be here;
yes, even as this month wastes away and the next sets in
he will return to his home, and will there take vengeance on
all those who treat his wife and splendid son with contempt.'

     Then in answer you addressed him, swineherd Eumaeus: 165
'Old man, neither will I pay you that reward for your good news
nor will Odysseus ever come home. Come now, drink your wine
at your ease, and let us turn our minds to other things. Do not
remind me of my troubles, for the heart in my breast is deeply
grieved whenever someone calls my considerate lord to mind.   170
As for your oath, let us put it from our minds; and yet, may
Odysseus come back, even as I wish, and Penelope wishes,
and aged Laertes, and Telemachus who looks like a god.
And that is another grief that will not leave me—Telemachus,
the son whom Odysseus sired. The gods made him spring up   175
like a young tree, and I thought he would be of no less account
than his father among men, admired for form as well as beauty;
but some immortal has wrecked the balanced wits in him, or
else it was some man. He has gone off in search of news of his
father, to sacred Pylos, and the lordly suitors are lying in wait   180
for him as he returns home, intending that godlike Arceisius'
clan* shall be wiped out on Ithaca and leave not a name behind.
Well, let us think no more about him, whether he will be taken
or perhaps escape and the hand of Cronus' son will shelter him.
But come now, aged man, and tell me about your own troubles: 185
and give me a true account, so that I may know all about them.
Who among men are you, and where are you from? Where are
your city and parents? What kind of ship did you come in? How
did sailors bring you to Ithaca? What men do they claim to be?
I do not suppose for a moment that you arrived here on foot.'   190

     Then in answer Odysseus of many wiles addressed him:

'Very well, I will give you a true account of all you ask.
I only wish we two now had an endless store of food and
sweet wine here in your hut, so that we could feast without
disturbance while other people carried on with the work!   195
If we did I could easily use up a whole year in telling the
troubles in my heart, and still not reach the end of them—
the full story of all I have endured through the gods' will.

   'I am proud to say that my family is from spacious Crete.
I am the son of a wealthy father, and he had many other   200
sons, conceived and raised in his halls, all born to his wife
in wedlock, whereas my mother was a bought concubine;
even so, he honoured me as much as his true-born sons.
He was Castor, Hylax' son, and I proudly claim his family
as mine. In those days he was honoured among the Cretans   205
as a god, for his good fortune and riches, and for his famous
sons. But all too soon grim death came and carried him off
to the house of Hades; his arrogant sons divided up Castor's
property, and cast lots for the portions they would have.
To me they assigned a very meagre inheritance and a house,   210
yet I got for myself a wife from a rich landowning family—
because of my manly prowess, as well as being no fool;
nor was I one to avoid a fight. Now all this has vanished—
though I fancy that by looking at the stubble you may judge
the corn's quality. Since then I have had misery in abundance.   215
Back then, though, Ares and Athena gave me daring in plenty,
and strength to break the battle-line; and when I picked the
best men for an ambush, sowing ruin's seed for my enemies,
my proud heart never feared the coming of death, but I would
spring out far in front of my men and with my spear kill   220
any opponent who could not outrun me in speed of foot.
That is what I was like in war. Farm-work never appealed
to me, nor running a household, though that is indeed the nurse
of fine children; but always my delight was in oar-driven
ships, and wars, and well-polished javelins and arrows—   225
terrible things, such as always bring a shudder to other men.
Still, I imagine these favoured pursuits were put into my
heart by a god; different men take pleasure in different things.
Before the sons of the Achaeans set foot on the land of Troy
I had nine times commanded men and swift-sailing ships   230

against men of other lands, and much treasure fell to me;
from this I chose for myself what pleased me, and much more
later came to me by lot. Very soon my household grew larger,
and from this time I was both feared and respected among the
Cretans. But when far-thundering Zeus planned that terrible   235
expedition, which weakened the knees of so many men,
then the Cretans kept urging me and far-famed Idomeneus
to take our ships to Ilium, and we had no means of refusing
them; the harsh voice of the people held us in its power.
So then for nine years we sons of the Achaeans fought there,   240
and in the tenth we sacked the city of Priam and made our way
home in our ships; but some god scattered the Achaean fleet.
For me, hapless man, Zeus the counsellor planned more trouble:
for a month, no longer, I enjoyed the company of my
children, my wedded wife, and my possessions, and then   245
my spirit urged me to make a foray by sea into Egypt; and so
I fitted out some ships, taking godlike companions with me.
Nine ships I equipped, and very soon crews were mustered.
For six days my trusty companions enjoyed their feasting;
I had made a present of many sacrificial beasts for them to   250
offer as victims to the gods, and to make a feast for themselves.
On the seventh day we embarked and left spacious Crete behind,
sailing along easily, with a fine steady North Wind astern; it was
 as if we were being borne along by a current. Not one of my
ships ran into any difficulty; we just sat there, secure and   255
untroubled, and always the wind and the steersmen guided us.
On the fifth day we reached Egypt, land of abundant water,
and anchored our well-balanced ships in the river Nile.
Then I gave my trusty companions strict orders to stay
where they were beside the ships and stand guard over them,   260
and detailed others to go and scout things out from high ground.
But my men yielded to arrogance, following their strong desire,
and straightaway began to ravage the fertile farmland of the
Egyptians and to carry off their women and infant children; and
they killed the men. Before long the clamour reached the city,   265
and its inhabitants, hearing the shouting, came at us just as dawn
broke. The whole plain was filled with foot-soldiers and chariots,
and with the flashing gleam of bronze. Thunder-delighting Zeus
flung evil panic among my companions, and no one had the nerve

to withstand this onslaught, for disaster stood all around them.   270
There they killed many of us with the sharp bronze, and carried
off others up-country, alive, to labour for them under duress.
As for me, Zeus himself put a scheme into my mind, as I shall
tell—but I wish I had died and met my doom there and then
in Egypt, for there was still suffering waiting in store for me!   275
At once I took the well-made helmet from my head, cast the
shield from my shoulder, and dropped the spear from my hand,
and made straight for their king and faced him on his chariot,
and kissed his knees. He showed pity and protected me, and
seating me in his chariot bore me away, weeping, to his palace.   280
To be sure, many of his men came rushing at me with ash spears,
desperate to kill me, for they were enraged beyond measure,
but he kept them off, having due regard for the anger of Zeus
the strangers' god, who is especially indignant at acts of savagery.
For seven years I stayed there, amassing huge amounts of treasure   285
among the Egyptians, for every one of them gave me gifts.
But when the eighth year in its circling course came round to me,
that was when a man of Phoenicia arrived, a practised liar and
a trickster, someone who had caused much mischief among men.
He won me over with his cunning talk, and so I went with him   290
to Phoenicia, where his house and his merchandise were.
I stayed there with him until one year had run its full course;
but when the days and months had completed their term, as
the year circled back and the seasons came round, he put me on
board a sea-traversing vessel bound for Libya; he had made me   295
a lying proposal—that I should join him in shipping a cargo—but
really so that he could sell me there and make an enormous profit.
Though suspicious, I embarked with him, since I had no choice.
The ship was speeding along before a fine steady North Wind,
in the open sea beyond Crete, when Zeus planned to wreck them.   300
We had left Crete astern, and there was no land at all to be seen,
nothing but sky and sea; and it was at this point that the son of
Cronus caused a dark cloud to hang above our hollow ship,
and the open sea beneath it was shrouded in blackness.
Zeus thundered, and at the same time hurled a bolt into the   305
ship; she shivered from stem to stern at the impact, and was
filled with the stench of sulphur; and everyone was thrown
overboard. Like cormorants they floated on the swell around

the black ship, and a god took away their homecoming. As
for me, though my heart was full of distress, Zeus himself   310
put into my hands the stout mast of this dark-prowed ship,
intending that I should escape further torment. I wrapped my
arms around it and was swept along, blown by cruel winds.
For nine days I was tossed about, and on the tenth black night
a huge rolling wave set me down on the land of Thesprotia.*   315
There the Thesprotians' king, the hero Pheidon, welcomed me
generously, without asking a reward. His son had found me,
overcome by cold and sleeplessness, and helping me up with
his hand had taken me home with him to his father's house;
and there he gave me a tunic and a cloak for me to wear.   320
It was there that I had news of Odysseus: Pheidon claimed he
had entertained and befriended him on his way back to his land.
He showed me the many treasures Odysseus had collected,
bronze and gold and iron that is difficult to work; all this could
keep his heirs and following generations, even up to the tenth,   325
so much was lying there waiting for him in the king's halls.
Pheidon told me that Odysseus had gone to Dodona, hoping to
hear the advice of Zeus from his high-branched oak tree,* as to
how, after his long absence, he should journey homeward
to the rich land of Ithaca, whether to go openly or in secret.   330
Furthermore, the king swore in my presence, pouring a drink-
offering in his palace, that a ship had been dragged down to sea,
and a trusty crew was ready to convey Odysseus to his own land.
But before this could happen he sent me on my way: a ship of
Thesprotians happened to be bound for wheat-rich Dulichium,   335
and he instructed the crew to convey me thither, to King Acastus,
in safety. But a wicked scheme against me tempted their hearts,
one that would cause me to endure yet more pain and misery.
When the sea-traversing ship had sailed a long way from land
they quickly set their minds to devising a life of slavery for me: 340
they stripped off my clothes, tunic and cloak, and gave me
different, wretched garments to wear, a ragged cape and tunic—
the same tattered garments you yourself see before your eyes.
With the evening they reached the farmland of clear-seen Ithaca,
and there in their well-benched ship they tied me down tightly   345
with a closely twisted rope, and then disembarked and
quickly set about making a meal on the shore of the sea.

But the gods of their own accord untangled the knots for me,
with ease; I wound my ragged cloak about my head, and slid
down the polished landing-plank into the sea, which reached   350
up to my chest, and swam away, striking out with both hands.
Very soon I was out of the water and a long way from them.
From there I struck inland until I reached a thicket of woodland
in full leaf, and there I lay crouched, while they with loud shouts
cast around for me; but then, when they realized that nothing   355
was to be gained by searching further, they retraced steps
and boarded the hollow ship. The gods themselves hid me,
easily, and so brought me on my way to the farmstead of a man
of discernment. So it is clearly my destiny to go on living.'
    Then in answer you addressed him, swineherd Eumaeus: 360
'Unhappy stranger! You have certainly stirred my heart with
all these tales of yours, of your many hardships and wanderings.
Yet in this one respect—when you mention Odysseus—I do not
think you are right, nor will you persuade me. Why should
someone like you tell such idle lies? No, I know all about   365
the return of my lord: he was hated by all the gods, utterly
hated, and so they did not beat him down among the Trojans,
or let him die in his friends' arms after spinning out war's thread.
The whole Achaean army would then have built him a barrow,
and he would have won great glory for his son too hereafter;   370
but as it is, whirlwinds have snatched him away, without glory.
As for me, I live a solitary life here with my pigs; I do not
go to the city, unless circumspect Penelope perhaps tells me
to come, when news arrives from somewhere or other. Then
the people sit around and question the newcomer, point by   375
point, both those grieved at their lord's long absence, and
those who are happy to consume his substance without payment.
But, I take no pleasure in questioning and asking for news,
especially since a man from Aetolia deceived me with his story.
He had killed a man, and had roved far and wide in the world,   380
and arrived at my house, and I gave him a warm welcome.
He said he had seen Odysseus in Crete, with Idomeneus,
repairing the ships he owned which storm-winds had damaged.
He said that by the end of summer or harvest Odysseus would
be here with his godlike crew, bringing vast treasure with him.   385
So I tell you too, much-suffering old man, since a god has brought

you to my house, not to please me with lies nor try to beguile
me; it is not for this that I shall respect and entertain you, but
because I fear Zeus, patron of strangers, and because I pity you.'

Then in answer Odysseus, man of many wiles, addressed him: 390
'Well, you certainly have a mind full of mistrust in your breast,
seeing that I cannot win you over, even with an oath, nor am I
able to persuade you! Still, let us now make a bargain, and later
the gods who live on Olympus will be witnesses for us both:
if ever your lord comes back to your house here, you must   395
give me clothes to wear, a cloak and a tunic, and then send me
on my way to Dulichium, where it is my heart's desire to be.
But if your lord does not come in the way I declare, you may
set your servants on me and throw me down from a high rock,
so that the next beggar after me may steer clear of telling lies.'   400

Then in answer the good swineherd addressed him:
'Stranger, it would doubtless bring me a fine reputation for
noble conduct among men, both now and in time to come,
if after welcoming you to my hut and offering you hospitality
I were then to kill you, taking away your dear life. To be sure,   405
after that I could pray with confidence to Cronus' son Zeus!
But now it is supper-time. I hope my companions will very soon
be back here, and then we can prepare a tasty supper in my hut.'

So they conversed, one with another, in this way; and
the swine, and the men who looked after them, came back.   410
The sows they shut up for sleep in their accustomed places,
and as they were bedded together an amazing din arose.
The good swineherd then called to his men: 'Bring me the
best of the hogs, that I may kill it in honour of this stranger
from far away. We too will enjoy ourselves, we who endure   415
long misery looking after these white-tusked swine, while
other men devour our labour, and that without payment.'

So he spoke, and split some logs with the pitiless bronze, while
the others brought in a five-year-old hog, well-coated with fat.
They stood it at the hearth, and the swineherd, a man of good   420
sense, did not forget the immortal gods; he began the rite
properly by cutting bristles from the head of the white-tusked
hog; these he threw into the fire, and then prayed to all the gods
that Odysseus of many designs might return to his home.
Then, drawing himself up, he clubbed the boar with an oak billet   425

that he had left unsplit, and the life left it. His men cut its throat
and singed and quickly butchered it; and then the swineherd took
chunks from all its limbs as first offerings and laid them raw on
the rich fat. These he threw into the fire, having sprinkled them
with barley-meal, then chopped the rest and threaded it on skewers. 430
They cooked this carefully and then drew it off the skewers,
and laid it piled up on platters. Then the swineherd stood up to
share it out, for he knew well in his heart what was correct.
He divided the whole amount into seven helpings; after a prayer
he set aside one portion for the nymphs, and one for Hermes,   435
son of Maia, and the remainder he shared out to each man;
but to Odysseus he gave the honour of the whole length of
the white-tusked boar's chine, so gratifying his lord's heart.
Odysseus, man of many wiles, then addressed him, saying:
   'I wish, Eumaeus, that father Zeus could look as kindly on you   440
as I do, for honouring me in my state with such good things.'
Then in answer you addressed him, swineherd Eumaeus:
'Stranger-guest, you are a curious man! Eat, and enjoy this food,
such as it is. A god will give one thing, but will refuse another,
according to the desire of his heart; for he can do everything.'   445
   So he spoke, and offered the first share to the ever-living gods.
Then, having made an offering of gleaming wine, he put the cup
in city-sacking Odysseus' hands, and sat down to his own portion.
Mesaulius handed round the bread, a man whom the swineherd
had got for himself after his master had left, acting on his own   450
without the knowledge of his mistress and the aged Laertes;
he had bought him from some Taphians with his own resources.
   They reached out for the good things that lay before them,
and when they had put away the desire for eating and drinking
Mesaulius took the food away from them, and they, replete   455
with bread and meat, were ready to go straight to their beds.
   But a bad night came on, darkening the moon, and Zeus rained
all through it, and a strong wet West Wind blew continuously.
Now Odysseus spoke among them, testing the swineherd,
to see if, in his great concern for him, he would take his cloak   460
off and give it to him, or persuade one of his men to do so.
   'Listen to me, Eumaeus and you, his companions. I am going
to speak somewhat boastfully. Befuddling wine leads me on,
wine that induces even a moderate man to sing out loud

and giggle feebly, and yes, even persuades him to dance,   465
and provokes from him some word that was better left unsaid.
Still—I have now raised my voice, and will not hold back.
How I wish I were in my prime again, the strength firm in me,
as when we mustered an ambush party under Troy's walls.
Its captains were Odysseus, and Menelaus, son of Atreus,   470
and I was the third leader; for they themselves had ordered it.
When we came up to the city and its steep walls, we hid
ourselves in the dense scrub that lay all around it, crouching
under our armour among the reeds of some marshland;
But an evil, freezing night came upon us; the North Wind   475
dropped and snow fell from the sky like hoarfrost—it was
bitterly cold, and the ice set hard all over our shields.
Now everyone else had cloaks and tunics, and therefore
slept in comfort, their shoulders wedged into their shields;
but I in my folly had left my cloak with companions when I   480
set out, for I did not think there was a chance of being cold.
So I went with them, with only a shield and shining loin-plate.
When the night had two-thirds gone, and the stars had passed
their zenith, I nudged Odysseus with my elbow—he was next
to me—and spoke to him, and he instantly listened to me: 485
"Son of Laertes, sprung from Zeus, Odysseus of many wiles,
believe me, I shall soon be dead! This cold is killing
me, because I do not have a cloak; some god tricked me into
wearing only a tunic, and now there is no way I can survive."

  'So I spoke, and he had a plan ready in his mind, typical   490
of the man he was in both scheming and in fighting.
Keeping his voice low, he spoke and addressed me:
"Be quiet now, in case one of the other Achaeans hears you."
So he spoke, and propping his head on his elbow called out:
"Friends, listen! While I was sleeping a god-sent dream came to me.   495
We have come a long way from the ships, so I wonder if someone
might go and tell Atreus' son Agamemnon, shepherd of the people,
to rouse up some more men, to come up from the ships and help us."
So he spoke, and there rose to his feet Thoas, son of Andraemon.
Without pausing he threw down his purple cloak, and set off   500
at a run towards the ships; and I lay there in his clothes, full of
gratitude, until Dawn appeared on her throne of gold.
So I wish I were in my prime as I was then, with the strength firm

in me, and that one of the swineherds on this farm might give me
a cloak, out of friendship and respect for an honourable man.   505
Seeing me in these wretched clothes, they treat me with scorn.'
    Then in answer you addressed him, swineherd Eumaeus:
'Old man, no one could find fault with the tale you have told,
and no word you said was out of place or missed the point!
For this reason you will not go without clothing or anything else   510
that it is right for a sorely tried suppliant to meet with—for
now; but at dawn you will have to pull on your own rags again.
You see, there are not many cloaks here for people to wear,
nor changes of tunic, because each man has only the one.
But when the dear son of Odysseus comes, he will of his   515
own accord give you a cloak and tunic for you to wear, and
will send you wherever your heart and spirit desire to go.'
    So he spoke, and sprang up, and laid a bed for Odysseus
near the fire, throwing on to it the skins of sheep and goats.
There Odysseus lay down to sleep; and over him Eumaeus   520
spread a huge, thick cloak, which he kept by himself as a
change of clothing for times of unusually cold weather.
    So Odysseus lay down to rest there, and around him the
young men did the same. But the swineherd was not at all
comfortable lying down to sleep indoors, far away from his pigs,   525
and got himself ready to go outside; and Odysseus was glad,
because he took good care of his absent lord's property.
First Eumaeus hung a sharp sword over his sturdy shoulders,
and then put on a very thick cloak that kept the wind out,
and over it arranged the skin of a huge, well-fed goat; lastly he   530
picked up a sharp spear, his protector against dogs and men.
So he set off to lie down to sleep where his white-tusked
swine slept, under an arching rock sheltered from the North Wind.

BOOK FIFTEEN

Now Pallas Athena set off for Lacedaemon of the wide dancing-
places, to remind the illustrious son of great-hearted Odysseus
about his journey home, and to urge him to be on his way.
She found Telemachus and the splendid son of Nestor
lying in bed in the forecourt of the house of renowned Menelaus.   5
Nestor's son was indeed overcome by soft sleep, but sweet
slumber had no hold on Telemachus; all through the immortal
night anxieties in his heart for his father kept him awake.
Grey-eyed Athena came and stood close and addressed him:
'Telemachus, it is no longer a good thing to roam far from home,   10
leaving behind your possessions and men of such arrogance in
your house. You must not allow them to divide up your patrimony
and destroy it utterly, which would make your journey pointless.
So quickly rouse Menelaus, master of the war-cry, to send you
on your way, if you want to find your blameless mother at home;   15
even now her father and brothers are urging her to marry
Eurymachus, because he outbids every other suitor in presents,
offering ever more valuable marriage-gifts. Take care she does
not carry off some possession from the house without your leave,
for you know what the heart in a woman's breast is like: she   20
wishes to benefit the household of the man who marries her,
and no longer remembers or asks about her former children
or her dear wedded husband now that he is dead. No, you must
go back in person and hand everything over to the one among
the serving women you consider the best, until such time as   25
the gods reveal who will be your respected wedded wife.
I tell you one more thing, which you must store in your mind:
the best men among the suitors have a plan to ambush you
in the narrows between Ithaca and rocky Samos; they are
determined to kill you before you reach your fathers' land,   30
but I do not think they will succeed; sooner will the earth close
over many of those suitors who are consuming your livelihood.
So you must keep your well-built ship away from the islands;
keep sailing through the night as well, and that immortal who
guards you and keeps you safe will send a following breeze.   35

When you make the first cape of Ithaca, send your ship and
all your companions quickly on to the city, and yourself,
before anything else, go and meet the swineherd who
looks after your pigs, and is as ever loyal towards you.
You must rest there for the night; after that send him off   40
to the city with a message for circumspect Penelope,
to tell her that you are safe and have returned from Pylos.'
　So she spoke and departed, making for far-off Olympus;
and Telemachus woke Nestor's son from his sweet sleep,
rousing him with a kick, and spoke to him in this way: 45
'Peisistratus, Nestor's son, wake up! Fetch the single-hoofed
horses and yoke them under the chariot. We must be on our way!'
　Then in turn Peisistratus, son of Nestor, answered him:
'Telemachus, eager though we are for our journey, we cannot
drive through the pitch-dark night; and it will soon be dawn.   50
No; wait until the hero son of Atreus, spear-renowned Menelaus,
brings out presents for us and loads them on to our chariot,
speaks to us with kindly words, and sends us on our way.
As you know, a guest remembers for all his days the man who
has welcomed him hospitably and shown friendship towards him.'   55
　So he spoke, and very soon Dawn came on her golden throne.
Menelaus, master of the war-cry, rose from the bed he shared
with Helen of the beautiful hair, and came and stood near them.
When the hero, Odysseus' dear son, saw him approaching
he made haste to dress himself in his shining tunic, and   60
then threw his great cloak around his powerful shoulders.
He went to the door, and standing next to Menelaus spoke
to him—he, Telemachus, dear son of godlike Odysseus:
'Zeus-nurtured Menelaus, Atreus' son, captain of the people!
Send me now on my way to my beloved ancestral land,   65
for now my heart is full of longing to return to my home.'
　Then Menelaus, master of the war-cry, answered him:
'Telemachus, for my part I will certainly not keep you here
for long when you are anxious to return. I would indeed
disapprove of any host who is either over-hospitable or   70
too lacking in civility; moderation in all things is best. It is,
I think, an equal failing to speed a guest's departure when he is
reluctant to leave and to detain him when eager to go. One must
care for the guest in one's house, but send him on when he wishes.

But wait, please, until I fetch fine presents and load them on to   75
your chariot, a feast for your eyes, and tell the women to prepare
a meal in my halls out of the plentiful store they have within.
It brings both honour and glory, and advantage, if guests
have eaten well before setting out over the boundless earth.
If you wish to make a tour through Hellas and Argos' heart,   80
I myself could accompany you; I will yoke my horses for you,
and be your guide through the cities of men; no one will send us
away empty-handed, but will give us at least one gift to take
with us, either some tripod or cauldron of well-wrought
bronze, or a pair of mules, or a golden drinking-cup.'   85
    Then in turn thoughtful Telemachus spoke to him in reply:
'Zeus-nurtured Menelaus, Atreus' son, captain of the people,
I would rather return now to my own land. When I came here
I left no one behind to watch over my possessions; and I fear
that while I am seeking my godlike father I may perish myself,   90
or that some precious treasure may go missing from my halls.'
    Now when Menelaus, master of the war-cry, heard this,
he immediately ordered his wife and maidservants to prepare
a meal in his halls, from the plentiful store they had within.
Eteoneus, son of Boethus, came and stood near him, having   95
just risen from his bed, since he had his quarters not far away.
Menelaus, master of the war-cry, told him to light a fire and
cook some meat, and when Eteoneus heard he did not disobey.
Menelaus himself went down into a sweet-smelling storeroom,
not alone, but Helen went with him, and also Megapenthes.   100
When they reached the place where treasures were stored,
Atreus' son picked out a cup with two handles, and told
his son Megapenthes to bring with him a silver mixing-bowl.
Helen went over and stood by the chests which contained
some elaborately wrought dresses, which she herself had   105
worked, and she, bright among women, lifted out the one of
these that was her most beautiful handiwork, and the largest,
and it shone like a star, and lay stored underneath the rest.
Then they made their way back through the house, until they
found Telemachus, and fair-haired Menelaus addressed him: 110
    'Telemachus, as for your return home, may Zeus, Hera's loud-
thundering husband, bring it to pass as you desire in your heart.
But in the matter of gifts, I shall give you the most beautiful

and valuable of all the treasures that are stored in my house.
I shall give you a cunningly wrought mixing-bowl; it is made   115
of solid silver, and the rim around it is fashioned from gold.
It is the work of Hephaestus; the hero Phaedimus, king of
the Sidonians, gave it to me when his house sheltered me
as I was on my way home. This is what I wish to give you.'

So spoke the hero son of Atreus and put the two-handled cup   120
in his hands; and then mighty Megapenthes took the shining
mixing-bowl, made of silver, and set it in front of Telemachus.
Then Helen of the beautiful cheeks came and stood next to him,
bearing the dress in her hands, and spoke directly to him:
'Look, dear child, I too have a gift for you here: a keepsake   125
from Helen's hands, against the time of your much-desired
marriage, for your wife to wear; until then, let it lie in your
mother's room. And now, for you, I wish a happy return
to your well-established house and the land of your fathers.'

So she spoke, and put it in his hands, and he took it gladly.   130
The hero Peisistratus took all these gifts and put them in the
chariot's basket, and marvelled in his heart at them all.
Then fair-haired Menelaus led them towards the house,
and the two of them sat down on chairs and high seats.
A maidservant brought water in a beautiful golden pitcher   135
and poured it into a silver bowl for them to wash their hands,
and then drew up a polished table to stand beside them.
A respected housekeeper fetched bread and set it before them,
and added a heap of delicacies, giving freely from her store.
Boethus' son set about carving the meat and serving the   140
portions, and renowned Menelaus' son poured the wine.
They reached out for the good things that lay before them,
and only when they had put away the desire for eating and
drinking did Telemachus and the splendid son of Nestor
yoke their horses and climb into the decorated chariot, and   145
drive through the echoing courtyard and out of the gate.
Fair-haired Menelaus, son of Atreus, followed them out,
holding in his right hand a golden cup of mind-cheering
wine, for them to make a drink-offering before they went.
He stood in front of the chariot, and spoke, pledging them: 150
'Receive my greeting, young men, and give it to Nestor,
shepherd of the people! To me he was like a gentle father,

when we sons of the Achaeans were fighting around Troy.'

Then in turn thoughtful Telemachus answered him:
'Zeus-nurtured man, we shall indeed report all that you say   155
when we arrive there. For myself, my only wish is to return
home to Ithaca and to find Odysseus in my house; to tell
him how on my way I met with every kindness from you,
and that I am bringing much splendid treasure with me.'

Even as he was speaking, a bird flew up on his right hand,   160
an eagle, carrying in its talons a huge white goose, a tame
bird reared in the farmyard. Some men and women were
pursuing it with shouts, but it flew up close to them and
veered off to the right, in front of the chariot. Seeing it
they were glad, and the hearts within them were warmed.   165
The first among them to speak was Peisistratus, son of Nestor:
'Zeus-nurtured Menelaus, chieftain of men, explain this to us:
did the god reveal this portent for us two, or only for you?'

So he spoke, and Menelaus, dear to Ares, pondered as to
how he might consult his thoughts and reply correctly;   170
but Helen of the long robe forestalled him and answered:
'Listen to me! I shall make a prophecy just as the gods
have put it into my mind, and as I believe it will be fulfilled.
As this eagle has come from the mountain where it has its
birth and parentage, and has carried off a home-reared goose;   175
so Odysseus, after many hardships and much wandering,
will return to his house and take his vengeance—or he is
already at home, sowing the seed of ruin for all the suitors.'

Then in turn thoughtful Telemachus answered her: 'Now may
Zeus, Hera's deep-thundering husband, bring this to fulfilment;   180
and then, there in my home, I will pray to you as if to a god.'

So he spoke, and put the whip to the horses, and they at once
sped eagerly through the city, racing towards the plain; and
all day long they kept the yoke swaying on their twin necks.

The sun went down, and all the ways grew dark; and they   185
came to Pherae,* to the house of Diocles, who was the
son of Ortilochus, whom the river Alpheus had once sired.
There they slept the night, and he gave them gifts of hospitality.

When early-born Dawn with her rosy fingers appeared,
they yoked the horses and climbed into the decorated chariot,   190
and drove through the echoing courtyard, out of the gate.

He touched them with the whip to start them, and they flew on
willingly, and very soon they came to the steep citadel of Pylos.
At this point Telemachus addressed the son of Nestor:
'Son of Nestor, can you promise to answer a request from   195
me? Through our fathers' friendship we can truly say we are
long-standing guest-friends; we are also of the same age,
and this journey will bring us even closer in fellow-feeling.
Zeus-nurtured man, do not take me past my ship, but leave me
at it; I am afraid that your aged father, wishing to entertain me,   200
will detain me in his house. I must go home quicker than that.'
    So he spoke, and the son of Nestor considered in his heart
how he might fairly make this promise and carry it out.
And as he pondered this seemed to him the better course:
he wheeled the horses toward the swift ship and the shore   205
of the sea, and on to its stern loaded the fine presents, the
clothing and the gold that Menelaus had given Telemachus,
and then addressed him in winged words of encouragement:
'Make haste now and board your ship, and tell your crew
to do the same, before I arrive home and tell my aged father   210
the news. I know very well in my mind and in my heart
how imperious his spirit is; he will not let you go, but will
come here in person to invite you, and will not, I think, go
back without you. He will be very angry, in any case.'
    So he spoke, and drove the fine-maned horses away, back   215
towards the city of the Pylians, and soon reached the palace.
Meanwhile Telemachus gave urgent orders to his companions:
'Set all the tackle in order in the black ship, my companions,
and then let us go on board ourselves, to press on with our voyage.'
So he spoke, and they listened carefully and did what he said,   220
and without more ado embarked and took their seats at the oarlocks.
    Now while Telemachus was busy with this, and making a prayer
and a sacrifice to Athena by the ship's stern, there drew near
a man from far away, fleeing Argos because he had killed a man.
He was a seer,* by ancestry a descendant of Melampus, who long   225
ago used to live in Pylos, mother of sheep-flocks; he was a
rich man among the Pylians, and dwelt in a magnificent palace.
But later he came to a land of strangers, fleeing his own land
and great-hearted Neleus, most lordly of living men, who forcibly
seized his rich possessions and kept them for a whole year.   230

All this time Melampus was being held prisoner in the halls of
Phylacus, in cruel bonds, suffering harsh agonies for the sake of
the daughter of Neleus, and also because of the heavy delusion
which the Fury, the ghastly goddess, had thrust into his wits.
Even so, he escaped grim death, and drove the deep-lowing   235
cattle from Phylace to Pylos, where he revenged himself on
godlike Neleus for his ugly deed, and brought the girl back
to his brother's palace, to be his wife.* He himself went on to
another land, to horse-nurturing Argos, where it was fated
that he should live and rule over a great many Argives.   240
There he married a wife and built a high-roofed house,
and fathered Antiphates and Mantius, two mighty sons.
Now Antiphates was the father of great-hearted Oïcles, and
Oïcles sired Amphiaraus, driver of the war-host, whom Zeus
the aegis-wielder and Apollo loved greatly in their hearts,   245
favouring him in many ways; yet he never reached the threshold
of old age, but perished at Thebes, because of a bribed woman.*
Amphiaraus' sons were Alcmaeon and Amphilochus, while
Mantius in his turn was father to Polypheides and Cleitus.
Now it happened to Cleitus that golden-throned Dawn bore   250
him off because of his beauty, to live among the immortals;
while Apollo made the high-hearted Polypheides a seer, and
he was by far the best among mortals after Amphiaraus died;
he quarrelled with his father and moved his home to Hyperesia,
and there he lived and practised prophecy for all mortal men.   255

    It was this man's son, whose name was Theoclymenus, who
now came and stood next to Telemachus. He found him as
he was making a drink-offering and praying beside his swift
black ship, and spoke to him, uttering winged words:
'Friend, since I have come upon you sacrificing here,   260
I entreat you by these same offerings and by the gods, and
also by your own head, and by the men who accompany you;
answer my question truthfully, and do not conceal anything.
Who among men are you? Where is your city, and your parents?'

    Then in turn thoughtful Telemachus addressed him: 'I will   265
indeed, stranger, give you a true account of all you ask.
My family is from Ithaca, and my father is Odysseus—if ever
he was, though by now he has surely died a miserable death.
That is why I took my companions and my black ship and

have come here, searching for news of my long-absent father.'   270
    Then in answer godlike Theoclymenus addressed him:
'Just so, I too am far from my country; I killed a man of
my clan, and he had many brothers and kinsmen throughout
horse-rearing Argos, who have great power among the Achaeans.
Seeking to escape death and black destruction at their hands,   275
I am now an exile, for it is my fate to be a wanderer among men.
I entreat you as a fugitive; give me a place on your ship,
and do not let them kill me—I believe they are on my track.'
    Then in turn thoughtful Telemachus answered him:
'Be sure I shall not bar you from my trim ship if you wish to   280
join us. Come; in Ithaca you will enjoy what hospitality we have.'
    So he spoke, and took the bronze-tipped spear from him
and laid it on the deck of the balanced ship, and himself
went on board the vessel, traverser of the deep. This done,
he took his place at its stern, and next to him he settled   285
Theoclymenus; and his companions slipped the stern-cables.
He urged his crew on, ordering them to set their hands
to the rigging; and they bustled about and did what he said.
They raised the fir-tree mast, and stepped it inside its
hollow mast-box, and then secured it with forestays, and   290
with tightly twisted oxhide ropes hauled up the white sail.
Grey-eyed Athena sent them a following wind, which blew
with boisterous force through the upper air, to make the ship
speed over the sea's salt water and complete her course.
So they sailed past Crounoi and Chalcis with its fine rivers.   295
    The sun went down, and all the ways grew dark; and the
ship, sped on by the breeze from Zeus, made for Pheae
and ran past splendid Elis, where the Epeians hold power.
From there Telemachus steered her on towards the Pointed Isles,*
wondering if he would escape death, or would now be taken.   300
    Now the other two, Odysseus and the excellent swineherd, were
eating their supper in the hut; and the other men ate with them.
When they had put from themselves the desire for food and drink
Odysseus addressed them all, putting the swineherd to the test,
to see whether he would entertain him properly and invite him to   305
stay there on the farm, or would urge him to go on to the city:
'Listen to me now, Eumaeus and all you others, his companions;
I am eager to leave you when morning comes and to go

begging in the city, so as not to impoverish you and your men.
So give me some useful advice, and let me have a good guide   310
to conduct me there; once in the city I shall have to drift about
on my own, to see if anyone offers me a cup of wine and a crust.
I might perhaps find my way to godlike Odysseus' palace, and
bring some news to circumspect Penelope; and I might join
the company of those arrogant suitors, to see if they would   315
give me my supper, for they have good things in plenty.
Then I might do them some service, whatever they wanted.
I tell you this truly; listen and store it in your mind: by the
good favour of Hermes the guide, who dispenses grace and
glory to all men in their occupations, there is no other man   320
who can challenge me in the business of a serving-man,
in the lighting of a good fire and in the splitting of dry logs,
in carving meat, in cooking it, and serving as a pourer of
wine—all the tasks that lesser men perform for the well born.'

　　Greatly agitated, you addressed him, swineherd Eumaeus: 325
'Nonsense, stranger! How has this thought entered your head?
You must be utterly determined to die, there and then, if
it really is your wish to associate with that gang of suitors,
whose mindless arrogance and violence reach to the iron sky.
Those who serve them are not of the same kind as you;   330
they are young lads, smartly dressed in cloaks and tunics,
their heads sleek with oil, and their looks are handsome.
That is what their servants are like; and their well-polished
tables are heavily laden with bread and meat and wine.
No, stay here with us. No one is offended by your presence,   335
neither I myself nor any of the men I have here with me.
But when the dear son of Odysseus comes, he will himself
give you a tunic and a cloak for you to wear, and
will send you wherever your heart and spirit desire.'

　　Then much-enduring glorious Odysseus answered him: 340
'I wish, Eumaeus, that father Zeus looked on you as kindly as
I do, for you have put an end to my painful, miserable roving.
There is nothing worse for mortals than the wandering life,
but for the sake of their cursed belly men will endure hardship,
all the wandering and misery and pain that come their way.   345
But now, since you press me to stay here and bid me wait
for his son, tell me about the mother of godlike Odysseus,

and the father he left behind on the threshold of old age
when he went away—if they are still living in the sun's
rays, or if they are now dead, and in the house of Hades.'   350
    Then in turn you addressed him, swineherd, captain of men:
'I will indeed, stranger, give you a true account of all you ask.
As for Laertes, he is still alive, but all the time prays to Zeus
that the spirit may waste away from his body in his house;
terrible is his mourning over the son who has gone away,   355
and over his wise wedded wife, whose death caused him
such keen pain, and brought him to old age before his time.
It was through grief for her renowned son that she wasted
away, and died a miserable death—I hope no friend of mine
who lives here and deals with me kindly may die in this way.   360
As long as she was alive, though she was of course grieving,
I always liked to ask her questions and ask for news, because
she had brought me up herself with handsome Ctimene of the
long robe, the youngest child she had borne. I was raised
with Ctimene, and she honoured me only a little less than her.   365
But as soon as we both reached our captivating prime, they
sent her away in marriage to Same, and got a huge bride-price.
As for me, Anticleia gave me a cloak and a tunic, very fine
garments to wear, and sandals for my feet, and sent me away
to work on the farm; but she loved me dearly in her heart.   370
Now I have to manage without these things; but the blessed
gods still prosper the work which is here my lasting labour;
from it I have eaten and drunk, and have given to worthy men.
But from my mistress there is no comfort for us to hear,
neither word nor deed, ever since disaster fell upon the house—   375
I mean those arrogant men. Servants greatly miss the talking
and asking for news in their mistress' presence, the eating and
drinking there, and then taking some small gift with them into
the country, the kind of thing that always warms a servant's heart.'
    Then in answer Odysseus, man of many wiles, addressed him: 380
'Well! You must have been quite small, swineherd Eumaeus,
when you were driven away from your land and your parents.
Come, tell me this and give me a full and true account:
was your city of men, with its broad ways, utterly sacked,
that city where your father and revered mother lived, or did   385
some enemy band come upon you all alone with your sheep

or cattle, and drag you off to their ships, and then sell you into
the house of the man ruling here, getting a good price for you?'

  Then in turn the swineherd, captain of men, addressed him:
'Guest, you ask the question and seek to know about all this;   390
so now be silent, listen and enjoy the tale, as you sit here and
drink your wine. The nights are now very long; there is time
enough to sleep, and to enjoy hearing a story. You do not need
to go to bed before time; and too much sleep does you no good.
As for you others, let anyone whose heart and spirit move him   395
leave now and sleep outside, and as soon as dawn appears
let him eat his meal and then go out with our master's pigs.
We two will have our food and drink here in the hut and find
pleasure in each other's sad troubles, as we call them to mind;
for it is man's way to get enjoyment even from affliction, after   400
the event, if he is a man who has suffered much and roamed far.
So now I will tell you the story you ask about in your questions.

  'There is an island called Syria*—you may have heard of it—
to the north of Ortygia, where lie the turning-points of the sun:
not very thickly populated, but a good land, abounding in   405
cattle and sheep, with plentiful vines and rich in wheat.
Famine never visits the people there, nor does any
terrible disease spread itself among wretched mortals.
Rather, as the generations of men grow old in that city
Apollo of the silver bow visits them, together with Artemis,   410
and goes after them with his gentle shafts, and kills them.
There are two cities there, and the whole land is divided
between them; and over both cities my father was king—
Ctesius, son of Ormenus, a man who looked like the immortals.

  'To this place there came some Phoenicians, famed for their   415
seamanship, tricksters, in a black ship crammed with trinkets.
Now there was in my father's house a woman of Phoenicia,
tall and beautiful, and skilled in exquisite crafts; and she it was
on whom the scheming Phoenicians began to work their deceit.
It started when she was washing clothes by their hollow ship: 420
one of them coupled with her in love—for this always beguiles
the minds of womankind, even those who live upright lives.
Later on he asked who she was, and where she came from,
and she without more ado pointed out my father's high-roofed house:
"I am proud", she said, "to hail from Sidon, rich in bronze,   425

and I am the daughter of Arybas, a man awash with wealth.
But once when I was returning from the fields some Taphian
pirates seized and brought me to this place, and sold me into
the house of the ruler here; and he paid a good price for me."

'Then the man who had secretly coupled with her answered: 430
"Would you like to return with us to your home, to see
again the high-roofed palace of your father and mother, and
them too? They are indeed still alive, and spoken of as wealthy."

'Then in turn the woman answered and addressed him:
"I should like that very much, but only if you sailors will   435
promise on oath to take me back home quite unharmed."

'So she spoke, and they all swore as she had charged them.
When they had sworn their oath, and brought it to an end,
the woman spoke to them once again, addressing them:
"Keep silent now, and let none of your companions speak   440
to me in greeting if he chances to meet me, either in the street
or perhaps at the well, in case some man should go to the
old man's palace and inform him, and he should suspect and
imprison me in painful bonds, and plot destruction for you.
So hold these words in your minds, and press on with buying   445
your home-cargo. But when the ship is loaded full of stores,
then let a message for me come straightaway to the palace;
and I shall bring gold with me, all that I can lay my hands on.
And there is something else I would gladly give to pay for my
passage: I am nurse to a boy in the halls, a son of the master—   450
such a smart lad, who trots along beside me whenever I go out.
I could bring him on board, and he would earn you a huge price
wherever you sell him to men who speak in foreign tongues."

'So she spoke, and went away towards the splendid palace.
Now these Phoenicians stayed on among us a whole year, and   455
by trading gathered a great deal of wealth in their hollow ship.
But when the hollow ship was fully laden, ready for them to
sail, they sent a messenger to carry the news to the woman.
A man came, a very shrewd fellow, to my father's palace
with a necklace made of gold, and strung with amber beads.   460
While the maids and my mother in the hall were passing it
through their hands, gazing at it closely and suggesting a price
to him, he without speaking nodded to the woman; as soon as
he had made the sign he set off for the hollow ship, and

she seized me by the hand and led me out of the house.   465
In the forecourt she found the cups and tables of the guests
attending my father who had been feasting there, and had
left for an assembly in the place where the people debate;
she quickly hid three drinking-cups in the fold of her dress
and carried them off, and I in my innocence followed her.   470
The sun went down, and all the ways grew dark, and
we made haste and quickly reached the famous harbour,
where the swift ship of the men of Phoenicia was lying.
They put us on board, embarked themselves and sailed away
over the watery pathways; and Zeus sent a following breeze.   475
For six days we sailed on, night and day without ceasing,
but when Zeus the son of Cronus added a seventh day
Artemis shooter of arrows struck the woman down; she
dropped like a sea-tern and fell with a crash into the bilge.
The crew threw her overboard, to become the prey of seals   480
and fishes, and I was left behind, grieving in my heart.
They were carried on by wind and currents, which brought
them to Ithaca, where Laertes used his wealth to buy me.
And that is how my eyes came to look upon this land.'

   Then in turn Odysseus, sprung from Zeus, addressed him: 485
'To be sure, Eumaeus, you have stirred feelings within me
with your tale of all these hardships your heart has endured.
But for all that Zeus has sent you good fortune to set beside
the bad, in that after much toil you came to the house of a
kindly man, who as I see generously provides you with   490
food and drink; you live a good life, whereas I have roamed
through many cities of men before fetching up here.'

   So they conversed, one with another, in this way, and then
settled themselves for sleep—for a short time, not for long,
because very soon Dawn on her golden throne arrived. Meanwhile   495
near the shore Telemachus' companions struck their sail, quickly
lowered the mast and rowed the ship on to a mooring-place.
They threw out the anchor-stones and made the stern-cables
fast, and disembarked at the place where the breakers reached;
and there they prepared a meal and mixed some gleaming wine.   500
When they had put from themselves the desire for food and
drink thoughtful Telemachus was the first to speak to them:
'Now you must row the black ship quickly on to the city,

while I shall make for my estate and the herdsmen there, and
in the evening, having seen my lands, I shall return to the city.   505
In the morning I shall put before you payment for this voyage:
a good feast of meat and of wine that is sweet to drink.'
   Then in turn godlike Theoclymenus addressed him:
'But where then shall I go, dear boy? Whose house shall I
make my way to, of those men who are lords in rocky Ithaca?   510
Or should I head straight for your and your mother's house?'
   Then in turn thoughtful Telemachus answered him: 'If things
were different I would indeed urge you to go to my house, for
there is no lack of provision for guests there; but that would be
the worse for you, since I shall not be there, and my mother   515
will not see you, for she does not often appear in the house
before the suitors, but stays apart, weaving upstairs at her loom.
Still, I can tell you of another man to whom you could go—
Eurymachus, the splendid son of prudent Polybus,
on whom the people of Ithaca look as if he were a god.   520
He is by far the best man among them, and more than the rest
is eager to marry my mother and assume Odysseus' powers;
but Zeus the Olympian who dwells in the clear air knows
if he will bring about the evil day for them before that marriage.'
   No sooner had he spoken than a bird flew by on the right,   525
a hawk, Apollo's swift messenger; in its talons it was gripping
a dove and tearing at it, so that the feathers drifted down to
earth midway between the ship and Telemachus himself.
Theoclymenus called him to come away from his companions,
and grasping him firmly by the hand addressed him directly: 530
'Telemachus, it was not without a god's purpose that this bird
flew by on the right; when I saw it I knew it was an omen.
There is no family in the land of Ithaca more kingly than
yours; you and your kin will remain in power for ever.'
   Then in turn thoughtful Telemachus answered him: 535
'Stranger, may these words of yours turn out to be true!
If so, you will soon meet with kindness from me, and many
a gift, so that anyone encountering you will call you blessed.'
   So he spoke, and addressed Peiraeus, his faithful companion:
'Peiraeus, Clytius' son! Of all the friends who went with me   540
to Pylos you have been the most loyal to me in everything.
So now please take this stranger to your home with you, and

make sure you treat him with kindness and respect until I come.'

Then in answer Peiraeus, famed with the spear, addressed him:
'Telemachus, I will; even if you stay here for a long time I will   545
look after this man, and he will lack for nothing in hospitality.'
So he spoke, and boarded the ship, and ordered the crew
to embark as well and to slip the stern-cables; and they
quickly went on board and took their places at the oarlocks.

Then Telemachus bound his fine sandals under his feet;   550
from the ship's deck he picked up his stout spear, capped
with sharp bronze, while his men slipped the stern-cables,
and pushing the ship off sailed towards the city, just as
Telemachus, the dear son of godlike Odysseus, had ordered.

He strode out swiftly, and his feet carried him until he reached   555
the farmyard where his countless pigs lived; and among them
the noble swineherd used to sleep, a man loyal to his masters.

BOOK SIXTEEN

Now the two in the hut, Odysseus and the good swineherd,
had kindled a fire at dawn and were preparing their breakfast,
and had sent out the drovers with their herds of swine.
When Telemachus approached, the baying dogs came fawning
around him and did not bark. Glorious Odysseus saw the   5
dogs fawning, and the sound of footsteps fell around his ears.
At once he addressed Eumaeus in winged words: 'Eumaeus,
there is someone coming. It must be a friend of yours,
or someone known to you, for the dogs are not barking but
fawning around him; I can just catch the thud of footsteps.'   10

Before he finished speaking these words his dear son stood
at the porch. Up sprang the swineherd in amazement, and
the bowls in which he had been busy mixing the gleaming
wine fell from his hands. He went straight up to his master,
and kissed his head and both his bright eyes and   15
both his hands; and a huge tear fell from his eyes.
As when a father, with love in his heart, welcomes his dear
son on his return in the tenth year from a far-off land—his
only son, much loved, for whom he has suffered much pain—
so now the excellent swineherd greeted godlike Telemachus,   20
hugging and kissing him all over, as if he had escaped death.
Breaking into tears, he addressed him in winged words:
'So you have come, Telemachus, sweet light! I did not think
I would ever see you again after you left in your ship for Pylos.
Come in now, dear child, so that I may make my heart glad   25
by gazing at you, just back from abroad, here in my house;
you do not often visit your estate or your herdsmen, but
you stay in the city; this, I suppose, suits your purpose,
to keep a watchful eye on that murderous gang of suitors.'

Then in turn thoughtful Telemachus answered him: 30
'I will indeed come in, old friend; it is because of you I am here,
to see you with my own eyes and to hear what you have to say,
whether my mother is still living in her halls, or if some man
has by now married her, and Odysseus' bed no doubt lies empty
with no one to sleep in it, a home to grimy spiders' webs.'   35

Then in turn the swineherd, captain of men, addressed him:
'She is certainly still there, waiting in your halls, her heart
patient and steadfast; she weeps unceasingly, and as they
come and pass away her nights and days are full of misery.'

So he spoke, and took the other's bronze-tipped spear from   40
him, and Telemachus stepped inside over the stone threshold.
As he entered Odysseus rose from his seat to make room for him;
but Telemachus from across the room restrained him, saying:
'Sit, stranger! We shall find somewhere else to sit, in our
own farmhouse; and the man is here who will see to it.'   45

So he spoke, and Odysseus went and sat again; and the
swineherd spread green brushwood, and over it a fleece,
and on it the dear son of Odysseus then took his seat.
The swineherd set before them platters of cooked meat,
left uneaten from their meal on the day before, and hastily   50
piled up bread in baskets beside them. He mixed some
honey-sweet wine in an ivy-patterned bowl, and sat
down himself opposite Odysseus, the godlike man. They
reached out for the good things that lay before them, and
only when they had put away the desire for food and drink   55
did Telemachus address the good swineherd: 'Old friend,
where do you say this stranger comes from? How did sailors
bring him to Ithaca? What men did they claim to be? I do
not suppose for a moment that he arrived here on foot.'

Then in answer you addressed him, swineherd Eumaeus: 60
'I will indeed, my boy, give you a true account of all you ask.
It is from spacious Crete that he claims his family comes,
and he says he is a rover, one who has roamed widely
among mortal men's cities, for so a god has spun his thread.
And now he has run away from a ship of Thesprotian men   65
and has fetched up at my farm. I hand him over to you now,
to treat him as you please; he claims to be your suppliant.'

Then in turn thoughtful Telemachus addressed him:
'Eumaeus, what you have said causes my heart much pain,
for how can I welcome this stranger into my house?   70
To begin with, I am still young, and cannot yet rely on my
hands to fight off any man who may pick a quarrel with me;
then, my mother's heart and mind are divided, brooding in
two ways, whether to stay here with me and manage the house,

respecting her marriage-bed and fearing the people's voice,   75
or to go away with the best man of those Achaeans who are
courting her in her halls, the one who offers the most gifts.
But as to this stranger: since it is your house he has come to,
I will give him a tunic and a cloak, fine clothes to wear,
and I will give him a two-edged sword, and sandals for his   80
feet, and will send him wherever his heart and spirit desire.
Or, if you will, keep him here on the farm yourself and look
after him, and I will send the clothes here, and all the food he
needs to eat, so that he will not impoverish you and your men.
But as for going there into the suitors' company, I will never   85
allow it, for their reckless arrogance knows no bounds.
I fear they may taunt him, and that would be a bitter grief
for me; it is difficult, even for a powerful man, to do anything
against a crowd, since they are much stronger than him.'
  Then in turn much-enduring glorious Odysseus addressed him: 90
'My friend, it is surely proper for me to speak in answer:
truly, my heart is torn apart, as I listen to you speaking
of the kind of reckless acts that these suitors devise in
your halls, against the will of a man as fine as you are.
Tell me, are you willing to be browbeaten, or do the people   95
in your land hate you, following some prompting from a god?
Or do you have reason to blame your brothers, the very people
on whom a man relies as fighters, however great the feud?
I wish I was as young and vigorous as you, to match my anger,
or a son of excellent Odysseus, or even the man himself,   100
returned from his wandering—there is still room for hope.
If so, any foreigner would be right to cut off my head here
and now if I did not go into the hall of Odysseus, son of
Laertes, and come as a terrible affliction on all the men there.
But if they did overwhelm me, one man against so many,   105
I would rather be cut down in my own halls than day after day
witness those vile deeds that you describe: guests subjected
to brutal treatment, serving-women shamefully dragged
through the fine palace, and the suitors drawing off huge
quantities of wine and devouring food in utter recklessness,   110
to no purpose, for an aim that will never be accomplished.'
  Then in turn thoughtful Telemachus addressed him:
'I will indeed, stranger, give you a true account of all you ask.

It is not that the whole people hate and are angry with me,
nor that I blame my brothers, the very people on whom   115
a man relies in a matter of fighting, however great the feud.
Cronus' son has made our line one of single inheritance—
one son only was fathered by Arceisius, and he was Laertes;
one son after that was born to Laertes—Odysseus—and
one son Odysseus sired, and left in his halls: me, of whom   120
he had no joy. And so enemies without number now occupy
his palace—all those chieftains who rule over the islands,
Dulichium and Same and wooded Zacynthos, as well as
those who are lords in rugged Ithaca. All these are courting
my mother, and grinding down my household's wealth.   125
She neither refuses a marriage hateful to her, nor is she able
to bring things to a head; meanwhile they devour my household
and waste it away, and soon they will prove to be my ruin too.
But of course all these things lie on the knees of the gods.
Old friend, go quickly now and report to faithful Penelope   130
the good news that I have returned from Pylos safe and sound.
I will stay on here, and you must come back again when you
have given your message to her alone; none of the Achaeans
must find out, for many of them are plotting evil against me.'

     Then in answer you addressed him, swineherd Eumaeus: 135
'I understand very well; your orders fall on receptive ears.
But tell me this, and give me a full and true account:
should I go on and take the message as well to ill-fated
Laertes? For a while, though grieving deeply over Odysseus,
he went on overseeing his farm's work, and ate and drank at   140
home with his servants when the spirit in his breast moved him;
but now, ever since you went off in your ship to Pylos,
they say he no longer eats or drinks as he used to, or looks
to his farm's work, but sits there full of lamentation, sighing
and wailing; and about his bones the flesh wastes away.'   145

     Then in turn thoughtful Telemachus addressed him: 'It is
hard, but we should let him be, for all our distress. If men
could somehow have everything they wanted, my first
choice would be to see my father's day of homecoming.
Now go, and return when you have delivered the message;   150
do not wander off across the fields after Laertes, but tell my
mother to send her housekeeper there as quickly as possible,

and in secret; this woman can take the news to the old man.'

    So he spoke, and urged the swineherd to go; he picked up
his sandals, bound them under his feet, and set off towards   155
the city. But the swineherd's departure from the farm did not
go unnoticed by Athena, and she drew close in the likeness of a
tall, beautiful woman, one skilled in fine handicraft. She stood
in the gateway opposite the hut, appearing only to Odysseus;
Telemachus did not see or perceive her standing before him,   160
for the gods by no means make themselves manifest to all men.
But Odysseus saw her, as did the dogs, though they did not bark,
but slunk, whimpering and fearful, to the other side of the farm.
She raised her eyebrows at glorious Odysseus, and he understood,
and went out of the room, passing along and beyond the yard's   165
great wall, and stood in front of her; and Athena addressed him:
'Zeus-nurtured son of Laertes, Odysseus of many wiles, now
is the time to speak without concealment to your son, so that
you two may scheme death and destruction, fit for the suitors,
and then go to the far-famed city. And I shall not stay away   170
from you for much longer, since I am impatient for the fight.'

    So spoke Athena, and tapped him with her golden staff.
First of all she made the cloak and tunic that covered his
chest freshly washed, and enhanced his stature and manly
vigour; his dark complexion returned, his jaw filled out,   175
and about his chin the beard once again grew black.
After making this transformation she left, and Odysseus
went back into the hut. His dear son was amazed at the sight,
and turned his eyes away, fearing that it was some god;
he addressed Odysseus, speaking with winged words: 180
'You are changed, I see, guest, from just a moment ago:
your clothes are different, and your skin is no longer the same;
surely you must be one of the gods who dwell in the broad sky.
Be gracious, I beg, and we will bring you sacrificial offerings
to please you, and finely wrought gifts of gold; only spare us!'   185

    At this much-enduring glorious Odysseus answered him:
'No, I am not a god. Why do you liken me to the immortals?
I am your father, the man for whose sake you grieve and suffer
so many miseries, patiently bearing the violence of other men.'

    So he spoke, and kissed his son, and tears ran down his cheeks   190
to the ground; before this, he had resolutely held them back.

But now Telemachus, for he was not persuaded it was his father,
once again spoke in answer, addressing him in these words:
    'You cannot be my father Odysseus; it is some divinity that
bewitches me, to make me weep and lament the more.   195
In no way could a mortal have contrived this, simply by his
own invention, unless a god were to come to him in person
and easily make him a young man or an old, just as he wishes.
A moment ago you were an old man in squalid clothes, and now
you seem like one of the gods who live in the broad high sky.'   200
    Then in answer Odysseus of many wiles addressed him:
'Telemachus, it does not become you, when your father is here
in this house, to wonder overmuch at him, or to be amazed;
there is no second Odysseus on his way here, you may be sure.
No, I am he, as you see me; after dreadful sufferings and much   205
wandering I have returned in the twentieth year to my own land.
You must know that this is the work of Athena, leader of the
war-host, who shapes me as she wishes, for she has the power:
at one time in the likeness of a beggar, and at another in a
young man's form, wearing fine clothes about his body.   210
It is an easy matter for the gods who live in the broad high sky
now to cover a man in glory and then to make him despicable.'
    So he spoke, and returned to his seat, and Telemachus flung
his arms about his noble father and wept, letting the tears fall.
In them both there welled up a longing for sorrowful wailing,   215
and they both wept loudly, more unremittingly than birds,
sea-eagles or hook-taloned vultures, whose children hunters
have stolen away before they are fledged and ready for flight.
Just so did they let fall many pitiable tears from their eyes.
And indeed the sun's light would have set on their lamentation,   220
had not Telemachus suddenly asked his father a question:
'Dear father, what kind of ship did sailors bring you in
here to Ithaca? What kind of men did they claim to be?
I do not suppose for a moment that you arrived here on foot.'
    Then in turn glorious much-enduring Odysseus addressed him: 225
'I shall indeed, my son, give you a true account of what you ask.
Phaeacians, men famed for their seamanship, brought me here,
as they give passage to any other men who come to their land.
They conveyed me, sleeping, over the deep in their swift ship,
and set me down here in Ithaca. They gave me splendid gifts,   230

bronze and gold in abundance, and woven garments too.
All this treasure is, with the gods' help, stowed in caves;
and now, prompted by Athena, I have come here, so that
we may make plans together for the slaughter of our enemies.
So come, list for me the suitors and reckon up their number,   235
so that I may know how many and who they are, and
then, when I have given thought to it in my excellent mind,
I can determine whether we will be able to oppose them alone,
without anyone to help, or if we should seek the aid of others.'
     Then in turn thoughtful Telemachus addressed him: 240
'Father, I have always heard of your great fame as a strong
spearman, and how wise you are in counsel; but what you
speak of is too huge a task. I am bewildered, for two men
could not possibly fight against this number of mighty men.
The suitors are not simply a matter of ten, nor even twice that,   245
but many more. You will soon learn their number as I tell you:
from Dulichium there are fifty-two young lords, all chosen
men, and six manservants attend on them in addition;
from Same the number of men is twenty-four, and from
Zacynthos there are twenty young lords of the Achaeans.   250
From Ithaca itself the full count is twelve, all of high standing,
and along with them there are the herald Medon and the god-
inspired singer; then two serving-men, skilled carvers of meat.
If we are to confront all those inside the palace, I fear that the
vengeance you have come to take on their violence will turn out   255
bitter and painful. But if you can think of anyone to stand by us,
who might fight on our side with a willing heart, then tell me.'
     Then in turn much-enduring glorious Odysseus addressed him:
'I will indeed tell you; listen and mark my words. Consider
whether Athena, and with her father Zeus, will be enough   260
to protect us, or if I should also think of some other champion.'
     Then in turn thoughtful Telemachus addressed him:
'Those whom you name are certainly a fine pair of allies;
though they sit on high among the clouds, the power they
wield is over everyone else, both men and immortal gods!'   265
     Then in turn much-enduring glorious Odysseus addressed him:
'Well, these two will certainly not hold back from the
fierce conflict for long, once raging Ares has brought
the suitors and ourselves to a trial of strength in my halls.

Now, as soon as dawn breaks, you must go back to   270
the house and join the company of the arrogant suitors.
As for me, the swineherd will bring me to the city some time
later, in the likeness of an old man, a wretched beggar.
If they treat me with contempt in my palace, the heart in
your breast must endure this, even when I am badly used,   275
even if they drag me by the feet out of the house, or if they
throw things at me; you must look on and bear it patiently.
Speak to them with gentle words, and tell them to stop their
senseless behaviour—but still they will not pay you the
slightest heed, for the day of their destiny is close at hand.   280
And I tell you another thing, for you to store in your mind:
when Athena, she of many counsels, puts it into my mind,
I shall nod to you as a sign; and as soon as you see it you
must lift down all the weapons of war that are kept in the halls
and stow them away in a remote corner of a high storeroom,   285
every single weapon; then, when the suitors miss them and
start asking questions, put them off with soft, beguiling words:
"I have stowed them away from the smoke, for they are no
longer in the state Odysseus left them when he went to Troy,
but are damaged where the heat of the fire has got to them.   290
And there is, too, a more serious thought that Cronus' son has
put into my mind: that when full of wine you may come to
blows and injure each other, and so bring shame on to your
feasting and your courtship. Iron of itself draws a man on."
For us two alone you must leave behind a pair of spears and   295
two swords, and two oxhide shields for our hands, in a place
where we can make a direct dash and seize them. For the rest,
Pallas Athena and Zeus the counsellor will confuse their wits.
And I tell you another thing for you to store in your mind:
if you are truly my son, and share in our family blood, from   300
now on let no one hear from you that Odysseus is in his house;
do not let Laertes find this out, nor the swineherd, nor anyone
in my household, nor even Penelope herself; you and I
on our own will find out how the women regard us, and
we can also put some of our serving-men to the test, to see   305
which one respects and fears us in his heart, and who
has no regard for you, and holds your youth in contempt.'
   Then in answer Odysseus' splendid son addressed him:

'Father, as to my spirit, you will, I think, discover it in
good time; I am by no means a prisoner of irresolution.   310
But believe me, I do not think this scheme will serve us
well, either of us; and so I urge you to give it some thought.
You will waste much time if you go about our lands and
test each man, while those in your halls blithely consume
your substance in their great insolence, sparing nothing of it.   315
Instead, I urge you to find out about the serving-women, both
those who have no respect for you and those who are guiltless.
For my part, I do not think we should go around the farms and
put the men to the test, but should take on this task later—
if indeed you know of some true sign from aegis-wielding Zeus.'   320
   So they conversed, one with another, in this way. Meanwhile
the well-built ship was putting in at Ithaca town, the ship
that had brought Telemachus and his companions from Pylos.
When they had sailed it into the deep-water harbour,
they dragged the black ship up on to the seashore, and   325
high-spirited attendants carried their gear ashore for them,
and bore off the beautiful presents to the house of Clytius.
But they sent a herald to the palace of Odysseus,
with orders to take a message to circumspect Penelope,
that Telemachus was on his estate, but had told them   330
to sail the ship on to the city, in case the handsome queen
should be full of dread in her heart and let a soft tear fall.
Now the two men chanced upon each other, herald and good
swineherd, engaged on the same errand, to speak to the lady.
When they arrived at the palace of the godlike king, the   335
herald gave his message surrounded by serving-women:
'My queen, your dear son has come back, and is now here!'
But the swineherd went and stood close to Penelope, and
told her all that her dear son had instructed him to say to her.
When he had delivered the whole message entrusted to him,   340
he left the hall and the courtyard and set off back to his pigs.
   Now the suitors were troubled, and cast down in their spirits,
and they left the hall, passing along and beyond the yard's
great wall, and there they sat down, in front of the gates.
The first among them to speak was Eurymachus, son of Polybus: 345
'My friends, what an outrageous act this voyage of Telemachus
has turned out to be! And we thought he would not bring it off.

Come, let us drag a black ship down to the sea, the best we have,
and let us assemble seagoing men to row it, to take this news
immediately to our friends and tell them to return with all speed.'   350

     He had not finished speaking when Amphinomus turned in his
seat and caught sight of the ship, now inside the deep-water
harbour, with the crew lowering the sail and taking up their oars.
With a burst of cheerful laughter he addressed his companions:
'We need not now send any message; here they are in the harbour!   355
Either some god told them about it, or they themselves saw
Telemachus' ship sailing past, but were not able to catch it up.'

     So he spoke, and they rose to their feet and went down to the
seashore, and quickly dragged the black ship up on to land,
and high-spirited attendants carried their gear ashore. They   360
themselves went off in a body to the meeting-place, and would
not let anyone else sit in their company, either young men or old.
Then among them Antinous, the son of Eupeithes, spoke out:
'It is intolerable how the gods have saved this man from ruin!
By day lookouts have been sitting on windswept headlands,   365
one man succeeding the next; and at night, after the sun
set, we never slept on land, but would put out in our swift
ship on to the open sea, waiting for the glorious Dawn, lying
in wait for Telemachus, in the hope we might catch and kill
the man; but all this time some divinity was bringing him home.   370
So let us who are here devise a miserable death for him, for
Telemachus, so that he does not slip away from us. I do not
think that while he lives this business of ours will turn out well,
for he himself is skilled in both counsel and judgement, and
also the people are no longer entirely well disposed towards us.   375
So act now, before he brings the Achaeans together in an
assembly. I do not think he will let things go, but will give
rein to his anger, and stand up before everyone and will tell
them that we planned sheer murder for him but failed to
find him. When they hear of our wicked deeds they will not   380
approve them; and I am afraid they could do us some harm
and drive us from our country, to fetch up in other men's lands.
So let us move first, and take him in the fields, far from the city,
or else on the road; and then let us seize his goods and property,
dividing it up among us equitably, but the house we may give   385
to his mother to keep, with whichever man makes her his wife.

But if this proposal finds no favour with you, and you prefer
to allow him to live and enjoy the whole of his patrimony, let us
not go on meeting here, devouring his possessions in agreeable
luxury, but let us seek her in marriage, each from his own house,   390
and court her with wedding-gifts; and she may then marry
the man who offers the most and so comes as her appointed lord.'

So he spoke, and they all remained silent and still. Then
among them Amphinomus spoke out and addressed them.
He was the splendid son of Nisus, who was lord Aretias' son,   395
and he was the leader of the suitors from Dulichium, rich in
wheat and grass, and more than the others found favour with
Penelope through his words, for he was endowed with good sense.
With generous intent he spoke out and addressed them:
'My friends, I for one am unwilling to put Telemachus to   400
death—it is a terrible thing to kill someone from a kingly
family. No, we should first of all seek out the advice of the
gods; if the oracles of great Zeus approve the act, I myself
will kill him, and I shall order all the rest of you to help me.
But if the gods forbid us, I say we must give the idea up.'   405

So spoke Amphinomus, and his words found favour with them.
Without more ado they stood up and set off for Odysseus' house,
and went in and took their seats on their polished chairs.

But now circumspect Penelope had another idea: to appear
before the suitors, men of violent insolence, since she had   410
learned that they were plotting death for her son in the halls.
Medon the herald had heard their scheming and had told her this.
So she set off for the hall, accompanied by her serving-women.
Now when she, bright among women, reached the suitors,
she stood next to a pillar supporting the strongly built roof,   415
holding her shining veil in front of her face, and spoke in
rebuke to Antinous, addressing him directly: 'Antinous,
you are full of insolence, and a planner of evil; they say
among the people of Ithaca that you are the best of your peers
in counsel and speaking, but I see now you are clearly not so.   420
You madman! Why do you stitch a fabric of death and doom
for Telemachus, and pay no heed to suppliants, even though their
witness is Zeus? It is an impious thing to plot against each other.
Have you forgotten how your own father once came here as a
fugitive, in fear of his people? They were indeed exceedingly   425

angry, because he had joined forces with Taphian pirates and
had harried the men of Thesprotia, and they were our allies.
So they wanted to kill him, to tear his life from him, and
to devour all of his abundant livelihood; but Odysseus
held them off and checked them, inflamed though they were.   430
Now it is his house you devour, without payment; you court
his wife, you seek to kill his son, and you cause me great grief.
I command you to cease, and to order the rest to do likewise.'

Then in turn Eurymachus, son of Polybus, addressed her:
'Daughter of Icarius, circumspect Penelope, take courage,   435
and do not let these things be a trouble to your heart.
The man does not nor will not exist, nor can ever be born,
who could lay hostile hands on your son Telemachus, as
long as I am alive and look upon the light here on earth.
I tell you this plainly, and it will surely come to fulfilment: 440
instantly that man's blood will gush out around my spear—
yes, my spear. Many times did Odysseus the city-sacker
set me too on his knees and put pieces of cooked meat
into my hands, and hold the red wine up to my lips. For
this reason Telemachus is by far the dearest of men to me,   445
and that is why I say he should have no fear at all of death—
from the suitors, at any rate; death from the gods is unavoidable.'

So he spoke, meaning to cheer her, but was himself planning
death for Telemachus. She went up to her bright room above,
and fell to weeping for Odysseus, her dear husband, until   450
grey-eyed Athena threw a sweet sleep over her eyelids.

In the evening the good swineherd returned to Odysseus and
his son. They killed a year-old pig and set about making
supper, standing close to their task. And now Athena came
and stood alongside Odysseus Laertes' son, close by him, and   455
tapping him with her staff turned him as before into an old man;
she gave him foul clothes to wear about himself, fearing the
swineherd should recognize him, face to face, and, not guarding
the secret in his heart, might go and tell faithful Penelope.

Telemachus was the first to speak to the swineherd: 460
'So you have returned, good Eumaeus. What news is there
in the city? Are the proud suitors now home again from their
ambush, or are they still watching for me on my way home?'

Then in answer you addressed him, swineherd Eumaeus:

'I did not trouble to go about through the city, inquiring　　465
and asking after news; my heart prompted me to deliver
my message and come back here as quickly as I could.
But a swift messenger fell in with me, one of your companions,
a herald, who was in fact the first to tell your mother the news.
And here is something else I know; I saw it with my own eyes.　　470
I was already above the city on my errand, where the hill
of Hermes is, when I saw a swift ship putting in to our
harbour. There were many men on board, and she was
heavily laden with shields and curved-headed* spears.
I thought they must be suitors, but I did not know for sure.'　　475

　　So he spoke, and Telemachus, man of divine might, glanced
at his father and smiled, but avoided the swineherd's gaze.

　　Now when they had finished their task and prepared supper,
they feasted, and no man's heart lacked a fair share in the meal.
And when they had put away the desire for food and drink,　　480
they turned their minds to rest, and accepted the gift of sleep.

BOOK SEVENTEEN

When early-born Dawn with her rosy fingers appeared,
Telemachus, dear son of Odysseus who looked like a
god, bound his beautiful sandals under his feet.
He picked up the stout spear that fitted into his hand,
and, eager to set off for the city, addressed his swineherd;   5
'Old friend, I am now away to the city, so that my mother
can set her eyes on me; I do not think she will stop
her grievous weeping and tear-laden crying until she
sees me in person. Now these are my orders to you:
take our unfortunate guest here to the city, so that he can   10
beg there for his meals; anyone who wishes will offer him
a cup of wine and a crust. It is quite impossible for me to
provide for all men, when I have such pain in my heart.
If this makes our guest very angry, so much the worse
for him; speaking the plain truth is much my preferred way.'   15
    Then in answer Odysseus of many wiles addressed him:
'My friend, I too have no great wish to be detained here.
It is far better for a beggar to cadge his supper in the city than
in the country; anyone who wishes will offer me something, for
I am no longer of an age to spend my time on a farm, to follow   20
the bidding of some overseer in whatever he orders me to do.
Off you go; this man will take me as you instructed, as soon as
I have warmed myself at the fire, and the sun has grown hot.
These clothes I wear are terribly poor, and I fear the dawn
frost will be too much for me; and you say the city is far away.'   25
    So he spoke, and Telemachus set off through the farmyard,
striding out at a swift pace, and sowing the seeds of ruin for
the suitors. When he arrived at the pleasantly ordered palace
he took his spear and propped it against a tall pillar, and
himself stepped over the stone threshold and went inside.   30
    Easily the first to see him was the nurse Eurycleia, who
was spreading fleeces over the cunningly worked chairs.
Bursting into tears she made straight for him, and the other
maidservants of patient-spirited Odysseus gathered round,
greeting him warmly and kissing his head and shoulders.   35

Now circumspect Penelope came down from her chamber,
looking like Artemis or golden Aphrodite, and threw
her arms around her dear son, weeping all the while,
and kissed his head and both his handsome eyes, and
in melancholy tones addressed winged words to him: 40
'So you have returned, Telemachus, sweet light! I thought
I would never see you again after you left in your ship for
Pylos—in secret, against my wishes—to find news of your
father. Come now, give me a full account of what you saw.'
    Then in turn thoughtful Telemachus addressed her: 45
'Mother, do not move me to weeping, or trouble the heart
in my breast, when I have just escaped sheer destruction.
Rather, go and wash yourself and put on clean clothes, and
go up into your rooms with your women servants, and
vow an offering of unblemished hecatombs to all the gods,   50
in the hope that Zeus will bring about requital on our behalf.
I am going to the meeting-place, where I will welcome as
a guest someone* who has accompanied me on my voyage
from Pylos. I sent this man ahead with my godlike crew,
and I instructed Peiraeus to take him to his home and to   55
treat him with kindness and honour until I should come.'
    So he spoke, and his words flew quickly to their mark.
Penelope went and washed herself and put on clean clothes,
and vowed unblemished hecatombs to all the gods, in the
hope that Zeus would bring about requital on their behalf.   60
    Now Telemachus went striding through and out of the hall,
gripping his spear, and two swift dogs went along with him.
All over him Athena poured an astonishing grace, and
all the people gazed in wonder at him as he approached.
The proud suitors flocked around him with noble speeches,   65
but deep in their minds they were turning over evil schemes.
Telemachus avoided the great throng of them, and went
over to where Mentor and Antiphus and Halitherses,
longstanding companions of his father, were sitting; he sat
with them, and they questioned him about everything.   70
Peiraeus, renowned with the spear, drew near, bringing the
stranger through the city to the meeting-place; and Telemachus
did not ignore his guest for long, but came to meet him.
Peiraeus was the first of them to speak, and addressed him:

'Telemachus, dispatch some women to my house without delay,   75
so that I may send on the gifts that Menelaus gave you.'
     Then in turn thoughtful Telemachus addressed him:
'Not so, Peiraeus; we do not know how all this will fall out.
If the proud suitors are going to kill me by stealth in my own
halls and share out my ancestral wealth, I would rather you   80
yourself kept and enjoyed them, or any of these men here;
but if I can sow the seeds of death and doom for them,
bring them to my house, and both of us will enjoy them.'
     So he spoke, and led his sorely tried guest into the house.
When they reached the pleasantly ordered palace, they   85
laid aside their cloaks on the chairs and benches, and
stepped into well-polished bath-tubs and had their bath.
Then, when maidservants had bathed and rubbed them with
oil, and put tunics and thick woollen cloaks around them,
they stepped out of the baths and took their places on chairs.   90
A maidservant brought water in a beautiful golden pitcher
and poured it into a silver bowl for them to wash their hands,
and drew up a polished table to stand beside them.
A respected housekeeper brought bread and set it before them,
and added a heap of delicacies, giving freely from her store.   95
Telemachus' mother sat opposite them, by a pillar of the hall,
leaning back in her chair and twisting fine wool on her distaff.
They reached out for the good things lying before them,
and when they had put away the desire for food and drink
circumspect Penelope was the first of them to speak: 100
'Telemachus, I am going up to my rooms, where I shall lie
on my bed, my bed that is so full of misery, for ever
soaked by my tears since the time Odysseus went away to
Ilium, along with the sons of Atreus. You could not bring
yourself to tell me, before the proud suitors come back to the house,   105
if you have heard any sure news of your father's return.'
     Then in turn thoughtful Telemachus addressed her:
'Very well, mother, I shall now give you a full account.
We went to Pylos, to see Nestor, shepherd of his people,
and he received me in his lofty palace and treated me   110
in a kindly fashion, like a father welcoming his son
newly returned from foreign parts after a long absence.
So kindly did he entertain me, along with his famous sons.

But he said he had heard nothing about Odysseus of the
enduring spirit, whether alive or dead, from anyone on   115
this earth. Instead he gave me horses and a close-jointed
chariot and sent me on to Atreus' son, spear-famed Menelaus.
There I saw Argive Helen, for whose sake both Argives
and Trojans suffered so much, all by the will of the gods.
While there Menelaus master of the war-cry asked me   120
what was the object of my search in coming to splendid
Lacedaemon, and so I gave him a full and truthful account.
He then replied, addressing me in these words: "How
dreadful! For sure it was a strong-hearted man's bed they
hoped to sleep in, though they themselves are cowards.   125
As when a hind settles her newly born fawns who are still
drinking her milk to sleep in the woodland den of a mighty lion,
and herself goes out to scour the foothills and grassy hollows
in search of grazing—but the lion returns to his lair
and unleashes an ugly death on both hind and fawns—   130
so will Odysseus unleash an ugly death on those men.
Father Zeus and Athena and Apollo, I wish he could now be
the same man who once on well-founded Lesbos stood up
and wrestled Philomeleides* for a challenge, and threw
him violently down, and all the Achaeans were delighted!   135
I wish Odysseus could come like that among the suitors; it
would mean quick deaths and bitter marriage-hopes for them all.
As for your question and entreaty, I will not sidestep
the matter and answer you crookedly, nor will I deceive you.
And the tale the truth-telling Old Man of the Sea told me—   140
that story I shall not keep back or conceal from you.
He said he had seen Odysseus on an island, in the grip of
harsh suffering, in the halls of the nymph Calypso, who
holds him there by compulsion; he cannot return to his own
land, because he has no oared ships nor any companions   145
who might convey him over the broad back of the sea."
    'This is what Atreus' son, spear-famed Menelaus, told me.
When I had finished my task, I set out for home, and the gods
sent me a breeze and brought me quickly to my own land.'
    So he spoke, and stirred the heart in Penelope's breast. 150
Then the godlike Theoclymenus addressed them both:
'Lady, respected wife of Odysseus son of Laertes:

it must be that Menelaus does not understand clearly; mark
my words, for I shall prophesy truthfully, hiding nothing.
May Zeus, first of gods, be my witness, and your hospitable   155
table, and blameless Odysseus' hearth, to which I have come,
that Odysseus is actually in his native land, even now,
at rest or moving around, finding out about these evil deeds;
he is here, sowing seeds of destruction for all the suitors.
Such is the bird-omen I interpreted as I was sitting in the   160
well-benched ship, and declared it aloud to Telemachus.'
      Then in turn circumspect Penelope addressed him:
'Stranger, may these words of yours turn out to be true!
If so, you will soon meet with kindness from me, and many
a gift, so that anyone encountering you will call you blessed.'   165
      So they conversed, one with another, in this way.
Now the suitors were amusing themselves on level ground
in front of Odysseus' hall, throwing discuses and spears,
filled with the same arrogance that they had shown before.
But when it was time for supper, and sheep had arrived from   170
the fields round about, driven by the same men as always,
then Medon spoke to them. He was the most popular herald
with the suitors, and he used to wait on them at their feasts:
'Young lords, now that you have enjoyed yourselves with
sports, go into the palace, so that we can prepare your feast.   175
It is no bad thing to eat one's supper at the right time.'
      So he spoke, and they rose and set off, and did what he said.
When they reached the pleasantly ordered palace,
they laid their cloaks aside on chairs and seats, and
set about slaughtering some huge sheep and fat goats,   180
and killed some fatted swine and a heifer from the herd,
ready for the feast. Meanwhile Odysseus and the good
swineherd were getting ready to leave the country for the
city. First to speak was the swineherd, captain of men:
'My guest, you are clearly impatient to set out for the city   185
today, as my master instructed you. For my part, I would
have preferred you to stay here and look after the farm; but
I respect and fear him, troubled that he may hereafter take
me to task—and the rebukes of masters are hard to bear.
So let us go now; the greater part of the day is now gone,   190
and as evening comes on you may well find it colder.'

Then in answer Odysseus of many wiles addressed him:
'I understand very well. Your advice falls on receptive ears.
Let us go, then; and you must be my guide all the way.
And, if you have anywhere a staff already cut, give it to me   195
to lean on; you did say that the way was very slippery.'
   So he spoke, and hung round his shoulder the shabby satchel,
full of holes, which had a twisted cord to hold it up,
and Eumaeus gave him a stick that suited his needs.
So the pair of them set off, and dogs and herdsmen stayed   200
behind to protect the farm. Off to the city went Eumaeus,
leading his lord in the guise of a wretched beggar, an old
man, leaning on a stick and dressed in miserable garments.
   Their way lay along a rock-strewn path, and when they
were close to the city they came upon a clear-flowing,   205
well-made fountain, from which the citizens used to fetch
water. Ithacus had built it, with Neritus and Polyctor, and
around it was a copse of alders, trees that thrive on water,
set all in a circle; and a chill stream flowed into it, down
from a high rock. Above it an altar had been built to the   210
nymphs, and there all passers-by would make offerings.
Here Melanthius, Dolius' son, chanced to meet them, as
he was driving the finest nanny-goats in all his flocks to
make the suitors' supper; and two herdsmen were with him.
Seeing them he hailed them jeeringly in tones of shameful,   215
violent abuse, which roused Odysseus' heart to anger:
'Well, look! Here is one utter scoundrel leading another!
It's true that gods always bring like together with like.
Miserable swineherd, where can you be taking this empty-
bellied wretch, this tiresome beggar, this licker of plates—   220
the kind who is always hanging around, rubbing his shoulders
on doorposts, begging for scraps, never for swords or cauldrons?
If you would but give him to me, to watch over my farm and
muck out my byres and bring in green fodder for the kids, he
could drink some whey and build up the muscles on his thigh.   225
But since it is obvious that all he knows is how to make
trouble, he will not want to work hard, preferring to go
begging round the town after food to fill his insatiable belly.
I tell you this plainly, and I believe it will be fulfilled:
if he comes anywhere near the palace of godlike Odysseus   230

he will be thrashed through the house, and many a stool
flung from men's hands at his head will break about his ribs.'

So he spoke, and as he went past Odysseus kicked him, fool
that he was, on the hip; but he could not force him off the path,
for Odysseus firmly stood his ground. He pondered whether to   235
rush at Melanthius and take the life from him with his stick,
or lift him by the waist and smash his head on the ground.
But he held himself in check, and endured. The swineherd
stared at Melanthius and rebuked him; lifting his hands
he prayed: 'Nymphs of the spring, Zeus' daughters, if ever   240
Odysseus wrapped thigh-bones in rich fat and made you a
burnt offering of lambs or of kids, then fulfil this wish for me:
grant that the man may return home, with a god guiding him.
Then, Melanthius, he would chase away all these fancy airs
that you now so insolently put on, loafing all the time   245
about the city while worthless herdsmen ruin your flocks.'

Then in turn Melanthius, herdsman of goats, addressed him:
'Dear me—how this slippery-minded dog can talk! One day
I shall put him in a well-benched black ship and take him
far from Ithaca, somewhere he could fetch me a good profit.   250
And I pray that Apollo of the silver bow may shoot Telemachus
today in his halls, or that the suitors may beat him down,
as surely as Odysseus, far away, has lost his day of return!'

So he spoke, and left them to continue their quiet journey,
and himself went on, and quickly reached his master's house.   255
He went straight inside and sat down among the suitors,
opposite Eurymachus, who always showed him particular favour.
Industrious servants set before him a portion of meat, and
a respected housekeeper brought bread and put it by him to eat.
By now Odysseus and the good swineherd had arrived and   260
were standing near the palace; around them stole the sound
of the hollow lyre, for Phemius was striking up a prelude to his
song. Odysseus took the swineherd's hand and addressed him:
'Eumaeus, this must surely be the splendid palace of Odysseus.
It is easy to make out and identify even among many others;   265
one building joins on to another, its courtyard is furnished
with a wall and coping-stones, and the double doors provide
a secure defence. No one could take it by storm. And I can
tell that many men are holding a feast inside, for the savour of

cooking is in the air, and there is inside the sound of the lyre,   270
which the gods have created to be the companion of a feast.'
    Then in answer you addressed him, swineherd Eumaeus:
'You recognized it easily, for in other things too you are not
without wits. But let us consider now what to do next:
either you should be the first to enter this well-ordered palace   275
and mingle with the suitors, while I remain outside; or,
if you prefer it, stay out here and I will go in before you.
But do not loiter here, in case someone sees you outside and
throws something at you or chases you away. Do be careful.'
    Then much-enduring glorious Odysseus answered him: 280
'I understand very well. Your orders fall on receptive ears.
Now: you should go in before me, and I will wait here.
I am not unschooled in blows and missiles—I have
an enduring spirit, since I have borne much hardship, on
sea and in war. So let these sufferings be added to those.   285
For all that, there is no way one can hide a ravening belly,
an accursed thing that deals out much misery to men;
for its sake strong-benched ships are fitted out, to cross
the restless open sea and bring affliction to their enemies.'
    As they were conversing one with the other in this way,   290
a dog that was lying there, called Argus, raised its head
and ears; it was once the dog of patient-spirited Odysseus,
which he himself had bred, but left for sacred Ilium before
he could have any enjoyment of him. In the past young men
would take him to hunt wild goats and deer and hares;   295
but now, his master long gone, he lay neglected on a deep
heap of the dung of mules and cattle, which lay in great
piles in front of the doors, waiting for Odysseus' servants
to carry it away to be used as manure on his great estates.
So here Argus lay, covered in dog-devouring ticks.   300
But now, when he saw Odysseus standing nearby, he
wagged his tail and let both his ears droop, but no
longer had the strength to move any nearer his master—
who, turning his eyes from the sight, wiped away a tear,
easily hiding it from Eumaeus, to whom he quickly said: 305
'Eumaeus, this is truly remarkable, a dog like this lying in
the dung. He certainly has a handsome frame; but I cannot
tell if, to match his beauty, he was also a swift runner, or if

he was one of those dogs that lurk around men's tables,
the kind that lords keep simply in order to show them off.'   310
     Then in answer you addressed him, swineherd Eumaeus:
'This dog did indeed belong to someone who has died far
away. If his form and exploits were now such as when
Odysseus went away to Troy and left him behind, you
would soon be amazed when you saw his pace and mettle.   315
Never, in the deep parts of a wood, did any game he was
pursuing escape him; and he was also skilled at tracking.
But now he is in a sorry state: his master is dead, far from
home, and the women are neglectful and do not care for him.
When masters are no longer around to give orders, servants   320
are not inclined to carry out their proper tasks. Zeus who
thunders far and wide takes away the half of a man's
excellence the moment the day of slavery seizes on him.'
     So he spoke, and went into the pleasantly ordered palace,
and set off straight through the hall to join the lordly suitors.   325
But the doom of black death seized hold of Argus, at the
very moment he saw Odysseus again, after nineteen years.
     Now godlike Telemachus was by far the first to see the
swineherd coming up through the palace, and he quickly
nodded to call him over. Eumaeus looked about him, and   330
picked up a stool lying nearby, on which a carver sat when
serving heaps of meat to the suitors feasting in the house.
This he brought and set it down next to a table, opposite
Telemachus, and sat on it. A herald fetched a portion
and served it to him, and brought him bread from a basket.   335
     Close on his heels Odysseus followed him into the
house, in the guise of a wretched beggar, an old man,
leaning on a stick and dressed in miserable garments.
He sat down on the ash-wood threshold, inside the doors,
leaning against the cypress-wood doorpost, which a carpenter   340
had once planed skilfully and made straight against a line.
Telemachus called the swineherd over and spoke to him,
taking a whole loaf from the beautiful basket, and some
meat, as much as his hands could hold in their compass:
'Take this and give it to the stranger; and tell him to go   345
round to every single suitor in turn and ask for more.
Shame is no good companion for a needy beggar.'

So he spoke, and hearing these words the swineherd went
and stood by Odysseus and addressed him in winged words:
'Look, stranger; here is a gift from Telemachus. He tells you   350
to go round every single suitor in turn and to ask for more.
He says that shame is no good thing in a man who begs.'
   Then in answer Odysseus of many wiles addressed him:
'Lord Zeus, I pray Telemachus may prosper among men;
and may he be given everything that his heart desires.'   355
   So he spoke, and took the food in both hands and laid it
there in front of his feet, on top of his shabby satchel,
and ate while the bard was singing in the hall. When
he had finished his meal, and the god-inspired singer
had stopped, the suitors set up a great clamour in the hall;   360
but Athena came and stood next to Odysseus, Laertes' son,
and urged him to go round the suitors and collect crusts, to
find out which were right-minded and which lawless;
even so, she did not intend that any should escape ruin.
So off he went, from left to right, to beg from each man,   365
holding his hand out everywhere, as if he had long been a
beggar. They took pity and gave him food, and wondered
at him, asking each other who he was, and where he was from.
But Melanthius, herder of goats, spoke out among them:
'Listen to me, you suitors of our renowned queen, and I will   370
tell you about this stranger, because I have seen him before.
It was the swineherd who guided him here; but I do not
rightly know who he himself is, or what ancestry he claims.'
   So he spoke; and Antinous rebuked the swineherd, and said:
'Most eminent swineherd, why have you brought this man   375
to the city? Do we not have enough vagrants besides him
at our banquets—tiresome beggars, and lickers of plates?
Is it not enough for you, while men gather here and devour
your lord's livelihood, that you must invite this man in too?'
   Then in answer you addressed him, swineherd Eumaeus: 380
'Antinous, you may be noble, but this was not well spoken.
Who would go out of his way to invite a stranger in
from some other land, unless of course he was one who
works for the people: a seer, or a healer, or a shipwright, or
even a god-inspired singer, who gives pleasure with his song?   385
These men are invited everywhere on the boundless earth,

whereas no one welcomes a beggar who will eat him out of house
and home. You, above all other suitors, are always hard on
Odysseus' servants, and above all on me; but I do not care,
as long as I know that faithful Penelope is alive in these   390
halls, and with her Telemachus who looks like a god.'
   Then in turn thoughtful Telemachus addressed him:
'Be silent, please. That was too long a reply to this man.
It is Antinous' cruel custom to provoke others with
harsh words, and he encourages the rest to do the same.'   395
   So he spoke, and then addressed Antinous with winged words:
'Antinous, you take good thought for me, as a father for his
son, in telling me to have this stranger chased from the hall
with brutal words. But may the god not bring it to pass.
Take some food and give it to him; I do not begrudge it—   400
indeed I myself order you; and pay no heed to my mother,
or any of the servants in the house of godlike Odysseus.
But in fact you have no such thoughts in your breast; you
would far rather gorge yourself than give anything to another.'
   Then in turn Antinous answered and addressed him: 405
'Telemachus, you intemperate public loudmouth—what a thing
to say! If all the suitors were to offer him as much as I do he would
have enough to stay away from this house for all of three months.'
   So he spoke, and seizing the footstool where he rested his shining
feet while feasting, brought it out from where it lay under the table.   410
All the others gave Odysseus something and so filled his satchel
with bread and meat; and he was on the point of returning to his
doorway and tasting the Achaeans' gifts without payment
when he stopped by Antinous, and spoke to him in this way:
'Friend, give me something. You do not seem to me the worst   415
of the Achaeans, but the best; you have the look of a king, and
so it befits you to give me an even better portion of food than
the rest; and I will then sing your praises over the boundless earth.
I too was once prosperous, you know, and lived among men in
my own rich house, and would often give to a wanderer such as   420
I am, whatever kind of man he was and whatever his need.
And I had serving-men in their hundreds, and all the other things
by which men live a good life and gain a name for their wealth.
But Zeus, the son of Cronus, ruined me—he must have desired it—
sending me off to join sea-robbers who range far and wide, to   425

go on a long voyage to Egypt, on which he meant me to perish.
I brought my well-balanced ships to anchor in the Egyptian river,
and then gave my trusty companions strict orders to stay
where they were beside the ships and to stand guard over them,
and detailed others to go and scout things out from high ground.   430
But my men yielded to arrogance, following their strong desire,
and straightaway began to ravage the fertile farmland of the
Egyptians and to carry off their women and infant children; and
they killed the men. Before long the clamour reached the city—
its inhabitants, hearing the shouting, came at us just as dawn   435
broke. The whole plain was filled with foot-soldiers and chariots,
and with the flashing gleam of bronze. Thunder-delighting Zeus
flung evil panic among my companions, and no one had the nerve
to withstand this onslaught, for disaster stood all around them.
There the Egyptians killed many of us with the sharp bronze, and   440
carried off others up-country, alive, to labour for them under duress.
As for me, they gave me to a friend they encountered, to take me
to Cyprus—Dmetor, Iasus' son, who ruled over Cyprus in might.
From there I have come here, in a very poor state, as you see.'

    Then in turn Antinous answered him with these words: 445
'What divinity delivered this nuisance here, to spoil our feast?
Go, stand over there, in the middle, away from my table, or else
you may find yourself in an Egypt or a Cyprus you will not like.
You really are a barefaced sponger, quite without shame:
you go and stand by everyone in turn, and they give to you   450
without thought, for no one cares to hold back or feels remorse
at lavishing other men's goods, since everyone has plenty.'

    Odysseus, man of many wiles, fell back and addressed him:
'For shame! I see now you do not have the wits to match your
good looks. You would not give a servant a pinch of salt from your   455
own stores, you who sit at another's table but cannot be bothered
to take some bread and give it to me; and yet there is plenty here.'

    So he spoke, and Antinous was even more enraged in his heart,
and looking at him darkly addressed him in winged words:
'I do not think you will now be able to get away from this   460
hall without mishap, after giving voice to insults like these.'

    So he spoke, and picking up the stool threw it, hitting him on
the back under his right shoulder. But Odysseus stood unmoved,
like a rock, and did not lose balance at Antinous' missile, but

simply shook his head silently, brooding deeply on evil thoughts.   465
Back he went to his doorway and sat there, and laid down
his satchel, now well filled; and then addressed the suitors:
'Listen to me, you men who court our renowned queen,
and I will tell you what the spirit in my breast urges me.
There is, to be sure, no grief in his heart, nor any sorrow,   470
when a man takes a blow while fighting for his possessions,
in defence of either his cattle or his shining white sheep;
but Antinous struck me because of my wretched belly,
an accursed thing that deals out much misery to men.
If there exist anywhere gods or avenging spirits of beggars,   475
may the end of death come upon Antinous before he marries!'
     Then in turn Antinous, son of Eupeithes, addressed him:
'Sit quietly, stranger, and eat your food, or go somewhere else;
otherwise, your speechifying will end in young men dragging you
by foot or hand through the palace and tearing the skin from you.'   480
     So he spoke, but they were all exceedingly angry with him,
and this is what one of the arrogant young men would say:
'Antinous, you did not do well to strike this unlucky vagabond;
you will be accursed if he is in fact some god from the high sky.
We all know that gods take the form of strangers from other   485
lands, assuming all kinds of shapes and roaming through cities,
while they observe the acts both of the violent and of the just.'
     So spoke the suitors, but Antinous paid no heed to their words.
But Telemachus felt huge grief swelling in his heart for the
stricken man, yet shed not a tear from his eyes to the ground; he   490
shook his head silently, brooding on evil thoughts deep in his mind.
     When circumspect Penelope heard that the man had been struck
in her hall, she cried out to her maidservants: 'I hope Apollo,
famed with the bow, will strike you exactly as you struck him!'
     Then in turn the housekeeper Eurynome addressed her: 495
'May fulfilment attend our prayers! If it does, not one of
these men will live to see the Dawn on her lovely throne.'
     Then in turn wise Penelope addressed her: 'Nanny,
they are all our enemies, because they plot our ruin,
but Antinous more than the rest is like a black death-spirit.   500
There is an unfortunate stranger going about our house,
begging from men, because necessity is driving him on;
all the others gave to him and filled his satchel, but this man

alone threw and hit him with a stool under his right shoulder.'

So she conversed with her women servants, sitting in her   505
room, all the time that glorious Odysseus was eating his meal.
Then she summoned the good swineherd to her and said:
'Go on your way, good swineherd, and tell the stranger to
come here, so that I may offer him welcome, and ask if he
has anywhere heard about Odysseus of the enduring spirit, or   510
set eyes on him. He seems like a man who has wandered far.'

Then in answer you addressed her, swineherd Eumaeus:
'My queen, I wish all these Achaeans would fall silent—
the tales he has to tell, such as would bewitch your heart!
Three nights I kept him with me, and three days I lodged him   515
in my hut, for I was his first call after he fled from his ship;
and yet he has not yet reached the end of his tale of suffering.
As when a man gazes at a singer, the kind who has learnt
from the gods how to sing his ravishing songs to mortals,
and men are all afire to listen to him for ever while he sings;   520
just so this man bewitched me while he sat in my house.
He says he is a long-standing guest-friend of Odysseus' family,
and his home is in Crete, where the descendants of Minos live.
From there he has now come here, in a sorry state, as you see,
driven ever onwards; he solemnly declares he has heard that   525
Odysseus is near at hand, in the rich land of the Thesprotians—
alive, and bringing a great deal of treasure back to his house.'

Then in turn circumspect Penelope addressed him:
'Go now and summon him here, so that he may talk to me
face to face; as for the rest, let them sit by the doors or here   530
in the hall and amuse themselves; their hearts are cheerful,
because their own wealth, their food and sweet wine, is safely
stored in their houses, untouched except by their own servants.
Meanwhile they keep coming day after day to our house,
slaughtering our oxen and sheep and fat goats, holding   535
revels and drinking our gleaming wine, in utter heedlessness.
Most of this has gone to waste, for no longer is there a man here
such as Odysseus was to preserve this house from ruin. If only
Odysseus could come, returning to his own land; with his son's help
he would soon punish these men for their violence.'   540

So she spoke, and Telemachus gave a great sneeze, and
a loud echo rang all around the house. Penelope laughed,

and straightaway addressed Eumaeus in winged words:
'Go, please, and summon the stranger to meet me here.
Did you not see how my son's sneeze proves all that I said?   545
And so may certain death fall upon the suitors, every single one
of them, and none shall escape death and ruin. And
I tell you another thing, and you must store it in your mind:
if I discover that everything this man claims is the truth,
I shall give him a tunic and a cloak, fine clothes for him to wear.'   550
     So she spoke. When he heard what she said the swineherd left,
and standing close to Odysseus addressed him in winged words:
'Father guest, circumspect Penelope, Telemachus' mother, is
summoning you to meet her. Her heart urges her to question you
about her husband, even though she has suffered much already.   555
If she discovers that everything you say is the truth, she will
give you a tunic and a cloak to wear, something you are most
in need of. As for food, you must beg for it among the people,
and so fill your belly. Those who are willing will give to you.'
     Then in turn much-enduring glorious Odysseus addressed him: 560
'Eumaeus, I shall waste no time in telling Icarius' daughter,
circumspect Penelope, the whole truth; I know that man's
story very well, since we endured the same miseries together.
But I have some fear of that gang of ruthless suitors, whose
arrogance and violence reach as far as the iron high sky.   565
Even now, as I was walking through the hall, doing no harm
at all, a man over there threw a stool at me and caused me much
pain; and neither Telemachus nor anyone else could protect me.
So tell Penelope now, though she is anxious to see me, to
wait behind in the hall until the setting of the sun. Then she   570
may ask me about her husband's day of return; and let her
give me a seat nearer the fire, for my clothes are wretched things,
as you yourself know, since I came to you first as a suppliant.'
     So he spoke, and when he had heard him the swineherd went back.
But as he was stepping over the threshold Penelope addressed him: 575
'Eumaeus, are you not bringing him? What does the beggar mean
by this? Perhaps he is overly afraid of someone, or does he feel shy
in this house for some other reason? A shy beggar is a poor one.'
     Then in answer you addressed her, swineherd Eumaeus:
'He is right to say what he does, and another man might think   580
so too, since he wants to avoid the arrogance of these insolent

men. And so he tells you to wait until the setting of the sun;
this way will be much better for you too, my queen: to speak
with the stranger in private, and hear what he has to say.'

Then in turn circumspect Penelope addressed him: 'This   585
stranger is no fool in his thinking, however things turn out;
never yet among mortal mankind have there been men
who plot such arrogant and reckless violence as these do.'

So spoke Penelope, and the good swineherd went on his way
to join the suitors, now that he had delivered all his message.   590
Without delay he addressed Telemachus in winged words,
holding his head close to him, so that the others should not hear:
'My friend, I am going now, to look after my pigs and my duties
yonder—your livelihood and mine. You must look to events here.
Above all, take care of yourself, and think hard how you may   595
avoid hurt; there are many Achaeans here who wish you evil.
May Zeus destroy them utterly before any harm falls on us!'

Then in turn thoughtful Telemachus addressed him:
'So be it, old friend. When you have eaten your supper, go,
and in the morning come again, and bring some fine victims.   600
I shall see to everything here, with the help of the immortal gods.'

So he spoke, and Eumaeus went back and sat on a well-polished
chair. When he had satisfied his heart with food and drink
he went off to join his swine, leaving the courts and the hall
full of banqueters, who now fell to taking their pleasure in dance   605
and in singing; for already the late afternoon was upon them.

BOOK EIGHTEEN

Now there came up a common beggar, whose habit it was
to cadge around the city of Ithaca. He was notorious for his
ravenous belly and incessant eating and drinking; but he had
no muscle or strength, though he was a very big man to look at.
He was called Arnaeus, for that was the name his revered mother 5
had given him at birth, but the young men all called him Irus,
because he would run messages when anyone ordered him.*
This man came up to Odysseus, meaning to chase him out of
his own house, and, baiting him, addressed him in winged words:
'Get away from that doorway, old man, before someone drags 10
you off by the feet! Can you not see that they are all giving me
the wink to lug you away—even though I am ashamed to do it.
So get to your feet, or our quarrel may quickly end in blows.'

Looking at him darkly Odysseus of many wiles addressed him:
'Madman! I am doing you no harm in word or deed, nor 15
do I bear it ill if any man takes a good helping and gives it
to you. This doorway can hold us both, and you have no need
to begrudge me what others give. I take you to be a vagrant
like me; and handing out prosperity is the gods' function.
Do not insist on challenging me, or you will make me angry; 20
though I am an old man I could bloody your mouth and chest,
which would bring me some peace now, and even more
tomorrow, for I reckon you are very unlikely to come
back a second time to the hall of Odysseus, Laertes' son.'

At this the vagabond Irus grew angry, and addressed him: 25
'Well, look at this! How glibly the empty-bellied wretch babbles,
like some aged hag at the oven! I have a mind to do hurt to him—
beat him with both hands, and knock all the teeth from his jaws
to the ground, as if he was some sow foraging among crops.
Come on, tuck up your tunic, so that these here can see us fight. 30
You cannot possibly stand up to someone younger than you.'

And so there, on the polished threshold in front of the high
doors, they set to, goading each other as hard as they were able.
Antinous, a man of divine might, caught sight of the pair,
and with a gleeful laugh spoke out among the suitors: 35

'My friends, nothing like this has ever happened before—
some god has brought this sport into the house, the stranger
and Irus challenging each other to a fight, fist against fist.
Let us lose no time in pitting them, one against the other.'

So he spoke, and they all started up from their seats, laughing,   40
and crowded round the beggars in their ragged clothes.
Then Antinous, son of Eupeithes, spoke out among them:
'Listen to me, you proud suitors, to what I have to say.
Over there, lying by the fire, are some goats' paunches which
we have stuffed with fat and blood and set aside for our supper.   45
Let the one of these two who prevails and proves the stronger
stand forward and choose whichever of them he pleases; and
for ever after this he will take his meals with us; we shall not
allow any other charity-seeking beggar to join our company.'

So spoke Antinous, and his words found favour with them.   50
But then, with deceit in his mind, Odysseus of many wiles spoke:
'Friends, it is in no way possible for an old man, broken by cares,
to fight against a younger man. It is my troublesome belly
that drives me to it, to be beaten down by his blows.
Now, all of you, swear me a mighty oath, that none of you   55
will take Irus' part and recklessly use his heavy hand to strike me
down, crushing me brutally just to please himself.'
So he spoke, and they all swore an oath as he had ordered.
When they had sworn their oath and brought it to an end,
Telemachus, a man of divine strength, again addressed them: 60
'Stranger, if your heart and proud spirit urge you to match
yourself against this man, you must not fear any of the Achaeans,
for any man who strikes you will have to contend with many more;
it is I who entertain guests here, and these two princes agree
with me—Antinous and Eurymachus, both men of good sense.'   65

So he spoke, and they all approved his words. Then Odysseus
tucked up his rags about his loins, and exposed his handsome
great thighs; and his broad shoulders were also revealed, and
his chest and powerful arms. And Athena came and stood by
him, and filled out the limbs of the shepherd of the people.   70
All the suitors were exceedingly amazed; and this is
what one of them would say, looking at his neighbour:
'Irus will surely now be un-Irused!* He has brought this hurt on
himself; look at that thigh showing through the old man's rags!'

So they spoke, and Irus' heart was troubled with foreboding.   75
But the servants tucked up his tunic and dragged him out by
force, full of dread, and the flesh on his limbs was shaking.
Antinous flung a rebuke at him, hailing him in these words:
'Now, you great ox, you will wish you were dead, and had never
been born, if you are going to tremble at this fellow in desperate fear, 80
an old man, broken down by the suffering that has come his way.
I tell you this plainly, and it will certainly be fulfilled:
if this man defeats you and proves himself to be the stronger,
I shall throw you into a black ship and send you off to the
mainland, to Echetus* the king, bane of all mortal men, who will   85
chop off your nose and ears with the cruel bronze, and rip away
your genitals and give them raw to his dogs, for them to eat.'
    So he spoke, and a creeping tremor spread through Irus' limbs.
They dragged him into the middle, and both men raised their hands.
And now much-enduring glorious Odysseus considered whether   90
to strike him so that his life's breath would leave him where he fell,
or to lay him prostrate on the ground with a glancing blow.
And as he pondered this seemed to him the better course: to deal
him a glancing blow, so that the Achaeans should not suspect him.
So then they both drew themselves up. Irus struck at Odysseus'   95
right shoulder, but the other landed a blow on Irus' neck, below
the ear, and shattered the bones, driving them inward; at once red
blood spurted from his mouth and he collapsed, squealing, in the
dust, grinding his teeth; and his feet drummed on the ground.
The lordly suitors threw their hands in the air, and died of laughter. 100
Odysseus caught Irus by the foot, and dragged him through the
porch until he reached the courtyard doors, and there he set him
down, propped against the courtyard wall. He stuck Irus' staff
in his hand, and addressed him in winged words: 'Sit there
now, and scare off the pigs and dogs; pitiful creature, you can   105
give up any hope now of lording it over strangers and beggars,
or some even greater calamity may come your way.'
    So he spoke, and slung about his shoulders his shabby satchel,
full of holes, with a twisted cord serving as its shoulder-strap.
Then he went back to his doorway and sat down; and the others   110
went back inside, laughing gaily, and toasted him in these words:
'Stranger, may Zeus and the other immortal gods grant you
whatever you most desire and is dearest to your heart, in return

for putting an end to this gluttonous tramp's begging about
the town. Soon we shall take him over to the mainland,　　　115
to Echetus the king there, who is the bane of all mortal men.'

So they spoke, and glorious Odysseus was glad at the omen
of their words. Then Antinous set before him a huge paunch,
stuffed with fat and blood; and Amphinomus fetched two
loaves of bread from a basket and set them beside him,　　　120
and made a pledge to him in a golden cup, saying: 'Good
health to you, father stranger! May prosperity attend you in
future, though now you are in the grip of many afflictions.'

Then in answer Odysseus of many wiles addressed him:
'You are, I think, a man of very good sense; such too was　　　125
your father, whose excellent fame has come to my ears—
Nisus of Dulichium, a good man and a wealthy. Men say
you are his son, and you do seem like an intelligent man.
So I will speak to you, and you must listen and take note.
Of all creatures that move and breathe throughout the world,　　　130
there is nothing the earth nurtures more feeble than mankind.
No man ever thinks he will suffer adversity in time to come,
so long as the gods give him manly strength, and his knees
lift lightly. And when the blessed gods send misery his way,
even this he endures with a patient spirit, though unwillingly;　　　135
for the disposition of men who live upon this earth is to accept
whatever the father of men and gods sends them day by day.
You must know that I too was destined to be prosperous
among men; but, relying on my father and brothers, I gave way
to wild violence and committed many acts of recklessness.　　　140
For this reason let no man ever live a wholly lawless life, but
in quietness hold on to whatever gifts the gods bestow on him.
Yet I here see the suitors plotting reckless deeds like these,
plundering the possessions and treating with dishonour the wife
of a man who I believe will not be long away from his loved ones　　　145
and ancestral land; indeed, he is very close at hand. As for you,
I hope some divinity will take you quietly to your home, so that
you do not meet him when he returns to his dear native land.
I do not think that he and the suitors will settle their differences
without bloodshed, once he has come under his own roof.'　　　150

So he spoke, and poured an offering and drank the honey-sweet
wine, and put the cup back in the hands of Amphinomus, captain

of his people, who went back through the house, troubled in spirit
and shaking his head, because in his heart he could foresee evil.
Even so he did not escape death; he too was bound fast by Athena,   155
to be overcome by Telemachus' hands and the force of his spear.
He went back and sat again on the chair from which he had risen.

But now the goddess grey-eyed Athena put an idea into
the mind of circumspect Penelope, daughter of Icarius,
to show herself in the suitors' presence, in order to inflame   160
their passion more keenly, and to become more valued than
she had been before in the eyes of her son and her husband.
Forcing a laugh, she spoke directly to her servant Eurynome:
'Eurynome, my heart now craves—though it did not in the past—
to appear before the suitors, hateful though they are to me.   165
And I also wish to give some advice to my son, for his benefit:
that he should not always associate with these arrogant suitors;
their words are friendly, but they are plotting harm for him.'

Then in turn the housekeeper Eurynome addressed her:
'Everything you have said, my child, is right and proper.   170
Go and speak to your son, and do not hold anything back,
but first wash yourself and anoint your cheeks; you should
not go there with your face stained like this with tears, for
it is a bad thing to be always grieving, on and on without end.
And beside, remember that your son has now come of age, and   175
your particular prayer to the gods was to see him with a beard.'

Then in turn circumspect Penelope addressed her:
'Eurynome, I know you care for me, but do not try to
talk me into washing and anointing myself with creams.
Any beauty that I had, the gods who dwell on Olympus have   180
destroyed in me since the day that man left in his hollow ships.
No, go and tell Autonoë and Hippodameia to come to me here,
so that they may stand next to me as my attendants in the hall;
I will not go in alone to join the men; it would not be modest.'

So she spoke, and the old woman went off through the hall,   185
to take the message to the women and urge them to come.

But now the goddess grey-eyed Athena had different plans:
down over Icarius' daughter she shed sweet sleep; and she,
sinking back, fell into a slumber, and all her limbs went limp
as she lay there on the bed. Meanwhile the bright goddess   190
set about bestowing immortal gifts on her, so that the Achaeans

might look at her in wonder. First she cleansed her comely face
with an immortal balm, a cream such as fair-crowned Cytherea*
uses when she goes to join the Graces' charming dance.
Next she caused her to be taller and fuller in their sight,   195
making her look whiter than ivory that has been newly sawn.
When she, bright among goddesses, had done her work she left,
and the white-armed serving women came up from the hall,
chattering; and sweet sleep released its hold on Penelope.
Rubbing her hands over her cheeks she addressed them: 200
'This was a gentle sleep which lapped me round, in spite of
my misery! I wish Artemis would send me such a gentle death,
here and now, and then I would no longer waste my life away,
grieving in my heart and longing for my dear husband, supreme
in all manly virtues; he was outstanding among the Achaeans.'   205
    So she spoke, and came down from her bright upper room,
not alone, but two serving-women were attending her.
When she, bright among women, had reached the suitors,
she stood beside a pillar supporting the strongly built roof,
holding her shining veil in front of her face, and a loyal   210
woman servant took her place on either side of her. There
and then the suitors' knees gave way, and their hearts were
carried away with desire, and all prayed to lie beside her.
But she addressed Telemachus, her own dear son:
'Telemachus, your judgement and sense have taken leave   215
of you! As a boy you used your wits more shrewdly, but
now that you are fully grown and have reached manhood's
measure, and any foreigner, looking at your stature and
beauty, might take you for the son of a prosperous man,
your wits and judgement are no longer securely rooted.   220
Look at this thing that has been done in your hall, the way
you have allowed the stranger here to be so shamefully treated.
How would it be if, while sitting quietly in our palace, he
were to come to some harm because of this brutal handling?
It would mean shame and disgrace for you in men's eyes.'   225
    Then in turn thoughtful Telemachus addressed her:
'Mother, I do not blame you for being angry about this;
But I do see all these things in my mind and understand them,
and can tell good from bad, and am no longer the child I was.
Yet still I cannot hit on the wisest course in everything, for   230

these men hem me in on all sides and drive me to distraction.
Their intentions are wicked, and I have no one to take my part.
Even so, we saw that the fight between the stranger and Irus
did not go as the suitors wished; the other man was stronger.
Father Zeus and Athena and Apollo, how I wish that the   235
suitors could now suffer a beating in our hall like Irus,
and were sitting, some in the courtyard and others in the
house, every man's head lolling and his limbs undone,
just as Irus is now sitting over there propped against the
courtyard gates, his head hanging, looking like a drunkard.   240
He cannot stand upright on his feet, nor can he find his way
back home, wherever that is, because his limbs are undone.'
     So the pair conversed in this way, one with the other.
But then Eurymachus spoke up, addressing Penelope:
'Daughter of Icarius, circumspect Penelope! If all the   245
Achaeans who live in Ionian Argos were to see you now,
tomorrow morning there would be more suitors feasting
in your palace, for you surpass all other women in beauty
and in stature, and in the well-balanced mind within you.'
     Then circumspect Penelope spoke to him in answer: 250
'Eurymachus, as to the excellence of my beauty and form,
the gods destroyed them when the Argives took ship on
their way to Ilium, and among them went my husband Odysseus.
If he were to return and look after my livelihood, my fame
would thereby become greater and the more glorious; but   255
as it is I grieve, so many are the troubles a god has sent
against me. When he went away, leaving his native land
behind, he caught my right hand at the wrist and said:
"Wife, I do not think that all the well-greaved Achaeans
will return home from Troy safely and without injury;   260
they do say that the Trojans are men who can fight,
both as throwers of the spear and as drawers of the bow,
and as chariot-riders behind swift-footed horses—men
who can most quickly decide the great strife of levelling war.
So I do not know if a god will let me return, or if I shall   265
be slain there in Troy. You must take care of everything here;
be mindful of my father and my mother in these halls, as
you are now—or even more when I am far away from you.
When you see that our son has grown a beard, you may

marry whoever you wish, and leave your house behind."   270
That was what he said, and now it has all come to pass.
The night will come when a hateful marriage will face me;
I am accursed, and Zeus has taken my happiness away.
And there is one more cruel grief that assails my heart and
spirit: this was not the custom of suitors in times past, when   275
men who wished to pay court to a well-born woman, a
rich man's daughter, competed with each other for her.
Such men would bring their own oxen and fatted sheep,
to be a feast for the girl's friends; they would give her fine
gifts, and not eat up another's substance, without compensation.' 280

   So she spoke, and much-enduring glorious Odysseus was glad,
because she subtly wrested presents from them and beguiled
their hearts with winning words, while her mind had other plans.*

   Then in turn Antinous, son of Eupeithes, addressed her:
'Daughter of Icarius, circumspect Penelope! As for the gifts   285
that any man of the Achaeans may choose to bring here,
take them, because it is not a good thing to refuse a present;
but we will not go back to our estates, or anywhere else,
until you marry whichever of the Achaeans is the best.'

   So spoke Antinous, and his words found favour with them;   290
and so each man dispatched a herald with orders to fetch gifts.
For Antinous his man brought a robe, long and very beautiful,
and cunningly worked; on it were brooches, a dozen in all,
made of gold, with finely curved pins fitted on them. For
Eurymachus his man brought a skilfully wrought neck-chain,   295
made of gold and strung with amber beads, bright as the sun.
For Eurydamas two attendants brought in some earrings, each
having three drops like mulberries, shining and very beautiful.
And from the house of Peisandrus, son of lord Polyctor, his
attendant brought a necklace, a most lovely piece of jewellery.   300
And each of the other Achaeans brought his own beautiful gift.
Then Penelope, bright among women, went back to her room
above, and women servants carried the beautiful gifts for her.

   Now the suitors turned to dancing and pleasing song, taking
delight in them while they waited for evening to come; and   305
in the midst of their enjoyment the dark evening arrived.
Straightaway servants set up three braziers in the hall, to
provide them with light. On these they laid dry firewood,

long-seasoned and sapless, newly split by the bronze axe;
into these they pushed kindling, and the maidservants of   310
patient-spirited Odysseus kept them burning, turn by turn.
Then Zeus-nurtured Odysseus of many wiles spoke to them:
'You maidservants of Odysseus, your long-departed master,
go now to the room where your respected queen is; sit
in this room and cheer her spirits, and keep spinning   315
your thread beside her or carding the wool in your hands.
I myself will provide the light for these people here;
even if they want to carry on until Dawn comes on her
golden throne they will not weary me, for I can endure much.'

So he spoke, and they laughed and exchanged looks;   320
but fair-cheeked Melantho scolded him in shameful words.
Her father was Dolius, but Penelope had raised her, had
cherished her as her own child, and given her toys to amuse
her. For all that, she had no sympathy for Penelope's grief, but
used to sleep with Eurymachus, because he was her favourite.   325
And now she rebuked Odysseus in abusive words: 'Wretched
stranger, you must have had the wits knocked out of you!
Not content to go off to some smithy or lounging-place and
sleep there, you must stay here and spout at length before
all these men, full of impudence and with no trace of fear   330
in your heart. The wine has got to your wits—or perhaps you
were always this way inclined, to judge from the drivel you talk.
Have you been carried away because you beat the beggar Irus?
Be careful; another man, better than Irus, may soon stand up
against you, one whose heavy fists will smash your head in   335
and drive you out of this house, covered all over with blood.'

Odysseus of many wiles looked at her darkly, and said: 'You
shameless hussy! I shall go straight to Telemachus over there
and tell him what you have said, and he will chop you in pieces.'
So he spoke, and with these words terrified the women,   340
who ran off through the house; each one's limbs went slack
with fear, for they believed he would do what he had said.
But Odysseus stood there beside the blazing braziers, watching
them all and tending their fires; yet the heart within him was
brooding on schemes which would not indeed be unfulfilled.   345

As for the proud suitors, Athena did not intend them to hold
back entirely from heart-wounding insults, so that even greater

anguish might sink into the heart of Odysseus, son of Laertes.
Among them the first to speak was Eurymachus, son of Polybus,
who jeered at Odysseus, provoking laughter among his friends: 350
'Listen to me, you men who court our renowned queen, and
I will tell you what the spirit in my breast urges me. It is not
without the gods' will that this man has come to Odysseus' house;
at any rate, light from the torches' gleam seems to me to be leaping
from his head, since there are no hairs on it, not even a few.'   355
    So he spoke, and turning to Odysseus, sacker of cities, he said:
'Stranger, if I took you on, would you work for me as a day-
labourer, on the edge of my lands, for an adequate wage,
collecting stones to build walls and planting tall trees?
For my part, I would provide you with a regular supply   360
of food, and give you clothes to wear and shoes for your feet.
But no; since obviously all you know about is making trouble,
you would not be prepared to get down to hard work, preferring to
go around the town begging for food to fill your insatiable belly.'
    Then in answer Odysseus, man of many wiles, addressed him: 365
'Eurymachus, I wish there could be a farm-working contest
between us, in the spring season when the long days come round!
This would be in a grass meadow, and I would have a curved
sickle, and you another the same, and we would challenge
each other at the job, fasting until dark, and with plenty of grass   370
to cut. Or again, there could be oxen to drive, the best kind,
great tawny beasts, both with a bellyful of fodder, the same age,
with equal drawing-power, endowed with no negligible strength.
There would be four acres of sod yielding to the plough, and
you would see if I could cut a straight furrow in front of me.   375
And then again: if the son of Cronus were to stir up war
somewhere today, and if I had a shield and two spears and
a helmet made all of bronze, snug-fitting about my cheeks,
you would see me in the mêlée, among the front-fighters; and
then you would not make speeches that poke fun at my belly.   380
But no; you are an arrogant bully, and your mind is full of hatred.
You think you are so important, someone of power, because
the people around you are few in number, and of no worth.
Now if Odysseus were to come back to his ancestral land,
you would soon discover that these doors, though seemingly   385

wide, would turn out too narrow as you fled through the porch.'

So he spoke, and Eurymachus' heart became even more enraged,
and looking darkly at Odysseus he spoke with winged words:
'You miserable thing! I will make you suffer—and it will hurt—
for this impudent talk in front of this gathering, without a trace of　390
fear in your heart. The wine has got to your wits—or perhaps you
were always this way inclined, to judge from the drivel you talk.
Have you been carried away because you beat the beggar Irus?'

So he spoke, and picked up a footstool, but Odysseus went and
crouched at the knees of Amphinomus, the man from Dulichium,　　395
in fear of Eurymachus, who threw the stool but hit the wine-
steward on his right hand; the jug fell to the ground with a
clang, and he cried out and fell backwards in the dust. At this
the suitors raised a clamour down the shadowy hall, and this
is what one of them would say, looking at his neighbour:　　　　400
'I wish this vagabond had died somewhere else, and not come
here, and then he would not have caused such a commotion.
As it is, here we are quarrelling over beggars, and will get no
pleasure from this splendid feast, since bad behaviour prevails.'

Then Telemachus, a man of divine power, spoke out among them: 405
'What has possessed you? You are mad, and it is obvious you
have eaten and drunk to excess. Some god must be exciting you.
You have feasted well. Now return home and go to bed—but only
when the spirit moves you, for it is not my way to drive anyone out.'

So he spoke, and they all bit their lips hard, and looked with　　410
amazement at Telemachus, because he had spoken so boldly.
Then up spoke Amphinomus, and addressed them; he was
the splendid son of Nisus, whose father was the lord Aretias:
'My friends, surely no one of you, after so proper a speech,
could become angry and answer our host with offensive words.　　415
Do not act roughly towards this stranger, or towards any
of the servants who live in the palace of godlike Odysseus.
Come, let the wine-steward pour the first drops into our cups,
and when we have made an offering we will go home to sleep.
Let us leave the stranger in Odysseus' hall in Telemachus'　　　420
care, since it is to his house that he has come as a guest.'

So he spoke, and his words were acceptable to them all.
Then Mulius, the herald from Dulichium, mixed wine in a bowl

for them and served it to all, standing by each man in turn; and
they poured offerings of honey-sweet wine to the blessed gods.   425
When they had made their libations and drunk to their hearts'
content, they left, each man to his own house, to go to their rest.

BOOK NINETEEN

But glorious Odysseus stayed behind in the hall, plotting
how he might, with Athena's help, slaughter the suitors.
Without more ado he addressed Telemachus in winged words:
'Telemachus, you must hide away our war-gear in the house,
every piece; and then, when the suitors see it is gone and   5
start asking questions, put them off with soft, beguiling words:
"I have stowed them away from the smoke, for they are no
longer as Odysseus left them when he went to Troy, long ago,
but are damaged where the heat of the fire has got to them.
There is, too, a more serious thought that Cronus' son has put   10
into my mind: that when full of wine you may come to blows
and injure each other, and so bring shame on your feasting
and your courtship—for iron of itself draws a man on."'

  So he spoke, and Telemachus did what his dear father said;
he summoned the nurse Eurycleia and spoke to her: 'Nanny,   15
please do this for me: keep the women shut in their rooms
until I have stowed my father's fine weapons in a storeroom.
They have lain neglected about the house in my father's absence,
and I have let the smoke dull them; I was still a child then,
but now I wish to store them where the fire's heat cannot reach.'   20

  Then in turn his dear nurse Eurycleia addressed him: 'I wish,
my child, you could one day show the same good judgement
in caring for this house and watching over its possessions!
But tell me: who will go with you to carry a torch? The maids
would have lighted your way, but you will not let them.'   25

  Then in turn thoughtful Telemachus addressed her:
'This stranger will. I will not put up with idleness in anyone
who has eaten my bread, even if he has come from far away.'

  So he spoke, and his words flew quickly to their mark.
Eurycleia barred the doors of the well-built rooms, and   30
the two of them, Odysseus and his splendid son, sprang up
and set about bearing away the helmets, the studded shields,
and the pointed spears; and before them went Pallas Athena,
carrying a golden lamp which shed a wonderful radiance.
And now Telemachus quickly addressed his father: 35

'Father, here is indeed a great marvel I see before my eyes:
it seems to me as if the walls of the hall and its fine cross-
beams, the pine-wood roof-beams, and the high-reaching
pillars are actually shining as if in the light of a blazing fire.
Surely one of the gods who dwell in the broad high sky is here.'   40

   Then in reply Odysseus, man of many wiles, addressed him:
'Hush! Keep your thoughts to yourself and ask no questions;
I tell you, this is the way of the gods who dwell on Olympus.
Go now and lie down to sleep; I shall remain behind here,
so that I may further provoke the maids, and your mother too;   45
in her grief she will want to question me about everything in detail.'

   So he spoke, and Telemachus strode off through the hall, lighted
on his way by the bright torches, to the chamber where it was
his custom to rest whenever sweet sleep came over him.
There he lay down as before, and waited for the bright Dawn.   50
But glorious Odysseus remained behind in the hall, plotting
how with the help of Athena he might slaughter the suitors.

   Now circumspect Penelope came down from her chamber,
looking like Artemis or like golden Aphrodite. Her attendants
set a chair for her next to the fire, where it was her custom to sit;   55
decorated with spirals of ivory and gold, the craftsman Icmalius
had made it long ago, and had fashioned a footstool for her feet,
joined to the chair; and over it was thrown a great fleece.
And so on this chair circumspect Penelope took her seat.
White-armed serving-women arrived from their quarters,   60
and began to clear away the mounds of bread, the tables, and
the cups from which the arrogant suitors had been drinking.
They raked the embers from the braziers on to the floor, and
piled logs in abundance on them, to give light and warmth.
But then Melantho began to scold Odysseus a second time: 65
'Stranger, are you still here? Do you plan to bother us all
night, prowling about the house and leering at the women?
Get out of here, you wretch, and be grateful for your meal—
or someone might throw a torch at you and drive you outside.'

   Then Odysseus of many wiles looked at her darkly and said: 70
'Are you mad, that you attack me in such a spiteful spirit?
Is it simply because I am filthy, clad in wretched rags, and
go begging about the town? Well, necessity drives me to it;
this is the way of all those who are roving men and beggars.

I too was once prosperous, you know, and lived among men in   75
my own rich house, and would often give to a wanderer such as
I am, whatever kind of man he was and whatever his need.
And I had serving-men in their hundreds, and all the other things
by which men live a good life and win a name for their wealth.
But Zeus, the son of Cronus, ruined me—he must have desired it.   80
So, woman, take care in case one day you lose all the dazzling
beauty that now marks you out among the serving-women.
Take care that your mistress is not provoked to anger with you,
or Odysseus may come back—there is still room for hope.
And even if he is dead, as you hope, and will never return,   85
he still has a son here like him, by the good grace of Apollo,
Telemachus. None of these women's wanton conduct in the halls
will escape his notice, since he is no longer of an age to ignore it.'

So he spoke, and circumspect Penelope heard what he said,
and rebuked her woman servant, speaking directly to her: 90
'You impudent, shameless hussy! I am well aware of your
monstrous behaviour, which will be upon your own head.
You knew very well, for you heard it from my lips, that
I was minded to ask the stranger here in the hall for news
about my husband, sorely afflicted with grief for him as I am.'   95

So she spoke, and addressed her housekeeper Eurynome:
'Eurynome, bring a seat here and throw a fleece over it,
so that the stranger may sit and tell me his news and
hear what I have to say, for it is my wish to question him.'

So she spoke, and Eurynome bustled about, and brought a   100
well-polished chair and set it down, and threw a fleece over it;
and much-enduring glorious Odysseus took his seat there.
The first of them to speak was circumspect Penelope:
'Stranger, the first question I shall ask you is for myself:
Who among men are you? Where are your city and parents?'   105
Then in reply Odysseus, man of many wiles, addressed her:
'Lady, no one on the boundless earth could find fault with
you, for your fame surely reaches to the wide high sky; it is
like the renown of some blameless king, a god-fearing man,
who, ruling over a country of numerous, powerful people,   110
upholds just government; and his black earth brings forth
wheat and barley, and his trees are weighed down with fruit,
and his sheep give birth unfailingly, the sea supplies fish

thanks to his just conduct, and under him the people prosper.
So, now I am here in your house, ask me about anything else,   115
but do not question me about my parentage or ancestral land,
in case while I think on them you may fill my heart with even
greater misery. I am a man who has much to grieve over, and
it is not proper for me to sit in another's house wailing and
lamenting. It is a bad thing to go on mourning for ever; one of   120
your maids, or even you, may become indignant with me, and
say I am swimming in tears because my mind is heavy with wine.'
    Then circumspect Penelope answered and addressed him:
'Stranger, as to the excellence of my beauty and form,
the gods destroyed them when the Argives took ship on   125
their way to Ilium, and among them went my husband Odysseus.
If he were to return and look after my livelihood, my fame
would thereby become greater and more glorious; but
as it is, I grieve, so many are the troubles a god has sent
against me. All those chieftains who rule over the islands,   130
Dulichium and Same and wooded Zacynthos, and those
who are lords in clear-seen Ithaca, all these are courting me
against my will, and grinding down my household's wealth.
For this reason I have no time for guests or for suppliants,
or even for heralds, whose business is with public affairs.   135
Rather, I waste away my heart in my longing for Odysseus;
these men hasten my marriage, while I spin out my schemes.
My first ruse was the web, after a god had breathed into
my mind to set up a great loom in the hall and to weave on it
a web made with fine, very long threads. I said to them: 140
"Young princes, my suitors! Glorious Odysseus is dead; but
eager though you are for this marriage, wait until I finish
this robe, so that my weaving is not wasted, all in vain. It is
a burial-shroud* for the hero Laertes, meant for when the cruel
fate of death, bringer of long misery, takes him away, so that   145
no Achaean woman in our people will be indignant with me
because he who amassed much wealth is lying without a shroud."
That is what I said, and their proud hearts were persuaded.
From that time I would weave at the great loom by day, but
at night torches were set by me and I would undo my work.   150
So for three years my guile went unnoticed, and I fooled the
  Achaeans; but when with the seasons' round the fourth year

arrived, as the months waned and the long days came to an end,
then, with the help of my maids, irresponsible, shameless
hussies, they caught me by surprise and raised a loud complaint.   155
So, compelled against my will, I brought the work to completion.
And now I can neither escape from this marriage, nor can I think
of another stratagem. My parents keep urging me to marry,
and my son chafes with impatience while the suitors devour his
livelihood—and he knows it, for he is now a grown man, able to   160
look after his own house, someone to whom Zeus grants renown.
Enough; tell me about your family, and where you come from;
for you cannot be sprung from a rock or an oak,* as in the old story.'

   Then in answer Odysseus, man of many wiles, addressed her:
'Lady, revered wife of Odysseus the son of Laertes,   165
will you never give up questioning me about my ancestry?
Very well, I will tell you—but you will deliver me over to
more sorrows than those which now hold me; for so it is when
a man is absent from his native land as long as I have now been,
wandering and suffering hard times in many cities of mortals.   170
For all that, I will tell you what you ask and seek to know.
   'There is a land called Crete, in the middle of the wine-dark sea,
beautiful and fertile, washed all round by water; in it live many
men, beyond counting, and there too are ninety cities. It has
a mix of languages, all unlike each other: there are Achaeans   175
among them, and great-hearted True-Cretans, and Cydones,
and Dorians with long, flowing hair, and glorious Pelasgians.
Among these settlements is Cnossus, a great city, and there
Minos* ruled, who every nine years conversed with great Zeus;
and he was the father of my father, great-spirited Deucalion.   180
Now Deucalion had two sons, myself and lord Idomeneus;
Idomeneus went off in his beaked ships to fight before Ilium,
with the sons of Atreus. My renowned name is Aethon, and
I am the younger by birth; he was first-born and a better man.
I saw Odysseus there, in Crete, and gave him a guest-friend's   185
gifts, because violent winds had forced him to land there,
having driven him past Cape Malea* on his way to Troy.
He had put in at Amnisus, where is the cave of Eileithyia,*
a dangerous roadstead, and had only just escaped the storm.
He went at once up to the city and inquired after Idomeneus,   190
for he claimed to be a close, respected guest-friend of his;

but it was now the tenth or eleventh day since Idomeneus
had gone off in his beaked ships to fight before Ilium.
So I took him to my house and treated him generously,
showing him proper hospitality from my ample store within.   195
I also gave him, for the companions who accompanied him,
barley-meal and gleaming wine which I collected from the
public store, and oxen to sacrifice, all to satisfy their desires.
Here the glorious Achaeans stayed for twelve days, for the
mighty North Wind kept them weather-bound, and they could   200
not stand upright on the land; some hard god had stirred it up.
But on the thirteenth day the wind dropped and they put to sea.'

So in his tale Odysseus made his many lies seem like the truth;
and as Penelope listened the tears flowed and her body melted.
As when snow that has been piled up by the West Wind on   205
mountain peaks thaws when melted by the East Wind, and
as it melts the rivers fill up and run in spate, so Penelope's
beautiful cheeks melted as she shed her tears and wept
for the husband who was sitting by her side. Odysseus
felt pity in his heart for his wife as she wept, but his eyes   210
stayed fixed and unmoving under their lids, as if made of
horn or of iron, and by dissimulation he hid his own tears.
When she had had her pleasurable fill of tear-laden keening,
she answered Odysseus in turn and addressed him:
'Now, stranger, I am minded to put you to the test, to see if   215
you really did entertain my husband along with his godlike
companions there in your halls, as you boldly say. Tell me
what kind of clothes he was wearing about his person, and
what kind of man he was, and the companions with him.'

Then in reply Odysseus of many wiles addressed her: 220
'Lady, it is hard to tell you, when there has been so much
time in between, for it is now the twentieth year since he
set off from Crete, leaving my ancestral land behind him.
Still, I will tell you what kind of picture my mind has of him.
Glorious Odysseus was wearing a thick woollen cloak,   225
purple and folded double, and on it there was a golden pin
with double clasps, whose front part was cunningly made:
there was a hound gripping a dappled fawn in its forepaws,
holding it down as it struggled. All who saw it were amazed
at how, though made of gold, the hound gripped the fawn and   230

throttled it, while the fawn's feet thrashed about as it strove
to escape. Another thing: I noticed the shining tunic he wore,
how it looked like the skin that sits round a dried onion,
so soft it was, gleaming brightly just like the sun; and there
were indeed many women who looked at it with admiration.   235
And I will tell you another thing, for you to store in your mind:
I do not know if Odysseus wore these clothes when at home,
or if some companion gave them to him as he embarked in his
swift ship, or perhaps if some guest-friend did, for Odysseus
was loved by many people; few Achaeans were his equal.   240
I too gave him something—a bronze sword and a double cloak,
a fine purple garment, and a tunic with a fringe; then I sent
him off in the proper fashion in his well-benched ship.
And there is something else: there was ever a herald with him,
a little older than Odysseus, and I will tell you what he was like.   245
He was round-shouldered and dark-complexioned, with curly
hair, and his name was Eurybates. Odysseus valued him above
all his other companions, for they thought in the same way.'

So he spoke, and roused in Penelope a greater desire to weep,
recognizing as she did the sure tokens in Odysseus' words.   250
When she had had her pleasurable fill of tear-laden keening,
she answered, addressing him in these words:
'Stranger, even before this you were deserving of my pity,
but now you will be a dear and respected guest in this hall,
for I myself gave him those garments that you speak of;   255
I folded them in my chamber, and fastened the shining pin,
to be an adornment for him—but I shall never again
welcome him on his return home to his dear native land.
It was, I see, by a malignant destiny that Odysseus boarded
his hollow ship to set eyes on that vile Ilium, not to be named.'*   260

Then in answer Odysseus of many wiles addressed her:
'Lady, revered wife of Odysseus, son of Laertes; do not mar
your lovely skin any longer, nor let your heart waste away
in weeping for your husband; not that I blame you at all, for
many a woman has wept for the wedded husband she has lost,   265
with whom she has lain in love and borne his children—albeit
a lesser man than Odysseus, who they say was like the gods.
Come, put an end to your weeping, and mark my words.
I will tell you the absolute truth, nor shall I hide it from you

that only recently I heard of Odysseus' homeward journey: 270
that he is near at hand, in the rich land of the Thesprotians,*
alive; and moreover is bringing a great store of splendid
treasure, got by soliciting throughout that land. But he lost
his trusty crew, and his hollow ship, on the wine-dark sea, on
his way from the isle of Thrinacia; Zeus and Helios were at   275
odds with him because his crew killed the Sun-god's cattle.
They perished, every one of them, in the ever-surging sea,
but a wave cast him up on dry land, clinging to his ship's keel,
in the land of the Phaeacians, who are close in kin to the gods;
these men honoured him in their hearts as if he were a god,   280
and gave him many gifts, and were themselves ready to
escort him home unharmed. And indeed Odysseus would
have been here long since, had he not thought it more profitable
to amass treasure as he travelled the world—so skilled is he,
beyond all men who are doomed to die, in the acquisition   285
of possessions, nor can any mortal challenge him in this.
All this was told me by Pheidon, king of the Thesprotians; and
he also swore in my presence, while pouring a drink-offering in
his palace, that a ship was being dragged down to the sea and a
trusty crew was ready to convey Odysseus to his dear homeland.   290
But before this happened he sent me off, for it chanced that a
Thesprotian ship was passing, bound for wheat-rich Dulichium.
He showed me the many treasures Odysseus had collected,
enough to provide for his heirs, even to the tenth generation,
so much was lying there waiting for him in the king's halls.   295
As for the man, Pheidon told me he had gone to Dodona, hoping
to hear the advice of Zeus from his high-branched oak tree,*
as to how, after his long absence, he might return to his dear
ancestral land, whether this should be openly or in secret.
So you see from this that he is safe, and will soon be here,   300
and is in fact very near and will no longer be far from his
loved ones and his native land. I will add my oath to this:
may Zeus, the highest and the best of gods, be my witness,
and also the hearth of blameless Odysseus, to which I have
come, that all this will surely come to pass as I declare.   305
Some time in this very month, as one moon wanes
and another moon waxes, Odysseus will be here.'
    Then in turn circumspect Penelope addressed him:

'Stranger-guest, may these words turn out to be true!
If so, you will soon meet with kindness from me, and many   310
a gift, so that anyone encountering you will call you blessed.
But my heart has a foreboding that this is how it will really be:
Odysseus will never come home, nor will you get your passage
from here, because there are no longer masters in this house
such as Odysseus was among men—if he ever existed—   315
to welcome guests with respect and send them on their way.
But come, maids: give our guest a bath, and spread a bed
for him, a couch with cloaks and shining blankets, so that
he may be well warmed while waiting for Dawn on her golden
throne. Early tomorrow you may bathe and rub him with oil,   320
so that he may be ready to sit next to Telemachus in the hall
and take his supper there. And it will be the worse for any
ill-natured suitor who causes him distress; his business
here will come to nothing, however deeply angry he may be.
For how, stranger-guest, can you find out whether I surpass   325
other women at all in good sense and in thoughtful counsel,
if you are to join the feast here in my hall in a filthy state
and wearing dirty clothes? Man's life is short enough as it is;
if a man is unkind in himself, and has unkind thoughts in his
heart, everyone prays that he will suffer in torment as long   330
as he lives, and when he is dead everyone laughs at him.
But if a man is generous in himself, with generous thoughts
in his heart, his guest-friends spread his fame far and wide,
to men everywhere, and there are many to call him noble.'

   Then in answer Odysseus of many wiles addressed her: 335
'Lady, respected wife of Odysseus son of Laertes, I must
tell you that cloaks and shining blankets have long become
abhorrent to me, ever since I put behind me the snow-clad
mountains of Crete and embarked in my long-oared ship.
So I will lie as I have passed sleepless nights in the past;   340
many are the nights I have spent on some poor, mean bed,
waiting for the bright Dawn to appear on her lovely throne.
Moreover, baths for my feet no longer hold any pleasure
for me, nor shall any of the women who carry out tasks
for you in your house lay hands on my foot—unless   345
there is perhaps some aged woman of good character, one
who has endured as much suffering in her heart as I have;

I would not object to someone like her touching my feet.'
    Then in turn circumspect Penelope addressed him:
'Dear guest—so I must call you, since no one as considerate   350
or more welcome has ever come to my house from far away;
everything you say is so very thoughtful and well-expressed.
There is indeed someone here, an old woman of shrewd temper,
who was nurse to that unfortunate man, and brought him up,
taking him into her arms from the moment his mother bore him. 355
She will wash your feet, even though her strength is waning.
Come here, circumspect Eurycleia! Be up and wash the feet
of a man who is the same age as your master. It may be that
by this time Odysseus' feet and his hands look the same as his,
for in ill fortune mortal men quickly show the signs of age.'   360
    So she spoke, and the old woman covered her face in her hands,
shedding hot tears, and spoke to her in tones of lamentation:
'Ah, my child, how powerless I am to help you! Truly Zeus
hates you above all men, for all your god-fearing spirit.
No mortal ever made as many burnt offerings to Zeus   365
who delights in the thunder, of fatty thigh-bones or of
perfect hecatombs, as you used to do, praying to reach a
sleek old age and to bring up your splendid son to manhood.
But now, from you alone he has taken away all hope of a
return home. No doubt women have mocked him too, in the 370
grand palace of some far-off foreigner, when he called there,
just as these brazen hussies here mock you, all of them; it is
to avoid these women's insults and shameful abuse that you
will not let them wash your feet. But circumspect Penelope,
Icarius' daughter, has told me to do it, and I am not unwilling. 375
So wash your feet I will, both for your sake and for that of
Penelope herself, since the heart within me is troubled
with sadness. But listen, please, to what I have to say:
there have been many travel-worn strangers coming here,
but I do not think I have ever seen anyone who looks as much 380
like Odysseus as you do, in your build and voice and feet.'
    Then in answer Odysseus of many wiles addressed her:
'Old woman, that is what all those who have clapped eyes
on both of us say—that we are very much like each other,
exactly as you yourself have shrewdly observed and tell me.' 385
    So he spoke, and the old woman fetched a brightly shining

basin, which she always used when washing feet, and poured
into it plenty of cold water, then drew off some hot and added it.
Odysseus was sitting at the hearth, but at once turned to face
the dark, for he had a foreboding that when she held his foot she   390
would recognize his scar; and then everything would be revealed.
Eurycleia drew near and began to wash her master; instantly she
recognized the scar where a boar's white tusk had wounded him
when he was away in Parnassus, visiting Autolycus and his sons.
Now Autolycus was his mother's noble father, who excelled all   395
men in thievery and oath-twisting—a gift from a god himself,
because he had pleased him by making burnt offerings of the
thighs of lambs and kids; and so Hermes gladly favoured him.
Autolycus had once travelled to the rich land of Ithaca, and
there discovered that his daughter had recently borne a son.   400
As he was finishing his supper Eurycleia set the baby on
his knees, and addressed him, hailing him by his name:
'Autolycus, you yourself must find a name you can give to
the child of your own child; he has been much prayed for.'

　　Then in turn Autolycus addressed her in these words: 405
'My son-in-law and my daughter, give him the name I
tell you. Since I have come here as an object of odium
to many men and women on the much-nourishing earth,
let his given name be Odysseus.* When he reaches manhood
and visits me in my great house on Parnassus where his   410
mother was brought up, and where my possessions are,
I will make him a gift from them and send him away rejoicing.'

　　It was for this reason that Odysseus went there, to get his
magnificent gifts. Autolycus and his sons welcomed him
with clasping of hands and with words of kindness, and   415
his mother's mother, Amphithea, threw her arms around him
and repeatedly kissed his head and both his handsome eyes.
Autolycus summoned his splendid sons, and told them to
make supper ready; and they heard and did as he said.
At once they brought in a bull, five years old, which they   420
flayed and then set to work on, jointing the whole carcass.
They skilfully chopped the meat into pieces and threaded it
on to skewers, cooked it carefully, and shared the portions out.
And so, all day long until the setting of the sun, they feasted,
and no man's heart lacked a fair share in the meal.   425

But when the sun went down and darkness came over them,
they settled down to rest and took the gift of slumber.
    When early-born Dawn with her rosy fingers appeared,
they set off to go hunting, hounds and men, these sons
of Autolycus, and along with them went glorious Odysseus.   430
Starting up the steep mountain of thickly wooded Parnassus
before long they came to some hollows, swept by the wind.
The Sun-god had risen from the gently flowing waters of deep-
running Ocean, and was only now striking the ploughland,
when the beaters entered a wooded glen. Ahead of them   435
went the hounds, seeking a scent, and behind came the
sons of Autolycus, and with them was glorious Odysseus,
close on the hounds and hefting a far-shadowing spear.
And there, hidden in its densely covered lair, lay a huge boar.
The blustering winds' damp force never penetrated his den,   440
nor could the bright Sun-god strike into it with his rays,
nor could rain ever pass right through, so dense it was;
and there was a deep pile of leaves heaped up in it. As they
pressed forward, urging on the hounds, the thudding of men's
and dogs' feet drifted around the boar; right in front of them   445
it stood in its lair, back bristling and fire blazing from its
eyes, facing them and very close. Odysseus was the first
to rush forward, poising his long spear in his brawny hand,
raging to jab at it; but the boar was too quick for him, and
with a sideways lunge of its tusk gored him above the knee,   450
tearing the flesh wide open, though it did not reach the bone.
Then Odysseus took true aim and stabbed the boar in its right
shoulder, and his shining spear's point passed clean through;
down it fell in the dust, squealing, and the life flew from it.
Autolycus' dear sons busied themselves about the beast,   455
and also skilfully bound up the wound of godlike Odysseus,
checking the flow of dark blood with an incantation; and
very soon they arrived back at their dear father's house.
Autolycus and his sons, when they had fully healed Odysseus'
wound and presented him with magnificent gifts, lost no time   460
in sending him back, a happy man, to Ithaca, his beloved ancestral
land. When he reached home, his father and revered mother
were overjoyed at his coming and asked all about his visit,
how it was that he got the wound, and he gave them a full

account: that while he was on a hunting trip to Parnassus with   465
Autolycus' sons a boar had gashed him with its white tusk.

It was this wound that the old woman felt, as she ran her palms
over him, and recognizing the scar she suddenly let his foot
drop, and it fell into the basin; the bronze vessel rang out,
tipping on to its side, and the water spilled on to the ground.   470
Joy and grief together gripped her heart, and her eyes were
filled with tears, and all the strength went out of her voice.
Grasping Odysseus by the chin, she said to him: 'Of course!
You are Odysseus, my dear child; I did not know you before
this, not until I had passed my hands all over my master.'   475

So she spoke, and looked towards Penelope, wanting to
signal to her that her dear husband was now back home;
but Penelope could not meet her glance or notice her,
for Athena had turned her attention elsewhere. Meanwhile
Odysseus, feeling for it with his right hand, grabbed her by   480
the throat, and with the other drew her close to him, and said:
'Nanny, do you want to kill me, you who nursed me at your
own breast? Yes, after many hardships, I have indeed come
home now, in the twentieth year, to my ancestral land.
But now that you have recognized me, and a god has put it in   485
your heart, stay silent, so that no one else in my halls finds out.
I tell you this plainly, and it will surely come to fulfilment:
if you speak, and if at my hands a god beats down the lordly
suitors, though you are my nurse I will not spare you
when I come to kill the other women servants in my halls.'   490

Then in answer circumspect Eurycleia addressed him:
'My child, what words have escaped the barrier of your teeth!
You know well how steadfast and unwavering my spirit is,
and this is how I shall remain, stubborn as a rock or as iron.
And I will tell you one more thing, to store in your mind: 495
if indeed a god beats down the lordly suitors at your hands,
I shall give you a full account of those women in your halls
who have no respect for you, and those who are guiltless.'

Then in answer Odysseus of many wiles addressed her:
'Nanny, why do you speak of these women? There is no need.   500
I myself will take good note of each, and will find them out.
No, keep your tale to yourself, and leave things to the gods.'

So he spoke, and the old woman went away through the hall to

fetch water to wash his feet, for the first basinful was all spilled.
When she had washed him and rubbed him richly with oil,   505
Odysseus again drew his chair closer to the fire, meaning
to warm himself there; but he cloaked the scar under his rags.
Then circumspect Penelope was the first of them to speak:
'Guest, I will ask you one more small thing, for myself;
for soon, you know, it will be time for pleasant rest—at   510
least for those whom sweet sleep grips, for all their cares.
But for me, to whom some divinity has sent limitless grief;
during the day I find relief in grief, and I lament as I look
to my own work and that of the servants in my house; but
when night comes, and sleep has gripped everyone else,   515
I lie on my bed, and close around my overfilled heart bitter
anxieties come crowding, and disturb me in my sorrow.
Just as the tawny nightingale, daughter of Pandareus,*
perched in the trees' thick foliage, sings her beautiful
song when the spring season is just beginning, pouring   520
out her far-echoing melody with many a trill and turn in
mourning for her beloved son Itylus, son of lord Zethus,
whom in her madness she killed with the sharp bronze;
so my heart too is pulled two ways, this way and that:
should I stay here with my son, keeping everything safe and   525
sound—my possessions, my servants, and my high-roofed
house—out of regard for my husband's bed and the people's
voice, or should I now go with the best of these Achaeans
who court me in my halls, he who brings me countless gifts?
My son, when he was a child and not yet of secure mind,   530
would not let me marry and leave my husband's house; but
now he is fully grown and has reached manhood's measure,
he actually begs me to return home from these halls, chafing at
the loss of his property, which the Achaeans devour before him.

   'And now hear this dream; please listen and interpret it for me.   535
I have in this house twenty geese which come up from their
pond and feed on wheat-grains, and I delight in watching them.
But a great hook-beaked eagle flew down from the mountains
and killed them all, breaking their necks; they lay in a jumbled
heap in the hall, and the eagle flew back up into the bright air.   540
So even though it was a dream, I began to weep and wail,
lamenting piteously because the eagle had killed my geese;

and around me gathered the Achaean women with lovely hair.
But then it came back and settled on the jutting end of a roof-
beam, and in a human voice spoke and checked my wailing: 545
"Far-renowned daughter of Icarius, do not despair! This is
no dream, but a true vision, and you will see it fulfilled.
The geese are the suitors, and I, you see, who was an eagle
in your dream, am your own husband. I have now returned
and am about to unleash an ugly death on all the suitors."   550
    'So it spoke, and honey-sweet sleep released its hold on me,
and as I looked about me I saw the geese in the hall,
pecking at the wheat-grains by their trough, just as before.'
    Then in answer Odysseus, man of many wiles, addressed her:
'Lady, it is not possible to interpret this dream by twisting it   555
to a different sense: Odysseus himself has revealed to you
how he will bring it to fulfilment. Doom clearly waits for the
suitors, all of them; not one will escape death and destruction.'
    Then in turn circumspect Penelope addressed him:
'Guest, dreams are puzzling things, and hard to interpret,   560
and not all the promises they make to men come to fruition.
There are two portals through which fleeting dreams come,
and of these one is made of horn, and the other of ivory.
Those that issue forth from the gate of freshly sawn ivory,*
they are the ones that deceive, bringing tidings that come to   565
nothing, while those that pass through the gate of polished
horn bear a true message to any mortal who sees them.
I do not think this uncanny dream came from this gate,
though my son and I would certainly welcome it if it did.
And I will tell you another thing, to store in your mind: 570
the ill-fated day will soon dawn that will take me away from
Odysseus' house, since I am now minded to propose a contest—
the famous axes, which he used to set up in a row in his hall,
like props under a ship's keel, twelve in all; standing a
good way off, he would shoot an arrow clean through them.*   575
This is now the contest I mean to put before the suitors:
whoever can take the bow in his hands and string it most
easily, and shoot an arrow right through all twelve axes,
with him will I go, forsaking the house to which I came as
a bride; such a beautiful house, full of life's sustenance,   580
one which I think I will always remember, even in my dreams.'

Then in answer Odysseus, man of many wiles, addressed her:
'Lady, respected wife of Odysseus son of Laertes, now is the
time. Do not put off this contest in your palace any longer,
for long before these men have handled the well-polished bow   585
you speak of, and tried to string it and shoot an arrow through
the iron axes, Odysseus of many wiles will be in this place.'

Then in turn circumspect Penelope addressed him:
'Guest, if only you could sit here beside me in this hall and
entertain me, sleep would never be shed over my eyelids!   590
But it is in no way possible for men to remain without sleep
for ever, for to mortals who live on the grain-giving earth
the immortals have assigned a proper portion of everything.
So now I am going to my upper room, where I shall lie
on my bed that is so full of misery, for ever soaked with   595
my tears, ever since the time Odysseus went away to set
eyes on that Evil-Ilium, never to be named.* There I shall
lie, but you must sleep here in the house; either spread some
bedding on the ground, or let them make you up a couch.'

So she spoke, and went back to her bright upper room,   600
not alone, but the two serving-women accompanied her.
When she had gone up there with her serving-women
she fell to weeping for Odysseus, her dear husband, until
grey-eyed Athena cast sweet sleep over her eyelids.

BOOK TWENTY

Meanwhile glorious Odysseus was abed in the forecourt.
He had laid out an undressed oxhide, and over it many
fleeces from the sheep daily slaughtered by the Achaeans,
and after he lay down Eurynome had thrown a cloak over him.
There Odysseus lay, awake and plotting destruction in his   5
heart for the suitors. Now the women who had up to now
been accustomed to sleep with the suitors came out of the
hall, laughing with each other and full of high spirits;
and Odysseus' heart in his breast began to be stirred,
and he pondered long in his heart and in his mind, if   10
he should rush at them and kill them, each and every one,
or let them lie with the arrogant suitors for one last
final time. Deep within him his heart was growling;
as when a bitch, standing guard over her tender pups,
growls at an unfamiliar man, all eager to fight him, so   15
Odysseus' heart within him growled at their wicked deeds.
But he struck his breast and spoke to his heart in rebuke:
'Endure, my heart! You have borne more shameful treatment
than this before, on the day the irresistible Cyclops ate your
mighty crew. But you endured, until your cunning brought   20
you safe out of the cave. You thought you were going to die.'
    So he spoke, in urgent appeal to the heart in his breast, and
it remained firm and steadfast and obeyed him, without
flinching. But Odysseus himself kept tossing back and forth.
As when a man has stuffed a paunch full of fat and blood,   25
and keeps turning it back and forth on a blazing-hot fire,
because he wants it to be cooked as quickly as possible,
so Odysseus kept turning back and forth, pondering how
to lay his hands on the shameless suitors, though he was
only one against so many. Then down from the high sky   30
came Athena in the form of a woman and stood close to him.
Standing above his head she addressed him in these words:
'Still awake, yet again, you most ill-fated of mortals?
This is your house, your wife is here inside it, and your
son, such a son as any man anywhere would hope to have.'   35

Then in answer Odysseus of many wiles addressed her:
'Everything you have said, goddess, is right and proper;
but even so my heart and mind are pondering a question:
how I may lay my hands on these shameless suitors, when
I am but one against many, and they are always here in force.   40
And there is too this greater concern in my mind: if with
Zeus' and your consent I succeed in killing them, where can I
flee, to be clear away from them? I ask you to consider this.'
    Then in turn the goddess grey-eyed Athena addressed him:
'Stubborn man! Most men will readily put their trust in an inferior 45
comrade, a mere mortal, who is not as clever as I am;
but I am a goddess, the one who has been protecting you
all the way through your troubles. I tell you this, plainly:
if there were fifty companies of mortal men standing
about us two, and raging in their battle-fury to kill us, you   50
would still be able to drive off their cattle and sturdy sheep.
So let sleep take you; it is a vexatious thing to lie awake,
on watch all night. You will soon be free of your troubles.'
So she spoke, and shed sleep over his eyelids, and then she,
bright among goddesses, made her way back to Olympus.   55
    While sleep held its grip on Odysseus, loosening the cares
of his heart and relaxing his limbs, his loyal wife suddenly
woke, and sitting on her soft couch fell to weeping.
When she, bright among women, had sated her heart
with crying, her first act was to make a prayer to Artemis: 60
'Artemis, revered goddess, daughter of Zeus, I wish you
could now shoot an arrow into my breast and take the life
from me, this instant; or that some tempest could seize
and sweep me away along the misty paths of the sea,
casting me up at the waters of circling Ocean, as when   65
storm-winds carried off the daughters of Pandareus.*
The gods killed their parents, and they were left orphans
in their halls, but bright Aphrodite looked after them,
feeding them cheese and sweet honey and pleasing wine.
And Hera gave them the gift of beauty beyond all women,   70
and sound understanding, and holy Artemis made them tall,
and Athena taught them the making of wonderful works.
But when divine Aphrodite turned her steps to high Olympus,
to Zeus who delights in the thunder, to ask him for the final

grant of a fruitful marriage for the girls—for well he knows　　75
everything, both the good and the evil destinies of mankind—
on that very day storm-winds snatched the girls away and
handed them over to the hateful Furies, to do their bidding.
Just so I wish the dwellers in Olympian palaces might make
me disappear, or fair-haired Artemis might shoot me down,　　80
so that I could pass beneath the hateful earth with Odysseus
vivid in my mind, and never gladden the heart of a lesser man.
It is a grief that may be endured, when someone weeps in
the daytime, and sorrows fall thick on the heart, but then at
night is held fast by sleep—for sleep brings forgetfulness of　　85
everything, good and bad, once it has clouded the eyelids.
But for me, even the dreams a god sends are horrible: again
this very night someone like him was sleeping beside me,
looking as he did when he left with the expedition, and my
heart was glad. I did not think it was a dream, but a true vision.'　　90

　　So she spoke, and Dawn on her golden throne arrived.
Glorious Odysseus caught the sound of her weeping, and fell
to thinking, and it seemed in his mind that she was standing
by his head, and that she now knew who he was. He rolled
up the cloak and fleeces in which he had been sleeping, and　　95
taking them into the hall laid them on a chair; then he took the
oxhide outside, put it down, and prayed to Zeus with hands raised:
'Father Zeus, if it was the plan of you gods to bring me over dry
land and sea to my own country, after causing me great suffering,
then let someone now waking in the house speak a word of　　100
good omen for me; and let Zeus show me some sign out here.'

　　So he spoke in prayer, and Zeus the counsellor heard him,
and at once sent thunder from gleaming Olympus, from a
high place among the clouds; and glorious Odysseus was glad.
And now a woman, a corn-grinder, cried out an omen from a　　105
building nearby, where the mills of the people's shepherd* were.
It was the task of twelve women in all to work at these mills,
grinding barley-meal and wheat-flour, the marrow of men.
All the rest were asleep, because they had finished pounding
their grain, but she alone, the weakest, was still working.　　110
She stopped her mill and spoke words of omen for her master:
'Father Zeus, you who rule over both gods and men, you
thundered loudly from the starry high sky, and yet there is no

cloud anywhere; you must be revealing a sign to someone.
So fulfil for me now what I, in my wretched state, ask: 115
may this day be the very last and final time that the suitors
enjoy the pleasure of their feasting in Odysseus' halls!
They have broken my knees with heart-sapping labour
as I grind the barley for them! May this meal be their last!'

So she spoke, and glorious Odysseus was glad at the uttered omen, 120
and at Zeus' thunder; he believed the wrongdoers would be punished.
   Now all the other maids in the splendid palace of Odysseus
had gathered and were lighting tireless fire on the hearth,
and Telemachus, a godlike man, sprang up from his bed
and put on his clothes; from his shoulder he slung his sharp   125
sword, and under his shining feet he bound his fine sandals;
then he picked up his sturdy spear, capped with sharp bronze,
and went and stood at the hall doorway and spoke to Eurycleia:
'Nanny dear, have you shown respect to the guest in our house—
a bed and food—or is he simply lying somewhere untended?   130
Such is now my mother's way, sensible though she may be:
she can on impulse treat one man with respect, even an
inferior one, but sends a better one away without honour.'

   Then in turn circumspect Eurycleia addressed him:
'Child, you must not blame her when she is not to blame.   135
The man sat and drank his wine for as long as he wished,
but said he wanted no more food; for she had asked him.
And when at last his thoughts turned to rest and sleep,
she instructed her women to make a up bed for him;
but he, as expected in one utterly pitiable and ill-fated,   140
had no desire to sleep on a bed under coverlets, but lay
down to rest on an undressed oxhide and sheep's fleeces,
in the forecourt; it was we who spread a cloak over him.'

   So she spoke, and Telemachus went out through the hall
holding his spear, and two swift dogs went with him, on   145
his way to the assembly to meet the well-greaved Achaeans.
But Eurycleia, bright among women, daughter of Ops who
was the son of Peisenor, called out to the serving-women:
'To work! You, stir yourselves and sweep the house,
sprinkle water on the floor, and throw purple rugs over   150
the well-made chairs; you, wipe down the tables with
sponges, all of them, and then scour the mixing-bowls

and well-made two-handled cups. And you, go to the
spring to get water, and bring it back as fast as you can;
for the suitors will not be away from the hall for long,   155
but will be here very early as this is a general feast-day.'
    So she spoke, and they listened carefully and obeyed.
Twenty went off to a spring flowing with dark water,
while the others worked purposefully about the house.
Then the proud manservants came in, and with great skill   160
set about splitting wood for kindling, and the women came
back from the spring. Next after them came the swineherd
leading three fatted hogs, the best there were in his herd;
these he left to forage at large inside the fine enclosure,
and himself addressed Odysseus in friendly words: 165
'Stranger, do the Achaeans look on you more respectfully
here in the hall, or are they as uncivil as they were before?'
    Then in answer Odysseus of many wiles addressed him:
'Eumaeus, I only wish the gods might punish these arrogant
suitors for the reckless acts they plan here, in the house of   170
another man! There is not a scrap of shame anywhere in them.'
    While they were conversing, one with another, in this way,
up came Melanthius, the man who tended goats, leading
beasts that were by far the best in all his herds, to be the
suitors' supper; and two herdsmen came along with him.   175
These nanny-goats he tethered under the echoing portico,
and himself addressed Odysseus with jeering words:
'Still here, stranger? Are you still intent on pestering
people in the palace with your begging? Get out of here!
I fancy we two will not part until we have had a taste of   180
each other's fists. This begging is quite beyond the pale—
and anyway, there are other Achaeans dining elsewhere.'
    So he spoke, and Odysseus of many wiles did not answer, but
shook his head in silence, brooding deeply on evil thoughts.
    Then there came up a third man, Philoetius, captain of men,   185
bringing a heifer and some fat goats for the suitors.
Ferrymen had brought them over from the mainland, men
who give passage to people too, whoever comes to them.
Philoetius tethered these beasts under the echoing portico,
and went and stood next to the swineherd, and asked: 190
'Swineherd, who is this stranger who has recently come to

our house? What stock of men does he claim to be from?
Where is his family, and his ancestral land? He is out
of luck, and yet he looks in stature like some royal lord.
It is true that the gods bring suffering on men who rove   195
afar, when even for kings they spin the thread of misery.'
    So he spoke, and standing by Odysseus held out a friendly
right hand and addressed him, speaking in winged words:
'Welcome, father stranger! May prosperity attend you in
future, though now you are in the grip of many troubles.   200
Father Zeus, no other god is crueller than you: you have no
pity for men, though you yourself father them, but force
them to keep company with troubles and bitter pains.
When I saw you I broke into a sweat, and my eyes are filled
with tears. You remind me of Odysseus; I suppose he too is   205
wearing rags like these and wanders among men—if indeed
he is still alive somewhere, and looks upon the sun's light.
But if he is now dead and in Hades' halls, then I lament
for blameless Odysseus, who while I was still a lad set
me up in charge of his oxen in the Cephallenians' land.   210
And now these are beyond counting, and nowhere else has
a man's stock of broad-browed cattle seen such an increase.
But it is other men who order me to bring the beasts here for
them to eat; they have no respect at all for his son in the halls,
nor do they tremble at the gods' vengeance, being now eager   215
to share out the possessions that belong to my long-gone lord.
As for me, the heart in my breast time and again turns over
this thought: while the son is alive, it would surely be a
coward's way to take my cattle and go off to another land,
to live among strangers; and yet it is worse to stay on here   220
and suffer the misery of looking after other men's herds.
I would have run away long ago and gone to the house of
some other powerful king, for things are now beyond bearing,
but still I wonder about that luckless man, if he will appear
from somewhere and send the suitors scattering in his palace.'   225
    Then in answer Odysseus of many wiles addressed him:
'Cowherd, you seem to me a man neither bad nor foolish,
and I can see for myself that good sense lives in your mind.
So I will tell you this, and swear a great oath to support it:
may my witness be Zeus above all gods, and this hospitable   230

table, and blameless Odysseus' hearth, to which I have come,
that while you are still here Odysseus will return to his house.
If you wish it so, with your own eyes you will witness the
slaying of the suitors who now play the lord in this place.'

Then in turn the cowherd, keeper of his cattle, addressed him: 235
'Ah, stranger, I wish Cronus' son might fulfil these words!
You would soon know what strength there is in my hands.'
In the same way Eumaeus made a prayer to all the gods, that
Odysseus, man of many designs, might return to his own house.

While they were conversing, one with another, in this way,   240
the suitors were plotting death and ruin for Telemachus.
Suddenly there appeared over them a bird of omen,
on their left, a high-soaring eagle, clutching a timid dove;
and Antinous spoke out among them and addressed them:
'My friends, this plan of ours, the killing of Telemachus,   245
will not succeed. Let us rather turn our minds to feasting.'

So spoke Antinous, and his words found favour with them.
So they all went into the palace of godlike Odysseus,
and laid their cloaks down on chairs and seats, and set
about slaughtering some huge sheep and some fat goats,   250
and also some fattened swine and a heifer from the herd.
They cooked the entrails and shared them out, and mixed wine
in bowls, and the swineherd handed each man his cup; and
Philoetius, captain of men, passed around the bread in fine
baskets, while Melanthius poured out the wine. So the suitors   255
reached out their hands for the food lying ready before them.

Now Telemachus, looking to their advantage, gave Odysseus
a seat inside the strongly built hall, beside the stone doorway,
and placed in front of him a mean stool and a small table.
He then put before him a portion of entrails, and poured wine   260
into a cup made of gold, and addressed him in these words:
'Sit there now, and drink your wine in these men's company;
and I myself shall protect you from any blows or taunts
of the suitors, since this house is no public meeting-place,
but the house of Odysseus, and I have inherited it from him.   265
And you, suitors, hold yourselves back from insults and
blows, and in that way no strife or quarrelling will arise.'

So he spoke, and they all bit their lips hard, and looked in
surprise at Telemachus, because he had spoken so boldly.

Then Antinous, son of Eupeithes, spoke up among them:　270
'Telemachus' words were harsh, but we Achaeans should
accept them—though there were heavy threats in what he said.
Cronus' son has blocked our purpose, or else we would by now
have silenced him in his hall, eloquent orator though he is.'

So spoke Antinous, but Telemachus paid no heed to his words.　275
And now heralds were driving a sacred hecatomb for the gods
through the city, and flowing-haired Achaeans were gathering
in the shade of a grove sacred to Apollo who shoots from afar.
When they had cooked the outer meat and drawn it off the spits
they shared it out in portions and dined off the splendid feast.　280
And those whose task it was set before Odysseus a helping
equal to what they themselves received, for these were the orders
of Telemachus, the dear son of Odysseus who looked like a god.

But Athena did not altogether intend the lordly suitors to
refrain from heart-wounding insults, since she wanted even　285
harsher anguish to enter the heart of Odysseus, Laertes' son.
There was in the suitors' number a man of lawless temper,
whose name was Ctesippus, and he had his home in Same.
Trusting, doubtless, in his amazing wealth, he was a persistent
wooer of the wife of Odysseus, a man long gone from home.　290
It was this man who now addressed the arrogant suitors:
'Listen to me, you proud suitors, to what I have to say.
This stranger has for some time had his portion, as is right,
an equal one, for it is not a good or proper thing to treat
Telemachus' guests badly, whoever may come to this palace.　295
So look, I too will give him a guest's token, which he may
himself pass on as a prized gift—to a bath-attendant or to any
of the servants who live in the palace of godlike Odysseus.'

So he spoke, and in his brawny hand picked up a cow's
hoof that lay in a basket and threw it; but Odysseus leaned　300
his head slightly and dodged it,* hiding his anger with a
grim fierce smile, and the hoof hit the house's well-built
wall. Then Telemachus rebuked Ctesippus in these words:
'Ctesippus, it was lucky for you how that turned out!
You missed the stranger, and he dodged your missile;　305
otherwise I would have driven my sharp spear through
your midriff, and instead of a wedding your father would be
holding your funeral here. So let no one make a show of

boorishness in my house. I now see and understand things:
and can tell right from wrong; I am no longer a child.   310
And yet, for all that, we must endure the sight of all this:
sheep being slaughtered, and wine and bread consumed,
since it is hard for one man by himself to restrain many.
Come, give up your malice and stop your attacks on me;
but if you are really intent on killing me with the bronze,   315
that would be my wish also, since it would be far better
to die than day after day to be a witness of these vile acts—
guests subjected to brutal treatment and serving-women
shamefully dragged about through the fine palace.'
     So he spoke, and they all remained still and silent.   320
Finally Agelaus, Damastor's son, spoke out among them:
'My friends, surely no one after such a fair speech
could out of resentment answer it with violent words.
Do not treat this stranger roughly, or any of the servants
who live in the palace of Odysseus who looks like a god.   325
To Telemachus and to his mother I would speak a gentle
word, hoping it might be pleasing to the hearts of both:
as long as the spirits in your breasts were fixed in the hope
that Odysseus of many designs would return to his home,
for that time no one could blame you for biding your   330
time and restraining the suitors in the palace; that was the
better course, if Odysseus was to come back to his house.
But it has now become clear that he will never return.
So sit beside your mother and explain this carefully to her:
she must marry the best man here, who offers the most gifts,   335
and then you may happily manage all your patrimony, and
eat and drink, while she looks after another man's house.'
     Then in turn wise Telemachus answered and addressed him:
'By Zeus, Agelaus, and by the sufferings of my father, who
is lying dead somewhere far from Ithaca, or is still wandering,   340
I am not delaying my mother's marriage. I urge her to marry
whoever she wishes, and I offer countless gifts to go with her.
Even so, I am ashamed to drive her unwilling from my hall
with a harsh word. May the god never bring this to pass.'
     So spoke Telemachus; and among the suitors Pallas Athena   345
roused unquenchable laughter, and drove their wits astray.
Now their faces were distorted by maniacal laughter,

and the meat they were eating crawled with blood; their
eyes filled with tears, and their minds strained to cry aloud.
Theoclymenus, a god-fearing man, spoke out among them: 350
'Wretched men! What is this horror afflicting you? Your
heads, your faces, and your knees below are wrapped in night;
sounds of wailing blaze out, your cheeks are wet with tears,
and the walls and fine cross-beams are spattered with blood.
The porch and the court are filled with spectres hurrying   355
down to Erebus and darkness. The sun has been wiped from
the high sky, and an evil mist is spread over the world.'

So he spoke, but they all laughed gaily at him. Among them
Eurymachus, the son of Polybus, was the first to speak:
'Our newly arrived guest from abroad has lost his wits!   360
Quick, my young friends, show him out of the house and
send him to the meeting-place; he thinks it is night in here.'

Then in turn godlike Theoclymenus addressed him:
'Eurymachus, I am far from asking you to provide me with
guides; I have eyes and ears, and both my feet, as well as   365
a mind in my breast that is sound and by no means useless.
I will rely on these to leave this place, for I can see a calamity
advancing upon you, which not a single one of you suitors
will be able to avoid or elude, because of your arrogant
deeds and reckless plots in the house of godlike Odysseus.'   370

So he spoke, and went out of the well-situated palace, and
came to the house of Peiraeus, who readily welcomed him.
But now the suitors were all looking at each other, trying to
provoke Telemachus by treating his guests with ridicule;
and this is what one of the arrogant young men would say: 375
'Telemachus, no one is unluckier in his guests than you!
First, you keep a needy vagrant such as this man here,
always wanting food and wine, with no talent for hard work
or fighting, nothing more than a useless weight on the earth;
and then there is this other fellow who stood up and prophesied! 380
You would do much better to take some advice from me:
let us throw these strangers into a many-benched ship and send
them off to Sicily, where they would bring you a good price.'

This is what the suitors said, but he paid no heed to their words,
and kept looking in silence at his father, waiting always for   385
when he was ready to lay his hands on the shameless suitors.

Circumspect Penelope, daughter of Icarius, had positioned
her beautiful chair directly opposite the suitors, and was
listening to what each of the men was saying in the hall.
They had slaughtered a great number of cattle, and amid   390
much laughter had prepared a pleasant and satisfying meal;
but never could there have been a more unpalatable feast than
the supper which a goddess and a brave man would soon put
before them; for with them the shameful business had begun.

BOOK TWENTY-ONE

But now the goddess grey-eyed Athena put into the mind
of circumspect Penelope, daughter of Icarius, to lay
before the suitors the bow and grey iron in Odysseus'
halls, to be both a contest and the beginning of slaughter.
She climbed a tall staircase in the house, taking   5
in her sturdy hand a cunningly forged key, finely
made of bronze; and the handle on it was of ivory.
Then she set off with her women for the room that was
farthest away, where the treasures of her lord were laid up—
bronze and gold and iron wrought with much labour.   10
There too was stored his curved bow, and the quiver
that held his arrows; and in it were many grief-laden shafts.
His guest-friend Iphitus, Eurytus' son, a man like the gods,
had given it to him when they met once in Lacedaemon.
These two fell in with each other in Messene, in the house   15
of shrewd Ortilochus. Odysseus had gone there to recover
a debt which was owed him by the whole people: men of
Messene had stolen some sheep from Ithaca, three hundred,
with their shepherds, carrying them off in many-benched ships;
so on their account Odysseus, still young, had undertaken this   20
mission's long road, sent by his father and the other elders.
Iphitus on the other hand was looking for some horses he had
lost—twelve mares, with work-enduring mules at the teat.
These, however, later became his death and doom, at the
time when he encountered the mighty-spirited son of Zeus,   25
Heracles, a hero well-versed in monstrous deeds:
he killed Iphitus in his own house, though he was his host,
hard man that he was, paying no heed to the gods' vengeance,
nor to the table he had put before Iphitus. He killed the man,
and kept the strong-hoofed mares for himself in his halls.   30
It was while Iphitus was seeking these that he met Odysseus
and gave him the bow, which great Eurytus used to carry in
the past, and when he died in his high halls he left it to his son.
In return Odysseus gave him a sharp sword and a stout spear.
This was the beginning of a close friendship; but they did not   35

further their intimacy at table, for before they could Zeus'
son slew Iphitus, Eurytus' son, a man who resembled the gods.
He it was who gave glorious Odysseus the bow, though he
never took it with him when going to war in his black ships,
but it was always stored in its place in his halls, as a reminder   40
of his dear friend; but in his own country he always carried it.

    Now when Penelope, bright among women, reached the store,
she set her foot on the oaken threshold—which a carpenter
had once planed skilfully and made straight against a line,
and had sunk doorposts in it, on which he hung shining doors—   45
and straightaway she unwound the leather strap from its handle
and thrust the key inside, and, aiming straight at them,
knocked back the bolts.* With a sound like the roar of a bull
grazing in a meadow the handsome doors groaned when
knocked by the key, and they quickly opened up before her.   50
She stepped up on to the raised platform, where stood
her chests, in which sweet-smelling clothes were stored;
and reaching up, she took the bow down from its peg,
together with its shining case which protected it all around.
There and then she sat down and set the case on her knees,   55
and wept loudly as she lifted from it the bow of her lord.
Then, when she had comforted herself with weeping,
she set off for the hall to join the haughty suitors,
holding in her hands the curved bow and the quiver that
contained its arrows; and in it were many grief-laden shafts.   60
With her went serving-women, carrying a box in which
lay stored much iron and bronze, prizes won by her lord.
When she, bright among women, had reached the suitors,
she stood beside a pillar supporting the strongly built roof,
holding her shining veil in front of her face, and a loyal   65
woman servant took her place on either side of her.
Without more ado she addressed the suitors in these words:
'Listen to me, you proud suitors! You have been vexing
this house with your interminable eating and drinking,
now that its master has been gone for a long time; nor   70
could you find any words by way of an excuse except
that you desired to marry me and make me your wife.
So look, suitors—here is the prize, before your very eyes!
I shall set before you the great bow of godlike Odysseus,

and whoever can set his hands to the bow, string it with the   75
greatest ease, and shoot an arrow through all twelve axes,*
with him I shall go, forsaking the house to which I came
as a bride—such a beautiful house, full of life's sustenance,
one which I think I will always remember, even in dreams.'
   So she spoke, and ordered Eumaeus, the good swineherd,   80
to lay out the bow and the grey iron axes before the suitors.
As he took them and laid them down he burst into tears;
and the oxherd wept too, when he saw his master's bow.
Antinous flung a rebuke at them, hailing them in these words:
'Foolish bumpkins, whose thoughts last no longer than a day!   85
Wretches, both of you; why shed tears, and why disturb
this lady's heart in her breast, when even without this
her spirit is deep in grief, because she has lost her dear lord?
Sit down and eat in silence, or else go outside and do your
weeping there. But leave the bow and arrows where they are;   90
they are going to be a test for the suitors, a hard one, for
I do not think this well-polished bow can easily be strung;
there is no one among us all here who is equal to the man
Odysseus was—I saw him once myself, and I remember
him well, though I was only a child at the time.'   95
   So he spoke, though in fact the heart in his breast hoped
that he would string the bow and shoot through the iron axes.
And yet he was to be the first to taste an arrow from the hands
of blameless Odysseus, whom he now treated with contempt as
he sat in his halls, urging all his companions to do the same.   100
   Then Telemachus, man of divine strength, spoke among them:
'What am I doing? Cronus' son has surely taken away my wits!
My dear mother, sensible though she is, is saying she will go
with some other man, putting this house behind her, yet
here am I laughing and being glad in my witless mind.   105
So come forward, suitors—here is the prize set before you,
a woman whose like does not exist throughout the land of
Achaea, neither in holy Pylos, nor in Argos, nor in Mycenae,
nor in Ithaca itself, nor anywhere on the dark mainland.
But you yourselves know this; why need I praise my mother?   110
So come: do not drag things out with excuses, nor hold back
any longer from this bow-stringing; and then we shall see.
I too may try my hand with the bow, and if I chance to be

successful in the attempt, and shoot through the iron axes,
I would not grieve at my revered mother leaving this house   115
and going away with another man, so long as I remain here,
now man enough to win the fine prizes won by my father.'

   So he spoke, and springing up to his full height threw off the
purple cloak from his shoulders, and unslung his sharp sword.
First, he dug a trench of full length and set up the axes, one   120
long trench for them all, making it straight against a line, and
stamped the earth flat around them. Amazement gripped all the
onlookers at how neatly he ordered them, having never seen it done
before. Then he went and stood on the threshold and tried the bow.
Three times he set it quivering as he strained to bend it, and   125
three times he gave up the struggle, yet still hoping in his heart
to stretch the string and shoot through the iron axes. And indeed
the fourth time he would have succeeded, pulling strongly on it,
had not Odysseus cut his efforts short with a jerk of his head.
Then Telemachus, man of divine strength, spoke to them again: 130
'Curse the thing! I suppose I shall always be a coward and a
weakling, or else I am still too young, not yet confident in my
hands' strength to take on a man who picks a fight with me.
So step forward, you whose strength is surely superior to
mine, and try the bow. Then let us make an end of the contest.'   135

   So he spoke, and put the bow from him, down on the ground,
propping it against the well-polished, close-fitting doors,
and leaned the swift arrow there against the fine door-handle,
and went back and sat on the chair from which he had risen.

   Now Antinous, son of Eupeithes, addressed the company: 140
'Stand up, my friends, all of you, and take turns from left
to right, starting from the place where the wine is poured.'

   So spoke Antinous, and his words found favour with them.
The first to rise to his feet was Leodes, son of Oenops,
who interpreted their sacrifices, and always sat furthest away,   145
next to the fine mixing-bowl; he was the only one who hated
the suitors' reckless deeds, and was indignant with them all.
He then was the first to pick up the bow and its swift shaft.
He walked to the threshold and stood there and tried the bow,
but could not string it; too soon, he wore out his delicate,   150
unhardened hands with bending it, and spoke to the suitors:
'My friends, I cannot string it; let someone else take it up.

I tell you, this bow will deprive many a chieftain of his
breath and spirit, for it is surely much better for us to die
than to stay alive and fail to gain the prize for which we are   155
forever gathered here, living in expectation all our days.
There are many here who even now fervently hope in their
hearts to marry Penelope, the wedded wife of Odysseus;
but once they have tried the bow and seen the outcome,
they should then seek out some other fine-robed Achaean   160
woman and pay court to her with gifts. Then, let her marry
the man who offers most and comes as her destined lord.'
   So he spoke, and put the bow from him, propping it
against the well-polished, close-fitting doors, and leaned
the swift arrow there against the fine door-handle. Then   165
he went back and sat on the chair from which he had risen.
   But Antinous flung a rebuke at him, hailing him in these words:
'Leodes, what a word has escaped the barrier of your teeth—
a terrible thing to say, and hard to bear; I am outraged to
hear it! To think that this bow will deprive chieftains of their   170
breath and spirit, simply because you are unable to string it!
The truth is, your revered mother did not bear you to be
the kind of man who draws bows and shoots arrows. But
there are other lordly suitors here who will soon string it.'
   So he spoke, and gave orders to Melanthius, herder of goats: 175
'Look sharp now, Melanthius, and light a fire in the hall.
Set a great stool next to the fire and throw a fleece over it;
then bring a great round of tallow out from the stores within,
and we young men will warm the bow and grease it with fat.
Then let us try our hands at it, and so end the contest.'   180
   So he spoke, and without more ado Melanthius lit the tireless fire.
He drew up a stool and laid a fleece over it, and then brought
out a great round of tallow from the stores within. The young
men warmed it, greased the bow, and tried their luck; but they
could not string it, for their strength fell far short of the task.   185
Now Antinous and godlike Eurymachus, leaders of the suitors,
were still holding back, though they were by far the best of them.
   Meanwhile the two men, the oxherd and swineherd of godlike
Odysseus, went out of the house, both at the same time,
and glorious Odysseus too left the house and followed them.   190
When they were well clear of the doors and the courtyard,

Odysseus spoke up and addressed them with winning words:
'Oxherd, and you too, swineherd—shall I say something, or
shall I keep it to myself? No, my heart urges me to speak.
How would you be at fighting on Odysseus' side, if he were   195
suddenly to appear from somewhere, just like this, brought
here by some god? Would you fight for Odysseus, or the
suitors? Tell me what your heart and spirit urge you to do.'
     Then in turn the oxherd who tended his cattle addressed him:
'Father Zeus—if only you could bring this wish to fulfilment—   200
that this man could return home, guided by a god! Then
you would soon know what strength there is in my hands.'
In the same way Eumaeus made a prayer to all the gods, that
Odysseus, man of many designs, might return to his own home.
     When Odysseus understood the true temper of these men,   205
he answered them once again, speaking in these words:
'Here I am before you, the man himself! After much toil
I have come back in this twentieth year to my native land.
I know that you are the only ones among my servants who
longed for me to return, for I have not heard any of the   210
rest of them praying that I might come back home again.
So I will spell out for you exactly what is going to happen.
If at my hands a god is going to beat down the lordly suitors,
I shall provide both of you with a wife, and set you up with
possessions and houses close to mine; and henceforth in my   215
eyes you will be companions and brothers to Telemachus.
Now look; I will show you something, a clear sign, so that
you may be quite sure about me, and be convinced in your
hearts: the scar where a boar's white tusk gored me, long
ago when I went to Parnassus with the sons of Autolycus.'   220
     So he spoke, and pulled his rags aside from the huge scar.
When the two men had looked and examined it thoroughly,
they threw their arms around shrewd Odysseus and wept,
and kissed his head and shoulders, welcoming him back;
and Odysseus too kissed their heads and hands. And   225
indeed the sun's light would have gone down upon their
weeping, had not Odysseus himself checked them, saying:
'Stop your weeping and wailing, you two, in case someone
comes out of the hall and sees you, and tells those inside.
Go back in one by one, not together; I will go first,   230

and you must follow me. Now, let this be our signal:
all the others there, as many as are lordly suitors, will not
allow the bow and its quiver to be given to me; so you,
good Eumaeus, must bring the bow down through the hall
and put it in my hands. And you must tell the women   235
to bolt the close-fitting doors of their quarters; and if any
of them hears from there the sound of groaning or the noise
of men caught in our snares, she should not venture outside
but should remain there in silence and stay by her work.
Your task, good Philoetius, is to secure the courtyard   240
door with its bolt and quickly knot the fastening on it.'

So he spoke, and went back into the well-established palace,
and sat down on the seat from which he had arisen.
And the two servants of godlike Odysseus entered also.

Now Eurymachus was already turning the bow in his hands,   245
warming it round and round in the fire's blaze; but for all that
he could not string it, and groaned loudly from his proud heart.
In his frustration he cried aloud and called out to them all:
'Curse it! My pain is not for myself alone, but for everyone.
It is not so much the marriage I grieve for, bitter though this is;   250
there are many other women in Achaea, some in sea-girt
Ithaca itself, and others in cities elsewhere. No, it is the
thought that we are so obviously inferior in might to godlike
Odysseus, because we are not strong enough to string his bow.
And that will be a reproach for men of future times to hear of.'   255

Then in turn Antinous, son of Eupeithes, addressed him:
'Eurymachus, it will not be so—and you yourself know it.
Today is a holy feast among the people in honour of the god
of archery; and who would string bows at such a time? No,
put it quietly aside; as for the axes, perhaps we can leave them   260
all in place—I do not think that anyone else will come into
the hall of Odysseus, son of Laertes, and take them away.
So let the wine-steward pour the first drops into our cups,
and we will make offerings and put the curved bow aside.
Then in the morning tell Melanthius, the one who herds goats,   265
to drive here the very best beasts in all his flocks, and we shall
lay thigh-bones on the altar of Apollo, famed with the bow;
after that let us try our hands at this bow, and end the contest.'

So spoke Antinous, and his words found favour with them.

Heralds set about pouring water over their hands, and   270
young men brimmed the mixing-bowls with wine and
served it round to all, first pouring a drop into their cups.
When they had made offerings and drunk as much as each
man's heart desired, Odysseus of many wiles spoke to them
with guile in mind: 'Listen to me, suitors of our renowned   275
queen, and I will say what the heart in my breast commands.
It is Eurymachus especially I entreat, and godlike Antinous,
since what he said just now was also right and proper:
leave the bow alone for now, and hand it over to the gods;
in the morning some god will give the victory to whoever   280
he wills. But now, give me the well-polished bow, so that
here among you I may test my hands' strength, to see if
I still have the power that was once in my supple limbs,
or if wandering and lack of care have wrecked it for me.'
    So he spoke, and they were all greatly indignant at him,   285
fearing he might be able to string the well-polished bow.
Antinous flung a rebuke at him, hailing him in these words:
'Wretched stranger, there is no sense in you, not even a little.
Are you not content to eat here unmolested, among powerful
men, lacking no fair share in the feast and listening to our   290
discourse and conversation? There is no stranger or beggar
besides you who is allowed to listen to what we talk about.
It is the honey-sweet wine that is your undoing, wine that
always ruins anyone who takes it in gulps, not in moderation.
It was wine that drove the splendid centaur Eurytion into   295
madness in great-spirited Peirithous' palace, when he was
visiting the Lapiths.* His wits were driven crazy with it,
and he went berserk, and caused havoc in Peirithous' house.
Then anger seized the hero Lapiths, and they leapt up and
dragged him out through the porch, and sliced off his ears   300
and nose with the pitiless bronze; and he went on his way
deranged in mind, bearing the weight of his heart's folly.
At that time the feud between Centaurs and men began;
and he was the first to find his own torment in drunkenness.
Just so I predict great misery for you, too, if you happen to   305
string this bow, for you will meet with no act of kindness
from anyone in our land; we shall send you off smartly
in a black ship to Echetus,* the bane of all mortal men,

and nothing on earth can save you from him. So drink on
undisturbed, and do not pick fights with younger men.'   310
     Then in turn circumspect Penelope addressed him:
'Antinous, it is not a good or proper thing to maltreat
any guest of Telemachus who comes to this palace.
Do you really think that if the stranger is able to string
Odysseus' great bow, trusting in his hands' strength,   315
he will carry me off to his house and make me his wife?
Surely not even he expects in his heart that this will happen.
Let not any of you feasting here be distressed in your heart
on this account; it is not likely to happen, no, not at all.'
     Then in turn Eurymachus, son of Polybus, answered her: 320
'Daughter of Icarius, circumspect Penelope; of course we
do not suppose this man will take you in marriage; it is not
credible. But we feel shame at the talk of men and women,
in case one of the lower sort among the Achaeans might say,
"These men who are courting the wife of a blameless man   325
are far inferior to him! They could not string his well-polished
bow, while some other fellow, a vagabond beggar, came here
and strung it without effort and shot through the iron axes."
That is what they will say, and it will be a reproach to us.'
     Then in turn circumspect Penelope spoke to him: 'There can 330
be no question, Eurymachus, of enjoying a good reputation
among our people for those who openly dishonour and devour
a great man's estate; why then be concerned about disgrace?
This stranger here is a fine big man, and well built, and
he claims to be the son of a man of noble birth. So come,   335
give him the well-polished bow, and let us see what happens.
I tell you this plainly, and it will surely come to fulfilment:
if he strings the bow, and Apollo grants him his prayer,
I will give him a tunic and a cloak, fine clothes to wear, and
I will give him a sharp spear, a defence against dogs and   340
men, and I will give him a two-edged sword and sandals for
his feet, and send him wherever his heart and spirit desire.'
     Then in turn wise Telemachus addressed her directly:
'Mother—as to the bow, no man of the Achaeans has more
authority than I have to give or refuse it to whoever I wish—   345
neither all those who are lords in rugged Ithaca, nor
those who hold sway in the islands off horse-rearing Elis.

None of these will force me against my will, even if I choose
to give the bow to the stranger outright, for him to take away.
So go now to your quarters and take charge of your own tasks,   350
the loom and the distaff, and order your women servants to
go about their work. The bow must be men's concern, all of
them, and me especially, for the authority in the house is mine.'

Penelope was amazed, and went back into her own quarters,
and stored the discerning words of her son in her heart.   355
She went up into her rooms with her women servants and
there wept for Odysseus, her dear husband, until Athena
the grey-eyed let fall sweet sleep upon her eyelids.

Now the good swineherd had picked up the curved bow, to
hand it over, but the suitors in the hall all shouted threats at him;   360
and this is what one of the arrogant young men would say:
'Hey, you miserable swineherd, where are you taking that
curved bow, you madman? Soon enough the swift dogs you
bred will eat you up, alone among your pigs and far from men—
if Apollo and the other immortal gods will look kindly upon us.'   365

So they spoke, and Eumaeus put the bow down where he was,
afraid because many men were threatening him in the hall.
But Telemachus shouted a stern warning from the opposite side:
'Bring the bow on, old friend! You cannot easily obey everyone.
Watch out, or I might chase you out into the field with a shower   370
of stones. I may be younger than you, but I am stronger.
How I wish I were that much stronger, and a better fighter
with my hands, than all the suitors who sit here in my house!
I would soon give them a painful send-off back to their homes
and out of our palace where they hatch their wicked schemes.'   375

So he spoke, and all the suitors laughed merrily at him, and
indeed softened their bitter resentment against Telemachus.
And now the swineherd brought the bow down the hall,
and standing next to shrewd Odysseus put it into his hands.
He called to the nurse Eurycleia to come out, saying: 380
'Circumspect Eurycleia, Telemachus orders you to
drop the bolt on the close-fitting doors of your quarters,
and if anyone hears from there the sound of groaning or the noise
of men caught in our snares, she should not venture outside
but should remain there in silence and stay by her work.'   385
So he spoke, and his words went straight to their mark;

and Eurycleia barred the doors of their well-built quarters.
    Meanwhile Philoetius slipped quietly out of the hall, and
barred the outer doors of the strongly fenced courtyard.
There was lying under the portico a cable from a balanced   390
ship, made of papyrus, and with this he made fast the doors;
then he went back and sat on the stool from which he had risen,
watching Odysseus. He was already handling the bow,
turning it ever about, testing it this way and that, to see if
worms had eaten into the horn while its master was far away.   395
And this is what a suitor would say, looking at his neighbour:
'Clearly this is some fancier of bows, and wily with it!
I suppose he too has something like this in his house, or
plans to make one himself? Look at the way he is turning
it about in his hands—troublesome vagabond that he is.'   400
And another of the arrogant young men would say in his turn:
'I hope this fellow's chances of future good fortune are
as great as is his prospect now of ever stringing the bow.'
    So the suitors spoke. But Odysseus, man of many wiles,
lifted up the great bow, examining it from every side,   405
and then, just as a man skilled in lyre-playing and song
without difficulty stretches a string around a new peg,
tying the well-twisted gut of a sheep at both its ends,
so, without any effort, did Odysseus string the great bow.
Taking it up in his right hand he tested the string,   410
and it sang out sweetly, like the song of a swallow.
At this great distress fell upon the suitors, and the colour
left their faces. Zeus sent a sign, a loud clap of thunder;
and much-enduring glorious Odysseus was glad, because
Cronus' crooked-counselling son had sent him a portent.   415
He picked up a swift arrow that was lying loose on a table
next to him; the rest still lay in their hollow quiver, those
which the Achaeans were very soon destined to sample.
Laying this arrow on the bridge, he notched it to the string
and drew it back. Straight from the stool where he sat, he   420
took careful aim and shot the arrow. From the first handle on
he did not miss a single axe, and the bronze-weighted shaft
sped straight through and out at the other end. Then he said:
'Telemachus, the guest sitting in your halls does you no
discredit; I did not miss the mark, nor did I make hard work   425

of stringing the bow. My strength is still set firm in me,
not as the abusive suitors make light of in their scorn at me.
But now it is time for supper to be served to the Achaeans,
while it is light; afterwards we may find other entertainment,
with song and the lyre, for these are a feast's accompaniment.' 430

 So he spoke, and signed with his eyebrows; and Telemachus,
the dear son of godlike Odysseus, slung his sharp sword
about him and grasped his spear firmly, and took his stand
by his father, next to his seat, armed in flashing bronze.

BOOK TWENTY-TWO

Odysseus of many wiles threw back his rags, and leapt
on to the great threshold, holding the bow and quiver
full of arrows; and there he spilled the swift shafts,
right in front of his feet, and addressed the suitors:
'This terrible contest has now come to its end! But this   5
time I shall shoot at another mark, one that no man has
yet hit—if I can hit it, and if Apollo grants my prayer.'
    So he spoke, and lined up a bitter shaft at Antinous.
Now he was on the point of lifting up a fine, golden
two-handled cup, and was already turning it in his hands,   10
meaning to drink some wine. Violent death had no place in
his thoughts—for who would suppose that one man, alone
and outnumbered by the diners, however strong he was,
could contrive hideous death and black doom for him?
But Odysseus took aim, and shot the arrow into his neck,   15
and the point passed clean through his soft gullet.
The cup dropped from his hand as he was hit; he slumped
sideways, and at once a thick jet of life-blood spurted
from his nostrils. His foot shot out and kicked the table
away from him, spilling the food all over the ground,   20
bread and roast meat jumbled together in the dirt. Seeing
the man fall the suitors set up a clamour in the palace, and
starting up from their chairs they scattered about the hall,
looking anxiously along its well-built walls; but nowhere
was there a shield or a stout spear they could lay hands on.   25
They began to berate Odysseus furiously with angry words:
'Shooting at men, stranger—that was badly done! No more
contests for you; sheer destruction is now your certain fate.
You must know that the man you have just killed was by far
the best of Ithaca's young lords. For this vultures will eat you.' 30
    This is what each man imagined, for they thought he had
killed Antinous by accident—fools, who did not understand
that on every one of them death's ropes were now fastened tight.
Looking at them darkly Odysseus of many wiles spoke:
'You dogs! You never expected me to return home, back   35

from the land of the Trojans; and so you plundered my house,
you brutally forced my women servants to sleep with you,
and you courted my wife in stealth while I was still alive,
with no fear of the gods who inhabit the broad high sky,
nor that the vengeful anger of men would one day follow.   40
Now on every one of you death's ropes are fastened tight.'

So he spoke, and pale terror took hold of them all, and each
looked about him to find some escape from sheer doom.
Only Eurymachus gave Odysseus an answer, and said:
'If you really are Odysseus of Ithaca, come home, you were   45
right to speak as you did of all that the Achaeans have done—
many acts of recklessness in the palace, and many in the country.
But the man who was the instigator of it all now lies dead,
Antinous. It was he who set these deeds in motion, not so
much out of a desire for the marriage, nor needing it, but   50
with another purpose—which Cronus' son has not fulfilled—
to waylay your son and kill him, and then become king
himself over the land of well-established Ithaca. But now
he lies dead, as was his due. So spare us, who are your own
people; and afterwards we shall make public reparation to   55
you of all that has been drunk and eaten here in your halls.
Each of us in turn will pay you compensation, twenty oxen's
worth, and requite you in bronze and gold until your heart
is softened. But until then no one can blame your anger.'

Looking at him darkly, Odysseus of many wiles spoke: 60
'Eurymachus, not even if you suitors handed over all your
patrimony, everything you now own and anything else you
may add to it—not even then would I hold my hands back
from killing, until you suitors pay in full for your outrage.
Now, the choice is yours: either stand up and fight, or else   65
run away, to see if any of you can avoid death and doom—
not that I think anyone will escape sheer destruction.'

So he spoke, and at once their knees and hearts went slack.
But Eurymachus spoke among them for a second time:
'My friends, plainly this man will not restrain his irresistible   70
hands; now he has got the polished bow and quiver in his hands
he will shoot at us from the smooth threshold until he has
killed us all. So come, let us turn our minds to battle-craft.
Draw your swords, hold up the tables as shields against his

arrows of swift death. Let us all charge at him together, to see　　75
if we can shift him from the threshold and the doors, and then
disperse through the city; that way we can quickly raise an
alarm, and this man will soon have shot for the last time.'

So he spoke, and drew his keen-edged sword, bronze and
sharpened on both sides, and sprang at Odysseus with a　　80
fearful yell; but at the same time glorious Odysseus let
fly an arrow, and hit him on the chest next to the nipple,
driving the swift shaft into his liver. He let his sword drop
to the ground from his hand, and fell doubled up, sprawling
over the table, sweeping the food and two-handled cup　　85
to the floor. In his agony he beat his forehead repeatedly
against the ground, and with both feet kicked his chair
away and sent it tumbling; and a mist spread over his eyes.

And now Amphinomus sprang at renowned Odysseus,
charging straight at him with drawn sharp sword, hoping to　　90
force him away from the doors. But Telemachus was too quick
for him, hitting him between the shoulders from behind with
a bronze-tipped spear, and driving it clean through his chest.
He fell with a crash, smashing his brow full on the ground.
Telemachus leapt back, leaving the far-shadowing spear there　　95
in Amphinomus; he was afraid that while he was pulling
the far-shadowing spear out one of the Achaeans might rush
up and deal him a sword-blow, or strike him as he bent over.
He set off at a run, and very quickly reached his dear father,
and standing close addressed him in winged words:　　100
'Father, I will now go and fetch a shield and two spears for you,
and a helmet made all of bronze, fitting close to your temples;
and when I return I will also arm myself, and will equip the
swineherd and oxherd in the same way; it is better to be armed.'

Then in answer Odysseus, man of many wiles, addressed him:　　105
'Run and fetch them, then, while I have arrows to defend myself,
or else they may force me from the door while I am on my own.'

So he spoke, and Telemachus did as his dear father had said,
and set off for the room where the splendid arms were stored.
From it he brought four shields, eight spears, and also four　　110
helmets made of bronze, which had thick horsehair crests.
Back he came with them, and quickly reached his dear father.
He was the first to array himself in the bronze armour; and in

the same way the two servants clad themselves in fine gear,
and stood on either side of Odysseus, the cunning counsellor.   115

Now he, as long as he had arrows to defend himself, kept
aiming his bow and shooting down the suitors one by one
in his house; and they fell in heaps, one on top of another.
But when there were no arrows left for their lord to shoot,
he propped the bow against a pillar of the well-built hall,   120
facing the bright-shining side walls, and himself slung
a shield made from four folds of hide across his shoulders,
and on his mighty head set a well-made helmet with a
horsehair crest; and the plumes nodded terribly above him.
Then he picked up the two stout spears, tipped with bronze.   125

There was in the well-built wall a kind of side-entrance, on a
level with the raised plinth running round the well-made hall,
with a way through to a passage, shut off by snug-fitting doors.
Odysseus had ordered the good swineherd to stand near this,
to which there was only one approach, and keep watch on it.   130
But now Agelaus spoke among the suitors, calling to them all:
'Friends, could not someone go up through the side-door and
tell the people, so that the alarm could speedily be raised—
and then this man would soon have shot for the last time.'

Then in turn Melanthius, herder of goats, addressed him: 135
'Zeus-nurtured Agelaus, it cannot be done. The fine doors to
the court are dangerously close, and the passage's mouth is a
difficult place. One brave man could defend it against all of us.
But look, let me fetch war-gear from the storeroom for you to
arm yourselves; it is in that room, I believe, and nowhere else,   140
that Odysseus and his splendid son have hidden their weapons.'

So spoke the goat-herder Melanthius, and went up from the hall
by narrow passageways as far as the storerooms of Odysseus.
From there he picked out twelve shields, and the same number
of spears, and as many bronze helmets with horsehair crests.   145
Off he set with them, and very soon gave them to the suitors.
Now Odysseus' knees and the heart within him went slack
when he saw them arming in war-gear and brandishing long
spears in their hands; the challenge now seemed too great.
Straightaway he addressed Telemachus with winged words: 150
'Telemachus, it must be that one of the women in our halls is
setting up a surprise attack against us; or it may be Melanthius.'

Then in turn thoughtful Telemachus addressed him:
'Father, it was I alone who was at fault in this; no one else is
to blame. I left the close-fitting doors of the storeroom ajar,   155
and they had someone watching who was cleverer than me.
Quick, good Eumaeus, shut the storeroom door, and then
find out if indeed it was one of the women who did this,
or if it was Dolius' son Melanthius, whom I in fact suspect.'
    So the pair conversed in this way, one with the other.   160
Melanthius the goatherd set off again for the storeroom,
to fetch some more fine weapons, but the good swineherd
saw him, and at once spoke to Odysseus, standing near him:
'Son of Laertes, sprung from Zeus, Odysseus of many wiles,
there goes that dangerous man again, the one we suspect,   165
off back to the storeroom. Now give me clear instructions:
if I can get the better of him, shall I kill him, or shall I
bring him back here, so that he may pay the penalty
for the many outrages he has planned in your house?'
    Then in answer Odysseus of many wiles addressed him: 170
'I and Telemachus will keep the lordly suitors in check
here inside the hall, for all their raging; you two twist
Melanthius' feet and arms behind him and throw him into
the storeroom; set a plank to his back and lash him to it,
and then, when you have tied him securely with a braided   175
rope, hoist him high on a pillar, close to the roof-beams,
so that, while still alive, he may endure a long, cruel torment.'
    So he spoke, and they listened carefully and did what he said.
They set off for the storeroom; the goatherd was inside but did
not see them, as he was hunting for weapons in a corner of the   180
room, and they stood waiting on either side of the doorposts.
When Melanthius, herdsman of goats, emerged over the
threshold, carrying in one hand a fine helmet and in the
other an ancient broad shield, speckled with mould—it had
belonged to the hero Laertes, and he carried it when young,   185
but it was now lying neglected, the seams of its straps rotted—
then the pair sprang out and seized him, and dragged him by
his hair into the room, and threw him painfully to the floor.
They tied his feet and hands together in agonizing bonds,
twisting them together with great thoroughness, exactly as   190
ordered by Laertes' son, much-enduring glorious Odysseus.

Then they tied him securely with a braided rope and hoisted
him high up on a pillar, bringing him close to the roof-beams.
And then, swineherd Eumaeus, you spoke jeeringly to him:
'Now, Melanthius, you can keep a long watch, right through   195
the night, stretched out on a soft bed, just as you deserve!
Nor will you miss early-born Dawn when she arrives on her
golden throne from Ocean's streams, at the time you usually
drive your goats to the palace to provide the suitors' meal.'

So Melanthius was left there, racked in his deadly bonds,   200
while the other two donned their war-gear and shut the shining
door, and set off for wise Odysseus, man of cunning counsels.
So there they stood, four men on the threshold, breathing fury—
though those inside the house were both numerous and brave.

Now Athena, Zeus' daughter, came and stood close by them,   205
taking on the likeness of Mentor in both form and voice.
When he saw her Odysseus was glad, and addressed her:
'Mentor, defend us from harm, and remember the dear friend
who has been so good to you! You and I are of the same age!'

So he spoke, but suspected it was Athena, driver of armies.   210
The suitors on their side raised a clamour in the hall at her,
and the first to utter a rebuke was Agelaus, Damastor's son:
'Mentor, do not let Odysseus' words beguile you into
coming to his assistance and fighting against us suitors!
Let me tell you how all this will end, as I believe: when   215
we have killed these men, father and son, you too will be
slaughtered along with them, in return for what you are so
eager to do here in the hall. You will pay with your own life.
When we have put an end to your violence with the bronze,
we shall add all that you possess, in your house and on your   220
land, to the wealth of Odysseus. Nor shall we permit your
sons to go on living in your halls, nor your daughters
and wedded wife to go to and fro in the city of Ithaca.'

So he spoke, and Athena's anger grew great in her heart,
and she rebuked Odysseus in furious words: 'No longer,   225
Odysseus, is that fierce resolution and courage as firmly
fixed in you as when you fought for nine years relentlessly
against the Trojans for white-armed, nobly born Helen;
many men you killed in the terrible fighting, and it was by
your stratagem* that the broad-wayed city of Priam was taken.   230

So how can it be that now, at home among your possessions,
you complain of the need for courage when faced by suitors?
Come over here, old friend, stand by me and watch me at work;
you will soon know what kind of a man Mentor, Alcimus' son,
is, and how he repays good deeds in the face of your enemies.'   235

So she spoke, but would not yet shift the victory entirely
his way, for she still wanted to put to the test the strength
and courage of both Odysseus and his far-famed son.
So now, taking on the appearance of a swallow, she flew
aloft and perched on a beam of the smoke-blackened hall.   240

On the suitors' side, Agelaus, Damastor's son, began to urge
them on, with Eurynomus, Amphimedon, and Demoptolemus,
Polyctor's son Peisandrus, and also warlike Polybus, for
these were by far the best in prowess of the suitors who
had survived, and were now fighting for their lives; the rest   245
had by now been laid low by the bow and its rain of arrows.
Among them Agelaus now spoke up, addressing them all:
'Friends! This man must soon check his invincible hands;
for look, after uttering his empty boasts, Mentor has gone.
There are only these men left, standing in front of the doors.   250
So do not all now hurl your long spears at the same time;
rather, you six throw first of all, and perhaps Zeus will
grant that Odysseus is struck down, and we shall win glory.
Once this man falls the rest will be of no concern to us.'

So he spoke, and they all aimed carefully and threw their   255
spears as he had ordered, but Athena made them all miss
the mark: one man hit a pillar in the well-built hall,
while another struck the close-fitting doors, and a
third's bronze-heavy ash spear stuck fast in the wall.
Then, now that he had avoided the spears of the suitors,   260
much-enduring glorious Odysseus was the first to speak:
'My friends, now I would say is the time for us too to hurl
our spears into the mass of the suitors, afire as they are to
add slaying us to the outrages they have already committed.'

So he spoke, and so they all took careful aim and threw their   265
sharp spears at the others. Odysseus killed Demoptolemus,
and Telemachus slew Euryades; the swineherd killed Elatus,
and the man who tended the oxen killed Peisandrus.
All these fastened their teeth upon the boundless earth, and

the other suitors drew back to the furthest corner of the hall,   270
while the four ran up and pulled their spears from the dead.
  The suitors took aim again and threw their sharp spears,
but Athena made most of their casts miss the mark:
one man hit a pillar in the well-built hall, while
another struck the close-fitting doors, and a third man's   275
bronze-heavy ash spear stuck fast in the wall. But
Amphimedon hit Telemachus on the wrist with a glancing
blow, and the bronze point tore away his outer skin; and
Ctesippus' long spear passed over Eumaeus' shield and
grazed his shoulder, but it flew beyond and fell to the ground.   280
Again the companions of shrewd Odysseus, crafty counsellor,
threw their sharp spears into the mass of the suitors; and
this time Odysseus, sacker of cities, struck Eurydamas,
Telemachus hit Amphimedon, and the swineherd hit Polybus.
Then the man whose task was to herd oxen struck Ctesippus   285
in the chest, and spoke over him in exultation: 'Son of
Polytherses, lover of mockery—do not ever again be led
on by foolishness to talk so big! Leave the last word to
the gods, because they are much stronger than you are.
This is a guest-gift in return for the hoof* you just now   290
gave godlike Odysseus when he was begging in the palace.'
  So spoke the herdsman of crook-horned cattle. Odysseus
stabbed Damastor's son from close range with his long spear,
and Telemachus struck Leocritus, Euenor's son, with his spear
in his under-belly, and drove the bronze clean through;   295
he fell headlong, smashing his brow full on the ground.
And now at last Athena held aloft the man-slaying aegis,*
high in the roof; and the suitors were driven out of their wits.
They fled in terror through the hall like a herd of cattle
attacked and driven to stampede by a darting gadfly in   300
the season of spring, when the long days come round.
The others, like hook-taloned vultures with curving beaks
that swoop down from the mountains on to smaller birds—
these drop from the clouds and fly close to the ground,
but the vultures dive down and kill them, and there is no   305
defence or escape; and men take pleasure in their hunting—
so Odysseus and his men chased the suitors through the palace,
striking them down right and left; dreadful groans arose as

heads were broken, and the whole floor was awash with blood.

Now Leodes rushed over to Odysseus and took hold of   310
his knees, and spoke to him in winged words of entreaty:
'Odysseus, I am at your knees! Show me respect and pity.
Never yet, I swear, have I harmed any woman in your
halls, by word or deed, but I always tried to stop any of
the other suitors who acted like this; but they would not   315
listen to me and restrain their hands from wrongdoing.
For this, and their recklessness, they have met an ugly doom.
Yet I, who was their sacrifice-interpreter, and did no wrong,
will lie among them. There are no thanks for good deeds done.'

Odysseus, man of many wiles, looked at him darkly and said: 320
'If you really claim that you interpreted sacrifices for these
men, you must have prayed many times in these halls that
the day of my happy homecoming would be far away, and
that my dear wife would go with you and bear you children.
And so for this there is no way you can escape a bitter death.'   325

So he spoke, and set his brawny hand to a sharp sword that was
lying nearby, where Agelaus had let it fall to the ground when
he was killed. With this he slashed Leodes full in the throat,
and his head rolled in the dust before he had finished speaking.

The singer son of Terpes was still trying to escape black fate—   330
Phemius, who used to sing for the suitors under compulsion.
There he stood, clutching his clear-voiced lyre in his arms,
keeping close to the side-door. And as he considered his mind
was divided: should he slip out of the hall to the altar of great
Zeus of the Court built there, on which Laertes and Odysseus   335
had sacrificed the thigh-bones of thousands of oxen, and
crouch at it, or rush over and entreat Odysseus at his knees.
And as he pondered this seemed to him the better course,
to seize hold of the knees of Odysseus, son of Laertes.
And so he laid his hollow lyre on the ground, between   340
the mixing-bowl and his chair with its silver studs, and
threw himself at Odysseus and grasped him by the knees,
speaking to him in winged words of entreaty:
'Odysseus, I am at your knees! Show me respect and pity.
It will be a grief to you in time to come if you kill a singer   345
like me, whose custom it is to sing to gods and to men.
My only teacher is myself; some god has planted varied

song-paths in my mind, and I deserve to sing for you,
as if for a god. Do not then be resolved to cut off my head.
And indeed Telemachus, your dear son, will agree with me: 350
it was not by my own will or inclination that I kept coming
to your house to sing for the suitors at their feasts; but they
were stronger and outnumbered me, and forced me to comply.'

    So he spoke, and Telemachus, man of divine might, heard him,
and at once addressed his father, who was standing nearby: 355
'Stop! Do not strike this man with the bronze; he is innocent!
And we should also spare the herald Medon, who took care
of me in our house all through my childhood—unless
Philoetius or the swineherd has already killed him, or perhaps
he met you while you were rampaging through the palace.'   360

    So he spoke; and Medon, a man of sound sense, heard him.
He was lying crouched under a seat, and, seeking to avoid black
fate, had pulled about him the recently flayed hide of an ox.
At once he stood up from under the seat and threw off the
oxhide; launching himself at Telemachus he grasped him   365
by the knees, and spoke to him in winged words of entreaty:
'My friend, here I am! Hold back, and tell your father to do so
too, or in his overwhelming power he may slay me with the sharp
bronze, furious as he is with the suitors, who have been wasting
his substance in this hall, and, the fools, showing you no respect.'   370

    Odysseus, man of many wiles, smiled at him and said:
'Do not despair; Telemachus here has saved and protected
you, so that you may know in your heart and also tell others
that doing good deeds is a far better thing than doing wrong.
Go now, you and the singer skilled in songs, leave the hall   375
and sit outside in the courtyard away from this bloodshed,
until I have finished the work I have to do in the palace.'
So he spoke, and the pair made their way out of the hall and
sat as he had directed at the altar of great Zeus, looking
keenly all about them, expecting to be killed at any moment.   380

    And Odysseus too looked keenly about his house, to see
if anyone was lurking there alive, seeking to escape black
fate. But he found all of them lying in great heaps in the
blood and dust, like fish that fishermen have caught
in the grey sea in their many-meshed net and dragged   385
up on to a curving beach; and they all lie in heaps

on the sands, longing for the waves of the salt sea, but
the brightly shining Sun takes the life from them.
Just so the suitors lay in heaps, one on top of another.
Then Odysseus of many wiles addressed Telemachus: 390
'Quick, Telemachus, tell the nurse Eurycleia to come
here to me so that I may tell her what I have in mind.'

So he spoke, and Telemachus obeyed his father; he banged
on the door of her quarters and called to the nurse Eurycleia:
'Up with you, old woman, whose job it is to watch over   395
the serving-women in our halls, and come here! Hurry now—
my father is summoning you. He has something to tell you.'

So he spoke, and his words found their mark with her,
and she opened the doors of the well-appointed quarters
and set off; but Telemachus went ahead, leading the way.   400
She soon found Odysseus surrounded by bodies of the dead,
spattered with blood and clotted gore, like a lion that goes
on its way after feeding on some ox in the open pasture;
all of its chest and its jowls on either side are running
with blood, and it is a terrible sight to look upon. So   405
Odysseus' feet and his hands above were spattered.
When Eurycleia saw the dead bodies and the welter of
blood, she was about to raise the triumph-shout at the sight
of this great deed, but Odysseus made to hold her back,
eager though she was, and addressed her in winged words: 410
'Keep your joy in your heart, old woman; stop, do not
cry out. It is not a pious action to exult over slain men.
These men were beaten down by the gods' doom and their
own cruel deeds; they never respected any earth-dwelling man
who encountered them, neither the low-born nor the noble.   415
For this, and for their recklessness, they have met an ugly death.
So tell me: give me a full account of the women in my halls,
both those who do not respect me and those who are guiltless.'

Then in turn his dear nurse Eurycleia addressed him:
'I shall indeed give you a true account of this, my child.   420
In your halls there are fifty women who serve you, and
these we have trained in the performance of their tasks—
how to card wool, and how to bear the state of servitude.
Of these, twelve in all have gone the way of shamelessness,
showing respect neither to me nor to Penelope herself.   425

Telemachus has but recently come of age, and his mother
would not allow him to give orders to the serving-women.
But let me go up to the shining rooms above and tell
all this to your wife, on whom some god has shed sleep.'
Then in answer Odysseus of many wiles addressed her: 430
'No, do not wake her yet. Your task is to order the women
who in the past have behaved shamefully to come here.'
   So he spoke, and the old woman went out through the hall,
to take the message to the women and hasten their coming.
Odysseus now called Telemachus and the oxherd and   435
swineherd to him, and addressed them with winged words:
'Now, start carrying the dead men out; tell the women
to help you, and after that to wash down the beautiful
chairs and tables with water and with porous sponges.
Then, when you have restored order throughout the house   440
bring out the maidservants from the well-built hall to a place
between the round-house and the strong courtyard wall, and
hack at them with your long-bladed swords until you have
taken the lives of them all, and they have forgotten Aphrodite,
whom they followed in their secret coupling with the suitors.'   445
   So he spoke; and the twelve women came in huddled
together, lamenting bitterly and weeping copious tears.
First they carried out the dead men's bodies, and laid
them under the colonnade of the well-walled court,
propped one against another. Odysseus himself took charge,   450
and chivvied them on; and they had no choice but to carry
the bodies out. Next they washed down the beautiful chairs
and tables with water and with porous sponges.
Telemachus and the oxherd and swineherd then began to
scrape clean the floor of the well-constructed palace with   455
shovels; and the maidservants took the mess and put it outside.
Now, when they had restored order throughout the whole hall,
they led the maidservants out of the well-built edifice, between
the round-house and the strong courtyard wall, and herded
them into a narrow space from which there was no escape.   460
Thoughtful Telemachus spoke first to his companions:
'I have no wish to take away these women's lives by an
honourable death, for they openly poured abuse on my head
and on my mother's, and they have slept with the suitors.'

So he spoke, and tied the cable of a black-prowed ship to   465
a tall pillar, and threw the other end about the round-house,
securing it high up so that their feet could not touch the ground.
As when long-winged thrushes or doves fly headlong into
a net strung in a thicket to catch them—they are making for
their roosting-places, but it is a grim repose that awaits them—   470
so these women's heads were held fast in a row, with a noose
round each neck, so that their death would be most pitiable.
Their feet twitched for a short time, but not for very long.

Then they dragged Melanthius out through the door into the
the yard, and with the pitiless bronze sliced off his nose and   475
ears, tore away his genitals to be raw meat for the dogs to eat,
and in their raging fury lopped off his hands and feet as well.

After this they scoured the gore from their hands and feet,
and went into the house to meet Odysseus, their work done.
Odysseus then addressed Eurycleia, his dear nurse: 480
'Bring sulphur, cleanser of foulness, old woman, and
also bring fire for me to purify the hall. Then go and tell
Penelope to come here with her attendant women; and tell
all the maidservants in the palace to come here quickly.'

Then in turn his dear nurse Eurycleia addressed him: 485
'All that you say, my child, is surely right and proper.
But look, let me bring you a cloak and a tunic to wear;
do not stand in the hall with your broad shoulders covered
in rags like this, because people would blame you for that.'
Then in answer Odysseus of many wiles addressed her: 490
'Fire is what I need more than anything—now, in the hall.'
So he spoke, and his dear nurse Eurycleia did not disobey
him, but brought fire and sulphur; and Odysseus purified
everywhere—the hall and the house and the courtyard.

And now the old woman went away through Odysseus'   495
fine palace, to tell the women and to hasten their coming;
and they arrived from their quarters with torches in their
hands, and surged around Odysseus and embraced him in
welcome, greeting him warmly, holding and kissing his
head, shoulders, and hands; and a sweet desire to weep and   500
lament took hold of him, for now he recognized them all.

BOOK TWENTY-THREE

Chuckling to herself, the old woman climbed to the rooms above,
to tell her mistress that her dear husband was in the palace;
her knees moved swiftly, but her feet stumbled as she went.
Standing at the bed's head she spoke to Penelope in these words:
'Wake up, Penelope, dear child, so that you may see   5
before your eyes what you have been hoping for all these days.
Odysseus has returned! He is in his house, late though his coming
has been. He has killed the proud suitors, who for so long troubled
his house, devouring his property and browbeating his son.'

　　Then in turn circumspect Penelope addressed her: 10
'Nanny dear, the gods have driven you out of your mind;
they can render even the most sensible of men witless, though
they can also set the slack-brained on the way to understanding.
Now they have confused you, though before you were so level-headed.
Why do you mock me when my heart is so deeply distressed,   15
bringing me this meaningless news and waking me from a
sweet sleep that had shrouded my eyes and held me fast?
Never yet have I slept a sleep like this, not since Odysseus
went away to set eyes on that Evil-Ilium, never to be named.*
So come now, go back down and return to your quarters.   20
You know that if any other of the women who work for me
had come here with this tale and woken me from sleep,
I would have sent her off smartly with a harsh word, back to
her quarters; from this at least your old age will protect you.'

　　Then in turn her dear nurse Eurycleia addressed her: 25
'I do not mock you, dear child. It is all true. Odysseus
really has come home and is here in his house, as I say. He is
the stranger whom everyone in the halls has been ill-treating.
In fact, Telemachus has known for a long time that he is here,
but in his good sense has kept his father's plans hidden,   30
so as to make these arrogant men pay for their violence.'

　　So she spoke, and Penelope sprang full of joy from her bed,
and embraced the old woman, letting fall tears from her eyes,
and addressed her, speaking in winged words:
'Now, dear nanny, pay attention and tell me the truth: 35

if he really has come back to his house, as you say, how was it
he could lay hands on these shameless suitors, being but one
man while they were all the time lurking in the house, in force?'
    Then in turn her dear nurse Eurycleia addressed her:
'I did not see it, and no one told me; I heard only the groans   40
of men being killed. We were sitting terror-stricken in the
furthest part of our well-built rooms, and the close-fitting
doors confined us there, at least until your son Telemachus
summoned us; his father had sent him to tell me to come.
I found Odysseus standing over the dead men; they were   45
lying all about him in heaps on the hard-packed floor,
piled on one another. It would have cheered your heart
to see him, bespattered with blood and gore, just like a lion.
Now the dead have been stacked together by the courtyard
gate, while Odysseus has lit a great fire and is cleansing   50
the splendid palace with sulphur. He sent me to summon you.
Come with me, then, so that both your hearts may set out
on the path of happiness, after your many terrible sufferings;
now at last what you have long yearned for has come to pass.
The master has returned to his hearth, alive, and has found you   55
and his son in his halls; and in his own palace he has taken
his revenge on all the suitors for the wrong they did to him.'
    Then in turn circumspect Penelope addressed her: 'Nanny
dear, do not be too quick to laugh in triumph. You know how
gladly received in our halls he would be if he were to appear—   60
by everyone, and especially by me and the son we bore.
But there is no way that this tale you are telling me is true.
No, it was one of the immortals who killed the lordly suitors,
outraged at their heart-wounding arrogance and wicked deeds,
because they never showed respect to any earth-dwelling man   65
who encountered them, neither the low-born nor the noble.
So by their recklessness they have met an evil end. But Odysseus
has lost his homecoming and his life as well, far from Achaea.'
    Then in answer her dear nurse Eurycleia addressed her:
'My child, what words have escaped the barrier of your teeth!   70
Your husband is here in the house, at his hearth, and you say
he will never come home! Your heart was ever full of disbelief.
But look—I will now tell you something else, a clear sign:
a scar that was once gouged in him by a boar's white tusk.

I recognized it while I was washing him, and I wanted to tell   75
you as well; but he, in his cunning purpose, clapped his
hands over my mouth and would not let me to speak of it.
Please come with me; I will wager my life on it, and if I am
deceiving you, you may kill me in the most horrible way.'

 Then in answer circumspect Penelope addressed her: 80
'Dear nanny, you may be very clever, but it is hard for you
to puzzle out the purposes of the gods who live for ever.
For all that, let us go to find my son, so that I may see the men
who courted me lying dead, and the man who killed them.'

 So she spoke, and descended from her upper rooms, turning over   85
many things in her heart: whether to stand apart and question her
dear husband, or to approach him and kiss his head and hands.
When she had crossed the stone threshold and entered the hall,
she sat down in the brightness of the fire facing Odysseus,
by the wall opposite him. He was sitting leaning against a tall   90
pillar, eyes cast down, waiting to see if his handsome wife
would have anything to say when she set eyes on him.
But for a long time she sat in silence, bafflement in her heart;
sometimes when she looked him in the face she saw a likeness,
but then could not recognize him in the foul clothes he wore.   95

 Telemachus rebuked his mother, speaking directly to her:
'Mother—my hard mother, with an unbending heart in you!
How can you turn away from my father like this? Why not
sit beside him, ask him questions and find out about him?
No other woman would have had the stubbornness of spirit to   100
stay away from her husband, when after much hard suffering
he has returned to her in the twentieth year, back to his native land.
But your heart has always been more unyielding than a rock.'

 Then in turn circumspect Penelope addressed him:
'My child, the heart in my breast is dumbfounded;   105
I cannot say a single word to him, or ask him a question,
or look him full in the face. If he really is Odysseus, and
has come back to his house, we two have better ways to
recognize each other with certainty; we have shared tokens,
which we alone know, and which are hidden from others.'   110

 So she spoke, and much-enduring glorious Odysseus smiled,
and straightaway addressed Telemachus with winged words:
'Telemachus, leave your mother to put me to the test here

in the hall; soon she will come to a better understanding.
Now, because I am filthy and dressed in ragged clothing,   115
she despises me, and will not yet admit that I am Odysseus.
But we must now decide how things may turn out for the best.
We know that in any community if anyone kills just one man,
even one who has no great number to avenge him afterwards,
the killer goes into exile, abandoning his kin and land;   120
but we have slain the bulwark of the city, those who were
by far the best of Ithaca's young men. You must consider this.'
   Then in turn thoughtful Telemachus spoke in answer:
'Dear father, it is you who must see to this. They say
that among other men your ingenuity is unsurpassed,   125
and there is no mortal man who can compete with you.
We are afire to follow you, and I think we shall not
fall short in courage, in so far as it is in our power.'
   Then in reply Odysseus of many wiles addressed him:
'Very well; I will tell you what I think to be our best course.   130
First, you must wash yourselves, and put on your tunics,
and tell the maidservants in the halls to dress in clean clothes.
Next, let the god-inspired singer take up his clear-voiced
lyre and be our leader in the light-hearted dance, so that
anyone outside who hears it—a passing wayfarer, or one of   135
our neighbours—will think a wedding-feast is taking place.
We do not want report of the suitors' slaying to spread far
and wide through the town until we go out to visit our farm
on its thickly wooded estate. Once there, we can consider
whatever useful scheme the Olympian puts into our minds.'   140
   So he spoke, and they listened carefully and did what he said.
First, they washed themselves and put on fresh tunics,
and the women dressed in their best. Then the god-inspired
bard took up his hollow lyre and roused in them a desire
for sweet singing and for the pleasures of the dance.   145
All around them the great hall resounded to the beating
feet of men and fine-girdled women in the dance.
And this is what someone outside hearing them would say:
'One of her many suitors must have married the queen—
hard woman, who could not bring herself to watch patiently   150
over her wedded husband's great house until he should return.'
   This is what they said; but they did not know what had happened.

Meanwhile the housekeeper Eurynome had bathed great-hearted
Odysseus in his own home and rubbed him with olive oil, and
had clothed him in a splendid cloak and a tunic. And over   155
him from head to foot Athena poured great beauty, to make
him taller and more thickset to look upon; and from his head
she made his locks hang thickly, like the hyacinth flower.
As when a skilled man, one whom Hephaestus and Pallas
Athena have taught all manner of crafts, and graceful are   160
the works of art that he creates, overlays gold on silver,
so she poured grace down over his head and shoulders.
He rose from his bath looking in form like the immortals,
and went back to sit on the chair from which he had risen,
facing his wife. Then he addressed her in these words: 165
'Perverse woman! The gods in their palaces on Olympus
have given you a heart that is obdurate beyond all women.
No one else would have had the stubbornness of spirit to
keep away from her husband, when after much hard suffering
he has returned in this twentieth year to her and his native land.   170
Come, nanny, make up a bed for me to sleep on my own;
for surely this woman's heart in her breast is hard as iron.'

   Then in turn circumspect Penelope addressed him:
'It is you who are perverse! I am not being haughty or scornful,
nor am I greatly surprised at you; but I know very well what   175
you looked like when you left Ithaca in your long-oared ship.
Come now, Eurycleia; make up outside my well-built room
the strongly made bed the master built with his own hands.
Tell the women to move it out, and then throw over it
a covering of fleeces and cloaks and shining blankets.'   180

   So she spoke, testing her husband;* and Odysseus burst
out in anger, and addressed his faithful-minded wife:
'Lady, what you have just said causes me pain in my heart.
Who has moved my bed to another place? That would be hard
to do, even for a very skilled man, unless some god decided   185
to come here in person and easily set it down somewhere else.
There is no man alive, not even one in the prime of life,
who could shift it without difficulty, since there is a unique
token artfully built into it; it was my work, and mine alone.

   'There was inside the courtyard a long-leafed olive tree,   190
grown to its full height, and its trunk was thick as a pillar.

Around this I built our bridal chamber with close-set stones
until it was finished; and then I roofed it securely too,
and made well-jointed doors for it which fitted snugly.
Next I lopped off the top of the long-leafed olive tree,   195
and trimmed the trunk with a bronze adze from the root up,
dressing it well and skilfully all around, and truing it to a line;
and so I made it into a bedpost. Then with a drill I pierced
holes in it; working outwards I made my bed smooth until it
was finished, and decorated it with gold, silver, and ivory, and   200
across the frame I stretched oxhide straps, bright with red dye.
There now; I have revealed the token to you. I do not know,
lady, if this bed of mine is still firmly planted, or if some man
has now cut through the tree's base and moved it elsewhere.'

So he spoke, and her heart and knees at once went slack,   205
as she recognized the sure token Odysseus had revealed to her;
she burst into tears and ran straight to him, throwing her arms
around his neck and kissing his head and shoulders. She said:
'Do not be angry with me, Odysseus, for you were always
the wisest of men. It is the gods who have sent us this misery,   210
they who were reluctant to let us two enjoy our youth in
each other's company and so come to the threshold of old age.
So do not be angry with me any more, or hold it against me
that I did not greet you the moment I saw you as I do now.
It was because the heart in my breast was always fearful   215
that some man might come here and beguile me with his story;
there are many who plot wicked schemes to their advantage.
Argive Helen, daughter of Zeus, would never have coupled
in love with a foreigner from another country had she
known that the war-loving sons of the Achaeans were   220
fated to take her back to her home in her dear native land.
It was of course a god who incited her to this shameful act;
not until then had she admitted to her mind that cruel delusion,
which from the start has been the cause of our unhappiness too.
But now that you have given me a true account of our bed's   225
unmistakable token, which no other mortal has ever seen—
only you and I know about it, and one single woman servant,
Actor's daughter, whom my father gave me when I first came
here, and she has guarded the doors of our well-built bedroom—
now at last you persuade my heart, unbending though it is.'   230

So she spoke, and aroused in him a greater desire to weep;
he wept, holding his heart-gladdening, faithful wife to him.
As welcome as the sight of land* appearing to swimmers,
men whose strong-constructed ship, driven by winds
and heavy seas, Poseidon has shattered in open waters—   235
only a few escape the grey sea by swimming to the shore,
their skin covered with a thick crust of brine, and with joy
they set foot on land, for they have avoided a grim death—
just so did Penelope look with joy upon her husband, and
would not quite release her white arms' hold on his neck.   240
And rosy-fingered Dawn would have risen on their weeping,
had not the goddess grey-eyed Athena had other plans:
she held back the night, delaying it at its furthest limit, and
in the East checked golden-throned Dawn at the river Ocean,*
and did not allow her to yoke the swift-footed horses that bring   245
light to men—Lampus and Phaëthon, colts who draw her chariot.
Then at last Odysseus, man of many wiles, addressed his wife:
'Lady, we have not yet reached the end of all our trials;
there are still labours without measure for us in the future,
many difficult labours that I must bring to full completion.   250
I mean the predictions made to me by the shade of Teiresias
on the day that I went down into the house of Hades,
seeking a way home for my companions and for myself.
So come, lady, let us go to our bed, so that now we
may take pleasure in rest, in the hold of sweet sleep.'   255
    Then in turn circumspect Penelope addressed him:
'As for the bed, it will be ready for you whenever your heart
desires, now that the gods have brought about your return to
your own well-founded house in the land of your fathers.
But since a god has put it into your mind, and you have turned   260
your thoughts to it, tell me about this trial. I shall hear of it
later, I think; but it would be no bad thing to be told directly.'
    Then in answer Odysseus of many wiles addressed her:
'Strange woman! Why do you keep urging me so insistently
to speak of it? Still, I will tell you the tale, and hide nothing.   265
Your heart will derive no delight from it, nor will I have
any pleasure in its telling. Teiresias told me I must visit
many men's cities, carrying in my hand a well-shaped oar,
until such time as I encounter men who are ignorant of

the sea, and who eat food that is not seasoned with salt.   270
These people know nothing of ships with crimson prows,
or of well-shaped oars, which serve as the wings of ships.
He gave me a very clear sign, which I will not hide from you:
when I fall in with another traveller, someone who will tell
me I am carrying a winnowing-fan on my bright shoulder,   275
then at last, he said, I must plant my oar in the ground,
and make a splendid offering to lord Poseidon, of a ram,
a bull, and a boar-pig that is a mounter of sows.
After that I must return home and offer holy hecatombs
to the immortal gods whose dwelling is in the high sky,   280
to all of them in due order. Death will come to me far
from the sea, such a gentle death, taking me when I am
worn out, in sleek old age with my prosperous people
around me. All this, he told me, would be fulfilled.'

    Then in turn circumspect Penelope addressed him: 285
'If indeed the gods make your old age happier, there is
yet hope that you will find an escape from your troubles.'

    So they conversed on these matters, one with another.
Meanwhile Eurynome and the nurse were making the bed
ready with soft coverings, by the light of flaming torches.   290
When they had finished their work with the strongly made
bed, the old woman set off back to retire in her own quarters,
and Eurynome, the one who looked after their bedroom,
led them on their way to bed, holding a torch in her hand.
When she had escorted them to their bedroom she went back,   295
and the two went gladly to the place of their familiar bed.
Meanwhile Telemachus and the oxherd and the swineherd
had rested their feet from the dance and told the women to do
the same, and themselves went to their rest in the shadowy hall.

    When the other two had enjoyed their tender love-making,   300
they found delight in talk, telling each other their stories.
She, bright among women, related what she had endured in
the palace, having to witness the loathsome gang of suitors,
who on her account kept slaughtering so many cattle and
fat sheep, and drawing off quantities of wine from her jars.   305
In his turn Zeus-sprung Odysseus told her of all the grief he had
inflicted on other men, and the miseries he himself had endured,
leaving nothing out. She listened rapt with delight, nor did sleep

fall on her eyelids until he had given a full account of everything.*

He began with how he overcame the Cicones, and then   310
came to the rich ploughland of the men who ate the lotus-plant;
then he told what the Cyclops did, and how he himself
avenged the mighty companions he had so pitilessly eaten.
How he came to Aeolus, who received him kindly and tried
to send him on his way, though it was not yet his fate to   315
reach his native land, for a storm caught him up once again
and carried him over the fish-rich sea, groaning loudly.
How he came to Telepylus in the Laestrygonians' land, who
destroyed his ships and killed his well-greaved companions,
every one, while he alone managed to escape in his black ship.   320
He told her all about the trickery and deviousness of Circe,
and how he made his way in his many-benched ship to the
dank house of Hades, hoping to consult the shade of Theban
Teiresias; and there he saw all his former companions, and
the mother who bore and nursed him when a small child.   325
How he heard the voice of the ceaselessly singing Sirens,
and went on to the Wandering Rocks and terrible Charybdis,
and Scylla, whom no man had yet escaped from unscathed.
How his companions slaughtered the cattle of the Sun-god;
how Zeus the high-thunderer struck his swift ship with a   330
smoke-streaming thunderbolt, and his excellent companions
perished, all together, though he himself avoided an evil doom.
How he came to the island of Ogygia and the nymph Calypso,
who kept him there in her hollow cavern because she longed
to make him her husband; she cared for him, and promised   335
to make him ageless and immortal for all his days, but
she was never able to persuade the heart in his breast.
How after many hardships he came to the island of the
Phaeacians, who honoured him in their hearts like a god,
and sent him away in a ship with lavish gifts of bronze   340
and gold and clothing, back to the dear land of his birth.
This was the last tale he told, for sweet sleep that slackens
the limbs and frees the heart from cares fell suddenly on him.

But now the goddess grey-eyed Athena had a different plan:
when she considered Odysseus had in his heart enjoyed   345
his fill of both love and sleep in bed with his wife, she
straightaway roused early-born, golden-throned Dawn

to come from Oceanus and to bring light to men; and
Odysseus rose from his bed and gave orders to his wife:
'Lady, you and I have had our full share of trials, both   350
of us: you here, weeping over my trouble-ridden return
home, while Zeus and the other gods kept me agonizingly
far from my fathers' land, greatly though I yearned for it.
But now that we have both come to our much-desired bed,
your task is to look after the possessions I have in my halls;   355
as for the flocks which the arrogant suitors have wasted,
most I shall get back by raiding, and the Achaeans will
contribute the rest, until they have filled my sheepfolds.
But now I am going to my thickly wooded estate, to see my
noble father, who I think is sorely troubled on my account.   360
These are my instructions for you, lady, though you are too
wise to need them. As soon as the sun is up report will
go abroad about the suitors I have killed in my halls;
so take your serving-women and go to your rooms
above, and stay there; see no one, and ask no questions.'   365

　　So he spoke, and put his splendid armour over his shoulders,
and roused Telemachus and the oxherd and the swineherd,
and told them all to take up their war-gear in their hands.
They did not disobey, but armed themselves with bronze,
opened the doors and went out; and Odysseus led the way.   370
There was now daylight over the earth, but Athena enveloped
them in darkness, and escorted them quickly out of the city.

BOOK TWENTY-FOUR

And now Cyllenian Hermes summoned forth the shades of
the suitors, holding in his hand the beautiful golden rod
with which he charms the eyes of those men he chooses,
while others he rouses from sleep. With this he mustered the
shades and led them along, and they followed, squeaking.   5
As when bats flutter about the far corners of a huge cave,
squeaking, when one of them has fallen from the cluster
where they hang on to each other at the rocky face, so
these shades came on together, squeaking; and Hermes
the kindly god was their leader down the paths of decay.   10
Past the waters of Oceanus they came, and the rock of
Leucas, past the gates of the Sun and the country of dreams,*
and very soon reached the meadow of asphodel, which is
the dwelling-place of shades, phantoms of men done with life.

  There they found the shade of Achilles, son of Peleus, and   15
the shades of Patroclus, of blameless Antilochus, and of
Ajax, who was the finest man in form and appearance
of all the Danaans except for the blameless son of Peleus.
So as these were crowding around Achilles, there came up
to them the shade of Agamemnon, son of Atreus, full of grief; 20
and there were gathered around him other shades, those who
had died with him and met their doom in Aegisthus' house.
The first to speak to Agamemnon was the shade of Peleus' son:
'Son of Atreus, we used to think you were for all your days
loved beyond all heroes by Zeus who delights in the thunderbolt, 25
because you commanded a numerous people, mighty men, in
the Trojans' land, where we Achaeans suffered such hardship.
But as it turned out you too were fated to be claimed by cruel
death before your time—death that no man born can escape.
If only you had met your death and doom there in the Trojans'   30
land, in enjoyment of the high honour that you enjoyed!
Then all the Achaeans would have made you a burial-mound,
and you would have won great fame for your son in future.
But instead you were fated to be taken in a most pitiable death.'

  Then in turn the shade of Atreus' son addressed him: 35

'Son of Peleus, godlike Achilles, you are a fortunate man
to have died in Troy, far from Argos! Around you others
were killed, all the best sons of Trojans and Achaeans, as
they fought over your body, while you lay in the whirling
dust, mightily in your might, your chariot-skill all forgotten.   40
All through that day we struggled; and we would never have
given up the fighting had not Zeus ended it with a storm.
When we had carried you out of the battle to the ships
we laid you on a bier, having first washed your handsome
body with warm water and with unguents; and around you   45
the Danaans shed copious warm tears and cut their hair short.
When your mother heard the news she rose out of the sea
with her immortal sea-nymphs; an unearthly cry echoed over
the deep, and trembling seized the limbs of all the Achaeans.
And indeed they would have leapt up and run to the ships,   50
had not a man of deep ancient wisdom restrained them—
Nestor, whose counsel even before this had proved the best.
With generous intent he addressed them publicly, saying:
"Hold back, Argives! Do not run away, young Achaeans!
Look, here is Achilles' mother, rising from the sea with her   55
immortal sea-nymphs, to take her place beside her dead son."
    'So he spoke, and the great-spirited Achaeans checked their
flight. Around you stood the daughters of the Old Man of the
Sea, lamenting piteously, and clad you in deathless clothing.
All nine Muses began a dirge, singing antiphonally in their   60
sweet voices; and then you would not have seen any Argive
without tears, so strongly did the clear-voiced song move them.
For seventeen days, night and day continuously, we mourned you,
immortal gods and mortal men alike, and on the eighteenth
day we gave you to the fire; and around you we slaughtered   65
large numbers of fat sheep and crook-horned cattle.
You were burnt in clothing of the gods, with many unguents
and with sweet honey; and while you burned many Achaean
heroes paraded in armour around the pyre, both foot-soldiers
and those who fight from chariots; and a great din went up.   70
But when Hephaestus' flames had done their work with you,
in the morning we gathered up your white bones, Achilles,
and laid them in unmixed wine and unguents. For this your
mother gave us a golden, two-handled urn, which she said was

a gift from Dionysus, and the work of far-famed Hephaestus.   75
In this, splendid Achilles, your white bones lie, mingled
with the bones of the dead Patroclus, son of Menoetius, but
separate from those of Antilochus, whom you valued above
all your other companions—after the death of Patroclus.
Over these bones we, who were the mighty expedition of   80
Argive spearmen, heaped up a huge, splendid barrow, on
a jutting headland that looks over the broad Hellespont,
so that it could be seen from far away by men on the open
sea, by those now alive and also those born in time to come.
Your mother begged the gods to present exceptionally fine   85
prizes, which she then set in their midst for the Achaean
chieftains to compete for. In time past you attended the
funeral rites of many heroes, whenever at the death of some
king young men prepared themselves for the games; but
you would have been greatly amazed in your heart to see   90
the magnificent prizes which the goddess silver-footed Thetis
set up there in your honour. You were very dear to the gods.
So even in death you have not lost your good name, Achilles,
and your noble reputation will last among all men for ever.
But for me, what joy was there in seeing this war to its end?   95
While I was on my way home Zeus devised a miserable death
for me at the hands of Aegisthus and of my accursed wife.'
     So they conversed, one with the other, on these matters.
Now there came up to them the guide and slayer of Argus,
leading down the shades of the suitors killed by Odysseus.   100
Both were amazed at the sight and went straight over to
them. The shade of Agamemnon, Atreus' son, recognized
far-famed Amphimedon, the dear son of Melaneus,
who had once been his host in his house on Ithaca.
The shade of the son of Atreus was the first to speak: 105
'Amphimedon, what calamity has brought you down to this
murky land—all of you chosen men, and of the same age?
It is as if someone had picked out all the best men in the city.
Were you in your ships, and did Poseidon stir up a violent
tempest and enormous waves to batter you down? Or was it   110
perhaps on dry land, and some hostile band of men cut you
down as you were rounding up their fine sheep-flocks, or
were they were fighting to defend their city and womenfolk?

Answer my questions, for I claim to be your guest-friend.
Do you not remember when I came over to your house there   115
with godlike Menelaus, on a mission to urge Odysseus
to accompany us to Troy in his well-benched ships? It was
a whole month before we made our passage back across the
wide sea, so hard it was to win over Odysseus, sacker of cities.'

   Then in turn the shade of Amphimedon addressed him: 120
'Most glorious son of Atreus, Agamemnon lord of men, Zeus-
nurtured man! I do indeed remember all that you speak of,
and so I will give you a full account of all that has happened,
of the wretched manner by which our death came about.
We were courting the wife of Odysseus, now long absent.   125
She neither rejected marriage—hateful to her—nor agreed
to it, because she was plotting death and black doom for us;
and this was the deception she worked out in her mind:
she set up a great loom in her halls, and began to weave
on it using fine, very long thread. She then said to us: 130
"My princely suitors! Glorious Odysseus is dead; but eager
though you are to make this marriage, wait until I finish
this robe, and then my weaving will not be wasted, all in vain.
It is a burial shroud* for the hero Laertes, for when the cruel
fate of death, bringer of long misery, takes him away, so that no   135
Achaean woman among our people will hold it against me that a man
who amassed much wealth should be lying without a shroud."
That is what she said, and our proud hearts were persuaded.
From that time, she would weave at the great loom by day, but
at night torches were set beside her and she would undo her work.   140
So for three years her guile went unnoticed, and she fooled
the Achaeans; but when with the seasons' round the fourth year
came, as the months waned and the long days reached their end,
then at last one of her women, who knew her secret well, told us,
and we caught her in the act of undoing her bright weaving,   145
and so she finished it; she was reluctant, but we forced her.
She had just completed the great web, and was showing us the
robe, after washing it so that it shone like the sun or the moon,
when an evil divinity brought Odysseus back from somewhere,
to a remote part of his estate, where a swineherd had his house.   150
The next thing that happened was that godlike Odysseus' son
came back, having crossed in his black ship from sandy Pylos.

The two of them then planned an evil death for the suitors, and
made their way to our renowned city; or rather, Telemachus
went on ahead and Odysseus followed behind. The swineherd   155
acted as guide for Odysseus, who was dressed in filthy clothes,
disguised as a wretched beggar, an old man supporting
himself on a staff. The clothes he wore were so wretched
that no one among us, not even the older men, was able to
recognize him for who he was when he suddenly appeared;   160
instead we insulted him with unkind words and threw things
at him.* For some time he endured being the object of missiles
and insults in his own halls with a steadfast spirit; but
when the will of Zeus who wields the aegis roused him,
with the help of Telemachus he took down the splendid   165
war-gear and put it away in a storeroom and bolted the doors.
Next, in his great cunning he ordered his wife to put before
the suitors a bow and axes of grey iron, to be a contest for
us cruel-fated men; and it was the beginning of bloodshed.
Not one of us could stretch the string of this mighty bow,   170
for our strength fell a long way short of the challenge.
When the great bow came into the hands of Odysseus,
we all shouted threateningly at the servant, telling him
not to give him the bow, however loudly he might argue;
but Telemachus alone was insistent, and told him to do it.   175
Then much-enduring glorious Odysseus took the bow in his
hand and strung it with ease, and shot through the iron axes.
He then took his stand on the threshold, and with a fierce
glare spilled the swift arrows and shot down lord Antinous.
After that he took careful aim and let fly his grief-laden   180
shafts at the rest; and they fell there, one after the other.
Now it became clear that some god was helping them;
in their frenzy they ranged everywhere about the palace,
killing men right and left. Shameful groans arose as heads
were broken, and the whole floor was awash with blood.   185
This, Agamemnon, was how we perished, and our bodies
are even now lying unattended in Odysseus' halls; for each
man's loved ones, back at home, do not yet know the news—
those who might wash the black gore from our wounds and
lay us out with mourning; for that is the privilege of the dead.' 190
     Then in turn the shade of Atreus' son addressed him:

'Fortunate son of Laertes, Odysseus of many wiles!
You have surely got for yourself a wife of outstanding
virtue, such is the good sense that is in blameless Penelope,
daughter of Icarius! How well she has kept the memory   195
of Odysseus, her wedded husband! And so the fame of her
virtue will never die, and the ever-living gods will make a
beautiful song for men on earth in honour of faithful Penelope.
Not so was the daughter of Tyndareus,* who plotted a wicked
deed and murdered her wedded husband; full of hate will be   200
her song among men, and evil the reputation she will pass
on to womankind, even to those who live upright lives.'
    So these two conversed in this way, one with another,
standing there in Hades' house, in the secret depths of the earth.
    Odysseus and the others left the city, and soon reached   205
the fine, well-cultivated estate of Laertes, which he had
created long ago, and over which he had laboured much.
His house was there, and all around it were the sheds
in which his servants took their food and lived and slept,
working under compulsion and carrying out his wishes.   210
There was an old Sicilian woman living there, who looked
after the old man devotedly on the estate, far from the city.
Once there, Odysseus spoke to his servants and his son:
'Go now into this well-founded house, and without delay
slaughter the best pig you can find for our midday meal;   215
meanwhile I shall put my father to the test, to find out if
he knows who I am and recognizes me when he sees me, or
if he fails to remember me; I have been away a long time.'
    So he spoke, and handed his weapons of war to his servants.
They quickly went off towards the house, while Odysseus   220
made for the fruitful orchard in order to continue his search.
As he went down into the large garden he did not find Dolius*
or any of the other servants or their sons; they had gone out
to gather stones in order to build a wall for the vineyard,
and the old man had gone in front to show them the way.   225
But he found his father, alone in the well-tended vineyard,
busy hoeing round a tree; he was wearing a filthy tunic,
patched and shabby, and around his legs he had fastened
stitched oxhide leggings to protect him from scratches, and on
his hands he was wearing gloves, to save them from brambles;   230

and on his head, to complete his misery, was a goatskin cap.
When much-enduring glorious Odysseus caught sight of him,
worn down by old age and carrying huge grief in his heart,
he stopped underneath a tall pear tree and began to weep.
And then he considered in his mind and in his heart whether   235
he should embrace and kiss his father and tell him everything,
how he had returned, back to his ancestral land, or if he
should first question Laertes about everything and test him.
And as he pondered this seemed to him the better course,
first of all to put his father to the test with teasing words.*   240
With this in mind glorious Odysseus made straight for him.
Laertes, keeping his head down, continued hoeing round
the tree; and his splendid son drew close and addressed him:
'Old man, you lack no skill in tending your orchard; your
care shows in everything, and there is nothing at all here,   245
no plant or fig tree, no vine or olive tree, no pear tree, no
vegetable bed that is not carefully maintained in your garden.
But I have something to say to you; do not let it anger your heart.
You do not care for yourself so well; wretched old age has you
in its grip, you are unkempt, and the clothes on you are shabby.   250
It cannot be laziness that causes your master to neglect you,
and there is certainly nothing slave-like in your appearance,
in either form or stature; you look to me like a kingly man,
the kind of man who after he has bathed and eaten ought to
sleep in a soft bed—which is the due owed to aged men.   255
So come, tell me this, and give me a full and true account:
whose servant are you, and whose orchard do you tend?
You must tell me this truly, so that I may know for sure
if this really is Ithaca I have come to, as the man I met
yonder told me just now, while I was making my way here.   260
He was not especially civil, and did not take the trouble to
answer my questions exactly, nor to listen to what I said;
I was asking him about a guest-friend of mine, if he is still
living somewhere, or is now dead, in the house of Hades.
I tell you this, and you should listen and store it in your mind: 265
long ago in my ancestral land I entertained a man who came
to my home; and no mortal among those who came from
far away to my house has ever been more welcome than him.
He claimed that his family was from Ithaca, and said

that his father was Laertes, who was the son of Arceisius.   270
I took him into my house and entertained him hospitably,
with proper generosity from the abundant store I had,
and presented him with guest-gifts, fitting for such a man:
I gave him seven talents of artfully worked gold, and a
mixing-bowl of solid silver which had a flower decoration,   275
and twelve single-fold cloaks, and as many coverlets,
and in addition the same number of fine robes and tunics.
Beyond all these I gave him women, skilled in fine crafts,
four of them, all beautiful; and he chose them for himself.'

Then his father answered him, weeping tears: 'Stranger,   280
you have indeed reached the country you are asking about,
though it is held in the grip of arrogant and reckless men.
As for those lavishly given gifts, you bestowed them in vain.
If you had found him still alive in the land of Ithaca, he
he would have matched your gifts and hospitality and sent   285
you on your way, as is right for the man who gave first.
But tell me this, and give me a full and true account:
how many years is it since you entertained this man, your
unhappy guest-friend—my son, if I ever had one, ill-fated
man. Doubtless fishes have devoured him in the open sea,   290
far from friends and homeland, or else he has become the
prey of wild beasts and birds on land. His mother could not
solemnly bury and weep over him, nor I his father—we who
gave him birth. Nor could his richly dowered wife, faithful
Penelope, close his eyes and wail over her husband on his bier,   295
as would have been proper, for that is the privilege of the dead.
Now tell me this truthfully, so that I may know it: who among
men are you? Where are you from? Where is your city and
parents? Where is the swift ship moored that brought you and
your godlike companions here? Or were you a passenger in   300
someone else's ship, and they set you ashore and sailed away?'

Then in answer Odysseus of many wiles addressed him:
'I will indeed give you an accurate account* of all you ask.
I am from Alybas,* where I live in a famous palace; I am the
son of the king there, Apheides, Polypemon's son, and my   305
name is Eperitus. On my way from Sicania* some god
drove me off course against my will, and I fetched up here.
My ship is moored near open country, away from the city.

As for Odysseus, it is now the fifth year since he went from
my house and left my country behind, ill-fated man; and yet   310
the bird-signs were good when he went, appearing on the
right hand, and so I was happy to send him on his way, and
he was cheerful when he went. Both of us hoped in our hearts
to meet again in friendship and to exchange splendid gifts.'
    So he spoke, and a black cloud of grief enveloped Laertes.   315
With both hands he scooped up the sooty dust and poured
it over his grey head, groaning all the time. Odysseus'
heart was moved, and now, as he looked at his dear father
a sharp, powerful pang rose up to his nostrils. Rushing
forward, he threw his arms around him and kissed him.   320
'Look, father, here I am—the very man you are asking about;
I have come home, in the twentieth year, to my ancestral land!
Come now, stop your weeping and tear-laden lamentation,
for I tell you this plainly: there is need for haste, because I
have killed the suitors in my palace, and have taken revenge   325
for their heart-wounding insults and their wicked deeds.'
    Then in turn Laertes answered him and said:
'If it is really you, my son Odysseus, who have come back here,
give me now some clear token, so that I may be persuaded.'
    Then in answer Odysseus, man of many wiles, addressed him: 330
'First, cast your eyes on this scar here, which was gouged
in me by a boar's white tusk on Parnassus, while I was on
a visit there; you and my revered mother had sent me there
to see Autolycus, my mother's father, to be given the gifts
that he had formally promised to me when he came to Ithaca.   335
And listen: let me tell you about the trees in this well-tended
orchard which you once gave me as a child. I was following
you round the garden, constantly begging for this or that tree,
and as we walked through these very trees you told me the
names of all of them. Thirteen pear trees you gave me, and   340
ten apple trees, and forty fig trees, and you pointed out the
fifty vine-rows that would be mine; all had different kinds
of grape-cluster on them, and ripened at different times,
according as the seasons from Zeus weighed the vines down.'
    So he spoke, and Laertes' knees and heart at once went slack,   345
recognizing the sure tokens that Odysseus had shown him.
He threw his arms around his dear son, and much-enduring,

glorious Odysseus caught him, fainting, against himself.
When he had recovered his breath and had gathered his
spirit again, he once more addressed his son in these words: 350
'Father Zeus, you gods surely still exist on high Olympus,
if indeed the suitors have now paid for their wild arrogance.
But now I am terribly afraid in my heart that the Ithacans
will soon come here in great numbers to confront us,* and
will send messages through all the cities of the Cephallenians.'   355
     Then in answer Odysseus of many wiles addressed him:
'Take courage, and do not let these things trouble your heart.
Let us go rather to your house, which lies here near the orchard;
I sent Telemachus on there, with the oxherd and the swineherd,
to make our midday meal ready as quickly as they could.'   360
     Conversing in this way they made their way to the fine house;
and when they reached the well-situated dwelling they
found there Telemachus, with the oxherd and the swineherd,
chopping up great quantities of meat and mixing gleaming wine.
     While they did so the Sicilian woman bathed great-hearted   365
Laertes in his house and rubbed him with olive oil, and
clothed him in a handsome cloak; and Athena stood beside
him and filled out the limbs of this shepherd of the people,
making him taller and sturdier than before to look upon.
He rose from his bath, and his dear son gazed in amazement   370
when he saw him, looking like the immortal gods before him.
He addressed him, speaking in winged words:
'To be sure, father, one of the gods who live for ever has
made you more handsome to look upon in form and stature!'
     Then in turn thoughtful Laertes spoke to him: 375
'Father Zeus and Athena and Apollo—if only I could be as
I was when as ruler of the Cephallenians I captured Nericus,*
that well-founded citadel, set on a cape of the mainland!
If I had been so yesterday in the palace, with armour round
my shoulders, I could have stood against the suitors and   380
beaten them back; I would have loosened the knees of many
of them there, and you would have been glad in your heart.'
     So they conversed in this way, one with the other; and when
the other two had finished their work and prepared the meal,
they all took their seats in due order on benches and chairs.   385
They were reaching out for the food when the old man Dolius

arrived, and with him his sons, weary after their toil in the
fields. Their mother, the old Sicilian woman, had gone out
and summoned them in—she who looked after them and
ministered kindly to the old man, now in the grip of old age.   390
When they caught sight of Odysseus and recognized him,
they stood there in the hall, dumbfounded; but Odysseus
greeted them with courteous words, and spoke to them:
'Sit down to your meal, old man! And you others, do not
be startled; we have long been eager to put our hands to the   395
food, waiting in the house and all the time expecting you.'

   So he spoke, and Dolius went straight up to him, throwing
wide both arms; he seized Odysseus' hand and kissed him
on the wrist, and speaking in winged words addressed him:
'My friend—so you have come back to us! How we yearned, but   400
never thought to see you. The gods themselves have brought you.
Health and happiness to you—may the gods bring you prosperity!
And now, tell me this truly, so that I may know it for sure:
does circumspect Penelope know for certain that you have
come back here to us, or should we send her a messenger?'   405

   Then in answer Odysseus, man of many wiles, addressed him:
'Old man, she knows already. Why concern yourself with this?'
So he spoke, and Dolius sat down again on his well-polished
chair. And in the same way the sons of Dolius gathered round
far-famed Odysseus, welcoming him in words and clasping his   410
hands, and then took their seats in order, by their father Dolius.

   While all these busied themselves with their meal in the
house the messenger Rumour was roaming all over the city,
bringing news of the grisly death and fate of the suitors.
When the people heard it, they gathered from all sides with   415
moaning and groaning in front of the palace of Odysseus,
and began to carry the bodies out of the house and bury them,
each their own; those from other cities they laid in swift ships
and gave to seafarers to take away, each to his own home.
They themselves crowded to the meeting-place, grieving in   420
their hearts. When they were assembled and gathered together,
Eupeithes rose to his feet and addressed them; a violent
grief lay on his heart on account of his son Antinous,
who was the first man that glorious Odysseus had killed.
Weeping tears for Antinous, he spoke out among them: 425

'My friends, it is an evil deed this man has worked against
the Achaeans! First he took many noble men away in his
ships, but he lost the hollow ships and the people, and now,
returning, he has killed the very best of the Cephallenians.
Quickly, then, before he makes a swift escape over to Pylos   430
or to bright Elis, where the Epeians rule, let us be going.
If we do not, we shall be covered with shame for all time;
it will surely bring disgrace on us for future men to hear of,
if we do not take revenge on the murderers of our sons and
brothers. For me, at any rate, there will be no joy in my heart   435
to go on living—I would sooner die now and join the departed.
Let us go, then, before these men cross the sea and escape us.'
   So he spoke, in tears, and pity gripped all the Achaeans.
But now up came Medon and the god-inspired singer from
Odysseus' halls; sleep had released them, and they stood in the   440
midst of the crowd, and wonder seized hold of every man.
Among them Medon, a man of sound good sense, spoke out:
'Listen to me now, men of Ithaca! It was not without the will
of the immortal gods that Odysseus devised these schemes.
I myself saw a deathless god standing close to him, who   445
in every respect looked to me like Mentor. This immortal
god at one time appeared in front of Odysseus, and cheered
him on, and at another went charging through the hall and
caused havoc among the suitors, who fell one after another.'
   So he spoke, and pale terror laid hold on them all. Then   450
an aged man spoke out among them, the hero Halitherses,
Mastor's son, who alone saw into the future and the past.
With generous intent he spoke out and addressed them:
'Listen to me now, men of Ithaca, to what I have to say! It was
through your own wickedness, friends, that all this happened.   455
You would not listen to me, nor to Mentor, shepherd of the
people, and so put a stop to your sons' idiocy—they who
committed a great crime through their wicked recklessness,
plundering her possessions and dishonouring the wife
of the best of men, who you thought would never return.   460
So be persuaded by me, and let things now be as I say:
let us not go, or someone may bring hurt upon himself.'
   So he spoke; but more than half leapt up with a loud war-
shout, because his advice was not to their hearts' liking,

while the rest remained where they were, gathered all together.   465
They followed Eupeithes, and quickly rushed off for their arms.
When they had put on their glinting bronze war-gear, they
assembled in a body before the city of wide dancing-places.
Eupeithes took the lead, foolish man that he was; he
believed he could avenge his son's killing, though he was   470
destined not to return, but to meet his doom in this very battle.
    And now Athena spoke to Zeus, the son of Cronus:
'Our father, son of Cronus, supreme among rulers, give an
answer to my question: what thoughts lie hidden in you?
Do you intend to prolong this evil war and terrible strife   475
even further, or will you bring friendship to both parties?'
    Then in answer Zeus the cloud-gatherer addressed her:
'My child, why ask this question? Why interrogate me?
Was it not you yourself who conceived this idea, that
Odysseus should return and take vengeance on these men?   480
Do what you wish—but I will reveal to you the proper way.
Now that glorious Odysseus has punished the suitors, let
both parties make a secure treaty: he shall be king for ever,
and we for our part will cause them to forget the slaying of
sons and brothers. Let there be friendship between them   485
as before, and let peace and wealth be theirs in abundance.'
So he spoke, and roused Athena, who was already eager to go,
and she went swooping down from the peaks of Olympus.
    When the men had put away the desire for heart-cheering
food, much-enduring glorious Odysseus spoke first: 490
'Let someone go out and see if they are now approaching.'
So he spoke, and one of Dolius' sons left them as he had ordered;
he went and stood on the threshold, and saw they were all
nearby, and quickly addressed Odysseus in winged words:
'There they are, right on us! Quick, we must arm ourselves!'   495
So he spoke, and they rose and put on their war-gear—
Odysseus and his three companions, and Dolius' six sons.
Laertes and Dolius donned their armour along with them,
grey-haired though they were, now fighters by necessity.
When they had put on their glinting bronze armour, they   500
opened the doors and went out; and Odysseus led the way.
    Now Athena, daughter of Zeus, came and stood beside them,
taking on the likeness of Mentor in both form and voice.

When he saw her much-enduring glorious Odysseus was glad,
and without more ado addressed his dear son Telemachus: 505
'Now, Telemachus, you will surely learn—when you come to
where the best men measure themselves in battle—how not
to shame your fathers' family, we who in time past have been
pre-eminent throughout the world in courage and manliness.'
    Then in turn thoughtful Telemachus addressed him: 510
'Dear father, if you wish it, you will see that in my present
mood I will not shame your family, as your words declare.'
So he spoke, and Laertes was delighted, and gave voice:
'Dear gods, what a day this is! How happy I am to see
my son and grandson competing with each other in valour!'   515
    Now the goddess went and stood next to him and said:
'Son of Arceisius, by far the dearest to me of all my friends:
pray first to the grey-eyed maiden and to father Zeus, and
then quickly poise your far-shadowing spear and hurl it.'
    So spoke Pallas Athena, and breathed great vigour into him.   520
At once he prayed to the maiden daughter of mighty Zeus,
and poising his far-shadowing spear he hurled it, and hit
Eupeithes on the bronze cheek-piece of his helmet; it did not
keep the spear out, and the bronze tip went clean through,
and Eupeithes fell with a crash, his armour clattering about him.   525
Next Odysseus and his splendid son fell upon the front-fighters,
striking out continually with swords and curved-headed spears.
And indeed they would have slain them all, depriving them of a
homecoming, had not Athena, daughter of aegis-wielding Zeus,
let out a great shout and restrained the whole band of fighters: 530
'Men of Ithaca, stop! Give up this painful conflict! Stand
apart as fast as you can, and so avoid more bloodshed!'
    So spoke Athena, and pale fear gripped them, terrified at
the sound of the goddess's voice; their weapons flew
from their hands and dropped to the ground, and in their   535
anxiety to stay alive they turned and fled towards the city.
With a terrible war-cry, much-enduring glorious Odysseus
gathered himself like a high-flying eagle and swooped after
them. Then at last Cronus' son let fly a smoking thunderbolt,
which fell in front of the grey-eyed child of the mighty father.   540
    And now grey-eyed Athena addressed Odysseus: 'Zeus-born
son of Laertes, Odysseus of many wiles, stop! Put an end

to this quarrel, this levelling warfare, for fear that the son of
Cronus, wide-thundering Zeus, becomes angry with you.'

    So spoke Athena, and he obeyed her, and was glad in his heart.   545
Then Pallas Athena, daughter of Zeus who wields the aegis,
taking on the likeness of Mentor in both form and voice,
made a secure treaty for both sides, to hold for time to come.

EXPLANATORY NOTES

BOOK ONE

The poet invokes the Muse and outlines the subject and scope of his song, the resourceful Odysseus and his painful struggle to return home (1–10). The narrative begins with an assembly of the gods on Olympus at which Athena raises the issue of Odysseus' continued suffering, asking Zeus why he has abandoned him (11–62). Zeus blames Poseidon, whose anger at the blinding of his son Polyphemus pursues the hero (63–79). Taking advantage of Poseidon's absence, Athena proposes a plan (80–95). She goes to Ithaca, disguised as Mentes, an old guest-friend of Odysseus, where she is kindly received by Telemachus and offered hospitality (96–143). The suitors enter the hall and Telemachus outlines their outrageous conduct (144–77). Mentes explains how he came to know Odysseus and predicts his imminent return (178–212). When Telemachus describes the crisis in Odysseus' household, Mentes advises him on how he should handle both the suitors and Penelope, and instructs him to visit Odysseus' former comrades, Nestor and Menelaus, to see if they have news of his father (213–305). As she departs, Athena reveals her divine identity, filling Telemachus with new determination (306–24). Penelope descends from her chambers and instructs the bard Phemius, whose subject is the Greeks' return from Troy, to sing a different song, but Telemachus chastises her and Penelope withdraws (325–64). Telemachus then rebukes the suitors, who are surprised by his boldness. When they ask about Mentes, Telemachus deceives them; he then retires to bed, planning the journey that Athena had proposed (365–444).

10 *goddess daughter of Zeus*: the Muses were the offspring of Zeus and Mnemosyne ('Memory'). In the (later) canonical list of nine Muses, Calliope was the Muse of epic poetry, but Homer does not name his goddess.

24 *some... rising*: the Ethiopians are here divided into two groups, western and eastern. Poseidon's return journey is from the east (5.283). The Ethiopians, at the edge of the known world, are generally depicted positively in Greek thought as being better than ordinary people and enjoying a special relationship with the gods.

25 *hecatomb*: a sacrifice of 100 animals or, more generally, a large sacrifice.

29 *Aegisthus*: lover of Clytemnestra, who together killed her husband Agamemnon.

38 *keen-eyed slayer of Argus*: Zeus had ordered Hermes to kill Argus, a many-eyed monster posted by Hera to guard Io, one of Zeus' mistresses, whom Hera (or in some versions of the myth, Zeus) had turned into a cow.

50 *at the navel-point of the sea*: Calypso's island, Ogygia, is presented as lying at the centre of the sea. Some ancient commentators realized that the places mentioned in Odysseus' wanderings were fictional, but most

attempted to identify them with real islands or cities around (or beyond) the Mediterranean.

52 *murderous-minded Atlas*: the Titan was forced to hold up the sky, having led a failed rebellion against the Olympian gods. His bad temper foreshadows the threat posed to Odysseus' return by his daughter, Calypso.

62 *so odious to Odysseus*: the translation brings out the wordplay in Greek, which connects the hero's name to the verb *odussomai* ('to be angry with or against'); cf. 5.340, 423; 19.275, 407–9.

81 *son of Cronus*: Zeus, who (along with several other Olympian gods) was born of the marriage between the Titan Cronus and his sister Rhea.

105 *guest-friend*: for the importance of hospitality (*xenia*) to the shaping of the poem, see section 'Hospitality and recognition' in the Introduction.

105 *Taphians*: a people specializing in trading and piracy (cf. 1.181–4; 14.452; 15.427); the location of their kingdom is unknown.

154 *under compulsion*: Odysseus will eventually agree to spare Phemius for this reason (22.344–53).

184 *Temese*: possibly to be identified with Tamassos in Cyprus, famous for its copper, which, when combined with tin, makes bronze.

226 *a contribution dinner*: the suitors' greed and extravagance tell against this.

246 *Dulichium... Zacynthus*: islands close to Ithaca.

259 *Ephyre*: a town on the west coast of the Greek mainland north of Ithaca.

262 *bronze-tipped arrows*: the myth referred to here is otherwise unknown, but Odysseus' skill as an archer foreshadows the killing of the suitors.

297 *no longer a child*: for Telemachus' growth to manhood and responsibility, see section 'Marriage and family life' in the Introduction.

350 *Danaans*: like Achaeans and Argives, another name for the Greeks.

387 *your right by birth*: the admission marks the insolence of the suitors and their threat to Telemachus' future.

BOOK TWO

Telemachus summons the assembly, describes the ruin of Odysseus' household, and pleads with the suitors to stop (1–79). The suitor Antinous rejects Telemachus' attempt to shame them and blames the crisis instead on Penelope's refusal to remarry and on her deceit, as evidenced by the ruse of Laertes' shroud, which Penelope wove by day then undid by night (81–128). Telemachus, however, declares that he will never ask his mother to leave against her will (129–45). Zeus sends an omen, which Halitherses interprets as a warning to the suitors that their destruction is near, a conclusion rejected by the suitor Eurymachus (146–207). Telemachus requests a ship and crew to visit Pylos and Sparta for news of his father, and Mentor criticizes the Ithacans for failing to challenge the suitors in the past (208–59). Athena, answering Telemachus' prayer, appears as Mentor and assures Telemachus of his support (260–95).

Telemachus firmly rejects Antinous' invitation to dine with the suitors, who then mock him (296–336). Eurycleia, fearing for Telemachus' safety, agrees to keep his journey a secret from Penelope (337–81). Athena, disguised as Telemachus, organizes a ship and crew (382–92). Then, after putting the suitors to sleep, she takes the form of Mentor, urges Telemachus to depart, and they set sail (393–434).

99 *burial shroud*: Penelope's trick cleverly exploits a traditional female activity (weaving) and a laudable female duty (preparation of the dead for burial). It is condemned by the dead suitor Amphimedon in the underworld (24.128–46), who uses the same term (*dolos*, 'deception') as Antinous does here (93). Penelope herself laments its discovery when speaking to the disguised Odysseus (19.138–56).

120 *Tyro...crown*: Antinous compares Penelope favourably to three famous women of the past: Tyro was an ancestor of the heroes Nestor and Jason; Alcmene bore Heracles to Zeus; Mycene gave her name to the powerful kingdom of Mycenae.

175 *twentieth year*: i.e. ten years after the end of the Trojan War, which itself lasted ten years. For the poem's skilful handling of narrative time, whereby it covers only forty-one days in the twentieth year but nonetheless encompasses the whole of Odysseus' life, see section 'The *Odyssey* and early Greek epic' in the Introduction.

328 *Ephyre*: see note to 1.259; both passages refer to the town as a source of poison.

BOOK THREE

Telemachus arrives in Pylos and is advised by Mentor (Athena) on how to approach Nestor (1–28). They are kindly received by Nestor's son, Peisistratus, and after dinner Nestor enquires who they are (29–74). Telemachus explains that they have come from Ithaca in search of news about his father Odysseus (75–101). Nestor laments the losses of the Trojan War and recalls the homecomings, good and bad, of the other Greeks, but has not seen or heard news of Odysseus for ten years (102–200). Telemachus despairs of ever defeating the suitors, but is encouraged by Nestor and Mentor (201–38). Prompted by Telemachus, Nestor describes Agamemnon's death at the hands of Aegisthus and Clytemnestra, and explains why Menelaus was unable to prevent it (239–328). Telemachus and Mentor are eager to leave for Sparta, but Nestor insists they stay for the night (329–70). Athena reveals her true identity and Nestor promises her a sacrifice (371–403). The next day Nestor organizes a feast and sacrifices a gilded heifer to Athena (404–63). After his bath, Telemachus is given a chariot and horses, and Peisistratus drives them on their way to Sparta (464–97).

42 *the aegis*: a goat-skin shield and embodiment of Zeus' power.

43 *to the lord Poseidon*: there is great irony in Athena being asked to pray to the very god who is dead set against Odysseus' return.

91 *Amphitrite*: one of the Nereids (sea-nymphs), used by Homer to represent the sea itself.

109 *Ajax*: two Ajaxes fought for the Greeks at Troy. This one, the son of Telamon, was the second-best warrior after Achilles. When Achilles died, his arms were awarded to Odysseus rather than Ajax, causing the angry hero to commit suicide. For the other Ajax, see note to 3.135.

110 *Patroclus*: Achilles' closest friend, killed by the Trojan prince Hector.

112 *Antilochus*: he died defending his father against the Ethiopian king Memnon, an ally of the Trojans.

135 *deadly anger*: Ajax, son of Oileus, raped the Trojan princess Cassandra within Athena's shrine at Troy, and the Greeks failed to punish him; the goddess took her revenge by killing many of them on their way home.

136 *the two sons of Atreus*: Agamemnon and Menelaus.

167 *son of Tydeus*: Diomedes, one of the most skilled and successful warriors at Troy.

178 *Geraestus*: the most southerly point of the island Euboea.

190 *Philoctetes*: a festering wound from a snakebite led the Greeks to abandon Philoctetes on the island of Lemnos, where he spent the ten years of the Trojan War; the hero was finally healed and helped to sack Troy, killing the Trojan prince Paris, Helen's 'husband'.

191 *Idomeneus*: leader of the Cretan forces at Troy; cf. 14.237.

197 *Orestes*: Agamemnon's brave and loyal son serves as an exemplar for Telemachus; cf. 1.298–302.

222 *for all to see*: on Athena's particular affection for Odysseus, see section 'Mortals and immortals' in the Introduction.

267 *a singer*: acting as a chaperon to Clytemnestra. In a poem marked by praise of bards and singers (see section 'The *Odyssey* and early Greek epic' in the Introduction), his killing by Aegisthus emphasizes the latter's villainy.

288 *Malea*: on the south-easternmost promontory of the Peloponnese, where Agamemnon (4.514) and Odysseus (9.80) are also hit by storms.

326 *Lacedaemon*: Sparta.

367 *Caucones*: a people in the western Peloponnese.

378 *Tritogeneia*: an epithet of Athena, probably meaning 'true-born' and stressing her legitimacy despite her unusual (motherless) birth from the head of Zeus.

408 *gleamed with oil*: the king's seat is anointed as a symbol of its sanctity.

488 *Pherae*: a town midway between Pylos and Sparta.

BOOK FOUR

Telemachus and Peisistratus arrive in Sparta, where Menelaus' family is celebrating a double wedding (1–14). They are welcomed, bathed, and fed, and

Telemachus is amazed by the splendour of Menelaus' palace (15–75). Menelaus speaks of his eight years of wandering after the fall of Troy, and his grief
for Odysseus causes Telemachus to weep (76–119). Helen makes a grand
entrance and recognizes Telemachus immediately (120–54). Peisistratus confirms this, and when all (hosts and guests) weep at remembrance of their own
suffering, Helen produces a drug that banishes their grief (155–232). Helen
and Menelaus offer contrasting tales of Odysseus' exploits at Troy (233–305).
The next day Menelaus tells of his adventures off the coast of Egypt, revealing that, according to the Old Man of the Sea, Odysseus had been detained
by the nymph Calypso (306–586). As Telemachus prepares to leave Sparta,
the scene changes to Ithaca, where the suitors discover Telemachus' absence
and plot to ambush him on his return (587–674). When Penelope learns of all
this herself, she is comforted, first by Eurycleia, then by a phantom sent in
the night by Athena (675–841). Meanwhile, the suitors prepare their ambush
(842–7).

  10 *Megapenthes*: the name ('great grief') underlines the fact that he is not a
     true-born son but the offspring of a slave-woman, and Menelaus' mar-
     riage to Helen has not provided him with a legitimate son and heir. The
     name also expresses Menelaus' unhappiness at Helen's elopement with
     Paris and prepares us for the uneasy relationship between them. For the
     poem's presentation of their marriage as a foil to that of Odysseus and
     Penelope, see section 'Marriage and family life' in the Introduction.

  84 *Sidonians*: Sidon was a major city on the coast of Phoenicia (mod. Lebanon).

  84 *Erembi*: their exact location is unknown.

 187 *Antilochus*: see note to 3.112.

 232 *Paieon*: the god of healing, later identified with Apollo.

 261 *with grief*: for the very different accounts of Helen's attitude given by her
     and Menelaus, see section 'Marriage and family life' in the Introduction.

 276 *Deiphobus*: Paris' brother, who became Helen's new Trojan partner after
     his death.

 343 *Philomeleides*: a king of Lesbos, who challenged those arriving in his terri-
     tory to a wrestling match.

 499 *Ajax*: the inferior warrior of that name (see notes to 3.109 and 135), here
     punished by Poseidon.

 500 *Gyrae*: ancient scholars identified various possible locations, including the
     islands of Mykonos and Tenos.

 515 *Malea*: see note to 3.288.

 563 *the plain of Elysium*: Menelaus' blessed immortality, an exceptional hon-
     our, is not due to any achievement of his own, but to his relationship with
     Helen, as the daughter of Zeus, and is another marker of the unusual
     power dynamic between them.

 762 *the aegis*: see note to 3.42.

762 *Atrytone*: an obscure title of Athena, probably 'the Unwearied (or Invincible) One'.

798 *Pherae*: a town in Thessaly.

BOOK FIVE

The gods meet in assembly and Athena complains again about Odysseus' predicament (1–27). Zeus sends Hermes to Calypso with instructions that Odysseus must be released (28–42). Arriving on Calypso's island, Hermes admires its fertility and is kindly received by the goddess (43–91). When Hermes reports Zeus' demand, Calypso angrily criticizes the gods for their double standards, but reluctantly agrees to let Odysseus go (92–147). Odysseus is sceptical of Calypso's motives, and makes her swear an oath that she is not trying to trick him (148–91). Her offer of immortality is tactfully declined by Odysseus, and they make love one final time (192–227). With Calypso's help, Odysseus builds a raft, sets sail, and on the eighteenth day is within sight of the land of the Phaeacians (228–81). Poseidon spots him, however, and whips up a huge storm that smashes Odysseus' raft (282–332). The sea-goddess Ino takes pity on Odysseus and helps him survive the storm (333–81), and Athena stops the winds and guides Odysseus ashore (382–473). Exhausted, Odysseus hides beneath a pair of olive-bushes, covers himself with leaves, and falls into a deep sleep (474–93).

1 *Tithonus*: a Trojan prince, abducted by the goddess of the dawn to be her lover (cf. Orion at line 121 below). They had a son together, the Ethiopian king Memnon (see note to 3.112). The goddess asked Zeus for immortality for Tithonus but forgot to ask for eternal youth as well, so that he shrivelled away to a piping husk (the origin of the cicada).

34 *Scheria*: the magical kingdom of the Phaeacians. Scholars ancient and modern have (in literal-minded fashion) proposed a variety of locations, the most popular in antiquity being the island of Corfu.

43 *slayer of Argus*: see note to 1.38.

50 *Pieria*: a mountain north of Olympus.

93 *ambrosia...nectar*: food of the gods.

108 *affront to Athena*: see note to 1.135.

121 *Orion*: he was transformed into the constellation after his death.

122 *a grudge against her*: Dawn offended Aphrodite by sleeping with her lover, Ares.

126 *Iasion*: as a result of their union, Demeter gave birth to the god Wealth. Zeus' resentment is unfair, Calypso implies, since male gods have sex with mortals all the time.

161 *I am willing*: Calypso neglects to mention Zeus' command and makes her offer sound like spontaneous generosity.

185 *Styx*: a river of the underworld.

272 *Pleiades*: a cluster of seven stars (said to be daughters of Atlas), part of the Taurus constellation.

272 *Boötes*: the 'Oxherder' constellation, which includes the bright star Arcturus.

273 *Bear… Wain*: the Ursa Major (Great Bear) constellation. Appropriately, the Bear keeps a close watch on Orion, the hunter.

275 *no share… Ocean*: the Greeks thought of the sky as a dome covering the round flat earth, which was in turn surrounded by the river Ocean, and here the Bear is presented as the only constellation which does not sink into Ocean once it has crossed the sky.

283 *Solymi*: a people inhabiting ancient Lycia (an area in south-west Turkey).

310 *the dead son of Peleus*: Achilles; for the battle over his corpse, see 24.36–42.

381 *Aegae*: Poseidon's cult at Aegae is also mentioned in the *Iliad* (8.203; 13.21–2). There were several places called Aegae, but the likeliest for Poseidon's palace is a headland opposite the south-eastern corner of Lesbos.

422 *Amphitrite*: see note to 3.91.

BOOK SIX

As Odysseus sleeps, Athena goes to the palace of King Alcinous and appears to his daughter Nausicaa in a dream, urging her to wash clothes in preparation for her marriage (1–47). Nausicaa wakes up and asks her father for a wagon to transport the laundry (48–70). After washing the clothes, she and her maidservants play ball on the shore (71–109). Awakened by their cries, Odysseus supplicates Nausicaa, asking for some clothes and directions to the city (110–85). Nausicaa agrees, calms her terrified maids, and admires the washed and clothed Odysseus, whose appearance is enhanced by Athena (186–250). Nausicaa outlines her plan: Odysseus is to enter the city after the women so as to avoid gossip, and should then make for the palace, where he is to supplicate her mother, Queen Arete (251–315). Odysseus follows them to the outskirts of the city and waits, praying to Athena (316–31).

4 *Hypereia*: a fictional place, whose name (meaning 'the land beyond') suits its remote setting.

8 *Scheria*: see note to 5.34.

103 *Taygetus… Erymanthus*: mountain ranges in the Peloponnese.

106 *Leto*: mother of Artemis (and Apollo).

182 *harmony of minds*: for the importance of this theme, see section 'Marriage and family life' in the Introduction.

324 *Atrytone*: see note to 4.762.

BOOK SEVEN

As Nausicaa arrives home, Odysseus sets out for the palace; shrouded in a mist, he is guided by Athena, who is disguised as a Phaeacian girl. She explains the royal family's genealogy and instructs Odysseus to approach Queen Arete (1–77). Marvelling at the scale and richness of the palace and its estate, Odysseus arrives unseen and immediately supplicates Arete, asking for an escort back to his homeland (78–152). He is welcomed, fed, and promised safe passage home the following day (153–225). Arete, however, recognizes her handiwork in the clothes worn by Odysseus, and asks him where he got them. Still concealing his identity, Odysseus replies with an abbreviated account of his wanderings, culminating in his meeting with Nausicaa, whose idea that they not enter the city together (lest it provoke gossip) Odysseus politely pretends was his own (226–307). Alcinous hints that Odysseus might marry Nausicaa (should he choose to stay), but repeats the promise to send him on his way the following day. Odysseus prays to Zeus for a safe homecoming and all go to bed (308–47).

9 *Apeira*: meaning 'the boundless (or indeterminate) land', a fictional place (like Hypereia, the Phaeacians' original home: see note to 6.4).

66 *made her his wife*: Alcinous marries his niece. Marriage to an uncle was permitted in ancient Greek society (as was marriage to half-brothers by the same father or to cousins). With no father or brother living, an unmarried girl like Arete would in any case pass into the guardianship of her nearest male relative, who here also happens to be Alcinous.

81 *Erechtheus*: a mythical king of Athens, who was worshipped together with Athena in a joint temple (the Erechtheum) on the Athenian acropolis.

324 *Rhadamanthys...Gaia's son*: Rhadamanthys, son of Zeus and Europa, entered Elysium (see note to 4.563) and was revered as a wise judge of the dead in the underworld. Tityus, by contrast, was a notorious villain, who tried to rape Leto, and whose punishment in Hades (two vultures tear at his liver) has already been witnessed by Odysseus himself (see 11.576–81). The story linking them here is otherwise unknown.

BOOK EIGHT

The next day Alcinous summons the Phaeacians, who help prepare a ship for Odysseus and join in entertaining him before his departure (1–61). The blind bard Demodocus sings of the quarrel between Odysseus and Achilles, moving Odysseus to tears (62–95). Alcinous notices and calls for games to begin instead, and the Phaeacians compete in running, wrestling, long jump, discus, and boxing (96–130). Laodamas, one of Alcinous' sons, challenges Odysseus to compete, but he firmly refuses (131–57). Euryalus then insults Odysseus and is forcefully rebuked. Odysseus shows his strength by hurling the heaviest discus further than anyone, and angrily challenges all-comers (158–233). The situation is defused by Alcinous, who calls for dance and song (234–65). Demodocus sings of the adultery of Ares and Aphrodite, and of its discovery and punishment by Hephaestus (266–369). After more dancing displays, Alcinous calls on the Phaeacian leaders to bring gifts for Odysseus, and Euryalus apologizes personally to Odysseus (370–415). Alcinous and Arete add their own presents, placing all the gifts in a great chest, which Odysseus seals (416–48). Odysseus is bathed and dressed and says farewell to Nausicaa (449–68). At Odysseus' request, Demodocus sings the tale of the Trojan horse (469–520).

When Odysseus weeps once again, Alcinous asks him to explain exactly who he is and where he comes from (521–86).

62 *the worthy bard*: for the poem's positive depiction of bards, see section 'The *Odyssey* and early Greek epic' in the Introduction.

78 *the best of the Achaeans*: Agamemnon is pleased by their quarrel presumably because the oracle predicted it would herald the Greeks' ultimate victory at Troy.

111 *Acroneos*: the Phaeacian youths are given names that express their preoccupation with seafaring: Acroneos ('top ship'), Ocyalus ('sea-swift'), Elatreus ('rower'), etc.

219 *Philoctetes*: see note to 3.190.

288 *Cytherean*: an epithet of Aphrodite, who was born from the sea-foam on the shores of Cythera, an island off Cape Malea in the Peloponnese (see note to 3.288).

294 *Sintians...harsh tongue*: an obscure people, believed to be non-Greek-speaking Thracians who settled on the island of Lemnos. There was a major cult of Hephaestus on Lemnos, whose capital city was named Hephaestias.

393 *a talent*: a measure of weight, equivalent to around 26 or 38 kg in later systems of Greek coinage, but its exact size in Homer is unknown. In any case, Odysseus will here receive 13 talents in all, a considerable amount of gold.

481 *pathways of song*: for the significance of this idea within the oral tradition of epic poetry, see section 'The *Odyssey* and early Greek epic' in the Introduction.

BOOK NINE

Odysseus reveals his identity and begins his story (1–38). Starting from Troy with twelve ships, he and his companions raid the Cicones in Thrace, but Odysseus' crew ignore his orders to leave, leading to the loss of many men (39–61). A storm brings them to the land of the Lotus-eaters, where some eat the fruit of forgetfulness and have to be forced back on board (62–104). Reaching the land of the Cyclopes, they disembark on a nearby island, where they hunt and feast (105–69). Odysseus organizes a scouting party of twelve men and they enter the cave of Polyphemus, who is not at home. Odysseus' men urge him to leave immediately, but he foolishly ignores them, hoping for guest-gifts from the Cyclops (170–230). Polyphemus returns, blocking the cave entrance with a huge rock, and when Odysseus supplicates him to remember the respect due to guests, the Cyclops kills and eats two of Odysseus' crew for supper (231–306). With more men eaten for breakfast and dinner the next day, Odysseus hatches a plan: he gets Polyphemus drunk and tells him his name is 'No-man'; the Cyclops falls into a drunken stupor, and Odysseus and his men blind him with a heated wooden stake; when the other Cyclopes ask what the problem is, Polyphemus replies 'No-man is killing me' and the Cyclopes simply go away (307–414). To escape from the cave Odysseus clings to the belly of Polyphemus' favourite ram, having tied his men beneath some others, and they wait for the animals to be sent out to graze (416–61). As they sail off, Odysseus taunts Polyphemus repeatedly, ignoring his men's attempts to restrain him, and rashly reveals his name, which enables Polyphemus to pray to his father Poseidon for vengeance (462–535). Returning to the nearby island where his ships are stationed, Odysseus prays in vain to Zeus for a safe voyage, and they sail away, lamenting their lost comrades (536–66).

26 *the sun's rising*: the poet's knowledge of the Ionian islands is vague, since Ithaca is neither low (it has high peaks) nor the most westerly. Scholars ancient and modern have tried to map these names onto the islands in the region, but there is no reason to expect geographical precision in a poem of this kind. Homer's description is fictional, even if inspired by the island we know as Ithaca.

39 *Cicones*: allies of the Trojans from Ismarus in Thrace.

81 *Cythera*: see note to 8.288. This is the last real place to be mentioned, as Odysseus is now blown off the historical map into the realm of fantasy.

97 *forgetting their journey home*: the story-pattern (if one eats a certain food, one cannot return to normal life) is found in many cultures. Here the lotus plant threatens Odysseus' entire mission, namely his return to family and kingdom.

106 *the Cyclopes*: savage one-eyed giants, with (at least in Polyphemus' case) a penchant for cheese.

198 *Ismarus*: Maron was evidently spared by Odysseus during the raid on the Cicones (see 9.39–40).

209 *twenty measures of water*: ancient Greeks drank their wine diluted, usually one or two parts wine to three parts water, so Maron's wine is exceptionally strong, making it well suited to its eventual purpose (intoxicating the Cyclops).

405 *no mortal*: there is an ingenious pun in the Greek here, since the expression used by the Cyclopes for 'no mortal' and 'no one' is '*mē tis*', which evokes '*mētis*', i.e. guile or cunning, one of the core characteristics of 'Odysseus, man of many wiles' (*polymētis Odysseus*). Odysseus has called himself *Outis* (No-man/Nobody), and Polyphemus lacks the verbal wit to evade his trap.

BOOK TEN

Odysseus' fleet reach the floating island of Aeolus, ruler of the winds, who entertains them for a month and at their departure gives Odysseus a leather bag containing all the winds (1–27). After sailing for ten days and with Ithaca in sight, Odysseus falls asleep and his men open the bag in search of treasure; the resulting storm drives them back to Aeolus, who angrily refuses to have anything more to do with them (28–75). They struggle on to the Laestrygonians, who destroy eleven ships, complete with crew, and Odysseus' ship (which he had cautiously moored outside the harbour) is the only one to escape (76–134). Arriving at the island of Circe, Odysseus kills a huge stag and tries to encourage his desperate men (135–202). He splits them into two groups, and one led by Eurylochus heads for Circe's palace. Circe welcomes them inside, but then drugs them and turns them into pigs, and Eurylochus alone escapes (203–43). Leaving the terrified Eurylochus behind, Odysseus decides to go to the palace himself (244–73). As he does so, Hermes appears to him in disguise and explains how to counteract Circe's drugs and magic (274–306). Following the god's advice, Odysseus subdues Circe and agrees to go to bed with her only after she has sworn an oath not to plot against him (307–47). Despite Circe's generous hospitality, Odysseus is despondent until she agrees to transform his men back to their human form (348–405). The group left behind by Odysseus are reluctant to join him in Circe's palace, but are eventually persuaded, and they feast together (406–65). After a year with Circe, Odysseus needs to be reminded by his men to think of his return, and he asks to leave (466–86). Circe agrees, but explains that Odysseus must first visit the underworld, where he is to summon the shade of the blind prophet Teiresias, who will tell him of his route home (487–540). Odysseus' men are appalled at the news of their impending journey to Hades, one of them (Elpenor) dies in an accident, and they make their way in tears back to the last remaining ship (541–74).

81 *Lamus*: founder of the Laestrygonians' city, Telepylus.

137 *Aeëtes*: ruler of Aia, the kingdom of Colchis at the eastern end of the Black Sea. Jason was sent there to fetch the Golden Fleece, and overcame the deadly challenges set by Aeëtes with the help of his daughter, Medea, who then eloped with Jason.

235 *Pramnian*: it is likely that the word originally referred to the wine's origin, but no record of any town called 'Pramnos' has survived. Circe's alcoholic porridge sounds perfect for the weary traveller, until she adds her amnesiac drug.

517 *a cubit's length*: the distance from the elbow to the end of the knuckles of a closed fist.

528 *Erebus*: a region of darkness, often associated with Hades, i.e. the animals' heads are to be turned down towards the ground.

BOOK ELEVEN

Odysseus and his men sail to the remote spot described by Circe and call up the shades of the dead (1–50). The ghost of Elpenor explains how he died and begs to be buried when Odysseus and his men return to Circe's island (51–83). The shade of Odysseus' mother, Anticleia, approaches, but he cannot speak to her until he has seen the dead prophet Teiresias (84–9). Teiresias now appears, drinks the sacrificial blood, and explains that Odysseus and his crew may return safely home as long as they do not harm Helios' cattle; he also describes the chaos in Odysseus' household and predicts yet further travels after the suitors have been killed (90–137). Teiresias shows Odysseus how he may speak with the other shades, and Odysseus asks his mother how she died and enquires about Laertes, Telemachus, and Penelope. Anticleia details the misery and grief of Laertes, and reveals that she died of longing for Odysseus (138–203). When Odysseus attempts to embrace her, Anticleia describes the dissolution of the body after death (204–24). Odysseus then encounters a succession of famous women: Tyro, who bore Pelias and Neleus to Poseidon; Antiope, who bore Amphion and Zethus to Zeus; Alcmene, who bore Heracles to Zeus, and Heracles' wife Megara; Epicaste, who married her own son, Oedipus; Chloris, mother of Nestor; Leda, mother of Castor and Polydeuces; Iphimedeia, who bore the rebellious giants Otus and Ephialtes to Poseidon; and several others (225–332). Odysseus ends his tale; the Phaeacians, amazed, praise his skills as a storyteller. Promising to send him on his way with gifts the following day, Alcinous asks if Odysseus also met any of the heroes who fought at Troy (333–76). Odysseus obligingly recalls his exchanges with the shades of Agamemnon, Achilles, and Ajax, the last of whom refuses to speak with him (377–567). He also describes seeing other heroes, including the three great sinners Tityus, Tantalus, and Sisyphus (568–600). His final encounter is with Heracles, who recalls his own trip to Hades to fetch the dog Cerberus (601–26). As the dead clamour alarmingly around him, Odysseus returns to his ship and sets sail (627–40).

14 *Cimmerians*: a fairy-tale people at the edge of the world; their dark and gloomy land is a fitting stopover on the way to Hades.

198 *shooter of arrows*: Artemis, who was thought to bring sudden death to women, as her twin brother Apollo did to men.

220 *the spirit*: the spirit or soul (*psychē*) leaves the body at death and lives on in Hades as a shade, retaining the outward physical form it once animated in life.

238 *Enipeus*: a river in Thessaly.

254 *Pelias*: king of Iolcus, who devised the quest for the Golden Fleece as a way of ridding himself of Jason, the rightful claimant to his throne.

254 *Neleus*: father of Nestor (see 11.285–6).

271 *lovely Epicaste*: in contrast to Sophocles' influential version of the story in the *Oedipus Tyrannus*, produced in the fifth century BC, here Oedipus' mother is called Epicaste (not Jocasta), the incestuous couple do not appear to have had any children ('the gods soon made this public knowledge'), Oedipus does not blind himself, and he continues to rule in Thebes despite the revelation of his identity.

292 *the excellent seer*: Melampus, who eventually won the hand of Pero for his brother Bias.

303–4 *alive…dead*: the twins Castor and Polydeuces (better known by his Latin name Pollux) are given the unusual honour of alternating daily between life and death. For other privileges granted by Zeus to his children, see 4.561–9 (Helen's honour shared by Menelaus), 11.601–4 (Heracles' immortality).

319 *whom... Leto bore*: Apollo.

325 *the testimony of Dionysus*: this telling of the myth, in which the god bears witness against Ariadne, is obscure and otherwise unknown. In more popular versions Ariadne becomes the god's lover after being abandoned by Theseus on the island of Naxos.

327 *her husband's life*: Eriphyle accepted 'precious gold' (a necklace) in return for sending her husband Amphiaraus to fight at Thebes, where he was destined to be killed.

520 *Cetaean*: an alternative name for Mysian, Mysia being a kingdom near Troy. Eurypylus' mother accepted a bribe from King Priam to send her son to fight for the Trojans, but he was killed by Achilles' son, Neoptolemus.

522 *Memnon*: see note to 3.112.

568 *Minos*: he had been king of Crete.

572 *Orion*: the great hunter, killed by Artemis; see note to 5.121.

576 *Tityus*: see note to 7.324.

582 *Tantalus*: he had tried to serve up his son Pelops to the gods at a feast.

593 *Sisyphus*: a notorious trickster.

602 *or his phantom*: since Heracles himself has achieved immortality among the gods. See note to 11.303–4.

621–2 *a man far inferior to me*: Heracles was bound by the goddess Hera to Eurystheus, king of Mycenae, and had to perform twelve labours at his command.

BOOK TWELVE

Odysseus and his men return to Circe's island and bury Elpenor (1–15). Circe tells Odysseus in great detail how they should deal with the dangers awaiting them on the way home (16–141). Setting sail, Odysseus reveals to his men how to resist the Sirens' song, and they successfully escape (142–200). However, while steering clear of the whirlpool Charybdis, they lose six men to the monster Scylla (201–59). Odysseus' men then ignore the warnings of Teiresias and Circe about the island of the Sun and insist on resting and eating there (260–93). Odysseus makes them swear an oath that they will not touch Helios' cattle, but driven by hunger they slaughter and eat some of them (294–373). Helios complains to Zeus, who blasts Odysseus' ship with a thunderbolt, drowning all of his men (374–419). Odysseus survives by clinging on to wreckage from the ship, and after another narrow escape from Scylla and Charybdis, he finally reaches Calypso's island (420–53).

133 *Hyperion*: here used as an epithet of the sun-god, Helios, himself (cf. 1.8). Hyperion is also the name of Helios' father (see e.g. 12.176).

253 *horn tube*: fitted above the hook to prevent the line being bitten through.

358 *no white barley*: in Greek sacrificial ritual barley-grains were scattered by the participants just before the animal was killed (cf. e.g. 3.445–7). Here Odysseus' men are forced to substitute leaves for barley, and the abnormal ritual foreshadows their disastrous killing of the Sun-god's cattle.

BOOK THIRTEEN

Odysseus ends his tale and the Phaeacians give him even more gifts, stowing them aboard the ship which carries the sleeping Odysseus to Ithaca (1–124). Poseidon is granted Zeus' permission to punish the Phaeacians, turning their ship to stone and encircling their city behind a huge mountain (125–87). When Odysseus awakes, he is unable to recognize his homeland because of Athena's intervention. The goddess appears in disguise and Odysseus tries to deceive her, much to her amusement (187–286). She reveals her true identity, but Odysseus remains suspicious, and it is only when she shows him Ithaca that he believes he has returned home (287–360). Together they hide Odysseus' treasure in a cave and begin plotting against the suitors (361–91). Athena describes how she will disguise Odysseus and bring Telemachus back from Sparta, saving him from the suitors' ambush (392–428). She transforms Odysseus into a decrepit old beggar and heads off to Sparta to fetch Telemachus (429–40).

93 *that most brilliant star*: Venus, the morning star.

172 *my father's ancient prophecy*: already recalled by Alcinous at 8.564–71.

248–9 *Troy…Achaea*: Athena teases Odysseus with the reference to Troy, whose great distance from Greece he is all too aware of.

256 *even in spacious Crete*: the first of Odysseus' lying tales that present variations on his identity as a troubled Cretan; see section 'Odysseus as hero' in the Introduction.

259 *Idomeneus*: see note to 3.191.

285 *Sidon*: see note to 4.84.

300–1 *always stood by you… watched over you*: on Athena's particular affection for Odysseus, see section 'Mortals and immortals' in the Introduction.

388 *headdress*: the word is used in epic for a city's battlements.

BOOK FOURTEEN

Odysseus, disguised as an old beggar, approaches Eumaeus' pig-farm and is kindly welcomed (1–79). Eumaeus describes the suitors' crimes and their depletion of his master's property (80–108). When the beggar claims that Odysseus will return, Eumaeus refuses to believe him, since many other beggars have already tried to deceive Penelope with false tales about her husband (109–90). In a lengthy and eventful tale of how he came to Ithaca, Odysseus claims to be a once-wealthy Cretan who fought alongside Odysseus at Troy and later heard news of his return (191–359). Eumaeus remains sceptical, still fearing that Odysseus is dead, but prepares a generous meal for the beggar (360–456). Freezing with cold, Odysseus tells an amusing story of how Odysseus once procured a cloak for him at Troy, prompting Eumaeus to tuck him up for the night with extra warm coverings (457–522). Eumaeus finally goes to bed near the pigs, delighting Odysseus, who is pleased by the swineherd's concern for his property (523–33).

55 *you... swineherd Eumaeus*: Eumaeus is the only character addressed directly by the poet of the *Odyssey* (fifteen times in total), and the unusual technique reinforces the audience's affection and sympathy for this dutiful host and loyal servant.

181–2 *Arceisius' clan*: Arceisius was the father of Laertes (cf. 4.755; 16.118; 24.270, 517).

315 *Thesprotia*: part of Epirus, in north-west Greece beyond Ithaca.

328 *high-branched oak tree*: the oracle of Zeus at Dodona in Epirus (northwestern Greece), located in a sacred oak tree, seems to communicate here via its rustling leaves.

BOOK FIFTEEN

Athena goes to Sparta and sets Telemachus on his way, warning him of the suitors' ambush (1–42). Menelaus is persuaded to let him go home immediately (43–91). Menelaus and Helen present their parting gifts, and a bird omen is interpreted positively by Helen (92–181). When Telemachus reaches Pylos, Peisistratus helps him evade Nestor's hospitality (182–217). A seer called Theoclymenus, who is on the run, begs Telemachus to take him along, and they sail off towards Ithaca (218–300). At Eumaeus' pig-farm Odysseus tests the swineherd's hospitality (301–39). After asking about Penelope and Laertes, he enquires how Eumaeus came to be enslaved, prompting a long and painful tale (340–495). Telemachus reaches Ithaca and another bird omen is positively interpreted by Theoclymenus. Sending his ship on ahead to the city, Telemachus makes his way on foot to Eumaeus' pig-farm (496–557).

186 *Pherae*: see note to 3.488.

225 *a seer*: Theoclymenus' family history is lengthy and complex, but makes use of stories involving Melampus and Amphiaraus that the audience has heard before (see 11.281–97, 326–7).

238 *to be his wife*: see note to 11.292.

247 *a bribed woman*: see note to 11.327.

299 *the Pointed Isles*: no exact identification is possible, but they are evidently somewhere between the north-west Peloponnese (Elis) and Ithaca.

403 *Syria*: another fictional island.

BOOK SIXTEEN

Telemachus is welcomed back by Eumaeus and shares a meal with the disguised Odysseus, who questions him about the crisis on Ithaca (1–129).
Telemachus sends Eumaeus to Penelope with news of his return, and Athena
instructs Odysseus to reveal himself to his son (130–71). The goddess transforms Odysseus, but Telemachus, thinking him a god, at first refuses to recognize his father. Once reunited, they plan their vengeance upon the suitors, and
Odysseus reassures Telemachus they have the gods on their side (172–265).
Odysseus explains several details of their plot and instructs Telemachus not to
reveal his identity to anyone (266–320). Telemachus' ship returns to Ithaca
town and Penelope learns her son is safe (321–41). When the failed ambush
returns, the frustrated suitors call a meeting and argue inconclusively about
what to do next (342–408). Penelope rebukes the suitor Antinous for plotting
against her son, and Eurymachus pretends to be on her side (409–51). As
Eumaeus returns, Odysseus is changed once more into an old beggar, and
father and son take pleasure in the news of the failed ambush (452–81).

474 *curved-headed*: with a leaf-shaped blade, curved on both sides.

BOOK SEVENTEEN

Telemachus sets out for the palace and instructs Eumaeus to take the beggar
there too (1–25). Once home, Telemachus issues various orders and tells Penelope of his travels to Pylos and Sparta, ending with the report that Odysseus was
being detained by Calypso (26–149). However, the seer Theoclymenus insists
that Odysseus is already on Ithaca, and Penelope prays he is correct (150–65).
On their way Eumaeus and Odysseus encounter the goatherd Melanthius, a
supporter of the suitors, who insults then and kicks Odysseus (166–253). As
they approach the palace, Odysseus' old dog recognizes his master then dies
(254–327). Following Telemachus' instructions, Odysseus begs the suitors for
food, sparking an argument which culminates in Antinous throwing a footstool
at Odysseus (328–504). When Penelope asks to meet the beggar, Telemachus
sneezes, which she interprets as an omen of the suitors' destruction (505–50).
Odysseus advises that they meet later in private, Penelope agrees, and Eumaeus
heads home, having warned Telemachus to be careful (551–606).

53 *someone*: Theoclymenus; see 15.222–81.

134 *Philomeleides*: see note to 4.343.

BOOK EIGHTEEN

The beggar Irus insults Odysseus and they come to blows (1–31). The suitors
look forward to the spectacle of their boxing-match, and Odysseus makes them
swear an oath that they will not take Irus' side (32–65). Athena strengthens
Odysseus and the terrified Irus has to be forced to fight. Odysseus knocks him
out and claims his prize (66–123). The suitor Amphinomus is warned by Odysseus,

but he will not escape destruction (124–57). Prompted by Athena, Penelope decides to show herself to the suitors. Her beauty enhanced by the goddess, she drives the suitors wild and extracts valuable presents from them, delighting her husband (158–303). The disloyal maidservant Melantho insults Odysseus, as does the suitor Eurymachus; Odysseus answers his taunts and Eurymachus throws a footstool at him, but misses (304–404). Telemachus urges the suitors to leave, Amphinomus agrees, and they all go home (405–28).

6–7 *Irus...ordered him*: the beggar's comic nickname makes him the male equivalent of Iris, the messenger of the gods.

73 *Irus...un-Irused*: the wordplay in the Greek (*Iros Airos*, 'Irus non-Irus') exploits the name's derivation from *iros* meaning 'strong'.

85 *Echetus*: his name means 'Holder', underlining his scariness.

193 *Cytherea*: see note to 8.288.

283 *her mind had other plans*: Odysseus knows that Penelope does not wish to remarry and recognizes her delaying tactics, which also cleverly replenish his household's wealth.

BOOK NINETEEN

Odysseus and Telemachus remove the weapons from the hall, with Athena lighting their way (1–52). Melantho insults Odysseus again, but is rebuked by both him and Penelope (53–95). Penelope describes her predicament and asks the stranger who he is (96–163). Odysseus claims to be a Cretan prince who once entertained her husband (164–202). Testing the stranger, Penelope asks about details of Odysseus' visit and is convinced by his reply (203–60). Odysseus insists that her husband is on his way home and will be here imminently, but Penelope refuses to believe him (261–316). While washing his feet, Odysseus' old nurse Eurycleia recognizes her master by a scar, but Odysseus stops her telling Penelope (317–502). Penelope asks the stranger to interpret a dream and announces that she will stage a contest for the suitors, with the winner taking her as his wife, and Odysseus encourages her to do so. Penelope goes to bed in tears (503–604).

144 *burial-shroud*: see note to 2.99.

163 *from a rock or an oak*: a proverbial expression, referring to 'the old story' that the human race was created in this way.

179 *Minos*: see 11.568–71.

187 *Cape Malea*: see note to 3.288.

188 *Amnisus...Eileithyia*: a town on the north coast of Crete, not far from Cnossus, with a cave sanctuary of Eileithyia, the goddess of childbirth.

260 *vile Ilium, not to be named*: Troy is not nameable because of Penelope's hatred towards it, so she replaces its usual name *Ilion* with a pejorative version *Kakoilion* ('Evil-Ilium').

271 *Thesprotians*: see note to 14.315.

297 *high-branched oak tree*: see 14.328.

407–9 *odium... Odysseus*: see note to 1.62.

518 *daughter of Pandareus*: Aedon (= 'nightingale' in Greek), daughter of Pandareus, king of Crete, married Zethus, king of Thebes, and they had a son, Itylus. Jealous of her sister-in-law Niobe's larger family, Aedon tried to kill Niobe's eldest son but accidentally killed her own. Zeus took pity on her and turned her into a nightingale, perpetually mourning her child. This version of the mourning nightingale myth is attested only here. Penelope's use of it links the bird's varying song to her shifting thoughts ('so my heart too is pulled two ways'), but there are further connections: both women have lost loved ones, Aedon her son, Penelope her husband; and while Aedon killed her son unwittingly, Penelope's refusal to remarry threatens her son's safety.

563–4 *horn... ivory*: for Penelope at the gates of dreams, see also 4.809. There is some ingenious wordplay in the Greek here between 'ivory' (*elephas*) and 'deceive' (*elephairomai*), and between 'horn' (*keras*) and 'bear a true message' (*krainō*).

575 *clean through them*: the arrow passes through the hole in the axe-head where the handle would normally be fitted.

597 *Evil-Ilium, never to be named*: for the same expression, see note to 19.260.

BOOK TWENTY

Unable to sleep, Odysseus contemplates killing the wicked maidservants, but restrains himself. As he wonders how to overcome the more numerous suitors, Athena appears and reassures him, and he falls asleep (1–55). Penelope awakes and prays to Artemis; Odysseus awakes and prays to Zeus, who sends two favourable omens predicting his success (56–121). Eurycleia sets the servants to their tasks. The goatherd Melanthius taunts Odysseus again, but the cowherd Philoetius declares his loyalty to his absent master (122–239). The suitors plot once more to kill Telemachus, but are put off by a bad omen. They hurl more insults at Odysseus, and Ctesippus throws a cow's hoof at him. When Agelaus declares it is time for Penelope to make up her mind, Telemachus insists he will not force her (240–344). The suitors are overcome with maniacal laughter, and the seer Theoclymenus predicts their imminent doom (345–72). The suitors taunt Telemachus as well, but he ignores them, watching Odysseus instead for a signal (373–94).

66 *the daughters of Pandareus*: Penelope returns to the myth of Pandareus' daughters (see note to 19.515), here recounting how they were carried off by storm-winds before marriage, against their will, in contrast to Penelope herself, who would rather be swept away than forced to remarry.

106 *the people's shepherd*: 'shepherd of the people' is a typical Homeric epithet for heroes and rulers (here referring to Odysseus), expressing their

concern for the well-being of their people. For the social aspects of heroism, see section 'Odysseus as hero' in the Introduction.

301 *dodged it*: this is the third time things have been thrown at Odysseus, and the three episodes underline the diminishing power of the suitors and the growing confidence of Telemachus. When Antinous throws a stool, he hits Odysseus (17.462–3); when Eurymachus throws one, he misses and the stool hits a wine-pourer (18.396–8); here Ctesippus throws a cow's hoof, which harmlessly hits the wall. Telemachus was silent at the first incident (17.489–91), complained at the second (18.405–11), and here openly threatens Ctesippus with death (20.304–8).

BOOK TWENTY-ONE

Penelope fetches Odysseus' bow and announces the challenge: stringing the bow and shooting an arrow through twelve axes (1–79). Telemachus urges the suitors on and sets up the axe-heads, ready for the contest (80–139). Leodes is first to try, but fails; Antinous calls for the bow to be warmed and greased and other suitors try, still without success (140–87). After revealing his identity to Eumaeus and Philoetius, Odysseus gives them instructions for the vengeance to come (188–244). The suitor Eurymachus fails to string the bow, and Antinous postpones his turn until the following day. The suitors angrily object to the idea of letting the beggar have a go, and Telemachus sends Penelope away (245–358). The bow is finally brought to Odysseus, who inspects it expertly. Stringing the bow with ease, he shoots an arrow through all twelve axes and signals to Telemachus; father and son take their stand together, ready for the fight (359–434).

46–8 *the leather strap...bolts*: the strap was used to draw the bolts (on the inside of the door) into their socket (cf. e.g. 1.441–2), and could be tied to the handle to keep the door closed. Here the storeroom doors are fitted with a separate lock; Penelope's finely made key (cf. 21.6–7) is inserted into an opening, forcing the bolts out of their socket and releasing the lock.

76 *through all twelve axes*: see note to 19.575.

297 *visiting the Lapiths*: Peirithous, king of the Lapiths (a clan in Thessaly), invited the Centaurs (half-man, half-horse) to his wedding-feast, but the Centaur Eurytion got drunk and tried to rape the bride, Hippodameia. The battle of the Lapiths and Centaurs was a popular scene in Greek art, often symbolizing the battle between civilization and barbarism (see e.g. the Parthenon metopes conserved in the British Museum).

308 *Echetus*: see note to 18.85.

BOOK TWENTY-TWO

Odysseus shoots Antinous and reveals his identity to the astonished suitors (1–41). Eurymachus tries to blame everything on Antinous, but is killed (42–88).

Telemachus fetches armour, and together with Odysseus, Eumaeus, and Philoetius, prepares for hand-to-hand combat when Odysseus' arrows run out (89–125). The goatherd Melanthius manages to bring some armour to the suitors before being spotted and tied up (126–204). Appearing as Mentor, Athena spurs on Odysseus (205–40). The remaining suitors fight on, but are gradually picked off (241–309). After Leodes supplicates Odysseus in vain, the bard Phemius does so successfully, and the herald Medon is also spared (310–80). Eurycleia assembles the disloyal maidservants, who are forced to remove the suitors' bodies and wash down the hall before being hanged, while Melanthius is mutilated and killed (381–477). The house is purified and the loyal maidservants embrace Odysseus (478–501).

230 *your stratagem*: the Trojan horse; see 8.492–520.

290 *the hoof*: see note to 20.301.

297 *the man-slaying aegis*: see note to 3.42.

BOOK TWENTY-THREE

Eurycleia informs Penelope of her husband's return and revenge upon the suitors, but she refuses to believe the man is Odysseus (1–84). When Telemachus rebukes his mother for her stubbornness, Odysseus urges him to think instead of the fallout from the slaughter (85–151). Made extra handsome by Athena, Odysseus too criticizes Penelope's refusal to recognize him, whereupon she tricks Odysseus into confirming his identity by pretending that she has destroyed the marital bed Odysseus made for them (152–204). Reunited at last, Odysseus recounts Teiresias' prophecy of his future struggles (205–87). They make love and Odysseus recalls his adventures since leaving Troy (288–343). The next day, aided by Athena, Odysseus sets out to see his father (344–72).

19 *Evil-Ilium, never to be named*: see note to 19.260.

181 *testing her husband*: Penelope's ability to outwit the crafty Odysseus proves their *homophrosynē* or 'like-mindedness', a concept fundamental to the Homeric conception of a good marriage: see section 'Marriage and family life' in the Introduction.

233 *As welcome as the sight of land*: the simile used to describe Penelope's joy compares her to a sailor who has survived a shipwreck, evoking Odysseus' own struggles and linking his suffering to hers.

244 *river Ocean*: see note to 5.275.

309 *a full account of everything*: unsurprisingly, in recounting his adventures to Penelope, Odysseus does not mention his year of lovemaking with Circe, or that his men had to remind him of his need to leave her (see 10.469–75). In the case of Calypso, he emphasizes his refusal to stay as her husband rather than his pleasure in their lovemaking (see 5.153), and he makes no

mention at all of Nausicaa. The reunion of husband and wife is not the moment for such details. For Odysseus adapting his tales to suit his audience, see section 'Odysseus as hero' in the Introduction; for the poet doing the same, see there the section on 'The *Odyssey* and early Greek epic'.

BOOK TWENTY-FOUR

Hermes escorts the shades of the suitors down to the underworld (1–14). The shades of Achilles and Agamemnon talk with one another: Achilles laments Agamemnon's pitiable murder in his own land, while Agamemnon recalls Achilles' glorious death and funeral at Troy (15–97). Amazed by the arrival of the suitors, Agamemnon asks how they died. The shade of Amphimedon condemns Penelope's deception and Odysseus' ruthless revenge, but Agamemnon responds by praising Penelope's faithfulness (98–204). Odysseus goes to his father Laertes and decides to test him with a false story, a plan he soon regrets. Moved by his father's grief, he reveals himself and proves his identity (205–360). Following their reunion, Laertes is transformed by Athena and Odysseus is greeted by his father's loyal servants (361–411). The suitors' families bury their dead and the majority insist on revenge (412–71). Athena and Zeus, however, plan a treaty and lasting peace (472–88). A rejuvenated Laertes joins his son and grandson in the fray, and a few of the suitors' kinsmen are killed before Athena stops the fighting and secures peace (489–548).

11–12 *rock...dreams*: all places in the mythical far west, on the way to Hades.

134 *burial shroud*: see note to 2.99.

161–2 *threw things at him*: see note to 20.301.

199 *daughter of Tyndareus*: Clytemnestra; for her role in the murder of Agamemnon, see 3.248–310, 11.397–434, 24.24–34.

222 *Dolius*: Penelope's servant, a gardener, sent to Laertes for advice about Telemachus (see 4.735–41).

240 *with teasing words*: the scene with Laertes shows how lying has become an ingrained habit for Odysseus, and how his caution and guile may verge on cruelty because of his need to test everyone. Odysseus' attempt to control and delay the recognition here, however, will soon backfire when he is overwhelmed by his father's emotional response.

303 *an accurate account*: in contrast to his persona as a wandering beggar (as told to Athena, Eumaeus, the suitor Antinous, and Penelope), here the victorious Odysseus pretends to be a foreign prince.

304 *Alybas*: a fictional place, whose name (appropriately for Odysseus) suggests 'wandering' (*alaomai*, 'to wander'). Indeed, all the names fabricated here are significant: Apheides = 'generous man' (a compliment to Laertes); Polypemon = 'full of pain' (Laertes' current condition); Eperitus = 'the chosen one' (Odysseus' usual heroic modesty).

306 *Sicania*: Sicily.

354 *to confront us*: for earlier hints at the inevitable confrontation with the suitors' families, see e.g. 20.41–3; 23.117–22; 24.324–5.

377 *Nericus*: a town on the coast north of Ithaca.

INDEX OF PERSONAL NAMES

The index aims to give the reader a quick point of reference for the characters and their actions, but does not list every mention of each figure. References are to the book and line number in the translation.